CRIMINAL TRIALS AND MENTAL DISORDERS

DATE DUE

PRINTED IN U.S.A.

PSYCHOLOGY AND CRIME

General Editors: Brian Bornstein, University of Nebraska, and Monica Miller, University of Nevada, Reno

Criminal Trials and Mental Disorders

Thomas L. Hafemeister

NEW YORK UNIVERSITY PRESS
New York

NEW YORK UNIVERSITY PRESS
New York
www.nyupress.org

References to Internet websites (URLs) were accurate at the time of writing. Neither the author nor New York University Press is responsible for URLs that may have expired or changed since the manuscript was prepared.

Library of Congress Cataloging-in-Publication Data
Names: Hafemeister, Thomas L., author.
Title: Criminal trials and mental disorders / Thomas L. Hafemeister.
Description: New York : New York University Press, 2019. | Series: Psychology and crime |
Includes bibliographical references and index.
Identifiers: LCCN 2018020938| ISBN 9781479804856 (cl : alk. paper) |
ISBN 9781479861644 (pb : alk. paper)
Subjects: LCSH: Insanity (Law)—United States. | Insanity defense—United States. |
Mentally ill offenders—Legal status, laws, etc.—United States. |
Forensic psychiatry—United States.
Classification: LCC KF9242 .H34 2019 | DDC 345.73/04—dc23
LC record available at https://lccn.loc.gov/2018020938

New York University Press books are printed on acid-free paper, and their binding materials are chosen for strength and durability. We strive to use environmentally responsible suppliers and materials to the greatest extent possible in publishing our books.

Manufactured in the United States of America

10 9 8 7 6 5 4 3 2 1

Also available as an ebook

CONTENTS

Introduction

Seung-Hui Cho, more widely known as the "Virginia Tech Shooter," killed thirty-two people and wounded seventeen others on April 16, 2007, before killing himself during a rampage on a university campus.[1] Just prior to the event, he sent a self-made video to major news outlets showing him holding a gun to his head and saying: "You forced me into a corner and gave me only one option. The decision was yours. Now you have blood on your hands that will never wash off."[2]

Before taking his own life on December 14, 2012, Adam Lanza, the "Sandy Hook Elementary School Shooter," killed twenty elementary school students in their classrooms as well as six adult staff members in Newtown, Connecticut, after previously shooting and killing his mother at the home they shared. It was later reported that he would refuse to come out of his room, covered his windows with black garbage bags, and communicated with his mother via email.[3]

Tamerlan Anzorovich Tsarnaev, the older of two brothers who exploded a pair of bombs near the finish line of the Boston Marathon, killing three spectators and injuring more than 260 others, was killed following a massive manhunt on April 15, 2013. He was reported to have started hearing voices as a young man.[4]

The initial media inquiry after such horrific and seemingly senseless events tends to focus on whether the assailant had a mental disorder. If there is any such indication, it almost always plays a prominent role in the ensuing headlines and reports. It is no coincidence that the general public tends to associate violence with mental disorders. Nonetheless, although far less publicized, mental health experts have determined that most individuals with a mental disorder are not violent, that virtually no one wants nor chooses to have a mental disorder, that a mental disorder can overwhelm and transform a person, and that most defendants with a mental disorder who are caught up in the criminal justice system are not imminent threats to society.

High-profile cases such as those described above have drawn considerable attention to society's ongoing struggle with how to approach and manage cases involving criminal offenders with a mental disorder. Notwithstanding their horrific nature, the above cases were the "easy" ones for the criminal justice system in that each of these assailants died during the events that transpired. The cases described in this text are the "hard" ones in that the person charged with the crime survived and was brought before the criminal justice system. Questions that arise in these cases include whether it is fair and just to (a) conduct criminal proceedings while a defendant is experiencing a mental disorder and (b) hold individuals who were experiencing a mental disorder at the time of the crime fully accountable for their actions and punish them accordingly. What, if any, special rules and procedures should be employed in these cases? No set of issues poses a greater challenge to the criminal justice system than how to respond to individuals whose criminal actions can be attributed to a mental disorder or who are experiencing a mental disorder during their trial. Indeed, these cases illuminate who we are as a society.

The American criminal justice system is based on the bedrock principles of fairness and justice for all. In striving to ensure that all criminal defendants are treated equally under the law, it endeavors to handle like cases in like fashion, adhering to the proposition that the same rules and procedures should be employed regardless of a defendant's wealth or poverty, social status, race, ethnicity, or gender. Yet, exceptions have been recognized when special circumstances are perceived to have driven a defendant's behavior or are likely to skew the defendant's trial. Examples include the right to act in self-defense and to be provided an attorney if one cannot afford one. Another set of exceptions, but ones that are much more controversial, poorly articulated, and inconsistently applied, involves criminal defendants with a mental disorder. Some of these individuals are perceived to be less culpable, as well as less capable of exercising the rights all defendants retain within the justice system, more in need of mental health services than deserving of criminal prosecution, and warranting enhanced protections at trial. As a result, a series of special rules and procedures has evolved over the centuries, often without fanfare and even today with little systematic examination, to be applied to cases involving defendants with a mental disorder.

This book offers that systematic examination. It identifies the various stages of criminal justice proceedings when the mental status of a criminal defendant may be relevant, associated legal and policy issues, the history and evolution of these issues, and how they are currently resolved. To assist this examination, this text also offers an overview of mental disorders, the different models used to try to understand and explain them, how mental disorders are categorized, their relevance to criminal proceedings, and how forensic mental health assessments are conducted and employed during criminal proceedings.

It is important to note how pervasive and undertreated mental disorders are. According to current estimates, 4 percent to 7 percent (20 million) of all Americans experience a "serious" mental disorder that significantly disrupts their ability to function, 18 percent (44 million) experience a diagnosable mental illness each year,[5] almost half suffer some sort of mental disorder in their lifetime, and most are not treated, if treated at all, until years after the disorder's onset.[6] Within the criminal justice system, the pervasiveness of mental disorders is even more pronounced. Twenty percent of the nation's prison inmates are seriously mentally ill,[7] while 25 percent to 40 percent of individuals with a mental illness come into contact with the criminal justice system in some fashion every year, although often as victims of crime.[8] Indeed, it is often asserted that the criminal justice system has become the nation's de facto mental health care system given the vast number of people with a mental disorder who fall within its jurisdiction. As a result, issues regarding how to address defendants with a mental disorder within the criminal justice system are pressing and greatly in need of systematic examination.

As noted, because the criminal justice system is expected to provide criminal defendants with a fair and just trial, a defendant's mental disorder can play a potentially significant role in these proceedings. Although oftentimes difficult to assess and controversial, a defendant's mental status can be pivotal to the outcome of a case. It is a challenging undertaking to try to understand the workings of the mind and the impact of a mental disorder on human behavior in general and criminal behavior in particular. At the same time, trial officials may be under considerable pressure to move cases forward, with the existing system often ill-equipped to appropriately and promptly respond to the relatively unique and demanding issues posed by a criminal defendant with a mental disorder.

By offering an in-depth examination of the range of issues pertaining to the role of mental disorders in criminal trials, this book seeks to provide the reader with a greater understanding of the potential impact of these disorders on criminal defendants and their right to receive a fair and just trial, while balancing these considerations with society's need to hold guilty parties accountable for their crimes. To do so, an approach grounded in an analysis of actual cases is employed whenever possible. Drawing on this analysis, this text offers directions for future research and reforms regarding the processing, evaluation, and disposition of criminal defendants with a mental disorder.

To this end, chapter 1 provides core background information regarding mental disorders and their functional impact, particularly when associated with criminal behavior and defendants facing trial. This chapter dissects various myths pertaining to mental disorders, presents an overview of the different models used to understand, explain, and respond to mental disorders, and explores the diagnosis and differentiation of mental disorders.

Chapter 2 presents an overview of forensic mental health assessments and their deployment within the criminal justice system. This chapter describes how forensic mental health assessments are conducted, their distinctive nature, the multiple steps involved, and the challenges and tensions associated with providing them within the criminal justice system.

Chapter 3 begins a discussion of competency to stand trial (CST) determinations. It examines the initial United States Supreme Court (USSC) ruling establishing CST as a constitutional right, the underlying principles and forces that likely shaped the Court's determination, the pivotal role and foundational nature of CST determinations, and why this right was explicitly recognized only relatively recently and has received surprisingly little attention.

Chapter 4 further delineates the CST doctrine, including refinements to the USSC's basic approach, key aspects of these determinations, factors to be examined in these assessments, some criticisms of the existing CST doctrine, and possible alternative approaches.

Chapter 5 continues the discussion of CST issues but focuses on the procedural aspects of these determinations—an oftentimes overlooked but key component as these procedural matters can be outcome-determinative—and their evolution. It also addresses what forensic evaluators should incorporate in their CST assessments and potential complicating factors.

Chapter 6 addresses what happens after a CST hearing. If the defendant is found to be CST, trial proceedings usually resume where they left off, although scrutiny of the defendant's CST should continue. If found to be incompetent to stand trial (IST), the proceedings will generally remain suspended while custodial treatment is ordered for the defendant and the State is given an opportunity to restore the defendant's CST. A description of how these placements have evolved and related USSC rulings is also provided.

Chapter 7 addresses other competency issues that may arise in conjunction with criminal justice proceedings. These include competence to waive one's *Miranda* rights and confess to a crime or make other self-incriminating statements; competence to plead guilty and waive one's right to a trial; competence to waive one's right to an attorney and represent oneself; and competence to testify.

Chapter 8 addresses the insanity defense, its lengthy and controversial history, its basic threads and iterations, its evolution over time, the current tests employed, the lack of consensus over what the relevant standard should be, and the USSC's position regarding the defense.

Chapter 9 addresses variations and alternatives that have arisen because of reservations about the insanity defense, notwithstanding an underlying consensus that a defendant's mental disorder at the time of the offense should sometimes be relevant when determining criminal responsibility. These include deific decree, post-traumatic stress disorder (PTSD), battered spouse syndrome, and temporary insanity defenses, as well as efforts to abolish the insanity defense, preclude related mental health evidence, shift the burden of proof, heighten the required level of proof, and interject a guilty but mentally ill verdict. Determinations of criminal defendants' *mens rea* (that is, whether they had the requisite criminal intent) and *actus reus* (that is, whether they committed the requisite criminal act) are also discussed, including the automatism, "multiple personality," and sleepwalking "defenses."

Chapter 10 addresses the trial-related procedures used in conjunction with the insanity defense, the controversies associated with them, and USSC rulings regarding them.

Chapter 11 explores the dispositions of defendants who have been found not guilty by reason of insanity, the post-trial evaluations and judicial proceedings they must undergo to return to the community, bases for revoking a release, and associated evaluations and risk assessments.

Chapter 12 notes alternatives—such as diversion and mental health courts—to the commonly employed criminal justice proceedings, which are being explored in the hope that they may be more suitable for processing defendants with a mental disorder and thereby help to resolve some of the thorniest issues faced by the criminal justice system and society. It closes by reiterating the challenging nature of this field and stresses the important role that forensic mental health evaluators can play.

1

Mental Disorders and Criminal Behavior

If you don't know where you're going, you might not get there.
—Yogi Berra, baseball player and manager

Despite their pervasiveness, the impact of mental disorders is widely misunderstood, even though their impact often shapes the criminal justice system's response to defendants with a mental disorder.[1] For the criminal justice system to do a better job of addressing some of the most challenging and vulnerable defendants appearing before it, some common myths need to be identified and deconstructed.[2]

MYTH #1: MENTAL DISORDERS OCCUR RELATIVELY INFRE-QUENTLY. It has been estimated that in any given year a mental disorder is experienced by as many as one in four (nearly 60 million) American adults;[3] almost 20 percent (about 44 million) experience some form of diagnosable mental illness;[4] between 4 percent and 7 percent (as many as 20 million) experience a serious mental illness such as schizophrenia, major depression, or a bipolar disorder;[5] and more than 10 percent experience serious psychological distress.[6] Furthermore, almost half of all Americans will struggle with some form of mental disorder during their lifetime.[7] Of particular relevance to the criminal justice system is that among young adults ages eighteen to twenty-five, the age range during which a criminal act is most likely to be committed,[8] 20 percent experience a mental illness in a given year,[9] and 4 percent a serious mental illness.[10]

MYTH #2: MOST PEOPLE WITH A MENTAL DISORDER CAN READILY MANAGE THEIR AFFAIRS. The World Health Organization has determined that mental health disorders based on the "burden" of the disease are the leading cause of disability in the United States, with mental illness being the leading cause of disability for individuals between the ages of fifteen and forty-four.[11] People with a serious mental illness die on average twenty-five years earlier than the general population,[12] while a meta-analysis found that people with a mental disorder in general die ten years earlier than the general population, with this mortality gap increasing since the 1990s.[13] For individuals with schizophrenia, suicide is the leading cause of death.[14]

The disabling nature of mental illness is due in part to its frequent co-occurrence with another psychiatric disorder—about 45 percent of adults with a mental disorder have two or more mental disorders—and accompanying chronic medical conditions such as obesity, diabetes, chronic pain, and heart disease.[15] Complicating matters further, individuals with a mental disorder often have difficulty managing their chronic conditions because of poor diet, lack of exercise, problems maintaining prescribed medications, or an inability to get the health care they need, which may be attributed in part to their above-average rates of poverty and unemployment, as well as the lack of a "social support" network—family and friends—that often helps individuals manage a chronic medical illness.[16]

MYTH #3: MENTAL DISORDERS DEFINE A PERSON AND ARE MORE OR LESS THE SAME. Mental disorders encompass a widely diverse set of conditions, which manifest in many forms and affect individuals in many different ways. Their impact on cognition, emotions, and behavior, as well as on a person's capacities and abilities, varies enormously. A US surgeon general has pointed out that "many ingredients of mental health may be identifiable, but mental health is not easy to define."[17] The American Psychiatric Association, in its diagnostic manual—now in its fifth edition and referred to as the *DSM-5*—states that "it has not been possible to completely separate normal and pathological symptom expressions."[18] Furthermore, the symptoms associated with mental disorders, as well as their diagnoses, tend to fluctuate significantly over time and to variously interfere with some functions but not others.[19] This US surgeon general has also observed that "relatively few mental illnesses have an unremitting course marked by the most acute manifestations of illness; rather, for reasons that are not yet understood, the symptoms associated with a mental illness tend to wax and wane."[20]

MYTH #4: A MENTAL DISORDER REFLECTS A LACK OF EFFORT OR WILL ON THE PART OF THE PERSON WITH THE DISORDER. In a survey of 2,813 psychiatrists, 96.7 percent disagreed with the statement that one of the main causes of mental illness is a lack of self-discipline and willpower, and 92 percent agreed that virtually anyone can become mentally ill.[21] The Council of State Governments has observed that "a large number of people with mental illness in prison (and especially in jail) have been incarcerated because they displayed in public the symptoms of untreated mental illness. Experiencing delusions, immobilized by depression, or suffering other consequences of inadequate treatment, many of these individuals have [unsuccessfully] struggled, at times heroically, to fend off symptoms of mental illness."[22] As one mental health provider noted, "Don't let anyone tell you that mental illness is a character flaw that you can escape if you just try hard enough."[23] A mental disorder is often debilitating, disorienting, frightening, or overpowering, with the person often vulnerable to self-abuse or abuse by others.[24]

MYTH #5: PERSONS WITH A MENTAL DISORDER ARE LESS INTERESTED IN HUMAN RELATIONSHIPS AND LESS CAPABLE OF FORMING AND TREASURING SUCH RELATIONSHIPS. Human interactions generally remain important to individuals with a mental disorder, and how they are treated by others and society often has a significant impact on them.[25] For example, it has been pointed out that "the family is one of the most powerful forces in the universe. . . . [and] families can have a profound effect on . . . the course of a psychiatric disorder."[26] It has also been noted that "when you experience severe emotional problems, particularly those that get diagnosed as mental disorders or lead to psychiatric hospitalizations, [normal and expected] conflicts [with your family] are often heightened. . . . This [disruption] can throw your entire family into further turmoil, worsening your dilemma."[27] At the same time, it has been determined that adults with a disability are at greater risk of being a victim of violence within relationships and that individuals with a mental illness are particularly vulnerable, with 24 percent reporting they experienced physical, sexual, or intimate partner violence during the previous year.[28] Nevertheless, like most human beings, individuals with a mental disorder place considerable importance on maintaining these relationships.[29] Moreover, a strong association has been found between the occurrence of a mental disorder and a sense of loneliness.[30]

MYTH #6: A MENTAL DISORDER MAKES A PERSON MORE DANGEROUS. A US surgeon general has stated that "there is very little risk of violence or harm to a stranger from casual contact with an individual who has a mental disorder. . . . The overall contribution of mental disorders to the total level of violence in society is exceptionally small."[31] Indeed, individuals with a mental illness are more likely to be victims than perpetrators of violent crime.[32] Although most Americans believe that persons with a mental illness are dangerous and as a result are reluctant or unwilling to interact with them,[33] the contribution of people with a mental illness to overall rates of violence is small,[34] with violent behavior more common when other risk factors are present such as substance abuse or dependence.[35]

MYTH #7: GREATER SCRUTINY IS NEEDED OF PERSONS WITH A MENTAL DISORDER BECAUSE OF THE DANGER THEY POSE, AND MECHANISMS SHOULD BE PUT IN PLACE TO READILY PROTECT OTHERS. "Persons with a mental disorder should be afforded the respect and dignity to which all human beings are entitled": this is the position taken under the Convention on the Rights of Persons with Disabilities, an international human rights treaty adopted by the United Nations General Assembly in 2006 and ratified in 2008, with 160 signatories and 174 parties, including the European Union.[36] The stated purpose of the Convention is to "promote, protect and ensure the full and equal enjoyment of all human rights and fundamental freedoms by all persons with disabilities, and to promote respect for their inherent dignity"; it also specifically notes that "[p]ersons with disabilities include those who have long-term . . . mental [or] intellectual . . . impairments."[37]

MYTH #8: IF PROBLEMS ARISE INVOLVING A PERSON WITH A MENTAL DISORDER, THE MENTAL HEALTH SYSTEM WILL INTERVENE. It is estimated that 25 to 40 percent of individuals with a mental illness come into contact with the criminal justice system each year.[38] It is also estimated that 7 percent of police contacts in jurisdictions of 100,000 or more people involve persons believed to be mentally ill.[39] Mental disorders can result in disorganized thought processes, impaired reality testing and judgment, poor planning and problem-solving skills, and impulsivity associated with criminal behavior.[40] The criminal justice system continues to absorb and struggle with a massive number of individuals who "are falling through the cracks of this country's social safety net . . . [and] have been incarcerated because they displayed in public the symptoms of untreated mental illness."[41]

MYTH #9: MOST INDIVIDUALS WITH A MENTAL DISORDER WHO RUN AFOUL OF THE CRIMINAL JUSTICE SYSTEM HAVE COMMITTED A VIOLENT ACT. It has been determined that "during street encounters, police officers are almost twice as likely to arrest someone who appears to have a mental illness."[42] The underlying issue is often these individuals' immediate need for basic mental health services.[43] Half of all persons with a mental health diagnosis first experience symptoms by the age of fourteen, but on average they do not receive treatment until the age of twenty-four.[44] Two-thirds of primary care physicians cannot obtain outpatient mental health services for their patients—a rate that is at least twice as high as that for other services—due in part to health plan barriers and inadequate coverage.[45] Only 41 percent of individuals with a mental illness report receiving treatment, while a federal agency ascertained that 96.5 million Americans in 2014 were living in areas where there was a shortage of mental health providers, up from 91 million in 2012.[46]

MYTH #10: MOST INDIVIDUALS WITH A MENTAL DISORDER WHO COMMIT A CRIMINAL ACT ARE DIVERTED OUT OF THE CRIMINAL JUSTICE SYSTEM. It has been widely noted that "people with mental illnesses often cycle repeatedly through courtrooms, jails, and prisons that are ill-equipped to address their needs and, in particular, to provide adequate treatment."[47] Although virtually everyone will experience adverse consequences from such encounters, this contact "can be doubly traumatic for people with a mental illness, [as] the resulting criminal record can impede their later access to housing and mental health services."[48]

MYTH #11: PERSONS WITH A MENTAL DISORDER WHO BECOME INVOLVED IN THE CRIMINAL JUSTICE SYSTEM CANNOT COHERENTLY DESCRIBE WHAT HAPPENED. Individuals with a mental disorder sometimes feel that their criminal behavior was justified or understandable, and they may believe, sometimes justly, that they have been treated unfairly by the criminal justice system, society, or those around them.[49] For most individuals with a mental disorder, as for people in general, a perception that the criminal justice process is fair and that they have been given an opportunity to explain their situation are key factors in accepting the outcome, regardless of what it may be.[50]

MYTH #12: PERSONS WITH A MENTAL DISORDER WHO COM-
MIT A CRIMINAL ACT DO NOT FEEL GUILT OR REMORSE FOR
THEIR CRIME AND CANNOT BE REHABILITATED. Individuals with
a mental disorder can benefit from being held accountable for their
criminal behavior, be deterred from further criminal behavior, and
change their behavior, although they may have an impaired capacity to
do so that may require special assistance.[51] Persons with a mental disorder can also feel remorse for criminal behavior and empathy for victims
of that behavior, although they may have an impaired capacity for this
as well, which may also necessitate special assistance.[52]

MYTH #13: PERSONS WITH A MENTAL DISORDER KNOW WHAT
THEY ARE DOING WHEN THEY COMMIT A CRIME, COULD HAVE
DONE SOMETHING DIFFERENT, AND THUS SHOULD BE HELD
FULLY RESPONSIBLE FOR THEIR CRIME. In an approach that dates
back centuries, the diminished culpability of individuals with a mental
disorder can be established by showing an impairment of their ability to
(a) appreciate the nature, character, or consequences of their behavior;
(b) appreciate that their behavior was wrong; (c) conform their behavior
to the requirements of the law; or (d) choose between right and wrong,
although the standard employed across jurisdictions varies and this disposition does tend to be controversial.[53]

MYTH #14: EVALUATING AND CRAFTING THE NEEDED RESPONSE
FOR A CRIMINAL DEFENDANT WITH A MENTAL DISORDER IS RELA-
TIVELY STRAIGHTFORWARD. Mental disorders and the challenges they
entail tend to be multifaceted, with their evaluation, as well as the appropriate course of treatment, as much an art as a science. A leading treatise
notes, "The clinical evaluation of [mental state] is one of the more difficult
assessments in forensic work."[54] In addition to the challenge of understanding and assessing a mental disorder in general, complicating factors
include (a) a co-occurrence with a substance abuse disorder; (b) a lack
of employment, housing, or support; and (c) a history of experiencing
discrimination, stigma, prejudice, misunderstanding, and mistreatment.[55]
Crafting an appropriate response needs to take such factors into account.[56]

MYTH #15: SOCIETY AND INDIVIDUALS WITH A MENTAL DIS-
ORDER CONVICTED OF A CRIME ARE BEST SERVED IF THESE IN-
DIVIDUAL ARE INCARCERATED. For the past forty years the number
of incarcerated individuals in the United States has steadily grown to

the point where the per capita rate of incarceration exceeds that of every other country in the world,[57] with a significant proportion of incarcerated individuals experiencing a mental disorder.[58] It has been estimated that 16.9 percent of all people entering jails have a serious mental illness (14.5 percent of men and 31 percent of women),[59] that as many as 20 percent of prisoners are seriously mentally ill, with up to 5 percent being actively psychotic at any given time,[60] and that "more than half of all prison and jail inmates ha[ve] a mental health problem."[61] As noted earlier, American jails and prisons have become the de facto mental health system of this country, notwithstanding a widespread consensus that incarcerating these individuals is often inappropriate, counterproductive, and harmful, and that these facilities generally do not provide an appropriate environment for their care and treatment.[62]

MYTH #16: THERE ARE FEW AVAILABLE CREDIBLE OPTIONS BEYOND INCARCERATION FOR INDIVIDUALS WHO HAVE A MENTAL DISORDER AND HAVE COMMITTED A CRIME. There are a number of models for (a) diverting individuals with a mental disorder from the criminal justice system, (b) enhancing the likelihood that they will succeed upon returning to the community, and (c) minimizing the likelihood that they will reoffend or otherwise run afoul of the criminal justice system again.[63] The appropriate model will vary depending on the needs of the individual and the resources available, though it should be noted that the availability of related resources poses a continuing challenge.[64]

Explanatory Models of Mental Disorders

As should be apparent from this overview of myths regarding mental disorders and their impact on criminal defendants, a core challenge to enhancing and ensuring a fair, just, and appropriate response to these defendants is simply to make sure that these disorders are adequately understood and addressed. The identification of an applicable conceptual model is the first step in this process, although there is an ongoing debate over which model is best suited for this context. There are three predominant approaches.[65]

Medical Model

The first is the *medical model*, which in recent years has predominated for a number of reasons, not the least of which is that quicker and sometimes less costly results can be obtained when treatment is provided pursuant to this model. The medical model posits that a mental illness, like all illnesses, can be best understood and addressed by targeting the associated physiological or biological process. The medical model in general focuses on the various organs of the body and in the case of mental illness centers on the brain. Mental illness is perceived to be the product of a dysfunction of the brain, and just as there are specific adverse consequences when a heart, lung, or kidney does not function well, so, too, when the brain performs poorly, one of the results is mental illness.

In recent years, considerable progress has been made in identifying specific portions and mechanisms of the brain (known as *biomarkers*) linked to particular behaviors, functions, skills, and proclivities of the human being. This understanding, in turn, has improved the ability to diagnose mental disorders, ascertain their cause, predict the course of disorders and the effectiveness of treatments, and tailor treatment to a specific disorder.

Under the medical model, the emphasis tends to be on developing medications that change the functioning of the brain, typically by altering the actions or flow of neurotransmitters, chemical messengers that transmit information between neurons in the brain and direct its functioning. This model is less concerned with the etiology or cause of a mental disorder, including the impact of the surrounding environment, and instead places its primary emphasis on "fixing" whatever has gone wrong in the brain.

Various new technologies, such as brain imaging or neuroimagery, can now identify how the brain is functioning. Scientists are also gaining a greater understanding of the role and impact of genetics, proteins, chemical imbalances, and the structure or physiology of the brain on the emergence or manifestation of a mental disorder. One ongoing controversy is whether the "mind" is greater than the sum of the parts of the "brain," but even here proponents of the medical model tend to assert that the "mind" can best be understood by studying how the parts of the "brain" interact.

The criminal justice system over the years has increasingly gravitated toward the medical model, tending to view it as a "hard" science because its findings and assertions are more likely to be supported by empirical data. Nevertheless, concerns remain regarding this model's validity, reliability, and explanatory power, the availability of related services (e.g., the willingness of psychiatrists to fill relatively low-paying, unglamorous positions within the criminal justice system), and the growing expense of these services. In addition, prescribed treatments are not universally effective; multiple attempts, sometimes on an almost trial-and-error basis, may be needed to identify a treatment that ameliorates an individual's mental disorder, and even if a successful treatment is identified, its effectiveness may diminish over time. Furthermore, individuals who are prescribed these treatments may refuse or fail to adhere to their treatment plan, sometimes because the prescribed treatment has significant short-term or long-term adverse side effects.

Psychodynamic Model

A second model used to explain mental disorders, which had a widespread following in the past, is the *psychodynamic model*. This model posits that human behavior is the product of underlying internal conflicts, although we are often unaware of these conflicts. Proponents assert that past experiences, particularly those from childhood, shape how we feel about the world around us and behave. Sigmund Freud, the influential Austrian neurologist and founder of psychoanalysis who rose to prominence in the first part of the twentieth century, articulated concepts such as *id*, *ego*, and *superego* to explain our internal conflicts. He also developed various techniques, such as free association and dream analysis, to help people struggling with mental health problems to explore, understand, and work through their prior experiences and resulting conflicts. He believed that this process could help people gain insights into their problems and the sources of their conflicts, thereby change their thinking and behavior, and ultimately resolve their mental health issues.

Notwithstanding its lengthy history, the psychodynamic model has been the target of considerable criticism, much of which has particularly resonated within the criminal justice system. Criticisms include that it takes too long for the therapist and client to generate needed insights, with time a luxury the criminal justice system, particularly in conjunction with criminal trials, often lacks. In addition, it has been asserted that this model is not particularly effective in addressing psychoses—the mental disorders most likely to be the center of controversy in a criminal trial. Concerns have also been raised that this approach does not take into account ongoing environmental effects that may be instrumental in shaping the behavior of criminal offenders with a mental disorder. It has also been challenged for failing to address the underlying physiological functions of the brain and the effects that occur when the brain dysfunctions, such as may follow a head trauma. However, it is the expense associated with the psychodynamic model and its lengthy interventions that have particularly dampened demand for this model both in general and within the criminal justice system. The difficulty of applying its concepts to the criminal justice paradigm, particularly the tenet that criminal behavior may be the result of "invisible" unconscious motivations, has also limited any usefulness it may have in this context.

Behaviorism and the Social Learning Model

A third model that has gained a considerable following among mental health professionals comes from *behaviorism* and *social learning theory*. Individuals who provided the foundation for this approach include William James, Ivan Petrovich Pavlov, B. F. Skinner, and John Watson. Its supporters assert that our personality—who we are—is the sum of our responses to, and the impact of, the world around us. Those who embrace this model tend to reject the role of the unconscious and related dynamics embraced by the psychodynamic model. The proponents of this third model contend that the key element of human behavior is one's interactions with the environment in which one lives and what is learned from these interactions. When we learn inappropriate behavior, mental health professionals trained in this approach believe they can reshape our behavior by positively reinforcing more appropriate behavior and by withholding reinforcement for or by punishing inappropriate behavior. Positive reinforcement, it is asserted, will encourage desirable behavior, while punishing or withholding reinforcement will discourage and ultimately extinguish undesirable behavior. A spinoff from this approach is cognitive-behavioral therapy, an approach that relies on observational learning rather than just direct reinforcement to move clients toward more appropriate behavior.

A criticism of this model is its relative inability to help individuals experiencing a psychotic episode. This set of symptoms—which frequently must be addressed in connection with criminal defendants—not only impedes an individual's ability to learn, but often results in an active resistance to efforts to reinforce or otherwise encourage more appropriate behavior. In addition, although the treatment plans associated with this model tend to progress faster, are less costly, and are of more immediate help than those pursuant to the psychodynamic model, they are still often seen as relatively slow and ineffective by criminal justice officials. In recent years, treatment built upon this model tends to be used in conjunction with the medical model approach, with many mental health professionals asserting that a combination of the two is best.

Applying These Models

The key question regarding each of these models is its value for assessing and responding to defendants with a mental disorder within the criminal justice system. More specifically, how well do these models' diagnoses, explanations of the causes of behavior, and evaluations of the impact of mental disorders on behavior, cognition, emotions, and ability to communicate, as well as their approaches for treating mental disorders, fit the needs and demands of the criminal justice system? For example, which model is best suited for ascertaining whether a criminal defendant is sufficiently competent to stand trial or should be excused from criminal responsibility because the criminal behavior was the result of a mental disorder?

Finding the best approach is critical. As discussed, when a seemingly inexplicable violent crime occurs, media accounts typically probe whether the assailant's mental state played a role. The identified assailant may be portrayed as someone with a mental disorder who irrationally inflicted a tragic loss. At the same time, for every notorious case, there will be a score of cases involving defendants with a mental disorder that receive no media attention and whose trials are not subject to public scrutiny but which pose no less of a challenge to the criminal justice system.

There is, however, a growing recognition of the massive number of individuals with a mental disorder engulfed in criminal proceedings as the criminal justice system has become this country's de facto mental health system, with much of this attention stoked by criminal justice officials struggling with how to manage and respond to this population.[66] Indeed, the pervasiveness of this population, the challenges of meeting its basic needs, and the fact that they were not being met led the US Supreme Court to issue an unprecedented ruling in 2011, when it declared that California's failure to provide needed mental health services to its prison population could be the basis for a court order reducing inmate census not in just one facility, but in facilities across the state. This, in turn, forced California to release 25 percent of its prisoners back into the community before they would ordinarily have been deemed ready for such a return.[67]

Introduction to Mental Disorders

The ultimate question for a forensic mental health professional is how to obtain and present information that is sufficiently helpful and reliable for the courts to permit it to play a role in a criminal trial. A particular challenge is how to distinguish criminal defendants' genuine presentations of their mental status and perceptions of relevant events from intentional efforts to manipulate this information to serve their own ends.

Addressing this and related issues requires an understanding of mental disorders and associated nomenclature. It should be noted, however, that most relevant legal tests are primarily functional rather than diagnostic in nature. In other words, they assess how criminal defendants' mental state impacted their behavior regarding a specific issue before the court, rather than simply whether a psychiatric disorder was present or how mental disorders shape behavior in general. Nevertheless, judges presiding over criminal trials typically expect mental health experts to ground their opinions in a psychiatric framework. For example, although a diagnosis of schizophrenia or bipolar I disorder is generally not directly relevant to a determination of a defendant's competency or responsibility, this is the kind of foundation that judges typically expect forensic mental health experts to develop and draw upon in reaching their findings. Furthermore, both the lawyers introducing or challenging mental health–related evidence and the judges receiving this evidence will need some understanding of the underlying psychiatric framework.

Thus, to address related criminal trial issues, it is necessary to have at least some general familiarity with mental disorders and their diagnosis, their impact on behavior, and related terminology.

It is also important to recognize that beyond its direct effects, a mental disorder often has a significant impact on the psyche of a person, which is to say, how they see, define, or present themselves. Because the symptoms of a mental illness generally do not begin to manifest until individuals are at least in their teens, a person's self-identity is typically relatively well established by this time. Furthermore, the psychotic symptoms often associated with the more severe forms of mental illness—which are the focus of most mental health–related criminal trial issues—generally do not occur until individuals are in their twenties or thirties. As a result, there is often a sharp schism between such individuals' current lives and their lives before the mental disorder onset, which creates an ongoing struggle in these individuals over how to reconcile these two stages of their lives. Mental illness is frequently described as a changing of the person that induces fear and isolation. Individuals often struggle to cope both with their mental illness and their evolving relationships with family, friends, colleagues, and acquaintances, who, in turn, also struggle to understand and interact with someone who is both the same and a different person. It is an extremely confusing and frightening time for everyone involved.

Before turning to the different diagnoses used to categorize mental disorders, a few caveats should be noted. As a past US surgeon general cautioned, what constitutes mental health is not easy to define, is subject to many different interpretations, and is rooted in value judgments that may vary across cultures.[68] Indeed, some, including the "radical psychiatrist" Thomas Szasz, have even questioned these psychiatric labels and argued that they are simply tools to control unacceptable or unpopular behavior.[69] In a somewhat similar vein, Dr. Marcia Angell, a former editor of the *New England Journal of Medicine*, has contended that mental illness is unlike other illnesses in that its diagnoses are based on subjective descriptions of symptoms and behaviors, rather than the largely objective physical manifestations (which in turn serve as the basis for lab tests and other diagnostic tools) used to diagnose other illnesses; that is, less tangible and reliable indicators are generally used in diagnosing a mental illness.[70] Proponents of the medical model in particular, however, counter that scientific advances increasingly show that abnormal mental states arise from physiological or chemical irregularities within the brain.[71]

Regardless of these conflicting positions, the legal system for the most part recognizes the existence of mental disorders and applies them to a range of criminal trial–related issues. The criminal justice system, as noted, relies on mental health professionals to discern whether a criminal defendant has a mental disorder, the nature of that disorder, its impact on the defendant's thinking, behavior, and ability to communicate, and, although ultimately the responsibility of the judge or jury, whether a given legal standard has been met.

In evaluating mental disorders, some mental health professionals focus on the diagnosis, while others concentrate on the impact or resulting disability. There is also a debate over whether to focus on specific symptoms, the constellation of symptoms, how the person is behaving, or the person's underlying problems. Nevertheless, mental health professionals generally employ the diagnostic scheme provided by the American Psychiatric Association's *Diagnostic and Statistical Manual* (*DSM*), which has gone through a series of iterations over the years and become more expansive with each edition.

The most recent version, published in 2013, is referred to as the *DSM-5*, labeled as such because it is the fifth edition of the publication. Its focus is on a person's constellation of symptoms and the impact of these symptoms on the person's functioning. Typically it employs a "rule-in" rather than a "rule-out" approach. In other words, a person must demonstrate specific symptoms or a range of symptoms in order to be assigned a given psychiatric diagnosis; a particular diagnosis is not precluded by the presence of a seemingly inconsistent symptom.[72] The *DSM-5* is intended to generate consistent results across clinicians and researchers, but within a given diagnosis there is room for considerable variation in the symptoms manifested by individuals assigned this diagnosis. For example, a diagnosis may require only that two of five distinct listed symptoms be displayed, which means that individuals with this diagnosis can vary considerably in their symptom presentations.

The manual is a list of symptoms and traits that can serve as the basis for a diagnosis. It does not address likely causes. In addition, an assigned diagnosis is not necessarily permanent. As a clinician learns more about a client or as the mental disorder evolves, the identified prevalent symptoms may change, and a different diagnosis may become more appropriate. The manual is meant to provide a diagnostic guide, not a definitive resolution.

To enhance its value, the *DSM-5* sought to employ an operational or data-driven approach as the foundation for its classification scheme. However, while based on underlying empirical research, the determinations of diagnoses, relevant symptoms, and the like were made by a series of committees of mental health professionals. As a result, and because of the continuing uncertainty regarding the nature and manifestations of mental disorders, there were inevitably differences of opinion and some interjection of values and beliefs into this process. Nonetheless, although the manual is expressly intended solely as a guide for clinical diagnoses and research—with, as discussed below, a specific caveat that it is not intended for the legal arena—this has not prevented the legal system from relying heavily upon it.

The *DSM-5* defines a "mental disorder" as "a syndrome characterized by clinically significant disturbance in an individual's cognition, emotion regulation, or behavior that reflects a dysfunction in the psychological, biological, or developmental processes underlying mental functioning." It adds that "[m]ental disorders are usually associated with significant distress or disability in social, occupational, or other important activities." However, it also points out that "an expectable or culturally approved response to a common stressor or loss, such as the death of a loved one, is not a mental disorder." Finally, it notes that "socially deviant behavior (e.g., political, religious, or sexual) and conflicts that are primarily between the individual and society are not mental disorders unless the deviance or conflict results from a dysfunction in the individual."[73]

Nevertheless, the difficulty in establishing the specific parameters of a given mental disorder has been noted because (a) "mental disorders are not susceptible to precise definition," (b) "diagnoses rely significantly on the subjective impressions and judgment of the health-care provider," (c) "the 'symptoms' associated with a mental disorder often overlap with the 'normal' difficulties experienced by many," (d) "the symptoms of a specific mental disorder may vary from day to day and frequently overlap with the symptoms of other mental disorders," and (e) "mental disorders usually do not have physiologically detectible symptoms . . . that are susceptible to clinical measurement."[74]

In addition, even if precision can be obtained in a mental health diagnosis, this diagnosis often does not match the needs of the legal system.[75] As the *DSM-5* points out:

> When DSM-5 categories, criteria, and textual descriptions are employed for forensic purposes, there is a risk that diagnostic information will be misused or misunderstood. These dangers arise because of the imperfect fit between the questions of ultimate concern to the law and the information contained in a clinical diagnosis. In most situations, the clinical diagnosis of a DSM-5 mental disorder . . . does not imply that an individual with such a condition meets legal criteria for the presence of a mental disorder or a specific legal standard. . . . It is precisely because impairments, abilities, and disabilities vary widely within each diagnostic category that assignment of a particular diagnosis does not imply a specific level of impairment or disability. . . . Nonclinical decision makers should also be cautioned that a diagnosis does not carry any necessary implications regarding . . . the individual's degree of control over behaviors that may be associated with the disorder.[76]

Notwithstanding these caveats, psychiatric diagnoses tend to play a significant role in criminal justice proceedings when a defendant's mental disorder is relevant, largely because the mental health professionals who generate forensic evaluations are trained in this diagnostic framework and are far more conversant in and comfortable employing it. Judges and legal practitioners, in contrast, face an ongoing challenge in attempting to understand this diagnostic framework, its strengths and weaknesses, when and how such diagnoses are relevant to a legal determination, and how to press forensic mental health evaluators for needed clarification and application to the legal issues before the court.

Psychiatric Diagnoses

The *DSM-5* is organized into twenty diagnostic categories, although within these categories there are many syndromes and psychological patterns. What follows is a description of these diagnoses as set forth in the *DSM-5*, with examples provided of the diagnoses most frequently the focus of criminal proceedings. This discussion is intended to be instructive, not exhaustive.

Psychotic Disorders

A diagnostic category frequently associated with criminal trials, *psychotic disorders* are "abnormalities in one or more of the following five domains: delusions, hallucinations, disorganized thinking (speech), grossly disorganized or abnormal motor behavior (including catatonia), and negative symptoms."[77]

Delusions are fixed, false beliefs that do not change even when the person is presented with conflicting evidence. Delusions can be persecutory (that others are out to obstruct or harm you), referential (that random gestures, comments, events, and so on, refer specifically to you), grandiose (that you possess qualities superior to others), erotomanic (that another person is in love with you), nihilistic (that a major catastrophe is coming), and somatic (a preoccupation with one's health or organ function). *Hallucinations* are apparent sensory perceptions of things that are not present, with auditory hallucinations (such as voices) being the most frequent, while "frank" hallucinations (when the person sees something that is not there) are relatively rare. *Disorganized thinking* may result in incoherent speech or frequent derailment (the speaker going off-topic). *Disorganized motor behavior* includes mumbling to one's self, collecting odd objects, or catatonic behavior. The *negative symptoms* include avolition (a lack of motivation), lack of persistence (an inability to initiate and persist in an activity), affective blunting (diminished emotional expression), and alogia (poverty of speech, which is more frequent than disorganized speech).

Schizophrenia is the most prominent of the psychotic disorders. The National Institute of Mental Health defines schizophrenia as "a chronic and severe mental disorder that affects how a person thinks, feels, and behaves," and notes that "people with schizophrenia may seem like they have lost touch with reality."[78] For this diagnosis to be assigned, related symptoms must last at least six months, with two or more symptoms present for a significant portion of a one-month period. Untreated, schizophrenia tends to be a crippling, devastating disorder that most equate with mental illness and homelessness. It is estimated to affect roughly one out of every two hundred persons. The first psychotic episode associated with schizophrenia tends to occur when affected individuals are in their twenties, followed by "a slow and gradual development of a variety of clinically significant signs and symptoms."[79] Initial so-called "positive" symptoms such as hallucinations and delusions tend to gradually recede over time, while the disorder's "negative" symptoms gradually become more prominent and, if untreated, leave a person relatively unable to think, feel, or act. Because of its highly debilitating and chronic nature, there are few affected individuals who achieve prominence in their chosen vocation. One exception was the American Nobel prize-winning mathematician, John Forbes Nash Jr.—the focus of the biography *A Beautiful Mind* and a movie of the same name—who was hospitalized for several years and treated for paranoid schizophrenia early in his career.

Another psychotic disorder, one that particularly demonstrates the challenge of diagnosing mental disorders, is *schizoaffective disorder*. An individual with this disorder experiences both major mood episodes (either depressive or manic in nature) and schizophrenia. It tends to be one of the more perplexing diagnoses as—depending on which set of symptoms predominates at the time—an individual may variously be diagnosed with a mood disorder, schizophrenia, or a schizoaffective disorder.

Brief psychotic disorder—another perplexing diagnosis—is when an episode of delusions, hallucinations, or disorganized speech lasts at least one day but less than a month, with an eventual return to the person's previous mental state. When diagnosing this disorder, caution must be exercised to rule out the effects of substance abuse or an underlying medical condition such as a brain tumor. When reported as co-occurring with criminal behavior, its sudden onset and disappearance after a relatively brief time makes malingering a distinct possibility.

Other psychotic disorders listed in the *DSM-5* include *delusional disorder* (when one or more delusions are present for a month or longer); *schizophreniform disorder* (when an episode of delusions, hallucinations, or disorganized speech lasts at least a month but less than six months); *substance/medication-induced psychotic disorder* (in which delusions, hallucinations, or both develop during or soon after substance intoxication or withdrawal, or following exposure to a medication); and *psychotic disorder due to another medical condition*.

Neurocognitive Disorders

Another *DSM-5* diagnostic category encompasses what are called *neurocognitive disorders* (in the *DSM-IV* they were designated as "Dementia, Delirium, Amnestic, and Other Cognitive Disorders"). These mental disorders are relatively unique in that their underlying pathology, and frequently their etiology as well, can often be determined. Formerly referred to collectively as "dementia," these disorders involve a significant loss of consciousness and memory. The presence of one of these disorders can provide a foundation for concerns about the trial-related competency of a criminal defendant and on occasion for an assertion that an insanity or diminished capacity defense should be available.

Probably the most well-known of these disorders is *Alzheimer's disease*, which involves a gradual cognitive decline associated with a shrinking or hardening of the brain. Estimated to affect one in ten people over the age of sixty-five, it causes problems with memory and thinking and is generally untreatable, although considerable efforts are being devoted to finding a treatment.

Another relatively well-known neurocognitive disorder is *Parkinson's disease*, which is a chronic, slowly progressive neurological condition that affects movement and often includes tremors, rigidity, and difficulty walking. It is estimated that nearly 1 million people in the United States have this condition, including the actor Michael J. Fox and the now-deceased Muhammad Ali.

A third widespread variation is *neurocognitive disorder due to traumatic brain injury* (TBI), which is caused by an impact to the head or another incident that causes a rapid movement or displacement of the brain within the skull and precipitates either a loss of consciousness, post-traumatic amnesia, disorientation and confusion, or various neurological signs such as seizures. This disorder may result in irritability, tension, anxiety, being easily frustrated, angry outbursts, personality changes, sleep disorders, and seizures. In the United States, 1.7 to 2.5 million TBIs occur annually; they contribute to about 50,000 deaths per year or about 30 percent of all injury deaths. Roughly 2 percent of the population lives with a TBI-associated disability.[80] Although often associated with warfare, TBIs may be incurred from explosions in general, contact sports, automobile accidents, or a simple slip and fall. They have been cited increasingly in recent years as the basis for insanity or diminished capacity defenses.

Delirium, another neurocognitive disorder, involves a disturbance in attention (a reduced ability to direct, focus, sustain, or shift attention) or awareness (a reduced orientation to the environment) that develops over a short period of time (usually hours to a few days) and tends to fluctuate in severity during the course of a day. It can result in memory deficit, disorientation, language disruption, or distorted perception. It is generally attributed to substance intoxication, substance withdrawal, medication, or an underlying medical condition. If due to substance intoxication or substance withdrawal, the law has traditionally been reluctant to recognize this diagnosis as a basis for a legal excuse (such as insanity) for criminal behavior because of the perceived voluntary nature of the behavior that led to the condition, unless the condition has become permanent following prolonged substance abuse that typically lasted for years and resulted in permanent neurological damage.

It should be noted that the *DSM-5* includes the separate category of "Substance-Related and Addictive Disorders," which encompasses the use or ingestion of alcohol, caffeine, cannabis (marijuana), phencyclidine (PCP), other hallucinogens, inhalants, opioids, sedatives, hypnotics, anxiolytics (anti-anxiety), stimulants, and tobacco, as well as gambling disorder.

Bipolar Disorders

In the past, bipolar disorders were combined with depression and jointly listed as "Mood Disorders." The *DSM-5*, however, introduced a separate "Bipolar and Related Disorders" category and asserts that these disorders are distinct from both depressive disorders and psychotic disorders such as schizophrenia. Many famous people, including, it has been speculated, Isaac Newton, Ludwig van Beethoven, Vincent van Gogh, Ernest Hemingway, and Sylvia Plath, have wrestled with a bipolar disorder, accomplishing much during a manic or hypomanic phase, but later having to struggle with their "demons."

The *bipolar I disorder* includes what used to be referred to as "manic-depression" and involves manic or hypomanic (mildly manic) episodes, usually interspersed with major depressive episodes. During manic episodes, individuals may be pathologically happy and unaware of accompanying irritability or poor judgment. In addition, they may exhibit increased activity with little sleep; pressured, distracted, or nonsensical speech; flights of ideas or racing thoughts; grandiose thinking; impulsive behavior; delusions; poor insight; or excessive involvement in activities that have a high potential for painful or criminal consequences, such as unrestrained buying sprees, driving at high speeds, sexual indiscretions, or foolish business investments and activities. Individuals with this disorder can be at high risk of suicide, estimated to be at least fifteen times that of the general population, and may account for one-quarter of all completed suicides.[81]

A *bipolar II disorder* involves a major depressive episode followed by a hypomanic episode, during which time mood tends to be elevated, expansive, or irritable. There is an ongoing debate over whether bipolar II is better viewed as a depressive disorder, since many individuals with a diagnosis of major depression periodically go through periods of increased activity that can be viewed as an episode of mild mania. Individuals with a bipolar II disorder typically seek clinical help during a major depressive episode and are unlikely to complain initially of their hypomania, primarily because the latter does not impair or trouble them, whereas the depression does. The risk of suicide is also high among individuals with bipolar II disorder.

Individuals with a bipolar disorder (as well as those experiencing the depressive disorders described below) tend to self-treat, which sometimes leads to substance abuse. Individuals often fail or are unwilling to see it as an illness or a disorder, and instead attribute it to a lack of will. In addition, individuals sometimes fear that treatment will result in their losing the success or perceived success they attain during the manic phase.

Depressive Disorders

The common feature of the depressive disorders is the presence of a sad, empty, or irritable mood, accompanied by somatic (relating to the body) and cognitive changes that significantly affect the individual's capacity to function. Depression tends to be particularly undertreated, with one nationwide study finding that among US adults who screen positive for depression, less than 30 percent receive any type of treatment.[82]

Major depressive disorder is the most prominent of this set of disorders. It involves discrete episodes lasting at least two weeks, although most episodes last considerably longer. During these episodes, the person shows a clear-cut change in affect and cognition. These disorders can be traced back to antiquity, with some pharaohs as well as Saul in the Old Testament perhaps having struggled with this condition. It is also believed to have affected more recent well-known figures such as Abraham Lincoln, Edgar Allen Poe, Pablo Picasso, and Robin Williams. Today, this condition tends to be relatively treatable with medications, but it tends to recur, and the dread of this recurrence is itself very painful. Symptoms, which may be present almost every day, include insomnia, loss of appetite, chronic fatigue, decreased sex drive, loss of interest in one's normal activities, social withdrawal, joylessness, difficulty concentrating, loss of confidence, despair, feelings of guilt, and preoccupation with death. Depressed mood is present for most of the day.

Suicide is a significant risk with this disorder, with the most consistently described risk factor being a history of suicide attempts or threats. The most severe depressive episodes may be accompanied by delusions or hallucinations, but, unlike schizophrenia, they will typically be consistent with the person's mood (as in "I hear the devil telling me I'm worthless and doomed"). In the course of a year, 7 percent of the American population experiences this disorder, individuals eighteen to twenty-nine years of age are three times more likely to experience this disorder than individuals sixty years or older, and females are one-and-a-half to three times as likely to experience it as males.[83]

Dysthymia, or *persistent depressive disorder*, also falls within this category. This disorder involves two years or more of generally depressed mood (that is, on more days than not), but the depression is not as severe as that which is experienced in conjunction with major depressive disorder.

It is worth noting that these disorders are distinct from bereavement, which may involve great suffering but suffering that typically is not as pronounced as occurs with the depressive disorders. Also, many of the drugs associated with substance abuse, some prescribed medications, and several medical conditions can trigger depression-like symptoms, although they are addressed in their own diagnostic categories.

The remainder of the diagnoses described in this chapter tend not to be the primary focus of a criminal trial and thus are presented relatively briefly, although particularly because they can occur along with the disorders described above, basic related information is provided.

Dissociative Disorders

In a dissociative disorder, a "break" occurs in a person's usually integrated consciousness, memory, identity, emotion, perception, motor control, or behavior. The resulting dissociative symptoms are experienced as (a) an uninvited intrusion into awareness and behavior, with a loss of continuity in one's subjective experience, and/or (b) an inability to access information or control mental functions that are normally readily amenable to access or control.

Included in this category is *dissociative amnesia*, whereby a person experiences an inability to recall important autobiographical information that is more than just normal forgetting. Unlike dementia, it is usually the result of a traumatic or stressful event. The amnesia can range from a relatively limited inability to recall a specific aspect of an event, to not being able to recall the event or a period of time, to not being able to recall one's identity and life history, although this occurs relatively infrequently. Most individuals with this disorder are initially unaware of their amnesia ("amnesia for their amnesia"); they tend to become aware of it only when they discover evidence of events they experienced but cannot recall or when others tell them or ask them about such events. Such individuals also tend to be "chronically impaired in their ability to form and sustain satisfactory relationships . . . [and have] a history of self-mutilation, suicide attempts, and other high-risk behaviors."[84] It should be noted that this disorder is distinct from post-traumatic stress disorder, substance-related disorders, post-traumatic amnesia due to brain injury, and seizure disorders. Malingering is a specific concern with this disorder as "there is no test, battery of tests, or set of procedures that invariably distinguishes dissociative amnesia from feigned amnesia";[85] the *DSM-5* also notes that feigned amnesia is more common in individuals with financial, sexual, or legal problems.

Another disorder in this category is *dissociative identity disorder.* It is characterized by (a) the presence of two or more distinct personality states and (b) recurrent episodes of amnesia. Formerly known as "multiple personality disorder" (MPD), it gained notoriety in the 1950s following the publication of a case study that was then made into a movie, both with the title "Three Faces of Eve." Individuals with this disorder may experience (a) dissociated actions and speech, including intrusive thoughts, emotions, and impulses; (b) feeling like their attitudes, preferences, or actions are not their own; or (c) feeling detached from their body. In some cases, the fragmented identity is said to take the form of a possessing spirit, deity, demon, animal, or mythical figure. Stress may exacerbate these symptoms. In addition, a common feature of this disorder is dissociative fugue, whereby apparently purposeful travel or bewildered wandering occurs in conjunction with amnesia for one's identity or other important autobiographical information. Individuals with this disorder may suddenly and unexpectedly travel away from their home or job, be unable to recall their past, and must assume a new identity as a result. This is a controversial diagnosis and skepticism has ensued when defendants assert that this disorder was responsible for their criminal behavior (as in it was my "alter" personality that did it).[86]

Another type of dissociative disorder is *depersonalization,* or *derealization disorder.* Individuals with this disorder have a persistent feeling of being detached from their mind, body, feelings, sensations, or thoughts. They may feel robotic, or as if they lack control of their speech or movements even though they remain aware of the world around them. Alternatively, they may feel as if they are in a fog, dream, or bubble, with their surroundings artificial, colorless, or lifeless. Visual distortions may involve blurriness, heightened acuity, the world appearing either two-dimensional or three-dimensional in an exaggerated manner, alterations of distances, or changes in the sizes of objects. Auditory distortions may include muted or heightened voices or sounds. An association has been found between this disorder and childhood interpersonal traumas, particularly emotional abuse and neglect, although it is also associated with physical abuse, witnessing domestic violence, highly erratic parental behavior, or the unexpected death or suicide of a family member or close friend.

Trauma- and Stressor-Related Disorders

These are "disorders in which exposure to a traumatic or stressful event is listed explicitly as a diagnostic criterion."[87]

Included in this category is *acute stress disorder*. Individuals with this disorder have been exposed to actual or threatened death, serious injury, or sexual violation, which is followed by intrusive memories, negative mood, a sense of dissociation, avoidance of related thoughts, sleep disturbances, irritability, hypervigilance, problems with concentration, or exaggerated startle responses.

Similarly, *adjustment disorder* involves the development of emotional or behavioral symptoms following an identifiable stressful occurrence—such as the termination of a romantic relationship, business difficulties, marital problems, living in a crime-ridden neighborhood, experiencing a natural disaster, going away to school, or becoming a parent. However, the marked distress that results is out of proportion to the stressful occurrence or causes a significant impairment in functioning. This disorder often co-occurs with another mental disorder.[88]

The disorder in this category that has received the most attention in recent years in conjunction with criminal trials is *post-traumatic stress disorder* (PTSD). In 1980, responding to calls by Vietnam War veterans, the American Psychiatric Association added the diagnosis of PTSD to its third edition of the *Diagnostic and Statistical Manual of Mental Disorders*. PTSD typically develops after individuals experience or witness a life-threatening or extremely traumatic event, including—but not limited to—military combat, sexual violence, physical assault, a kidnapping, a natural or human-made disaster, a severe motor vehicle accident, or a terrorist attack. This disorder can have long-term psychological and behavioral effects, such as reliving the traumatic event, recurrent distressing dreams of the event, or intense distress when exposed to internal or external cues that resemble an aspect of the initial event.

Because individuals with this diagnosis may experience symptoms such as dissociation (flashbacks lasting from a few seconds to several days during which the individual feels or acts as if the traumatic event is recurring, sometimes with a complete loss of awareness of one's surroundings), exaggerated startle response, irritability, hypervigilance, and impulsive, reckless, or self-destructive behavior, which in turn may be linked to violent acts or other criminal behavior, a PTSD diagnosis may be the foundation of efforts to negate criminal culpability.[89]

The twelve-month prevalence of PTSD among United States adults is 3.5 percent, with a projected lifetime risk of 8.7 percent.[90] Rates of PTSD are higher among military veterans and emergency response personnel, with the highest rates—ranging from one-third to more than a half of those exposed—found among survivors of rape, military combat, and captivity.[91]

Anxiety Disorders

Anxiety disorders feature excessive fear and anxiety and related behavioral disturbances, with fear defined as "the emotional response to real or perceived imminent threat" and anxiety as the "anticipation of future threat."[92] This category formerly encompassed both obsessive-compulsive disorder and PTSD, but both now have their own diagnostic categories in the *DSM-5*. As currently conceptualized, anxiety disorders do not play a prominent role in the criminal justice system, although sometimes an assertion is made that a defendant's violent behavior was an unintended response stemming from an anxiety disorder.

One type of anxiety disorder is *panic disorder*, which features recurrent, unexpected panic attacks. The panic attack appears to come out of the blue, including when emerging from sleep (a nocturnal panic attack). It involves a period of intense fear or terror that reaches a peak within minutes and includes at least four of the following symptoms: pounding heart or accelerated heart rate; sweating; shaking or trembling; shortness of breath or sense of smothering; feeling of choking; chest pain; nausea or abdominal distress; dizziness or light-headedness; chills or heat sensations; numbness or tingling; feeling detached from oneself or experiencing a sense of unreality; fear of losing control or "going crazy"; or fear of dying. For a diagnosis of panic disorder, one of these panic attacks must be followed by a month or more of either a persistent concern or worry about additional panic attacks or a significant maladaptive change in behavior related to the attacks, including avoiding unfamiliar situations or restricting usual daily activities. The frequency of panic attacks varies considerably from daily to weekly to monthly, with short or long separating intervals. The severity of the attacks also varies considerably. The estimated twelve-month prevalence rate in the United States is 2 percent to 3 percent in adults and adolescents, with the median age of onset being twenty to twenty-four years of age.[93]

Another anxiety disorder is *specific phobia*. A person with this disorder has a marked fear or anxiety regarding a specific object or situation, which generally results in the person attempting to avoid the object or situation even if doing so causes the person considerable difficulties. Examples include fear of flying, heights, thunderstorms, elevators, specific animals (such as snakes or spiders), receiving an injection, or seeing blood. Exposure to the object or situation almost always provokes an immediate fear or anxiety out of proportion to any actual danger posed by it, and causes significant distress or impairs social, occupational, or other areas of functioning. Specific phobias sometimes develop following a traumatic event (such as being stuck in an elevator), observing someone else enduring such an event, or being exposed to extensive media coverage of such an event (such as a plane crash). However, many individuals with a specific phobia cannot recall the source of their phobia. It is common for a person to have multiple specific phobias, with the average being three. The twelve-month prevalence in the United States is 7 percent to 9 percent.[94] Individuals with this diagnosis are 60 percent more likely to attempt suicide, and the disorder is frequently associated with a range of other mental disorders.[95]

A third anxiety disorder is *social anxiety disorder*, or *social phobia*. This disorder involves "marked fear or anxiety about one or more social situations in which the individual is exposed to possible scrutiny by others," including meeting strangers, being watched while eating or drinking, or giving a speech or performing in public.[96] The disorder occurs in social situations in which (a) the individual may be scrutinized by others; (b) the individual fears that he or she will be humiliated, embarrassed, or rejected by or offend others; and (c) the individual's fear or anxiety is out of proportion to the actual threat posed by the social situation. Because of this disorder, the individual avoids social situations or endures them with intense fear or anxiety, which in turn impairs social, occupational, or other functioning. Anticipatory anxiety may occur far in advance of upcoming situations. The twelve-month prevalence in the United States is roughly 7 percent.[97] Childhood maltreatment and adversity are risk factors for social anxiety disorder, with males likely to use alcohol and illicit drugs to diminish symptoms of the disorder. The disorder is associated with higher rates of dropping out of school, decreased employment and workplace productivity, lower socioeconomic status, and an enhanced likelihood of not being married.

Other types of anxiety disorders include *separation anxiety disorder* (excessive fear or anxiety of separation from those to whom the individual is attached), *selective mutism* (a consistent failure to speak in specific social situations for which speaking is expected despite the person speaking in other situations), *agoraphobia* (a marked fear or anxiety about using public transportation, being in open spaces, being in confined places, standing in line or being in a crowd, or being outside of the home alone), and *generalized anxiety disorder* (excessive anxiety and worry more days than not for at least six months about a number of events or activities).

Obsessive-Compulsive and Related Disorders

As the name indicates, *obsessive-compulsive disorder* (OCD) is characterized by the presence of obsessions ("recurrent and persistent thoughts, urges, or images that are experienced as intrusive and unwanted") and compulsions ("repetitive behaviors or mental acts that an individual feels driven to perform in response to an obsession or according to rules that must be applied rigidly").[98] An individual with this disorder tries to ignore, suppress, or neutralize the obsession with some other thought or action (that is, by performing the compulsion). OCD symptoms often focus on cleaning, symmetry, forbidden or taboo thoughts, or fears of harm to oneself or others. The repetitive behaviors can include hand-washing, placing items in a specific order, checking repeatedly that everything is as it is supposed to be, counting, or repeating words silently. These behaviors are intended to prevent the dreaded event or situation from occurring, but they are not connected in a realistic way to what they are designed to prevent or are clearly excessive.

The obsessions and compulsions are time-consuming (they may take up more than an hour a day) or impair the person's social, occupational, or other functions. OCD is often accompanied by dysfunctional beliefs, such as an inflated sense of responsibility; an overestimation of the threat posed; perfectionism; intolerance of uncertainty; or the need to control one's thoughts. Most individuals with this disorder have at least some insight into the inaccuracy of their underlying beliefs, with only about 4 percent lacking any insight.[99] Nevertheless, it is common for people with OCD to avoid people, places, and things that trigger obsessions and compulsions. The twelve-month prevalence of OCD in the United States is 1.2 percent, with the mean age at onset being 19.5.[100] Left untreated, OCD is usually chronic, although symptoms often wax and wane. OCD is associated with a reduced quality of life and high levels of social and occupational impairment. About half of all individuals with OCD experience suicidal thoughts at some point, with up to one quarter attempting suicide.[101] Famous figures such as Charles Darwin and Michelangelo are believed to have struggled with OCD.

Other disorders in this category include *body dysmorphic disorder* (a preoccupation with a perceived flaw in physical appearance generally unobservable by others, with related repetitive behaviors such as mirror checking, excessive grooming, or reassurance seeking), *hoarding disorder*, *trichotillomania* (hair-pulling), and *excoriation* (skin-picking).

Personality Disorders

Although relatively unlikely to play a pivotal role in a criminal trial, the *DSM-5* category of personality disorders is worth noting because although virtually everyone shows some of the characteristics of a personality disorder, they tend to be more prevalent or pronounced in criminal defendants. There are ten specific personality disorders, each of which reflects "an enduring pattern of inner experience and behavior that deviates markedly from the expectations of the individual's culture."[102] Personality disorders are pervasive and inflexible, begin in adolescence or early adulthood and tend not to change over time, and cause significant distress or functional impairment. Approximately 15 percent of US adults have at least one personality disorder, although a person can have more than one.[103]

Personality disorders are often referred to as "traits" to reflect their enduring pattern, although they constitute a "disorder" only when they cause significant functional impairment or subjective distress. The previously discussed categories of mental disorders, in contrast, involve qualitatively distinct clinical syndromes that are amenable to change, including treatment. The enduring nature of personality disorders makes them very difficult to successfully treat (that is, change), a problem compounded by the fact that the person may not consider the associated traits to be problematic insofar as they are often consistent with their ideal self-image. To overcome this difficulty, other individuals, particularly those who know the person relatively well, may need to be brought in to describe the disorder's adverse impact on the person. The personality disorders are grouped into three clusters: Cluster A (paranoid, schizoid, and schizotypal), Cluster B (antisocial, borderline, histrionic, and narcissistic), and Cluster C (avoidant, dependent, and obsessive-compulsive).

A *paranoid personality disorder* involves a "pervasive distrust and suspiciousness of others such that their motives are interpreted as malevolent."[104] Individuals with this disorder suspect others are exploiting, harming, or deceiving them, but without a sufficient basis for this suspicion; are preoccupied with these unjustified doubts about the loyalty or trustworthiness of friends and associates; are reluctant to confide in others; read demeaning or threatening meanings into benign remarks or events; persistently carry grudges; perceive without justification that their character or reputation is being attacked and are quick to react angrily or counterattack; and have recurrent suspicions, again without justification, that their spouse or sexual partner is unfaithful. Because they interpret the motives of others to be malevolent, they are quick to counterattack and react with anger or will provoke others into a hostile response. They frequently become involved in legal disputes, while alcohol and other substance use disorders often co-occur. Particularly in response to stress, they may experience very brief psychotic episodes lasting minutes to hours.[105]

A *schizoid personality disorder* involves a "pervasive pattern of detachment from social relationships and a restricted range or expression of emotions in interpersonal settings."[106] Such individuals neither desire nor enjoy close relationships, almost always choose solitary activities, have little or no interest in sexual activities, enjoy few activities in general, lack close friends or confidants, appear indifferent to the praise or criticism of others, and display emotional coldness, detachment, or a limited range of emotional expression. They have difficulty expressing anger, even when directly provoked. Their lives may appear directionless to others in that they seem to "drift" without goals.[107]

A *schizotypal personality disorder* involves a "pervasive pattern of social and interpersonal deficits marked by acute discomfort with, and reduced capacity for, close relationships[,] as well as by cognitive or perceptual distortions and eccentricities of behavior."[108] Individuals with this disorder tend to interpret coincidences or random events as having strong personal significance; have odd beliefs, superstitions, or engage in magical thinking; embrace clairvoyance, telepathy, or the "sixth sense"; believe they have a magical control over others; have unusual perceptual sensations, such as the presence of another person or hearing a voice murmuring their name; be suspicious or paranoid; engage in odd thinking and speech; act in an eccentric or peculiar manner; and demonstrate excessive social anxiety. Such individuals are unlikely to have close friends.[109]

An *antisocial personality disorder* involves a "pervasive pattern of disregard for and violation of the rights of others."[110] This pattern typically begins in childhood or early adolescence and is sometimes referred to as "psychopathy" or "sociopathy." Deceit and manipulation are central features, as is a failure to conform to social norms. Other characteristics include repeated lying; conning others for personal profit or pleasure; impulsivity and a failure to plan ahead; irritability and aggressiveness, including frequent fights or assaults; reckless disregard for the safety of themselves or others; a failure to sustain consistent work behavior or honor financial obligations; and a lack of remorse for harming others. Such individuals are frequently defendants in criminal trials as they often engage in actions that are grounds for arrest, but an antisocial personality disorder will rarely be the basis for a finding of a lack of competence or criminal responsibility, absent the presence of another mental disorder that is not a personality disorder. It is much more common in males, and more than 70 percent of males in substance abuse clinics and prisons are believed to have this disorder.[111]

A *borderline personality disorder* involves a "pervasive pattern of instability in interpersonal relationships, self-image, and affects, and marked impulsivity."[112] Its characteristics include frantic efforts to avoid real or imagined abandonment; intense but unstable interpersonal relationships; an unstable self-image; impulsive spending, sex, and substance abuse; reckless driving; binge eating; recurrent suicidal or self-mutilating behavior; intense unease, dissatisfaction, irritability, or anxiety; chronic feelings of emptiness; frequent displays of temper, constant anger, or recurrent physical fights; and stress-related paranoid thoughts. The resulting unstable personal relationships are countered by a fear of being alone, which results in a trail of failed relationships and destructive behavior, which in turn may lead to arrest and criminal prosecution. Easily bored, these individuals tend to undermine themselves just as a goal is about to be realized. A completed suicide occurs in 8 percent to 10 percent of individuals with this disorder.[113]

A *histrionic personality disorder* involves a "pervasive pattern of excessive emotionality and attention seeking."[114] Individuals with this diagnosis generally need to be the center of attention; interact with others using inappropriate sexually seductive or provocative behavior; use their physical appearance to draw attention to themselves; display rapidly shifting and shallow expressions of emotions; employ a style of speech that expresses strong opinions but without supporting facts and details; are overly dramatic and theatrical, and engage in excessive public displays of emotions; are easily influenced by others, especially current fads and strong authority figures who they think will magically solve their problems; consider relationships to be more intimate than they actually are; are overly trusting; and tend to act on hunches and adopt convictions quickly. They may seek to control their partners through emotional manipulation or seductiveness, while also being dependent upon their partner; may alienate friends with their demands for constant attention; and may become upset and depressed when they are not the center of attention. Easily bored, they tend to crave novelty and excitement and are not interested in delayed gratification. They are at increased risk of suicidal gestures and using threats to get attention and coerce those around them.[115]

A *narcissistic personality disorder* encompasses a "pervasive pattern of grandiosity (in fantasy or behavior), need for admiration, and lack of empathy."[116] Individuals with this disorder tend to exaggerate their achievements and talents and expect to be recognized as superior; are preoccupied with fantasies of unlimited success, power, brilliance, beauty, or ideal love; believe they are "special" and unique and can be understood by or should only associate with similar people; require excessive admiration and have a sense of entitlement; take advantage of others to achieve their own ends and lack empathy for others; are envious of others or believe others are envious of them; and are arrogant or haughty. Often shuttling between elevated mood and depression, they tend to be very sensitive to criticism or defeat, which leaves them feeling humiliated, degraded, hollow, and empty, but they react with disdain, rage, or defiant counterattack. Their sense of entitlement, need for admiration, and disregard for the sensitivities of others typically impairs interpersonal relationships.[117]

An *avoidant personality disorder* involves a "pervasive pattern of social inhibition, feelings of inadequacy, and hypersensitivity to negative evaluation."[118] Individuals with this disorder avoid occupations that require significant interpersonal contact because they fear criticism, disapproval, or rejection; are reluctant to form new relationships because of their feelings of inadequacy and are unwilling to get involved with others unless they are sure they will be liked; are restrained within the relationships they do form because they fear they will be shamed or ridiculed; are preoccupied in social situations with the possibility of being criticized or rejected; view themselves as socially inept, unappealing, or inferior; and are unusually reluctant to take risks or try new things because doing so may prove embarrassing. These individuals often vigilantly appraise the movements and expressions of others. Sadly, their fearful and tense demeanor may elicit ridicule and derision, which only confirms their self-doubts. They tend to be described as "shy," "timid," "lonely," and "isolated," and to lack a large social support network that can help them weather crises.[119]

A *dependent personality disorder* involves a "pervasive and excessive need to be taken care of that leads to submissive and clinging behavior and fears of separation."[120] Individuals with this diagnosis may have difficulty making everyday decisions without excessive advice and reassurance from others; need others to assume responsibility for major areas of their lives; have difficulty expressing disagreement with others because they fear a loss of support or approval; have difficulty initiating projects or doing things on their own; go to excessive lengths to obtain nurturance and support from others, including volunteering to do unpleasant things; feel uncomfortable or helpless when alone; urgently seek another relationship when a close relationship ends; and are unrealistically preoccupied with fears of being left to take care of themselves. Such individuals are often dominated by pessimism and self-doubt, tend to belittle their abilities and assets, and may constantly refer to themselves as "stupid." Their performance at work may be impaired if independent initiative is required, and they may avoid positions of responsibility. As will be discussed, this diagnosis may become relevant when a criminal defense is built around a battered person or battered spouse syndrome.[121]

An *obsessive-compulsive personality disorder* involves a "pervasive pattern of preoccupation with orderliness, perfectionism, and mental and interpersonal control, at the expense of flexibility, openness, and efficiency."[122] Individuals with this disorder tend to have such a preoccupation with details, rules, lists, order, organization, or schedules that the purpose of the activity is lost; be such a perfectionist that task completion is impeded; have such an excessive devotion to work that leisure activities and friendships are excluded; be overly conscientious and inflexible about morality, ethics, or values; be unable to discard worn-out or worthless objects even if they have no sentimental value; be reluctant to delegate tasks or to work with others unless they do things exactly their way; be miserly, with money hoarded for future catastrophes; and be rigid and stubborn. If established rules do not provide the correct answer, decision-making can be time-consuming and even painful. They can become upset or angry if they cannot maintain control of their physical or interpersonal environment, although they may not express this anger directly. They tend to be very uncomfortable around others who are emotionally expressive, and have difficulty expressing tender feelings. They tend to hold themselves back until they can say something perfectly.[123]

Other Categories of Mental Disorders

The *DSM-5* incorporates eleven other categories of mental disorders that, for reasons of space, can only be listed briefly here. Consult the *DSM-5* if you wish to know more about them.

DISRUPTIVE, IMPULSE-CONTROL, AND CONDUCT DISORDERS. This category includes *oppositional defiant disorder, intermittent explosive disorder, conduct disorder, pyromania*, and *kleptomania*. Although many criminal defendants receive these diagnoses, related psychiatric issues are generally discussed in conjunction with the antisocial personality disorder diagnosis discussed above.

ELIMINATION DISORDERS. This category includes *enuresis* and *encopresis*, which can be the basis for a civil commitment order imposing involuntary hospitalization.

FEEDING AND EATING DISORDERS. Included in this category are *pica, rumination disorder, avoidant/restrictive food intake disorder, anorexia nervosa, bulimia nervosa,* and *binge-eating disorder*, which also can serve as the basis for a civil commitment order.

GENDER DYSPHORIA. This category includes *gender dysphoria in children* and *gender dysphoria in adolescents and adults*, and although issues addressed within this category have raised contentious political and legal issues, for the most part they have not been the focus of criminal proceedings.

NEURODEVELOPMENTAL DISORDERS. This category encompasses *intellectual disabilities, communication disorders, autism spectrum disorder, attention-deficit/hyperactivity disorder, specific learning disorder, motor disorders,* and *other neurodevelopmental disorders*, with some of these disorders germane to a defendant's competence to stand trial and other trial-related competencies.

PARAPHILIC DISORDERS. Within this category are *voyeuristic disorder, exhibitionistic disorder, frotteuristic disorder, sexual masochism disorder, sexual sadism disorder, pedophilic disorder, fetishistic disorder,* and *transvestic disorder*, with some of these disorders the focus of attention in criminal trials when the defendant is charged with a sex offense.

SEXUAL DYSFUNCTIONS. This category includes *delayed ejaculation, erectile disorder, female orgasmic disorder, female sexual interest/ arousal disorder, genito-pelvic pain/penetration disorder, male hypoactive sexual desire disorder,* and *premature ejaculation*. While these can be troubling disorders, for the most part they are not the focus of criminal proceedings.

SLEEP-WAKE DISORDERS. This category encompasses *insomnia disorder, hypersomnolence disorder, narcolepsy, sleep apnea, sleep-related hypoventilation, circadian rhythm sleep-wake disorders, non-rapid eye movement sleep arousal disorders, nightmare disorder, rapid eye movement sleep behavior disorder,* and *restless legs syndrome*. Some of these diagnoses, as will be discussed, pose challenging issues in trials involving a criminal act committed while the defendant was purportedly asleep.

SOMATIC SYMPTOM AND RELATED DISORDERS. This category includes *somatic symptom disorder, illness anxiety disorder, conversion disorder*, and *factious disorder*. This is a relatively new category that was recognized for the first time in the *DSM-5*. These disorders are encountered more frequently in medical settings than criminal trials.

SUBSTANCE-RELATED AND ADDICTIVE DISORDERS. Within this category are *alcohol-related disorders, caffeine-related disorders, cannabis-related disorders, hallucinogen-related disorders, inhalant-related disorders, opioid-related disorders, sedative-, hypnotic-, or anxiolytic-related disorders, stimulant-related disorders, tobacco-related disorders, other (or unknown) substance-related disorders*, and *gambling disorder*, with some of these disorders, as will be discussed, the focus of attention in trials in which the defendant's criminal responsibility is being considered.

OTHER MENTAL DISORDERS. This category addresses diagnoses that do not fit comfortably in any other *DSM-5* diagnostic category.

Conclusion

Mental disorders are widely misunderstood. Even though a number of explanatory models have been proposed and extensive efforts have been devoted to their diagnosis and classification, a wide range of symptoms and behaviors can be associated with a given diagnosis, and their impact on a person can vary from severe to mild. In addition, someone can experience multiple disorders, which substantially enhance the different ways in which a psychiatric condition can be manifested. Furthermore, a person's mental disorder may evolve or change over time,[124] and individuals can exhibit psychiatric symptoms at times without a psychiatric diagnosis being appropriate. Human beings are complex creatures, making the diagnosis of mental disorders and the assessment of their impact a challenging task. This is particularly evident within the context of criminal trials. The next chapter will explore how forensic mental health professionals evaluate mental disorders and their impact on human behavior and cognition as they attempt to assist and guide the criminal trial process.

2

Overview of Forensic Mental Health Assessments

Watch and learn.
—Author

Considerable misunderstanding, suspicion, and even mistrust divide the mental health professionals who perform forensic evaluations for criminal trials and the lawyers who conduct these trials. Indeed, there is considerable confusion and unease regarding the role and impact of forensic mental health professionals in general. Some see them as hired guns, as easily manipulated pawns, as capricious in their determinations, or as wielding undue sway in these proceedings and in effect serving as the de facto judge or jury. Others, however, regard them as providing an invaluable service that clarifies some of the most difficult and perplexing issues faced by the criminal justice system—namely, what role, if any, should a criminal defendant's mental state play in determining the defendant's criminal responsibility, decision-making capacity, and ability to receive a fair and just trial.

At the same time, forensic mental health professionals may be frustrated and upset that the information they need to fulfill their role is not readily forthcoming, that they are effectively required to proceed with one hand tied behind their back in conducting their evaluations, that they are not permitted to fully or even adequately express their insights and findings, that the challenges associated with their work are grossly underestimated and ignored, and that there is a lack of appreciation for the formidable and important nature of their task.

Enhancing understanding of forensic mental health assessments can close these divides, while promoting the fairness and justice of criminal trials involving defendants with a mental disorder.

Current Trends

Because the number of criminal defendants with a mental disorder remains at a historically high level, forensic mental health evaluations play a significant role in criminal trials. These evaluations may be needed to determine defendants' competence to stand trial, confess, plead guilty, waive the right to counsel, appear *pro se* (that is, without a lawyer), or testify, as well as their criminal responsibility pursuant to an insanity defense or variations on this defense such as guilty but mentally ill, diminished capacity, automatism/unconsciousness, or lack of mens rea.

It is important to note that this field continues to evolve. For example, as the scientific understanding of the brain and related technologies emerge—including enhanced brain imaging, the identification of abnormal physiological conditions, the availability of biomarkers, and an expanded understanding of related DNA, RNA, and genetics—insights drawn from the biological aspects of mental disorders will increase. At the same time, there is a continuing recognition of the impact of environmental factors on the development and manifestation of mental disorders. As a result, the old "nature versus nurture" dichotomy has been replaced by a dual model that incorporates both biological and environmental factors when assessing mental disorders.[1]

Similarly, the notion that mental disorders are distinct from physical disorders has largely been discredited. For example, factors such as the enlargement of the ventricles of the brain; irregularities in the ratio of brain tissue to fluid; the diminishment of those portions of the brain responsible for memory, attention, emotional expression, and information integration; and deficiencies in the areas of the brain associated with self-awareness have been found to be associated with mental illness. Thus, the *DSM-IV*, the predecessor to the current *DSM-5*, declared that to attempt a distinction between mental and physical disorders "is a reductionistic anachronism of mind/body dualism. A compelling literature documents that there is much 'physical' in 'mental' disorders and much 'mental' in 'physical' disorder."[2]

Features of Forensic Mental Health Evaluations

Although the criminal trial system is highly dependent on forensic mental health evaluations, these evaluations remain controversial.[3] One commentator, a psychologist, refers to the mental health professionals who provide expert testimony as "whores of the court," although her focus was high-profile cases, a milieu that she felt tended to corrupt involved mental health evaluators.[4] Judges and attorneys may indeed look at these evaluations skeptically, but they generally agree that the information provided is pivotal, that the evaluations address matters beyond the understanding of the judges and jurors who must ultimately decide these cases, and it is the best related information available. At the same time, generating a reliable and useful forensic mental health report and testimony is a particularly challenging task. Notwithstanding ongoing efforts to derive objective testing instruments, there are few definitive measures available for assessing a mental disorder and its impact on a person's cognition and behavior. These evaluations continue to be dependent on the insights and judgment of the mental health evaluator, who, in turn, must draw heavily upon the verbal and nonverbal presentation of the criminal defendant, notwithstanding a defendant's vested interest in shaping the outcome.

Clinical Evaluations and Mental Health Treatment

It is also important to recognize how different forensic evaluations are from clinical evaluations and mental health treatment in general, and how distinct and unique the role of a forensic mental health evaluator is. A clinician is *there to help* the client/patient and can say so honestly from the beginning of their interactions. Indeed, a clinician owes a fiduciary duty to the client and must place no other interest, including the clinician's own interest, above that of the client. Clinicians generally start by attempting to gain the trust of their clients, seeking a rapport with them and engaging them in open and frank discussions.

The goal of clinicians is typically to *obtain as much information as possible* from their client, seeking to learn about virtually anything that might be contributing to and explain the client's mental health problems. To facilitate this exchange, they will typically inform their client that they are bound by a legal and ethical obligation of *confidentiality* that generally ensures their discussions will not be disclosed to others.

Furthermore, clinicians are *not particularly concerned about the truthfulness* of what a client says. The nature of the client's presentation is more important than its veracity, with distortions and fabrications often being of particular interest and value. Clinicians are trying to better understand their clients' mental disorder and they recognize that these distortions may well be a key aspect of the disorder and provide insight into it.

Clinicians, in general, try to be *nonjudgmental and exploratory* in their approach. They are heavily dependent on the information obtained from their clients when formulating diagnoses and treatment plans. While they may contact third parties for supplemental information, typically their focus is on *the presentation of the client.*

In addition, clinicians typically *meet on multiple occasions* with a client. This enables them to further build trust as well as expand the information obtained. The aim is to increase both their own and their client's insights into the nature of the client's mental health problems.

It is also worth emphasizing that for a clinician, the diagnosis of a client's mental disorder is not the highest priority. Although an attempt will be made to accurately diagnose the client so that an appropriate corresponding treatment plan can be readily put into place, not only are diagnoses difficult to definitively establish, but a client's presentations and in some cases the mental disorder itself *may change over time*, requiring a new diagnosis and a change in the treatment plan. Efforts to provide mental health care and treatment tend to be a humbling endeavor, but to the extent a clinician observes *a client's improvement*, which is the ultimate goal, it can be a highly rewarding experience.

Forensic Mental Health Evaluations

The approach of mental health professionals conducting a forensic evaluation, as described below, differs significantly from that of clinicians. There are nine key distinguishing characteristics.

NARROW FOCUS

Rather than undertaking a broad exploration of all the possible mental health problems of a defendant, forensic mental health professionals must focus on select, relatively narrow issues. They are typically assigned a specific task, such as assessing a defendant's competence to stand trial, which considerably contracts the scope of their evaluation. Their sole function is to address the legal issue before the court, including the legal standard and accompanying criteria, and anything beyond this is considered irrelevant, is not admissible at trial, and should not be included in any report submitted to the court. Even if privately hired by one of the parties (that is, the defense or the prosecution) and not charged with testifying or submitting a report to the court, the party generally wants the evaluator only to generate information that addresses the legal issues likely to be raised at trial.

A limited exception to this narrow focus may occur if the evaluator is hired by the defense prior to trial to determine if there are any mental health–related legal issues that might be raised. In this instance, the scope of the evaluation may expand somewhat. However, it will still be limited to potentially relevant legal issues, and the defense will not be interested in having the mental health problems of the defendant addressed in general. Although the evaluator should be amenable to exploring what may initially seem like a tangential mental health issue if this may shed light on a germane legal issue, forensic mental health evaluators must keep their curiosity on a short leash. If a path of exploration does not produce material that is germane to a legal issue relatively quickly, forensic mental health evaluators are expected to abandon these tangents promptly.

It should be recognized, however, that keeping this focus during an evaluation can be a challenge as the person being interviewed may be prone to veering off into unrelated issues, particularly if a mental disorder is present. The challenge forensic mental health evaluators often face is how to keep a conversation on track without alienating the person being interviewed.

A CONFIDENTIAL RELATIONSHIP IS NOT ESTABLISHED

A second important distinction concerning forensic evaluations is that a confidential relationship with the defendant in the traditional sense is not established. While clinicians are typically deemed to be working for their clients and are focused exclusively on their treatment, forensic mental health evaluators are considered to be working for the court that appointed them or the party that hired them. In clinical care, where open and frank disclosures by the client are considered a key to successful treatment, it is paramount that the discussions between the client and the clinician be kept confidential. In contrast, the purpose of a forensic mental health evaluation is to shed light on relevant legal issues rather than promote the treatment of the defendant. Thus, the defendant cannot expect that statements made to and discoveries uncovered by the forensic evaluator will be kept private and confidential. From the forensic evaluator's perspective, this should also shift the mental health professional's approach from a broad-ranging search for insights into a client's mental health problems to a targeted study of the possible impact of a defendant's mental disorder on a relevant criminal trial issue.

The primary exception to this approach is when the criminal defendant is being evaluated by a forensic mental health professional in conjunction with a possible insanity defense. The defense has the prerogative of not pursuing this defense and if it is not placed in issue at trial, the defendant's interactions with the evaluator will be considered to be part of the defense attorney's trial preparation and thus be encompassed by the attorney-client privilege and shielded from disclosure. However, if the insanity defense is raised, the work of the forensic mental health evaluator is subject to examination by the prosecution and disclosure during the criminal proceedings. Because of this possibility, forensic mental health evaluators generally are, and should be, guarded in what they explore with the defendant in conjunction with a possible insanity defense.

OBJECTIVE AND NONPARTISAN APPROACH

Another distinction is that forensic mental health evaluators are expected to remain objective and nonpartisan. If appointed by the court, they are considered to be serving the court, not the defendant; they are not there to help or treat the defendant, and the defendant is not their client. Of course, forensic mental health professionals should generally try not to exacerbate a defendant's mental disorder, and will typically try to calm or reassure an anxious defendant, although this is done in part to enhance their ability to receive needed information from the defendant. However, there are times when a forensic mental health evaluator must confront a defendant, particularly if the evaluator thinks the defendant may be malingering. In addition, even though forensic mental health evaluators will seek to understand the defendant's perspective and perceptions, particularly as they relate to any relevant trial matter, they must refrain from becoming too emotionally involved. Such engagement can bias a forensic mental health evaluator and compromise the objectivity of subsequent determinations. Forensic mental health evaluators must be able to step back from what they hear and learn, view this information objectively, and generate a nonpartisan report.

INVESTIGATIVE ROLE

Forensic mental health evaluators must also recognize and embrace their investigative role. Their task is to address and answer questions pertaining to the court proceedings. Thus, they cannot be passive in their approach and must be prepared to push beyond what the defendant— and any third parties—readily volunteer. In contrast to a clinician, who—to maintain trust and rapport—will typically refrain from challenging a client's account unless it is deemed necessary to break past the client's psychological defenses, a forensic mental health evaluator generally does not have the luxury of time necessary for such a circuitous route. The demands of the court and the parties for relevant information in a timely manner, as well as the limited opportunities to interview criminal defendants, particularly if they are incarcerated, generally limit the amount of time available to conduct the investigation and generate the requisite report; moreover, a maximum period is sometimes set by statute, court rule, or judicial order.[5]

Thus, after a short period of introduction, explanations, and efforts to build a certain level of rapport and comfort with the defendant, forensic mental health evaluators will typically get to the point and target the issues they are there to address. There is a balance to be maintained here, of course, as pushing too hard, too soon, may confuse or alienate the defendant and prove counterproductive if, as a result, the defendant refuses to cooperate or provides inaccurate information. Forensic mental health evaluators therefore attempt, at least initially, to positively engage the person being interviewed. Nonetheless, evaluators must be proactive in exploring relevant issues, even if these are sensitive matters that make the defendant uncomfortable. Indeed, as noted, at times forensic mental health evaluators must be confrontational in order to overcome a facade and draw out more genuine descriptions of the defendant's mental status and related events. Forensic evaluators will often stress that they have been sent by the court (or one of the parties) to find out certain information and that it is generally in everyone's best interests to help them obtain an accurate picture of the defendant's past or present state of mind and its impact on the defendant's thinking, behavior, or ability to communicate. The evaluator may also note that a refusal to cooperate or provide truthful responses will be reported.

POTENTIAL FOR MALINGERING

In these interviews forensic mental health evaluators must always be mindful of the potential for malingering—that is, the misrepresenting, distorting, or withholding of relevant information.[6] The stakes can be very high for criminal defendants who are being evaluated, and this may lead them to present themselves and related events in a way they believe will lead to a more favorable trial outcome.[7] Even third parties may have a vested interest in the outcome, and this may lead them to provide less than a frank and full disclosure. For example, friends or relatives sympathetic to the defendant may be hoping to help the defendant escape or receive a reduced punishment, while individuals injured by or otherwise disposed against the defendant may selectively disclose information they think will enhance the likelihood that the defendant will be convicted or be punished more severely.

As a result, forensic mental health evaluators must sustain a questioning attitude and take what they hear with a grain of salt. Although they will be cautious, at least initially, about directly challenging an account for fear of dampening or ending a conversation, they will often return to a questionable assertion later in the interview to see if it is maintained and then point out details that are inconsistent with common knowledge, with what was said earlier, or with what the evaluator has learned from prior research. At a minimum, the evaluator may gain useful insights from strained explanations offered to "talk-away" such inconsistencies.

RELATIVELY UNIQUE POPULATION

Forensic mental health evaluators also tend to work with a population that is quite different from the one that clinicians serve, which in turn necessitates some differences in their approach. Clinicians working with a community-based population generally have clients who are at least moderately well-off economically, can communicate at a relatively high level, and are meeting with the clinician voluntarily, although somebody may be pushing them to do so. These circumstances can make it much easier for the clinician to establish a rapport with the client, engage the client in a relevant conversation, and explore the client's needs and difficulties.

In contrast, the criminal defendants with whom forensic mental health evaluators typically interact tend to have a history of social impediments and barriers, their communication and cognitive skills may be limited, and, because they are not there voluntarily and face a very stressful situation, they may be suspicious of the evaluator and reluctant to open up. To a certain extent, these considerations may also come into play with any third party with whom a forensic evaluator meets. Engaging these individuals in a frank, open, and revealing conversation may be a significant challenge, and thus accurately assessing them and their disclosures may be quite difficult. Such an understanding, however, is a key to a successful forensic mental health evaluation. The professionals providing these evaluations have generally received specific training to enable them to bridge these gaps, but even so, such challenges need to be overcome in virtually every case. It takes a dedicated and determined evaluator to sustain the focus and creativity needed to clear these hurdles on a routine basis.

AUDIENCE TO WHOM THE FINDINGS ARE REPORTED

Clinicians typically report their findings only to their clients. Ideally, the clinician has developed a level of rapport and sufficiently gained the trust of the client so that the client accepts and perhaps even embraces the clinician's findings. In addition, even if a client does not agree with the report, he or she is rarely able to effectively challenge or repudiate it. Generally, clinicians' views are not subject to second-guessing or public criticism, and they need be concerned only about their client's response and the therapeutic impact of their report.

Forensic mental health evaluators, in contrast, report their findings to a very different audience. Depending on who secured their services, they initially deliver their findings to the judge, the prosecutor, or the defendant's attorney, each of whom is likely to closely scrutinize the report and may be skeptical of and challenge the results, particularly if the report does not match his or her expectations, with the evaluator generally required to respond in turn. Furthermore, the evaluator may then have to go on to defend his or her findings in open court and be subjected to a series of confrontational and caustic questions posed by highly skilled opposing counsel seeking to undercut the evaluator's determinations.

At the same time, judges, lawyers, and juries generally have at best a limited understanding of mental disorders, their impact on behavior and cognition, related terminology, and the process of evaluation. These limitations may greatly hinder an evaluator's ability to convey his or her findings and may necessitate that the evaluator spend considerable time explaining basic concepts to them. Further hindering communication are the time pressures judges and attorneys often work under, which can limit their availability to study and grasp the nuances of the evaluator's report.

As a result, forensic mental health evaluators are typically expected to "translate" their findings into terms judges and lawyers can readily understand and employ. Like all professions, the legal profession has its own language and culture. In addition, the purpose of the evaluation is primarily to ascertain whether a criminal defendant meets a given legal standard, with these standards generally framed in legal not clinical terms. Indeed, they may be framed in terms that have no direct clinical equivalent or meaning. Forensic mental health evaluators must recast their findings in terms that address the legal standard in question, something for which their clinical training may provide little guidance.

HIGH STAKES

Beyond this initial audience, however, an even more daunting one may await. Although much is at stake when a clinician treats a client, as the client's well-being and even life, if suicide is a possibility, may hang in the balance, the clinician's responsibilities are generally limited to the client and the clinician's efforts usually do not undergo public scrutiny.

This is not the case if a forensic mental health evaluator's report is entered into evidence or the evaluator provides testimony at a defendant's criminal trial. If the case is notorious and widely publicized—particularly if an unpopular verdict is issued and the evaluator's report is viewed as providing the foundation for the verdict—considerable unwanted public attention may be focused on the evaluator and his or her findings. In addition to possible media intrusions, if the evaluator maintains a private practice as a clinician, which many do, this adverse publicity may negatively impact this practice.

Of greater weight, however, is that in addition to recognizing the need of any victim and society to see justice done, the forensic mental health evaluator knows the criminal defendant's ability to receive a fair and just trial—as well as the defendant's liberty and, in death penalty cases, life—may hinge on the evaluator's report and testimony. If a clinician is mistaken in his or her assessment of a client, the clinician will generally have an opportunity later to identify the mistake and make any necessary changes to the course of treatment. Such a reappraisal is typically not available to forensic mental health evaluators. Once they have submitted their report or provided their testimony, these become part of the trial record and, for better or worse, are part of the foundation on which the judge or jury base their verdict. Evaluators may later seek to amend or retract their report or testimony, but such changes are not warmly received, especially once the trial has begun and particularly after a verdict is issued, in part because such an amendment or retraction can be the basis for a mistrial.[8] The expectation is that forensic mental health evaluators will get it right the first time, notwithstanding the limited amount of time they have to spend with the defendant and investigate related issues, and the fragmented and sometimes misleading information on which they must base their evaluation. Plus, equivocation is not a quality well regarded in forensic mental health evaluators. Judges and lawyers expect a clear-cut determination regarding whether the legal standard has been met, with qualifications to the determination generally neither invited nor welcomed. A forensic mental health evaluator is expected to provide a timely and definitive opinion, but woe to those whose judgment errs or fails to find favor with the public. This is not a profession for those who are thin-skinned or faint of heart.

HEIGHTENED LEVEL OF PUBLICITY AND STRESS

While clinicians work in virtual anonymity, with their comments and observations largely cloaked by rules and standards governing confidentiality and privacy, the forensic mental health evaluator may be required to take the witness stand and testify in open court. Moreover, in some jurisdictions, this testimony may be broadcast directly to the public, while in others it tends to at least be subject to media reports. Mental health professionals uneasy with this level of scrutiny may want to think twice before undertaking a forensic mental health evaluation. This role may also not be suitable for someone uncomfortable examining the darker side of human behavior. Criminal trials, and thus forensic mental health evaluations, often focus on this aspect of life. Those who are squeamish should not apply.

Multifaceted Process

The role of the clinician is relatively straightforward: identify the client's mental health problems and devise means to ameliorate these problems.[9] Although the process is complex and challenging, the focus is always on the client. In addition, relevant information comes primarily from the client. Indeed, clients may prefer that clinicians not talk to third parties about their problems, and because of the constraints of confidentiality, clinicians are significantly limited with whom they may talk without the consent of the client. Furthermore, although records are often kept, they are typically limited to recording the nature of a counseling session and the clinician's impressions; generally they are not to be distributed to others. Finally, unless the clinician seeks assistance from another professional, and usually only with the permission of the client, the clinician typically works largely unimpeded (and unassisted) by others.

The forensic mental health evaluator works in a very different world, where the tasks performed are multifaceted.

Court Order/Attorney's Request

The work of a clinician in private practice typically begins when the clinician is contacted directly by a prospective client or meets with a client or patient who has contacted the clinic or been admitted to the facility with which the clinician is affiliated. A forensic mental health evaluator's duties begin with either the receipt of a court order or an attorney's request for an evaluation of a criminal defendant. Assuming the evaluator agrees to undertake the evaluation, the question of who is the forensic mental evaluator's client arises. Is it the defendant, or is it the court or lawyer seeking an evaluation? As noted, the nature of the task the forensic mental health evaluator is requested to undertake is also quite different from that of the clinician. While the clinician is asked to help and improve the condition of the client, the forensic mental health evaluator is tasked with answering a given legal question regarding the defendant's competency or criminal responsibility. As a result, the approach and means to be employed by the two will be vastly different, with the evaluator ordinarily being reactive and the clinician proactive.

Acquisition and Review of Background Information

The next step taken by the forensic mental health evaluator is generally the acquisition and review of background information regarding the defendant and the defendant's criminal case. Whereas the first step for clinicians is usually a meeting with their client to obtain a description of any mental health problems, for the forensic evaluator the legal question being posed is the initial critical issue. The evaluator will also need the surrounding context to ascertain how to approach the legal question, as well as the criteria relevant to the legal question. In addition, because malingering is usually a possibility when evaluating criminal defendants,[10] the evaluator will need relevant background information so that when he or she meets with the defendant, the evaluator is prepared to question or challenge the defendant regarding dubious remarks and behavior. At the same time, in acquiring this background information, evaluators should be sensitive to the possibility that this information may ultimately serve as part of the foundation for their report to the court and any related testimony. As a result, care must be exercised in recording the sources of this information and its specific content in case the evaluator must later document the foundation for his or her opinion. In supplying this foundation, evaluators typically need at least a working knowledge of the rules of evidence governing criminal trials, so they can anticipate what information is admissible into evidence and what is likely to be excluded.

Provide the Defendant with Notice

After gathering this background information, the forensic mental health evaluator will typically meet with and interview the criminal defendant.

This raises a third distinction in the process used by forensic evaluators and clinicians. A clinician's meeting with a client usually begins with the clinician obtaining the client's informed consent, generally in writing, to commence treatment. Because the forensic mental health evaluator is not providing the defendant with treatment and because a client-therapist relationship is not being established, informed consent per se is not required. Similarly, because evaluators are not law enforcement officials seeking to obtain information—including a confession—pursuant to or in anticipation of an arrest, they are generally not required to give the defendant *Miranda* warnings.

Nevertheless, most forensic mental health evaluators provide the defendant with notice regarding the purpose and nature of the interview.[11] Forensic evaluators generally introduce themselves and provide a brief recital of their credentials; explain who has requested this evaluation, why, and what its purpose is; supply a brief overview of how the interview is expected to proceed, noting that there will be an exchange of questions and answers and any tests that may be administered; tell the defendant that breaks can be taken if needed; and inform the defendant that although participation is encouraged, the defendant is free not to participate and can end the interview at any time, although a failure to cooperate may be noted in the evaluator's report.[12] If the interview is going to be recorded, generally the defendant is informed of this as well. The evaluator may then ask the defendant if he or she has any questions, answer any questions as honestly as possible, and, after any questions posed have been answered, ask the defendant to sign a document that includes the essence of what has just been discussed and indicates that this information has been explained to the defendant. The evaluator will then ask the defendant if he or she is ready to begin. Typically, evaluators will provide this notice in as pleasant and encouraging a tone as possible in the hope that the defendant will readily agree to fully and candidly participate in the evaluation. To the extent that evaluators are initially evasive, abrupt, condescending, or impatient, defendants are more likely to be on guard, suspicious, and less forthcoming in their responses.

Similarly, the place where the evaluation is to take place will be set up in a manner designed to make the defendant feel as comfortable and relaxed as possible. Preferably, it will be a pleasant room that is not cramped, has good acoustics, is well ventilated and maintained at an agreeable temperature, has comfortable chairs without a desk or other furniture creating a barrier between the evaluator and the defendant, is insulated from extraneous noise and interruptions, and permits the evaluator and the defendant to sit facing each other at eye level, with beverages and breaks made available to the defendant.

Single or Limited Number of Interviews

Another distinction in the process employed is that forensic mental health evaluators must often rely heavily on a single interview, or a limited number of such interviews, with the defendant.[13] While a clinician will typically meet frequently with a client, often on a regularly scheduled basis, the forensic evaluator will usually have only limited access to the defendant. As a result, forensic evaluators have less opportunity to explore defendants' mental disorders and their impact, which can create a significant challenge in conducting these evaluations. Among the reasons for the limited number of such interviews are that (a) the period of time before the scheduled beginning of a defendant's trial is often relatively short; (b) there may have been a delay in obtaining the forensic evaluator's services; (c) many defendants are incarcerated while awaiting trial, with access to them being constrained and difficult to arrange; and (d) if the evaluation is the result of a court order or a referral from a defendant of modest means, the funds available to compensate evaluators for these meetings may be limited.

Additional Collateral Information

To compensate for the limited access to the defendant, forensic mental health evaluators typically rely heavily on third-party accounts and other information sources regarding the defendant, as well as the defendant's behavior in formulating their findings and determinations.[14] As discussed, clinicians rely primarily on the accounts provided by their clients, with recourse to third parties and other information sources undertaken on a relatively infrequent basis and usually only to gain greater insight into their clients' accounts, not to verify or challenge them. For forensic evaluators, ascertaining what actually happened and determining whether defendants' accounts regarding events and their mental state are distorted or fabricated are critical parts of their job. The account provided by a defendant may be incomplete, reflect a narrow or limited perspective, not supply important relevant context, or be the product of malingering. As a result, it is generally imperative that forensic evaluators gather additional collateral information after interviewing a defendant.

Information regarding relevant events and the defendant's mental state may come from family members, friends, or acquaintances of the defendant, as well as from responding law enforcement officials or other witnesses. To gain further insight into the defendant's mental state, the evaluator may contact jail officials or mental health professionals who have provided the defendant with treatment in the past, although the latter will generally necessitate obtaining the defendant's written consent. Obtaining this additional collateral information can be a relatively time-consuming endeavor—sometimes made more daunting because of the time constraints under which the evaluator is working—and accessibility to these sources may not be readily available, if available at all. In addition, the forensic evaluator will need to weigh the respective value of the information obtained from these collateral sources, which in turn will require assessing its accuracy, reliability, and admissibility as a foundation for his or her findings.

Report-Writing

Report-writing plays a pivotal role in forensic evaluations. While clinicians may write reports summarizing their findings regarding a client, this is not a key aspect of what they do, and generated reports tend to have a limited impact on the client's future on those few occasions when such reports are released. In contrast, the evaluator's report, along with any associated trial testimony, is the sine qua non of the forensic evaluator's role.

As discussed earlier, the forensic mental health evaluator is not there to treat the defendant, but to answer a legal question. It is generally expected that this answer and its foundations will be incorporated into a formal report prepared by the evaluator and delivered to whoever initially secured the evaluator's services, whether it be the judge, the defendant's attorney, or the prosecutor. If delivered to the judge, the report will typically become part of the trial record. If delivered to the defense or the prosecution, they will decide whether to attempt to incorporate it into the trial record. In any case, whoever receives it will generally closely scrutinize the report. Sometimes follow-up questions will be asked, but not always. Because the evaluator cannot assume that there will be an opportunity to clarify what has been placed in the report, the evaluator needs to attempt to make it a self-sustaining, self-explanatory document. The applicable legal standard will typically be incorporated in the report, as well as whether the related legal criteria have been met and why.

Beyond this, forensic mental health evaluators tend to disagree on how much detail such reports should contain and how long they should be. Some believe that too much detail runs the risk that the lay persons reading the document will misunderstand its content or make unfounded inferences based on the details provided. They contend that if questions or uncertainty arise, they should be consulted directly for explanations, justifications, and clarifications. Other forensic evaluators take the position that because they may not be consulted again, everything that is germane to their determination should be incorporated in the report. That way the court or the party receiving it will have the benefit of all relevant information and if the report is incorporated in the trial record, this information will appear there as well.

Attorney Consultations

Another key aspect of forensic mental health evaluations that clinicians rarely face is consulting with an attorney. As discussed, it is often an attorney for the defense and sometimes for the prosecution who initiates the request for an evaluation and to whom evaluators report their findings. These attorneys generally will have one or more specific questions, legal or factual, that they want the evaluator to address. As a result, the evaluation process often begins and concludes with a consultation with an attorney. In addition, the attorney may request updates from the evaluator during the evaluation process; seek explanations, clarifications, and even suggestions; raise additional issues, facts, or collateral sources that the attorney wants the evaluator to explore; and, sometimes, challenge the evaluator's findings. The presence of the referring attorney effectively looking over the shoulder of and attempting to "assist" the evaluator is a scenario that is very different from that typically experienced by clinicians, who generally enjoy a great deal of autonomy in their practice.

Further compounding the potentially challenging nature of this arrangement for the forensic mental health evaluator is the fact that the lawyer may have little, if any, understanding of mental disorders, their impact on an individual's behavior, and the process and limits of forensic mental health evaluations. Although some attorneys may have experience with or specialized training in these issues and be relatively knowledgeable about them, forensic evaluators may find it difficult and frustrating to attempt to explain and justify their findings to individuals who are effectively laypersons, albeit ones who are very vested in the outcome of these evaluations. A significant question that may arise is whether the referring attorney should be present during the evaluation. Many forensic evaluators find the presence of the referring attorney to be an impediment to conducting an effective evaluation. A potentially thornier issue arises when it is the prosecuting attorney or the judge who requested the evaluation, and the defense attorney wants to be present to ensure the rights of the defendant are respected and protected.[15]

Provide Testimony

A final key distinction is that forensic mental health evaluators are often expected to provide testimony regarding the defendant whom they evaluated. Clinicians rarely provide such testimony, and for mental health providers entering the world of forensic evaluations, this can be an unsettling and intimidating experience. Mental health providers generally have little knowledge of the rules of evidence that govern these proceedings and place limits on what they can testify about. The rules of evidence, which vary from jurisdiction to jurisdiction, govern what information can be introduced into evidence and be considered by a judge or jury and what information is considered, for example, too unreliable, prejudicial, irrelevant, or inflammatory to be allowed into evidence.

For instance, a jurisdiction may not allow expert witnesses to testify regarding the "ultimate issue," namely, the legal question to be decided.[16] This restriction is imposed because deciding the ultimate issue is viewed as the job of the factfinder (that is, the jury or, if there is no jury, the judge). If, for example, the expert testifies regarding whether the defendant's mental state satisfied the requirements for the insanity test, it may be feared that the judge or jury will simply adopt the expert's opinion, particularly when the matter under consideration, such as the impact of a mental disorder on a defendant's behavior, falls outside the usual knowledge and insights of these factfinders.[17] Questions may also arise as to whether the expert witness can provide testimony based on "hearsay" or when derived from various "novel" clinical techniques such as polygraph results, narcoanalysis, or hypnosis.[18]

In addition, forensic evaluators may find providing testimony to be a relatively alien and uncomfortable experience. Instead of just providing a narrative of their findings, forensic evaluators must limit their testimony to answering the questions posed by the trial attorneys. If they go off on a tangent or provide an answer that is not responsive to the question asked, counsel may object. The judge may then strike the answer from the record, direct any jury to disregard the answer, and admonish the evaluator to limit his or her answers so that they are responsive to the questions posed. Particularly if the attorney asking the questions is not familiar with mental health evaluations or mental disorders and their impact on behavior, evaluators can become very frustrated that they are not being asked questions that will allow them to provide the factfinder with the information they believe the factfinder needs to reach a just and fair verdict. Furthermore, forensic evaluators may well prefer to simply explain matters in their own words and pursuant to their own narrative. They may find the interruptions resulting from an attorney's questions to be distracting and annoying.

Inexperienced evaluators are also likely to have never dealt with the type of questioning opposing counsel (that is, the attorneys representing the side that did not call the evaluator to the stand) may employ on cross-examination. Sometimes this line of questioning is relatively polite and to the point, simply asking the evaluator to clarify a previously made statement. At other times the attorney bores deeper and asks the evaluator to concede that his or her position is not supported by, and indeed may be contradicted by, previously introduced evidence or the evaluator's own findings and call on the evaluator to change his or her position. Sometimes the questions seem merely designed to confuse the evaluator into inadvertently saying something that undercuts the position that he or she is espousing. Alternatively, the attorney may question the credentials of the evaluator, seeking to establish that the evaluator lacks the requisite expertise or skill in these matters and that his or her findings should thus be disregarded. This line of questioning may be accusatory, derogatory, or dismissive. Finally, and perhaps most frustrating of all, because forensic evaluators can generally respond only to the questions posed, they may be cut off before they can provide a full and complete answer on a given point, thereby creating—evaluators fear—misconceptions in the minds of the factfinders. Ideally, once the cross-examination has ended, the attorney who originally called the evaluator to the stand will ask further questions that will enable the evaluator to clarify any misconceptions that may have arisen. This does not always occur, however, and evaluators may be left feeling that their findings have been "turned on their head."

Again, serving as a forensic mental health expert is not for the faint of heart. Mental health professionals who do not like to be directed, interrupted, questioned, or challenged regarding their findings or who do not appreciate the rules of the courtroom or enjoy the give-and-take exchanges with opposing counsel may want to refrain from accepting an invitation to serve as a forensic mental health evaluator. On the other hand, if they like the joust and the spotlight, if they like being called upon to solve a mystery or a puzzle, if they like being able to smile and say, "Watch and learn," then this may be the calling for them.

Malingering and Its Indicators

One of the most important and challenging tasks facing forensic mental health evaluators is determining whether a criminal defendant is malingering.[19] Some evaluators tend to see indications of malingering in virtually all criminal defendants, whether because the stakes are so high, because they think defendants feel they have nothing to lose by malingering or are unlikely to be detected doing so, or for other reasons. Such evaluators tend to be favored by prosecutors seeking to counter assertions that a defendant is incompetent or not criminally responsible as the result of a mental disorder. Other evaluators rarely discern malingering in criminal defendants, tending instead to routinely view their accounts as genuine. These evaluators tend to be favored by attorneys representing criminal defendants. Legal realists assert that judges, although expected to be unbiased, may also gravitate toward one extreme or the other, although they may be relatively unaware of their bias.

The actuality tends to be far more complex. Some criminal defendants will indeed malinger and fabricate a mental disorder or, if they are experiencing a mental disorder, exaggerate or distort its symptoms or its impact on them. Conversely, some defendants will understate or try to hide the effects of a mental disorder for various reasons, including hoping to avoid the internal or external stigma associated with having a mental disorder. A third group of defendants simply struggles to accurately describe their mental state. They may be unable in general to articulate coherently their thoughts and perceptions. Alternatively, they may be unable to express the nature and impact of their mental disorder because they do not understand it or cannot find words to describe it. The disorder may seem alien to their previously established identity or may overwhelm their ability to think clearly, understand questions, process what they are experiencing or previously experienced, and convey relevant information to the evaluator. A fourth group of defendants, in contrast, will be relatively forthcoming and able to accurately discuss any mental disorder and its impact on them.

Discerning the presence and impact of a mental disorder and being able to differentiate false or distorted accounts are key to a forensic mental health evaluation. At the same time, an evaluator should be cautious about readily labeling a criminal defendant as a malingerer. Even if this characterization is attached to a relatively small and unimportant portion of the defendant's account, it can determine the outcome of the trial. Many judges and jurors are skeptical of mental disorder–related claims in general and will readily dismiss such a claim based on an evaluator's assertion that the defendant failed to provide a fully accurate account, even if there is substantial evidence supporting the claim overall. Furthermore, a mental health evaluator's determination that a defendant is feigning symptoms of a mental disorder may be the basis for a judge ordering a sentence enhancement if the defendant is ultimately found guilty.[20] This possibility has raised concerns that attorneys may be discouraged from requesting forensic evaluations "out of fear that their client might be subject to a harsher penalty if by chance the [evaluator] concludes that there is a lack of cooperation or the presence of feigning but no mental illness."[21] As a result, some evaluators resist labeling a defendant as a malingerer. Instead, they simply describe in their reports their concerns about specific portions of a defendant's account without using such conclusory language, thereby requiring the judge or jury to sift through all the evidence and, hopefully, reach an informed and balanced conclusion.

The following describes possible indicators that a criminal defendant is malingering.[22] However, to suggest the complexity of this determination, a counterargument for why it may reflect a genuine expression of a mental disorder follows each indicator.

Overplayed and Dramatic Presentation

Malingering may be present if the defendant adopts a theatrical style that embellishes mental disorder symptoms and their impact, if the defendant seems especially eager to discuss them, if the defendant seems to be watching for or picking up on signals from the evaluator regarding what needs to be included or emphasized, or if the defendant seems to overreact to questions posed by the evaluator regarding the defendant's account. Because a mental disorder is typically a relatively painful experience that often results in ostracism, isolation, hardship, and abuse, individuals with a mental disorder tend to be reluctant to discuss their disorder and attempt to hide it from others, particularly from individuals they do not know well, such as a forensic evaluator. Furthermore, to the extent the defendant reports extreme or implausible combinations of symptoms, or seems to indiscriminately embrace any symptom the evaluator suggests, this should give the evaluator reason to pause and consider whether the account is genuine.

It is important to also recognize, however, that defendants may well be experiencing a considerable emotional surge that induces expansive responses during the evaluation. This may be because they realize the stakes are quite high, because they are exhilarated at being outside their jail or prison environment if currently incarcerated, or because they are relieved to finally be able to tell their story to someone who appears to be trying to help or understand them, which is a persona most forensic evaluators at least project. In addition, defendants may see the evaluator as an expert and an authority figure and think they should agree with whatever the evaluator suggests. Alternatively, defendants may simply be trying to please the evaluator by giving the evaluator what they believe the evaluator wants. Finally, the defendant may express himself or herself dramatically in general (something the evaluator can ascertain by talking to others who interact with the defendant in other settings), or, conversely, such a dramatic presentation may actually reflect the effects of a mental disorder (such as bipolar disorder I).

Overly Deliberate or Cautious Responses

Malingering may also be present if the defendant pauses noticeably before answering questions, particularly key ones pertaining to the asserted presence of a mental disorder and its impact, and appears to carefully digest what is being asked and mentally rehearse how to answer in a manner consistent with his or her account. Similarly, if the defendant routinely repeats questions before responding, the evaluator may conclude that the defendant is playing for time while searching for the best response consistent with the presentation being made. If a defendant also seems to add an inordinate number of qualifiers to his or her responses, this may suggest the defendant is uncertain as to what the "correct" answer is and hopes that the use of these qualifiers will "cover all the bases" needed to obtain the desired evaluation report.

The evaluator, however, will be cautious about drawing a determination of malingering solely from a defendant's deliberate and careful response style. Many mental disorders, particularly those associated with a cognitive impairment, cause slow or delayed responses. In addition, defendants may recognize the importance of the evaluation and simply be attempting to choose their words carefully, so that their responses will be as accurate and precise as possible. Alternatively, many defendants may find such an interview and environment unfamiliar and unsettling, which may add to their hesitancy in responding. Also, they may have little experience with the questions posed and struggle to understand and answer them. Particularly if evaluators employ relatively formal speech or terminology (such as legal or psychiatric jargon) with which the defendant is unfamiliar—which is often the case—and especially if the defendant is reluctant to ask for clarification, he or she may be mentally "translating" the questions before answering. Finally, many defendants will be suspicious of evaluators and the evaluation process in general, not to mention the entire criminal justice system, all of which can lead to a heightened level of deliberateness and care in responding to the questions posed.

Inconsistent or Unlikely Account

If a criminal defendant is describing symptoms inconsistent with a current psychiatric diagnosis or if the symptoms do not fit any known mental disorder, a forensic mental health evaluator will be very suspicious of the defendant's account. Similarly, an evaluator will skeptically view an assertion of rapid symptom onset by a criminal defendant who has not previously been diagnosed with a mental disorder, particularly if the defendant also asserts that the symptoms have since rapidly ceased and there has been no residual effect. If the symptoms appeared just before the criminal behavior and ended just after it, and the defendant is raising an insanity defense, the evaluator will be especially skeptical of the account given. Defendants' reports of rare, inconsistent, or extraordinary symptoms, a large number or unusual combination of symptoms, or rapid onset and prompt, total cessation of symptoms will all be viewed as possible indicators of malingering.

At the same time, mental disorders are often difficult to define and describe precisely and may be associated with unusual variations, symptoms, or presentations. For most mental disorders, there will be a first time when certain symptoms appear, and some individuals with a mental disorder will indeed experience a period when symptoms remit, either spontaneously or following treatment. Occasionally, there will indeed be an individual possessed by a dozen different demons. Furthermore, sometimes symptoms do evolve or change over time, or a person's description of the symptoms, given while simultaneously attempting to deal with those symptoms, may be incomplete, inconsistent, or bizarre.

Inconsistent Self-Reports

One of the reasons a forensic mental health evaluator generally wants to meet with a defendant on multiple occasions is to observe whether the defendant's reports of symptoms remain consistent. When defendants fabricate symptoms, odds are that they will forget exactly what they said previously and at subsequent meetings describe their symptoms differently, incorporate new symptoms, or fail to include previously reported symptoms. Sometimes in the interim a defendant may think of or hear about what seems to be a particularly convincing symptom and try to incorporate it at the next meeting with the evaluator. Another telltale sign is if there is a significant disparity between self-reported and observed symptomology, which is why forensic mental health evaluators often contact individuals who periodically interact with the defendant, such as jail or prison guards or mental health staff, to learn whether a defendant's behavior is consistent with their account. It can be quite difficult to "act crazy" in a consistent fashion over an extended period, across different settings, and while interacting with a range of individuals. Feigned symptoms consistent with a psychosis can be particularly difficult to sustain. Checking in with individuals who routinely interact with the defendant can provide information that the defendant has "broken character" and at various times is not demonstrating the symptoms the defendant described while meeting with the evaluator.

On the other hand, the symptoms of many mental disorders do tend to fluctuate over time, with some receding or changing, and certain situations or environments more likely to trigger or diminish the symptoms than others. Particularly if an individual has a serious mental disorder, he or she is also likely to be struggling to understand what is going on, and this confusion may result in some inconsistency in a defendant's account of the mental disorder and its effects. In addition, observers may find the individual's behavior and language to be bizarre and irrational in general, making it difficult for them to identify consistencies occurring over time.

Endorsement of Obvious Symptoms and a Failure to Report More Subtle, Less Commonly Known Symptoms

A forensic mental health evaluator interviewing a defendant will "listen" carefully for what is not said. For example, a defendant may readily report the "positive" symptoms of schizophrenia (such as delusions and hallucinations), but not report less well-known but frequently accompanying "negative" symptoms (such as avolition). Defendants who are malingering tend to describe relatively blatant symptoms, which they are more likely to have heard of and which may be easier to fabricate because they are intermittent and dramatic, but fail to mention the subtler symptoms that often accompany a mental disorder. Although these subtler symptoms tend to receive little publicity, they are generally present on a consistent basis, are often quite distressing, and can significantly impair an individual's day-to-day living. Furthermore, over time, these symptoms can have a significant impact on cognition, emotion, or behavior. Over and above the need for the defendant to remain "in character" around the clock, replicating these subtler symptoms may be especially difficult.

However, negative symptoms and other subtler changes in the person tend to occur later in the course of a mental disorder, while most criminal defendants, including those with a mental disorder, are relatively young. As a result, the subtler symptoms of their disorder may not have manifested yet. Also, in the early stages of a mental disorder, the more blatant symptoms tend to predominate over those that are relatively subtle. Because the former are more noticeable and disruptive, the individual, and those in the individual's social network, tend to focus their attention on them and recount them. Only later do they become cognizant of the subtler symptoms, sometimes because the dramatic symptoms have receded while the subtler ones have emerged to play a more dominant role. In addition, the attorney or judge who has requested the forensic evaluator's assistance is more likely to be cognizant of and recount the defendant's dramatic symptoms and expect the evaluator to address them. Unsurprisingly, the criminal defendant may also think these dramatic symptoms are what the forensic evaluator is most interested in, and if the evaluator does not directly ask about subtler symptoms, the defendant may not realize that they should be recounted as well. Alternatively, the defendant may be relatively embarrassed by this category of symptoms and be reluctant to disclose them.

Strategies for Assessing Malingering

Forensic mental health evaluators have many strategies for detecting whether a criminal defendant is malingering.[23] The following is a brief overview of some of these strategies.

STAY ON THE LOOKOUT FOR AND RULE OUT MALINGERING. The stakes are too high and the temptation for defendants to malinger too great for the evaluator to simply turn a blind eye to this possibility. A failure to detect malingering will typically skew the evaluator's report and possibly subsequent criminal proceedings, not to mention injure the reputation of the evaluator and that of forensic mental health evaluators in general. Thus, forensic evaluators generally take steps either to rule out the presence of malingering or to document and report its existence. To this end, they engage in a continuous process of "reality testing" in which they second-guess both the defendant's remarks and their own observations.

REFRAIN FROM RELYING SOLELY ON THE DEFENDANT'S REMARKS; CAREFULLY REVIEW RELEVANT MENTAL HEALTH RECORDS AND PSYCHIATRIC HISTORY. In reviewing a defendant's mental health records and psychiatric history, which are obtained from independent third parties whenever possible, the evaluator is looking for collaboration or disconfirmation of the defendant's account. Mental disorders tend to be relatively long-standing and at least somewhat consistent in their manifestations over time. Although the full onset of some mental disorders may not occur until an individual reaches his or her twenties or later, there are usually earlier indicators that suggest the presence of a mental health problem.[24] Prior manifestations of a mental disorder and its nature are often evident from these records and history, and the defendant's account should be relatively in line with them. Although changes in the course of a mental disorder do occur, any discrepancies raise a cautionary flag for the evaluator and should trigger further investigation.

INCORPORATE OBSERVATIONS BY THIRD PARTIES. As noted, forensic evaluators generally do not rely solely on the account of the defendant, but seek collaboration from third parties—preferably independent third parties. In addition, ascertaining how third parties perceive the defendant and the defendant's behavior can provide valuable insights and an important check on the evaluator's observations. The evaluator typically meets with the defendant for a relatively brief period in a setting that may not be particularly conducive to a thorough exploration of the defendant's mental state and behavior. As also discussed, the defendant may be able to feign a mental disorder in this context but not sustain it outside this setting. Third parties, such as jail or prison staff, can provide an invaluable check on the defendant's account.

USE OPEN-ENDED QUESTIONS. Open-ended questions force defendants to describe their mental disorders and symptoms, as well as their impact on their behavior, in their own words. Questions that provide defining terms—such as "yes-no" questions that ask "Do you ever . . . ?" or "When did you last . . . ?"—can provide defendants cues and clues regarding what to say when trying to fabricate or embellish their condition and are generally avoided.

AVOID SUGGESTING POSSIBLE SYMPTOMS. Evaluators generally avoid running through a check-list of possible symptoms of a given mental disorder as this also provides defendants a road-map for manipulating the evaluator into embracing the conclusion the defendant seeks. Instead, mental health evaluators often suggest bizarre symptoms or symptoms unrelated to a potential diagnosis to see if defendants give themselves away by adopting these symptoms as their own.

INVESTIGATE WHETHER THE DEFENDANT HAS RECENTLY OBSERVED OR HEARD ABOUT SOMEONE WITH A SIMILAR CONDITION OR SYMPTOMS. Defendants incarcerated while awaiting trial may observe other inmates exhibiting symptoms of a mental disorder or hear accounts regarding them. Alternatively, if not incarcerated, they may observe individuals with a mental disorder living in the community. If it is determined that the defendant spent time around or heard about an individual with a mental disorder, the forensic evaluator will generally probe whether the defendant is simply imitating this person's psychological presentation. Similarly, the evaluator will often explore whether the defendant has been in contact with someone who has such knowledge and may have coached the defendant on how to feign a mental disorder.

CONDUCT A LENGTHY INTERVIEW OR MULTIPLE INTERVIEWS WITH THE DEFENDANT AND REPEAT PREVIOUSLY ASKED QUESTIONS. It is harder to maintain a feigned psychiatric condition over a lengthy period, or to replicate it on multiple occasions, when inconsistences and contradictions are more likely to appear. Although arranging a number of meetings with a defendant may be a challenge, particularly if the defendant is incarcerated or a quick turnaround is demanded by the court or the party who secured the evaluator's services, forensic evaluators generally seek multiple or extended sessions with the defendant to test the reliability of the defendant's account. The evaluator will, of course, remain alert for the possibility that inconsistencies stem from fatigue or the mental disorder itself and be careful not to push too hard lest a defendant's symptoms be exacerbated by the interview. Nevertheless, with periodic breaks, the revisiting of previously addressed topics can help the evaluator determine the genuineness of the defendant's account.

INCORPORATE OBJECTIVE ASSESSMENT TESTS. Although some concerns have been raised about the validity and reliability of standardized instruments for the assessment of mental disorders, which suggest they should not be used in isolation, such measures can provide a useful check on or confirmation of the evaluator's subjective impressions, as well as identify topics that should be explored more fully during interviews with the defendant.[25]

PROVIDE CLARIFICATION. Defendants who malinger during the evaluation process may be motivated by misconceptions about the criminal process, such as a belief that they will be released and allowed to go free, either temporarily or permanently, if they are found to be incompetent to stand trial or not guilty by reason of insanity, or that any resulting placement will be shorter and preferable to conviction and sentencing. Accurately explaining what is likely to ensue following such a determination may lead to a discontinuation of efforts to malinger.[26] It can also be pointed out to a defendant suspected of malingering that sentences of convicted criminal defendants have been enhanced when the trial judge determined the defendant had been malingering symptoms of a mental disorder in conjunction with a forensic evaluation.[27]

CONFRONT THE DEFENDANT. As discussed, forensic mental health evaluators will typically consider a strategy of confrontation if they believe a defendant is not being candid in his or her presentation. However, this strategy needs to be used judiciously. If defendants become upset, insulted, angry, or otherwise alienated, they may "shut down" and leave the evaluator unable to get much in the way of useful information from them. Generally, evaluators try to employ this strategy in such a way that a defendant who has not been candid can "save face." The evaluator may suggest, in as amiable a fashion as possible, that the defendant has forgotten, misremembered, or misinterpreted key details. In addition, an evaluator will usually not challenge a defendant on a minor or extraneous matter, unless this is likely to encourage the defendant to be more candid in general.[28]

CONSIDER A PLACEMENT THAT ALLOWS FOR A MORE EXTENSIVE OBSERVATION OF THE DEFENDANT. If evaluators suspect they are not obtaining an accurate picture of a defendant's mental status from the interview process, they may recommend that an incarcerated defendant be transferred to a mental health unit at the correctional facility where he or she is currently housed or to a psychiatric facility for closer observation. If not incarcerated, the evaluator may recommend voluntary or involuntary placement in a community mental health program or a psychiatric unit or facility. Objections to such requests may come from the court or the party who secured the evaluator's services if they are seeking a quick turnaround; from defendants who fear that stigma may be attached to such a placement, or that it will extend the time they are held in custody, or because of their antipathy toward such placements in general; or from public officials who object to the cost of or tying up these relatively scarce commodities. To the extent the evaluator can establish these services are necessary for the psychological well-being of the defendant, these objections will generally be withdrawn or overridden.

Malingered versus Genuine Hallucinations

Malingering concerns often arise when a defendant claims to have experienced hallucinations.[29] Hallucinations are often associated with severe mental disorders, which can lead to a finding that a defendant lacks the requisite trial-related competency or should not be held criminally responsible for a crime. Because defendants contemplating malingering may be aware of this, as well as the fact that the presence of a hallucination is not readily subject to external verification, and because such defendants may think they can easily fabricate this symptom, hallucinations are often the symptom of choice for a malingering criminal defendant.

Malingering criminal defendants may be particularly likely to try to fake an auditory hallucination, claiming, for example, that "voices" told them to engage in the behavior that resulted in their arrest. However, there are tell-tale signs that may indicate such a claim is not genuine and for which the forensic evaluator will be on the lookout.

For example, genuine auditory hallucinations are generally associated with a delusion. They are not usually just random voices that suddenly appear; rather, they fit within a delusional context. If the defendant does not describe an accompanying delusion, evaluators will generally be skeptical about an auditory hallucination claim. Furthermore, such hallucinations usually have some psychic purpose or some meaning for the defendant, even though it may be bizarre and disconnected from reality.

In addition, auditory hallucinations tend to be intermittent, rather than occurring on a continuous basis. When defendants claim they hear the voices constantly, evaluators routinely question this assertion. An auditory hallucination is also usually perceived to originate outside the person's "head." When defendants indicate they hear the voices inside their head, this tends to give the evaluator reason to pause. Finally, auditory hallucinations generally go away or at least diminish when the person is active. When defendants assert they hear the voices regardless of what they are doing at the time, this is another reason for an evaluator to question a defendant's account.

Regarding hallucinatory commands in general, whether auditory, visual, or associated with another sensory modality, a genuine hallucinatory command can often be ignored, at least for a time. In addition, such commands tend to direct the person to engage in self-destructive behavior, rather than harm someone else. For example, a defendant's assertion that a hallucination told him to kill a neighbor who was selling him drugs would be greeted with skepticism. Plus, hallucinations are usually not this direct or narrow in scope.

Conclusion

There are several "take-home" points that should be kept in mind regarding the forensic mental health assessments of criminal defendants.

First, the *defendant should not be perceived as a patient or client* of the evaluator. While evaluators may be sympathetic to a defendant's plight and even be tempted to put on their "clinician's hat" and embrace a treatment perspective in an effort to help the defendant, forensic mental health evaluators must remain objective, maintain a psychological distance between themselves and the defendant, and adhere to a questioning, relatively skeptical approach.

Second, there are *legitimate reasons why a defendant may be a reluctant or reticent participant* in a forensic mental health evaluation. Defendants may not understand the process or fear the outcome, distrust mental health evaluations or mental health professionals, or be generally suspicious of anything and everything to do with criminal trials and the criminal justice system. There may be socioeconomic, cultural, racial, or gender barriers. For whatever reason, the defendant may resist the evaluation process. In addition, the defendant may be upset or worried about issues unrelated to the evaluation, or not feel well, including suffering from a lack of sleep. As a result, the forensic evaluator generally expects to receive guarded responses from the defendant and incomplete information. A successful forensic mental health evaluator must be able to overcome the defendant's reticence relatively quickly, without losing the ability to remain impartial and objective.

Third, the evaluator should employ a *low threshold for questioning* a defendant's account. As discussed, there is a lot at stake in these evaluations, which may lead defendants to feign a mental disorder and its impact. Alternatively, some defendants have an inordinate desire to please either the evaluator or people in general, which may be an aspect of their mental disorder. The evaluator may seem like a nice, attractive, successful, or impressive person, or the defendant may believe the evaluator can cure or solve the defendant's problems. Defendants may tell the evaluator what they think the evaluator wants or expects to hear, even though this is not an accurate account. Regardless of the defendant's rationale, the evaluator should always be prepared for the possibility that a defendant will provide disingenuous responses and take necessary remedial steps. At the same time, the evaluator must typically maintain an empathic and open approach that encourages defendants to be forthcoming. This can be a tricky balance to maintain, but it is one at which skilled evaluators excel.

Fourth, skilled forensic mental health evaluators almost never rely solely on their interviews with the defendant in reaching their determinations, but routinely accumulate *information from other sources* to check the validity and reliability of the defendant's responses and, if indicated, use this information to challenge the defendant's account. As discussed, such challenges must be tactfully employed to avoid "losing" the defendant, but their use is almost inevitable at some point if for no other reason than to encourage and perhaps push defendants to clarify their remarks. Thus, it is imperative that forensic mental health evaluators have a thorough knowledge of the local criminal justice and mental health systems, as well as other possible sources, so that they know where to turn to obtain needed additional information.

Fifth, it should be noted *assessing anxiety and depression* in criminal defendants can be particularly challenging. Defendants are likely to be distressed in general as a result of their current circumstances. Besides facing possible conviction and criminal penalties such as incarceration, many are wrestling with a host of problems in the outside world. Discerning whether a mental disorder is present, as opposed to a relatively normal but transient reaction to a set of very distressing circumstances, is one of the more difficult aspects of forensic mental health evaluations but may be pivotal to an evaluator's report. It takes considerable expertise to make this call.

Sixth, forensic mental health evaluators should *not assume symptom exaggeration establishes the absence of a mental disorder.* As discussed, there are reasons why defendants may exaggerate their psychiatric symptoms—reasons that do not indicate malingering. Sometimes exaggeration is a call for help on the part of a defendant who is overwhelmed and perhaps suicidal, and not an attempt to manipulate the forensic mental health evaluator. Furthermore, inserting the "M" word (for "malingering") in a forensic mental health report can be outcome-determinative in that a judge or jury may conclude there is no reason to consider this matter any further. As a result, the term should be used cautiously and judiciously, with some arguing it should never be used because the ultimate determination of the underlying legal issue remains the responsibility of the judge or jury, and they should be required to sift through all the facts before reaching their decision.

Seventh, despite the challenge of identifying malingering, there are relatively reliable *indicators* of its occurrence. They include an overplayed or dramatic presentation; pronounced deliberateness and caution before providing responses; a presentation that is inconsistent with the defendant's current diagnosis or clinical functioning; the ready endorsement of obvious or offered symptoms; and an overly broad assertion of visual or auditory hallucinations.

Keeping these key points in mind, skillful forensic mental health evaluators are an invaluable resource for judges and juries charged with reaching determinations and verdicts in criminal trials wherein a mental status issue has been raised. The following chapters address the range of legal issues in criminal trials in which mental disorders and related evaluations are pivotal.

3

Underpinnings of the Competence to Stand Trial Standard

According to Shakespeare, mercy must be freely given; you cannot force someone to be merciful. When addressing criminal defendants with a mental disorder and their right to be competent to stand trial (CST), the criminal justice system often struggles to balance its responsibility to be both merciful and just—in other words, to adhere to the sometimes dueling principles of fairness and justice.

Many are surprised to learn that the question of whether a criminal defendant is CST is adjudicated more frequently than the insanity defense. Indeed, CST evaluations are the most frequent and arguably the most significant mental health inquiry associated with criminal justice system proceedings.

CST is a "bedrock" inquiry without which criminal proceedings should not go forward according to the United States Supreme Court (USSC), which has ruled that a defendant's constitutional right to a fair trial is violated if the trial proceeds while the defendant is incompetent to stand trial (IST).[1] Further emphasizing its importance, this right applies even if the defense does not raise the issue, and if it is later determined that the defendant was IST during the trial, a guilty verdict will be overturned.[2] The CST requirement applies to all defendants regardless of whether or not someone raises the issue at the trial. As a result, the prosecutor in a criminal trial may raise the question of CST—even if the defendant does not—to avoid having a guilty verdict later overturned because an appellate court subsequently determined that the defendant was IST.

It has been estimated that there are 60,000 to 80,000 CST evaluations conducted in connection with felony trials in the United States each year. Between 2 percent and 8 percent of all felony defendants are evaluated, although only 10 percent to 30 percent of these evaluations result in an IST determination.[3] With such a relatively small percentage of defendants found IST, this process may seem inefficient, particularly since trial proceedings are largely suspended while a CST determination is being made. However, its frequent deployment reflects a view that it is "better to be safe than sorry" (thereby avoiding the risk of a conviction being overturned on appeal), as well as an understanding that requiring criminal defendants to stand trial when they are unable to understand the proceedings or participate in their defense runs counter to our basic notions of a fair trial.

At the same time, there are data indicating that defendants' CST is not addressed as frequently as it might or should be. For example, although the defendant's CST is raised in 2 percent to 8 percent of all felony cases, surveys of defense attorneys found they question their clients' CST in 10 percent to 15 percent of cases.[4] What explains this discrepancy? As will be discussed, although both the prosecutor and the judge can request a CST evaluation, generally the request comes from the defendant's attorney—that is, the trial participant who interacts directly and has the most contact with the defendant and is generally best positioned to ascertain whether his or her CST is questionable. Defense attorneys, however, may not request a CST evaluation because (a) they think they can work around their client's mental impairment by getting relevant information from other sources; (b) they do not want to delay the trial as they feel pressure to proceed from the judge, their client, or their own caseload; (c) they lack the time or resources to convince the judge to order a CST evaluation; (d) they are relatively inexperienced and do not realize what they can or should do if they suspect their client is IST; or (e) they fear that the defendant will incur adverse consequences as the result of a CST evaluation request, including being the object of resentment or sanctions for delaying the proceedings, being labeled or stigmatized as having a mental disorder, or being subjected to extended confinement for evaluation or treatment.

Unlike cases in which the insanity defense is raised, CST issues tend to receive little attention from the media or appellate courts. This may be because even when defendants are initially found IST, most of them will typically have their CST "restored" after a relatively short period of treatment, and trial proceedings will essentially resume where they left off. In addition, the details associated with CST evaluations tend not to be particularly salacious as they address defendants' current mental state rather than their mental state at the time of the crime.

Notorious Cases

The main exception to the general lack of notoriety given to IST cases is when the crime itself received considerable media coverage. A brief description of four such cases follows.

THE LONG ISLAND RAIL ROAD SHOOTER. On December 7, 1993, at the height of the afternoon rush hour, Colin Ferguson, an African American, boarded a Long Island Rail Road commuter train leaving New York City's Penn Station.[5] After the train crossed over into Nassau County, he pulled out a pistol and began selectively shooting passengers, killing six and wounding nineteen others. As he reloaded his gun for the third time, he was subdued. Trial evidence indicated that he planned the shootings in response to a number of personal slights and a perception that various people and institutions were working against him. Although his paranoid grievances involved people of diverse races and occurred in New York City, his anger was largely focused on Caucasians. He purportedly waited until the train was in Nassau County so that his crime would not embarrass the current New York City mayor, David Dinkins, its first elected African American mayor.

Before his trial, Ferguson's would-be attorneys argued that (a) he had been driven to mental illness by years of living in an oppressive and racist society, and (b) his insistence on representing himself and not entering an insanity plea showed that he was IST. The trial judge nonetheless found Ferguson CST and permitted him to represent himself. At trial, Ferguson argued that the ninety-three counts with which he was charged reflected the year of the crime (1993) and that the charges were thus fabricated. He also initially argued that another black man living at the same residential address as his had committed the crimes. Later in the trial he asserted that a white man had committed all the crimes. He called witnesses who identified him as the killer and questioned them in such a way that they repeated this identification over and over. Reporters described Ferguson's defense as "bizarre" and "surreal." He was ultimately found guilty and sentenced to 315 years in prison (New York does not employ the death penalty).

THE UNABOMBER. Ted Kaczynski was considered a genius at an early age, received a PhD in mathematics from the University of Michigan, and obtained a position as an assistant professor at the University of California–Berkeley.[6] He subsequently resigned this position, however, and moved to a remote cabin in Montana, from where he sent a series of bombs through the mail from 1978 through 1995 to individuals at universities and airlines across the country, killing three people and injuring another twenty-three, all the while avoiding identification and apprehension by law enforcement officials. In 1995 he sent a "Manifesto" to the *New York Times* and the *Washington Post* in which he referred to himself as the "Unabomber" (constructed from the phrase "university and airline bomber"), claimed technology was eroding human freedoms, stated he was responsible for the bombings, and said he would stop the bombings if his manifesto was published. After extensive editorial debate, the newspapers did indeed publish it. Kaczynski was subsequently captured following a tip to the FBI from his brother, whose wife recognized the published writings as Kaczynski's.

After his arrest, Kaczynski was examined by Dr. Sally Johnson, who was appointed by a federal district court judge to evaluate his mental status. She determined that Kaczynski was a highly intelligent but socially withdrawn individual who had experienced rapid decline due to paranoid schizophrenia and whose delusional thinking centered on being controlled by modern technology. Notwithstanding the psychiatric diagnosis, Johnson concluded that Kaczynski was CST—a determination the federal court judge adopted.[7] Prior to his trial in 1997, Kaczynski directed his lawyers to not pursue a mental illness defense because he feared that assertions he suffered from schizophrenia might undercut the validity of the points he made in his manifesto. He ultimately fired his attorneys; pled guilty to thirteen counts of bombing and murder, which enabled him to avoid the death penalty; and was sentenced to eight consecutive life terms.

THE KIDNAPPING OF ELIZABETH SMART. In the early morning hours of June 5, 2002, a fourteen-year-old girl was abducted from her bedroom—which she shared with her nine-year-old sister—in an affluent suburban home outside Salt Lake City, notwithstanding that the outside doors were locked and both of her parents were at home.[8] The brazen nature of the act, the intrusion into a family home in a seemingly safe environment, and the wide distribution of the victim's photograph—which showed a young smiling blonde girl—captured the nation's attention and triggered a massive search. She was ultimately spotted nine months later walking along a street in Salt Lake City with her two abductors, Brian David Mitchell and Wanda Barzee. Mitchell was a homeless street preacher and Barzee his consort. They had initially taken Smart to their hideout in the foothills outside Salt Lake City, then to homeless camps in San Diego, before returning to Salt Lake City.

In September of 2003, Mitchell and Barzee were indicted by a Utah grand jury on charges of aggravated kidnapping, aggravated sexual assault, and aggravated burglary. Barzee, age fifty-nine, was found to be delusional and IST on January 9, 2004, and sent to the Utah State Hospital in an attempt to restore her CST. Because she refused all efforts to treat her there, the trial court ordered treatment over her objection. Following a lengthy series of appeals, this order was upheld, she was treated, and at the end of 2009 she was deemed CST.[9] In 2010 she entered into a plea bargain in return for testifying against Mitchell and received a fifteen-year sentence, with credit given for the seven years she had been in custody.

Mitchell's trial in a Utah state court began in December 2004. Fifty-one years old, he was removed from the courtroom ten times over the next seven months for interrupting proceedings by singing hymns and shouting biblical commands and warnings. In July 2005 in a sixty-page decision—extraordinarily long for a trial court CST determination but no doubt reflecting the attention given to this trial—the judge found Mitchell to be IST and sent him as well to the Utah State Hospital for treatment to restore his CST. Mitchell also refused treatment. A hearing in September of 2007 was held to determine whether he should be treated over his objection, but the state judge refused to issue this order as he concluded that the likelihood of restoring Mitchell's CST was too small.

Following this apparent stalemate, the US attorney in Utah filed federal kidnapping charges against Mitchell, thereby commencing proceedings in the federal judicial system. A CST hearing was held in November of 2009, in which Smart testified and Mitchell was removed when he began singing hymns. In March of 2010 Mitchell was found to be CST in a 149-page ruling that determined he was not psychotic or delusional but rather an "effectively misleading psychopath" whose singing during trial was a contrivance to derail the proceedings.[10] At Mitchell's criminal trial, which began in November, his attorneys raised an insanity defense.

On December 14, 2010, after deliberating for five hours, the jury rejected Mitchell's insanity defense and found him guilty on the federal kidnapping charge. On May 25, 2011, Mitchell received a life sentence without the possibility of parole.

JARED LOUGHNER. On January 8, 2011, Gabrielle Giffords, who at the time represented Arizona in the US House of Representatives, was hosting a political "meet-and-greet" event at a shopping mall in Tucson, Arizona.[11] Jared Loughner, while waiting in line, pulled out a gun and began shooting, killing six and wounding another thirteen. Loughner severely injured Giffords, who was his target, and killed, among others, Chief US District Court Judge John Roll. Apprehended at the site of the shooting, Loughner was tried in federal court. In May, Loughner was declared IST, with the presiding judge citing the findings of two medical experts that Loughner was suffering from schizophrenia, disordered thinking, and delusions. He was described in news reports as agitated during the hearings, mumbling that they were "treasonous" and a "freak show." After the presiding judge gave him the option of restraining his outbursts or being removed from the courtroom, he watched the end of the hearings via closed-circuit television. The government was initially given four months to restore Loughner's CST, which was then extended another four months, and then another four months. Ultimately, in August of 2012, the trial court found Loughner CST. Loughner then entered a plea agreement to avoid the death penalty and was sentenced to seven consecutive life terms plus 140 years in prison without parole.

Concepts Underlying the CST Doctrine

Understanding how CST is determined requires some general knowledge of the law's approach when addressing competence and incompetence in general.

The law distinguishes between individuals who have the capacity to make a given decision for themselves and those who do not, with the focus generally on whether a person has the requisite decision-making ability regarding a specific law-related task, including the ability to make his or her own decision. In other words, it examines whether a person has the necessary basic skills to make a given decision, with the requisite skills varying with the nature of the decision.

The law recognizes two broad domains of incompetence. The first is *categorical incompetence*. Within this domain, all members of a class or group are considered per se incompetent; in other words, they are automatically deemed incompetent because they fall within a specified class or group. For example, a US federal law effectively establishes that all individuals in this country under the age of twenty-one are incompetent to make decisions to purchase alcoholic beverages and thus cannot purchase such beverages no matter how informed, intelligent, or mature they may be.[12] Laws similarly establish that you must reach a certain age before you can lawfully operate a motor vehicle, purchase tobacco, marry, or vote. Likewise, someone convicted of certain felonies will be deemed incompetent to vote. There used to be more categorical exclusions. At one time, an individual who was civilly committed (that is, involuntarily hospitalized for mental health treatment) automatically lost the right to vote, contract, marry, divorce, execute a will, drive, and obtain a professional license. Because of the restraining and sometimes devastating effect categorical exclusions may have on a person's ability to live his or her life as others do, they are largely limited to minors today.

An alternative sometimes employed is a *presumption of incompetence* for a class of individuals, a presumption that governs unless an individual takes required steps to establish his or her competence and thereby defeat the presumption. For instance, it has been suggested that all individuals over a given age (such as eighty-five) should be deemed incompetent to drive unless they take a specially designed driver's test that establishes they are physically and mentally fit to drive.[13]

Nonetheless, individuals are generally free to make their own decisions even if most people would agree that the decision is unwise or foolish and even though it may have significant long-term adverse consequences for the individual. For example, once they reach the age of majority, individuals do not have to establish they are competent to get married or to buy a house. The norm is to presume competence and to limit a person's ability to make his or her own decisions only if a judicial proceeding is initiated in which it is determined the individual lacks the competence to make that decision. These *case-by-case determinations* are often limited to the specific task under consideration; in other words, even if you are found incompetent to buy a house, this does not establish you are incompetent to marry someone. An exception to this rule occurs when it is established before a judge that for the foreseeable future a person is incompetent (because of a cognitive impairment, for example) to make a range of relatively similar decisions, in which case a guardian or a conservator will be appointed by the judge to make those decisions for the individual.

Sometimes different standards are employed depending on the type of decision being made, with more demanding standards applied to those decisions with greater consequences for the individual. For example, before someone can execute a binding will they must have testamentary capacity, which may require them to understand (a) the nature and extent of their assets, (b) the natural heirs of their bounty, (c) the fact that a will governs the distribution of their assets after their death, and (d) who receives their assets under the terms of the will. Relatively distinct standards also determine a person's competence to contract, to buy or sell property, and to consent to medical treatment.

Standards/Tests for Establishing Competence

Nevertheless, standards for determining competence in general, and CST in particular, tend to ask three basic questions.[14] First, what is the nature of the decision to be made by the person (in other words, what are the key aspects of the decision)? Second, what is the person's ability to acquire and use information to make this decision in a relatively normal, rational fashion? Third, what is the person's ability to convey or communicate his or her decision? The courts have employed five basic tests to answer these questions and thereby determine competence.

Ability to Reach a Decision

The most straightforward and easy to satisfy test asks whether the person has the *ability to reach a decision*. In other words, a person is deemed incompetent if the person lacks the capacity to make up his or her mind regarding a given matter. If the person vacillates so much that his or her decision cannot be ascertained, or the person is essentially paralyzed by his or her thought process and cannot make a decision, a judge under this test must rule the person incompetent. However, individuals will not be deemed incompetent simply because they cannot speak;

if they can express their decision by nonverbal means such as writing down their decision, making hand gestures, or nodding their head in response to a question they will be considered competent. What this test focuses on is whether the person can decide what he or she wants to do. Whether it is a foolish, irrational, misinformed, misguided, or impulsive decision is irrelevant. The test simply asks whether the person can reach a decision. If the person can, then he or she is deemed competent and allowed to execute his or her decision. This test is obviously not very probing or protective. An analysis of the choice itself is not undertaken. If the person makes a decision, basically that's it; the person is allowed to act on that decision and it will be respected and upheld by the courts.

Ability to Communicate a Choice

A similarly undemanding test asks whether the person can *communicate his or her choice* regarding a given decision. If the person cannot speak or indicate a choice by nonverbal means, the person is deemed incompetent. This means that individuals who are in a coma or who are exhibiting the psychiatric symptoms of stupor or mutism—often associated with a diagnosis of catatonia—will be determined to be incompetent.[15] This test also does not probe the wisdom of the expressed choice or provide protection from misinformed, misguided, or impulsive decisions. As with the previous test, the emphasis here is on allowing individuals to make decisions for themselves and respecting their autonomy even though most people would say the decision being made is a really bad choice.

Ability to Understand Relevant Information

The most common test applied by courts and legislatures is the ability to *understand relevant information* standard. This test examines a person's ability to comprehend the basic concepts involved in a given type of decision. For example, in determining whether a person is competent to sell a house, a judge employing this standard will ascertain whether the person understands what a contract is and what it means to own and sell property; has a rough understanding of the value of the house, although this does not mean the individual has to demand full value in the asking price for the house; and whether the person understands that someone is buying the house and that he or she will have to vacate the property after selling it. This test, however, does not examine the person's motive for selling the house. For instance, the court will not consider the fact that the person is selling the house for an amount far below its value because he or she "hears" voices directing the person to do so. Thus, this test is a bit more probing and protective than the first two, but the examination of the person's competence is still pretty limited in that the person's motive is not questioned and he or she does not need to have much appreciation of the consequences of the decision being made. In effect, this standard gives individuals considerable freedom to make their own decisions and permits them to make bad decisions so long as they have a basic understanding of what they are doing.

Ability to Appreciate the Nature of the Situation and the Likely Consequences

A fourth test—*ability to appreciate the nature of the situation and the likely consequences*—is typically employed in conjunction with the preceding test. It basically takes the "ability to understand relevant information" test and applies it to the individual's specific circumstances, with a person deemed incompetent if he or she is denying objective evidence that should shape the decision. For example, if the person is experiencing delusions that impact his or her decision (as in the case of Colin Ferguson, discussed previously), that person will be found to be incompetent under this test. However, if these delusions are not germane to the decision being made, they are irrelevant to this determination. Accordingly, it is not relevant that a person selling a house thinks the moon is made of green cheese as this delusion is not relevant to the selling of the house (unless this belief is somehow influencing the decision to sell the house or the terms of the contract). This test, unlike the preceding ones, tends to focus more on why the decision is being made.

Ability to Manipulate Information Rationally

The *ability to manipulate information rationally* test is the most demanding test for establishing that a person has the requisite competence to make a given decision. It is, however, rarely formally used as it is the most difficult to operationalize and apply. It requires a judge to essentially "climb inside the mind" of the person whose competence is questioned to ascertain why the person is making this particular decision. This inquiry is also made more difficult by the fact that individuals tend to manipulate information differently depending on their prior experience and values, so there is not a readily available standard for assessing an individual's capacity to manipulate information rationally and to which the individual's decision-making can be compared. Finally, it is hard to appraise individuals' reasoning capacity, which includes an assessment of their ability to think "logically" and compare the risks and benefits associated with a given decision. Note that this test is supposed to focus on the decision-making process of the person, not the outcome. However, the likely or actual outcome may slip into this analysis as the temptation is to start with a determination that this is a really bad idea and then work backward to say the person's decision-making capacity must be impaired. How else could he or she reach this decision? Yet, sometimes rich people, for example, really do want to be penniless. There can be a host of reasons why a person wants to do something with some, if not many, of these reasons seeming irrational to outsiders. As a result, courts and legislatures have been reluctant to formally embrace this standard, even though it may often be employed in practice.[16]

A Functional Test

One final point is worth stressing in conjunction with this discussion of how the law approaches questions of competence in general. Usually, regardless of the specific test employed, the legal standard for competence is a *functional test*. In other words, the test varies with the task and focuses on those aspects of the task that are relevant to the decision, not abstract categories or definitions. For example, when someone is selling a house, the law will typically assess whether the person understands what it means to make and execute a contract to sell his or her house, not whether the person understands real estate transactions in general.

One way of articulating this framework is that it examines a person's ability or capacity to conduct *the functions necessary to make a given choice*, with, as discussed above, some attention given to the functions necessary to make a *rational* choice. This approach seeks to recognize the idiosyncrasies of decision-making and embraces the notion that competence should not be based on how others view the actual or likely outcome of that person's decision. Thus, a competence test should not be outcome-based—which inevitably inserts the value-based judgments of others regarding the correctness of a given choice—but should instead focus on the decision-making process and the ability of the person to exercise his or her mind. Note, though, that this test is not totally subjective; rather, it assesses the ability of a person to exercise his or her mind *as minds generally work* when making a given decision. Thus, it attempts to strike a compromise by injecting both an objective and a subjective element into the analysis.

The Legal Standard Governing CST as Initially Set Out by the USSC in *Dusky v. United States*

With this discussion of competence standards as background, consider the standard governing the CST of criminal defendants. An articulation of this test dates back at least to seventeenth-century England, where a distinction was made between "mute by visitation by God," which was considered to render a defendant IST, and "mute by malice," which was considered to leave the defendant CST.[17] In the United States, however, little attention was given to the CST standard until 1960, when, with relatively little fanfare, the USSC ruled on the issue in *Dusky v. United States*. Before this ruling, when questions of CST arose the focus was primarily on the presence or absence of mental illness, and the CST standard was largely interchangeable with that for the insanity defense, with the main difference being that the latter focused on the defendant's state of mind at the time of the crime, while the former addressed the defendant's state of mind at the time of the trial.

Factual and Procedural Foundation

Milton Dusky was a thirty-three-year-old man charged in federal court with unlawfully transporting a fifteen-year-old girl in interstate commerce. The victim had been walking to a neighborhood drug store in a Kansas City, Missouri, suburb to have lunch with a friend, when the defendant, with two boys ages fourteen and sixteen, drove by and offered her a ride to the drug store. The girl, who knew the boys, accepted the invitation. They dropped her off at the drug store and went to a nearby drive-in restaurant, where they drank vodka supplied by Dusky and discussed "what kind of girl" the victim was and whether they could have sexual relations with her. They then returned to the drug store, waited for her to come out, and offered to drive her home. When she agreed, they drove her to Kansas instead, stopping on a back road where the two boys raped the girl and Dusky tried to do so unsuccessfully. Afterward, Dusky drove everyone back to Missouri, where the victim was able to leave the car and summon help.

At Dusky's arraignment, his lawyer suggested there might be some question as to the defendant's CST. At this point, the judge, on his own motion, committed the defendant for examination to the US Medical Center for Federal Prisoners. Although the psychiatric reports indicated that the defendant was experiencing schizophrenia (that is, a significant mental illness), after a hearing, the judge ruled that Dusky was CST. At the ensuing trial, the defendant was found guilty and sentenced to forty-five years in prison. On appeal to the Eighth Circuit, the defendant argued he had been IST. The Eighth Circuit upheld the trial court's CST finding, stating that the lower court's determination could not be set aside unless it was "clearly arbitrary or unwarranted," that the trial court was not bound by the experts' opinion, and that the court did not err despite ruling contrary to the psychiatric opinion.[18] Dusky then appealed these judgments to the USSC.

The Court's Ruling in Dusky

The following is the entire 1960 holding of the USSC in *Dusky*:

> PER CURIAM.
> The motion for leave to proceed *in forma pauperis* and the petition for a writ of certiorari are granted. Upon consideration of the entire record, we agree with the Solicitor General that "the record in this case does not sufficiently support the findings of competency to stand trial," for, to support those findings under 18 U.S.C. § 4244, 18 U.S.C.A. § 4244, the district judge "would need more information than this record presents." We also

agree with the suggestion of the Solicitor General that it is not enough for the district judge to find that "the defendant [is] oriented to time and place and [has] some recollection of events," but that the "test must be whether he has sufficient present ability to consult with his lawyer with a reasonable degree of rational understanding—and whether he has a rational as well as factual understanding of the proceedings against him."

In view of the doubts and ambiguities regarding the legal significance of the psychiatric testimony in this case and the resulting difficulties of retrospectively determining [Dusky's] competency as of more than a year ago, we reverse the judgment of the Court of Appeals affirming the judgment of conviction, and remand the case to the District Court for a new hearing to ascertain [Dusky's] present competency to stand trial, and for a new trial if [Dusky] is found competent.

It is so ordered.

Reversed and remanded with directions.[19]

Analysis of Dusky

WHY DID THE USSC WAIT SO LONG TO ADDRESS CST?

With this 1960 ruling, the USSC issued its first declaration regarding the standard governing CST determinations. Why did it take the USSC, which has been in existence since 1789, so long to address a bedrock question that determines whether a criminal trial can proceed, especially when English courts had issued rulings on this topic dating back to 1685? Perhaps this was a topic the Court was avoiding, preferring to leave it to the discretion of trial judges to resolve on a case-by-case basis. Perhaps it was an issue largely ignored in practice, with defense attorneys, not the defendant, expected to conduct and make all defense-related decisions relevant to the criminal trial. Perhaps it was generally resolved informally, with the defendant diverted out of the criminal justice system and placed instead in a psychiatric facility or the presiding judge implicitly taking it into account when issuing the verdict or the punishment. Perhaps it was folded into the insanity defense for simplicity's sake, posing one rather than two questions for the trial judge to resolve, with the assumption made that any underlying mental disorder that might trigger an IST ruling is a life-long condition and thus would have also been present at the time of the crime and therefore would be addressed in conjunction with the insanity defense.

WHY 1960?

After remaining silent on the issue for so long, why did the Court choose to issue a ruling in 1960? Of course, the USSC must generally wait for a request (a writ of certiorari) from a litigant to be filed with the Court to review a lower court ruling before it can consider a specific legal issue (in other words, it cannot act proactively and unilaterally). Furthermore, many, if not most, criminal defendants, particularly those with a mental disorder, traditionally lacked the funds to hire an attorney to defend them at trial, much less take a matter all the way to the Supreme Court. Indeed, it was not until three years after the *Dusky* ruling that the USSC established that states are required under the Fourteenth Amendment of the US Constitution to provide access to an attorney to those defendants unable to pay for their own attorney.[20] It is worth noting, as pointed out by the Supreme Court in its ruling, that Dusky appeared before the Court *in forma pauperis* (Latin for "in the form of a pauper"), which meant the Court waived the normal costs of appeal he would otherwise have incurred and appointed counsel to represent him on a pro bono basis.[21]

Perhaps the Court had become more conscious of the adverse effects mental disorders have on individuals and their decisions and actions and, like others, was beginning to question the adequacy of society's response, notwithstanding that mental disorders have troubled individuals since time immemorial and "laws [in this country] dealing with mentally ill people date back to colonial America."[22] One prominent psychiatrist has noted:

> Unquestionably attitudes toward the mentally ill and toward the psychiatric system responsible for their care were undergoing a remarkable transition in the middle of the twentieth century. Psychiatry had generally been treated with deference since the late nineteenth century, perhaps as a *quid pro quo* for its willingness to care for a segment of society that most citizens would just as soon ignore. In the late 1950s, however, that deference gave way to a questioning of psychiatry's most basic presumptions.[23]

Also, deinstitutionalization—the American policy of moving people with a severe mental illness out of large state institutions and back into the community—had begun in 1955 with the widespread introduction of Thorazine, the first relatively effective antipsychotic medication.[24] At the peak of institutionalization, over 550,000 people with mental disorders largely had been forced to reside in these facilities, oftentimes in very poor conditions and at considerable expense to the states that typically operated these facilities. Residing in the community instead was thought to be beneficial for these individuals, and because it was a much cheaper alternative, deinstitutionalization initially drew considerable and widespread enthusiasm. However, community programs that were promised to help released individuals—who often lacked or had lost the skills necessary to survive in the community—were oftentimes not forthcoming as many states struggled to balance their budgets during this era. In addition, while the new medications might initially abate symptoms, for many individuals there were relapses, which were associated with disorderly or impulsive behavior that harmed or alarmed others with whom they interacted. This, in turn, often led to their arrest and greater presence in criminal courtrooms, which increasingly brought them to the attention of judges throughout the country.[25]

Finally, this was an era when civil rights issues were being raised across the country and placed before the judiciary, including the rights of criminal defendants. There was also a greater recognition of how the rights of individuals with a mental disorder had long been disregarded in the name of an increasingly questionable paternalism. The USSC, like many courts, may have begun to recognize a need to articulate standards for how individuals with a mental disorder are addressed within the criminal justice process.

WHY WAS THE RULING SO SHORT?

The Supreme Court's ruling in *Dusky* is particularly noteworthy for its brevity and lack of citations to supporting authority. Rulings by the Court typically span many pages and include thousands of words, dozens of footnotes, and many citations. The longest majority opinion issued by the Supreme Court is 65,398 words in length,[26] with the median length of majority opinions in 1960 being roughly 2,400 words.[27] *Dusky* covers half a page, is two paragraphs long, consists of 237 words, and contains no footnotes or citations. Why in a ruling of first impression was the Court so succinct? Did it think its ruling was so obvious that there was no need for elaboration? This seems unlikely in that the Court was overturning the rulings of both the trial court and the Eighth Circuit. Did it see this as such a momentous ruling that it needed to approach the matter cautiously and leave the resolution of the details to a later day when a greater understanding of the issues would be available? Did its brevity indicate the members of the Court felt they lacked sufficient knowledge about mental health issues in general to wade very deep into these waters, particularly at a time when the mental health field was in considerable flux? Did it reflect division(s) among the nine members of the Court, which kept them from agreeing on accompanying details, notwithstanding that it was a unanimous opinion?

WHY DID THE COURT NOT ADOPT A MENTAL STATUS TEST?

Prior to *Dusky*, evaluations of a criminal defendant's CST, when conducted at all, tended to focus simply on whether a significant mental disorder was present.[28] There are various possible explanations for why the Court essentially rejected this approach and instead, as will be discussed, embraced a "functional" test targeting the defendant's understanding of the judicial proceedings and ability to consult with his or her lawyer. Perhaps the Court was concerned about effectively leaving this decision solely in the hands of mental health professionals, as would be the case if the presence or absence of a psychiatric diagnosis was the standard employed, and wanted to reframe this issue in terms trial judges could determine. Although mental health professionals under this standard can still provide relevant testimony regarding whether the defendant is affected by a significant mental disorder, a functional test focused on a criminal defendant's orientation to the judicial proceedings in which the defendant is immersed is something the Court may have believed trial judges were well-positioned and qualified to appraise. The Court may have wanted to ensure thereby that this pivotal issue—pivotal because a trial cannot and should not proceed if a defendant is determined to be IST—remained a legal determination over which trial judges retain ultimate control.

Furthermore, it is worth noting this was an era when there was considerable skepticism regarding the reliability, validity, and legal significance of psychiatric testimony, as well as the ability of mental health practitioners to fully understand and adequately address mental disorders. For example, popular stand-up comedian Woody Allen repeatedly incorporated in his monologues that he had been seeing a psychiatrist weekly for many years with no apparent improvement. In 1955, Erich Fromm published a book called *The Sane Society* in which he criticized fellow mental health providers for too readily labeling individuals who fail to conform to society as mentally ill and overlooking the possibility that the problem may lie with an unhealthy society that exploits, diminishes, or abuses various segments of the population. In 1961, sociologist Irving Goffman published *Asylums*, a bestseller that decried the current state of mental health treatment, attacked the placement of individuals with a mental disorder in psychiatric facilities for long periods of time, and supported deinstitutionalization. That same year, psychiatrist Thomas Szasz contended that psychiatric diagnoses were often inaccurate in his influential book *The Myth of Mental Illness*. Further demonstrating the growing distrust of mental health professionals was the publication in 1962 of the widely-read novel *One Flew over the Cuckoo's Nest* by Ken Kesey. These emerging viewpoints that mental health experts are often mistaken in their judgments may have increased skepticism among members of the Court regarding these experts' ability to provide reliable forensic evaluations of criminal defendants. This skepticism, in turn, may have furnished the cryptic rationale for the *Dusky* Court's ruling when it declared: "In view of the doubts and ambiguities regarding the legal significance of the psychiatric testimony . . . , we reverse the judgment of the Court of Appeals."[29]

Alternatively, the Court may have been concerned about making IST determinations too available. Although a state (or the federal government if the defendant is being tried in a federal court) is generally permitted to retain custody of a defendant found IST while attempting to restore the defendant's CST (as discussed in chapter 6), if the State is unable to accomplish this within a reasonable period of time, it must generally drop the defendant's criminal charges, which can deny the State the opportunity to hold a guilty party accountable, deprive victims of the satisfaction of knowing that the guilty party has been punished, and divest society of relief when a guilty party is incarcerated. Mental health professionals may have been perceived as too ready to diagnose criminal defendants as having a mental disorder, resulting in too many IST determinations at a time when psychiatric institutionalization was increasingly unavailable and individuals with an untreated mental disorder were increasingly likely to be returned to the community, where they might again run afoul of the criminal justice system.

A more generous explanation is that the Court may have reached a more sophisticated understanding of mental disorders in general and come to recognize that the effects of mental illness are not monolithic. Previously, disruptive individuals with a mental disorder were rapidly and routinely removed from society via involuntary hospitalization or incarceration with the result that most people rarely interacted with them and had no reason to think they were distinguishable from one another. As insights into mental disorders expanded and individuals with a mental disorder increasingly came out of society's "closet" as a result of deinstitutionalization, greater recognition of their differences and the differential impact of the various psychiatric conditions grew, along with an increased understanding that an individual could be experiencing a mental disorder and still have a relatively full understanding of the events in which he or she is engulfed. Thus, it may have become more widely recognized that the diagnosis of a mental disorder is not per se determinative of a defendant's CST; rather, the key is the nature of the mental disorder's effect on the defendant. This distinction may have led the Court to conclude that these determinations need to be made on a case-by-case basis, guided by a functional test applied by the trial judge, rather than based simply on a diagnostic test administered by a mental health professional.

Whatever the reason, the Court's ruling in *Dusky* had four major implications going forward. *Dusky* established that (1) the CST standard is a functional—not a diagnostic—test; (2) the CST standard is a legal question, not a medical inquiry; (3) a criminal defendant can be experiencing a psychiatric disorder at the time of the trial and still have the mental capacity necessary to participate in and receive a fair trial; and (4) it is the trial judge, not a mental health professional, who should make the final determination of whether a criminal defendant is CST.

The *Dusky* Test

To reiterate, when determining whether a criminal defendant is CST, a finding that a defendant is oriented to time and place and has some recollection of events is insufficient. Rather, the question is whether the defendant has "sufficient present ability to consult with his lawyer with a reasonable degree of rational understanding—and whether he has a rational as well as factual understanding of the proceedings against him."[30] Thus, the CST test articulated by the Supreme Court in *Dusky* has three components, namely, an examination of the criminal defendant's (1) factual understanding of the proceedings, (2) rational understanding of the proceedings, and (3) ability to consult with his or her attorney.

But what does this mean? What is the requisite mental capacity under this test? Unfortunately for judges who must apply the *Dusky* test, the above-quoted language was all the Court provided as guidance. Nevertheless, a few inferences can be drawn.

Does the test mean that criminal defendants must understand the world around them and make good decisions based on this understanding? No; the focus is limited to the criminal defendant's *understanding of the judicial proceedings* in which he or she is currently involved. The defendant can be convinced that the moon, and the earth for that matter, is made of green cheese, but if this does not impact the defendant's understanding of the criminal proceedings and ability to make related decisions, the defendant's cosmic beliefs are irrelevant.

But how well must the defendant understand the judicial proceedings? For example, does the defendant need to know whether judges in this jurisdiction are elected or appointed? Whether jury verdicts need to be unanimous? Whether defense attorneys are supplied by a public defender's office or are court-appointed? The answer to these questions is generally no. The defendant needs to have only *a basic understanding of how criminal trials work*. This typically includes knowing who the major players are (that is, the judge, jury, prosecutor, defense attorney, and sworn witnesses) and what their roles are in general; what constitutes evidence in a broad sense and basically how it is introduced during a trial; what criminal charges are and what charges the defendant faces; that the defendant has a right to a fair trial and roughly what this includes (for example, that a defendant is presumed to be not guilty and that the prosecutor must prove every element of a charged crime before a defendant can be convicted); how a verdict is reached and the consequences of various possible verdicts in the defendant's case; what it means to plea bargain; and any unique aspects of this case likely to be germane to the defendant's trial. Furthermore, a defendant will not be found IST simply because he or she does not understand all of this initially. Few will. Typically, forensic evaluators explain and clarify crucial information the defendant does not understand, and then they assess the defendant a short time later to determine whether he or she has retained this information.

Must criminal defendants be able to make trial-related decisions in a fully self-interested manner? Probably not. By focusing on the defendant's *sufficient ability to consult with a lawyer*, the Court seems to assume that the defendant's attorney will do most of the trial-related work and decision-making on the defendant's behalf and the defendant is required only to be able to communicate with the defense attorney and give the equivalent of a thumbs-up or thumbs-down to major decisions proposed by the attorney based on the defendant's general understanding of what is involved. Note that the Court did not use more proactive terms such as "assist" or "work with" the lawyer, although this may have been an oversight. Fifteen years later, in *Drope v. Missouri*, which will be discussed in chapter 4, the term "assist" was interjected.

Furthermore, in stating that the defendant must have a *reasonable degree of understanding*, the Court similarly suggested that defendants need only a relatively limited understanding of the proceedings when making their trial-related decisions. They do not need to understand the nuances of their attorney's proposed strategy, just the big picture. Use of the term "consult" suggests the Court expects the defendant's attorney to explain the planned course of action in general and not ignore the defendant (that is, not treat the defendant like a potted plant), but the defendant does not have to be an active participant in planning specific trial strategy. Indeed, the Court was likely cognizant of the fact that sometimes defendants, for various reasons, are unwilling—rather than unable—to actively participate in their own defense and that their attorneys are therefore forced to make trial-related decisions by default.

Because trial judges are not required to closely examine the nature of the interactions between criminal defendants and their attorneys, they are spared from having to evaluate how well defendants understand the multitude of trial-related decisions their attorneys make. This was a potential morass that the Court may well have wanted to avoid and a standard that few defendants, regardless of their mental status, could meet. So long as defendants can interact with their attorney, have a basic understanding of the proceedings, and possess the ability to veto overall trial strategy if they so desire, a trial court pursuant to *Dusky* can comfortably deem a defendant to be CST without worrying about being second-guessed on appeal.

It is worth noting, however, that the Court's thinking may have been premised upon the assumption that an attorney is representing the defendant. Without the assistance of counsel, criminal defendants arguably need a greater understanding of the proceedings and ability to make trial-related decisions to ensure they receive a fair trial. Some defendants, including those with a mental disorder, do indeed choose to appear pro se (without an attorney) in their criminal proceedings. Should the test of a defendant's CST change when this occurs?[31]

It is also worth exploring the difference between a *factual understanding* and a *rational understanding* of the proceedings. While the Court did not explain the distinction, a logical inference is that it perceived a mere factual understanding of the proceedings as insufficient to adequately protect a criminal defendant's constitutional right to a fair trial. A defendant may be able to parrot back to an evaluator or the judge the meaning of various court-related terms, but not really understand how a trial works. For example, the defendant may be able to recite that a judge presides over the trial, and may even be able to explain that this means the judge essentially runs the trial, but because of paranoid delusions the defendant may think the judge is part of some grand conspiracy that is "out to get" the defendant, and therefore believes that it will not be a fair trial no matter what defense is offered. Alternatively, a defendant may understand the rudiments of a trial in isolation, but not be able to put them together and use them in a self-interested manner. For instance, the defendant may understand the basic functioning of a trial but not understand the gist of the prosecutor's case, and thus will be unable to mount or help to mount an effective defense in response.

Finally, perhaps the most notable feature of the *Dusky* ruling is the Court's *failure to identify specific factors to be examined and how to as-*

certain whether a defendant is CST. Why might the Court have refrained from providing such valuable information? It may be that because this was the Court's initial foray into this thicket and because a large body of case law generated by lower courts on this topic was lacking, the Court was uncertain about how to proceed and was hesitant to reach too far with its holding, lest it thereby induce confusion if it determined upon further reflection and experience that different guiding factors and procedures would be wiser or more effective. Alternately, perhaps the nine members of the Court could agree only on the basic parameters of the CST doctrine and were unable to agree on the specific factors and procedures that should guide CST determinations. Or, as noted above, the Court may have believed this was a matter best resolved at the trial court level, where the judge has the benefit of directly observing and interacting with the defendant, and can obtain input from individuals who may closely interact with and observe the defendant, such as the defendant's attorney, jail officials, and sometimes even the prosecutor. Rather than hamstring the trial judge with abstract factors and procedures that might prove irrelevant or, worse, ultimately lead to unjust and unwise outcomes, the Court may have wanted to encourage trial judges to actively exercise their discretion in making these determinations. Finally, as will be discussed in later chapters, the Court may have wanted to defer, at least initialy, to the "laboratory of the states."

Conclusion

Notwithstanding that CST is a "bedrock" inquiry and the most frequently addressed mental health–related issue within criminal trial proceedings, it is still often overlooked and has received little attention from the USSC. Although over time the Court has somewhat fleshed out the CST standard and associated procedures, as the next two chapters will discuss, it has apparently been unwilling to interject itself deeply into CST determinations, preferring instead that their resolution rest primarily within the discretion of the judges presiding over criminal trials and the state, within which these trials are held.

4

Refining and Applying the Competence to Stand Trial Standard

While deciding whether a criminal defendant is competent to stand trial may seem on its face to be a relatively straightforward question, for both the mental health expert providing the initial assessment and the judge or jury responsible for reaching the final decision, making this determination is relatively nuanced. It requires the consideration of multiple factors, all of which need to be examined before a criminal trial can proceed, to ensure that a fair and just determination is reached on what the USSC has established as a bedrock issue, but none of which standing alone is typically dispositive.

Rationale for the CST Requirement

Why is it so important that a criminal defendant be competent to stand trial (CST)? As discussed, this requirement dates from early English common law and is based on the principles of fairness and justice. The long-standing belief is that criminal defendants must be given an opportunity to meaningfully participate in their defense; otherwise, the right to a trial—one of the long-standing tenets of both English common law and American jurisprudence—becomes an empty right. Over time, this concern for fairness and justice in conjunction with the defendant's CST has evolved to encompass three basic concepts.[1]

Accuracy

The first is that a CST requirement is necessary to ensure the accuracy of the trial outcome. Unlike some European nations, where the judge is investigator, inquisitor, and decision-maker all rolled into one (known as the *inquisitorial system*), English common law and subsequently

American jurisprudence decided that fair and just trials are most likely to result when opposing parties with vested interests in the verdict argue the case to the best of their abilities, restrained only by rules of evidence and procedures designed to ensure that the information introduced is relevant and not distorted or misleading, the proceedings are fair, and that a proper level of decorum is maintained, while a third party—the judge or a jury—ultimately decides the case based on the opposing parties' presentations (known as the *adversarial system*). For the adversarial system to function properly, it is believed that the judge or jury needs to fully hear from both sides. In conjunction with criminal proceedings, the concern is that the relevant information, knowledge, and insights possessed by a defendant who is incompetent to stand trial (IST) may not be raised for consideration by the judge or jury. Even if the IST defendant is represented by an attorney, the defendant's impairment may prevent the attorney from having access to all the information that might otherwise be forthcoming from the defendant and that needs to be presented during the trial to promote and enhance the likelihood of an accurate and just verdict.

Dignity

The second reason for requiring that a criminal defendant be CST is to protect the dignity of the legal system. The belief is that the validity and fairness of a verdict and the judicial system in general will be questioned if criminal defendants who cannot understand the proceedings and participate in their defense are placed on trial. Just as it is generally considered improper to try defendants who are physically absent, and thus cannot defend themselves, it is also considered improper to try defendants who are effectively "mentally absent" and similarly unable to defend themselves. The concern is that the morality of the judicial system will be questioned if it permits criminal defendants to be convicted who cannot understand or respond to the accusations being made. Additionally, an IST defendant may be unable to adhere to court rules designed to maintain order and decorum; if the defendant becomes unruly and disruptive during the proceedings as the result of a mental disorder, the dignity and integrity of the judicial system may likewise be brought into question.

Autonomy

The third explanation for imposing the CST requirement is our belief that the autonomy of all human beings, including criminal defendants, must be nurtured and respected whenever possible. Thus, just as we believe that adults should generally be allowed to make key decisions for themselves, so we also believe that criminal defendants should be capable of making key decisions about something as vital as their criminal defense. The belief is that defendants cannot exercise their autonomy if they cannot understand the proceedings or help prepare their defense.

The US Supreme Court (USSC) has left the basic components of the CST standard relatively untouched since its ruling in *Dusky* in 1960. However, it has gradually fleshed out the approach that should be employed when determining whether a criminal defendant is CST.

Pate v. Robinson (1966)

Factual and Procedural Foundation

The second of the USSC's three rulings addressing the CST standard involved Theodore Robinson, a criminal defendant charged with the murder of his common law wife, Flossie May. According to the Court, Robinson had a long history of "disturbed behavior" beginning at the age of seven after a brick dropped from a third floor hit him on the head.[2] As a young adult, his behavior became "noticeably erratic."

At one point, according to his mother, he "lost his mind and was pacing the floor saying something was after him," at which time he was taken to a hospital and was so violent he had to be strapped in a wheel chair. He was then transferred to a psychiatric hospital where he was described as hearing threatening voices and seeing things such as animals and snakes.

After his release, Robinson's "irrational episodes became more serious," and he would periodically go into a daze and not speak or respond to questions, although after an episode ended, he seemed fine. While married, he would become so violent that his wife would flee their home. A short time after the couple separated, he shot and killed his eighteen-month-old son, attempted to commit suicide by shooting himself in the head, and then confessed to what he had done to a police officer from whom he sought a cigarette. He was released from prison after four years, but shortly thereafter beat up his mother's brother-in-law.

The following year he went to a small barbecue house where his common-law wife, Flossie May, worked. In front of many witnesses, he leaped over the counter and, without saying a word, shot and killed her.

At trial, the defense called four witnesses who testified that Robinson was insane at the time of the crime and argued he should be found not guilty by reason of insanity. The prosecution had an expert in attendance at the trial who was prepared to testify Robinson was CST, but because the defense never claimed he was IST, the expert was not called as a witness. At the close of the trial, Robinson was found guilty and sentenced to life in prison.

On appeal, Robinson's CST was challenged. The prosecution argued that because the defendant failed to request a CST hearing at trial, the issue was thereby waived. The prosecution further argued that the trial evidence was insufficient to impose on the judge a duty to order a CST hearing *sua sponte* (of his own accord); essentially the prosecution asserted that if the defense does not ask for a CST hearing, there must be clear evidence a defendant is IST before a trial judge is required to order such a hearing unilaterally.

The Court's Ruling in Pate v. Robinson

The Supreme Court rejected the prosecutor's arguments and vacated the defendant's conviction, although it gave the prosecution the option—within a reasonable period of time—to put the defendant back on trial to face the same charges if the defendant's CST was restored. The Court began its analysis by noting that the due process clause of the US Constitution provides the legal foundation for the CST requirement, something that was not directly referenced in *Dusky*, and added "that state procedures must be adequate to protect this right."[3]

The Court then established a relatively unique aspect of the CST doctrine—namely, that a criminal defendant *cannot waive the right to be CST*. There are many constitutional rights a criminal defendant can waive, such as the right to a trial (defendants can enter a plea bargain instead), the right to a jury trial (defendants can opt to have a judge determine the verdict), the right to an attorney (defendants can appear pro se), and the right to cross-examine witnesses (defendants do not have to ask the prosecution's witnesses questions, or even call their own witnesses). In this context, though, the Court declared that "it is contradictory [for the prosecutor] to argue that a defendant may be incompetent, and yet knowingly or intelligently 'waive' his right to have the court determine his capacity to stand trial."[4] The Court thereby further established the bedrock nature of the CST requirement—namely, that regardless of whether criminal defendants raise the issue, they must be CST before criminal proceedings can continue.

The Court also signaled that trial judges must *be relatively flexible in permitting defendants to raise* the question of IST. The Court noted that although Robinson's attorney may not have formally made a motion challenging the defendant's CST or used terminology typically associated with questioning a defendant's CST during a trial (that is, the defendant's attorney did not specifically indicate the defendant's current lack of competence or capacity to stand trial), the record showed that the issue of defendant's CST was adequately placed before the judge when the defendant's attorney raised questions regarding the defendant's insanity, notwithstanding that this is a term generally reserved for asserting a defendant lacked the requisite mental state at the time of the crime rather than at the time of the trial. The CST issue was particularly placed before the judge, the Court added, when counsel asked Robinson's mother during her testimony about Robinson's "present" insanity.

The Court further underscored the importance of CST when it noted that even if the defense does not raise the issue, trial judges have an *affirmative obligation* to consider a defendant's CST, and if there is a "bona fide doubt" regarding the defendant's CST they must raise the issue sua sponte. In Robinson's case, the Court concluded there was no justification for the trial judge to ignore the testimony regarding Robinson's history of pronounced irrational behavior, which had not been contradicted. While the Court acknowledged the defendant's demeanor at trial is relevant in making this determination, which in Robinson's case apparently provided little indication he might be IST, it said that courtroom demeanor is not the only factor to consider.

The Court effectively ordained a "better safe, than sorry" approach, meaning that if there is any genuine reason to think a defendant might be IST, the judge must explore the issue further—typically by ordering an evaluation of the defendant by a mental health expert—and make a determination based on the resulting findings. The Court may have embraced this approach in part because the costs of temporarily suspending a trial to have a defendant's CST evaluated are not generally substantial. Usually such an evaluation can be conducted relatively quickly, with the proceedings only briefly interrupted. Once completed, the proceedings can resume where they left off if the defendant is found to be CST.

The Dissenting Opinion

Although two members of the Court disagreed with this ruling, they did not contest the basic CST doctrine.[5] Rather, their argument was that the facts known to the judge in Robinson's case did not justify a sua sponte order that a CST hearing be held. They contended that Robinson's psychiatric history indicated he functioned adequately most of the time, which was only sporadically "interrupted by periods of severe derangement that would have been quite apparent had they occurred at trial."[6] The dissent concluded that because (a) Robinson's behavior in the courtroom was relatively composed, which included engaging in conversations with the judge; (b) an expert witness who examined the defendant several months earlier was prepared, if called, to testify Robinson was CST; and (c) Robinson's lawyers, the two individuals who were in closest contact with the defendant during the trial, never raised the issue, the trial judge, "who had opportunities for personal observation of the defendant that we do not possess," did not violate the requirements of due process when he did not halt the proceedings and hold a CST hearing on his own motion.[7]

Analysis of Pate v. Robinson

What does the second of the USSC's three rulings regarding the CST standard teach us? *Pate v. Robinson* (1966) reiterates that a criminal defendant's CST is a bedrock matter without which a trial should not be allowed to proceed, and thus should be closely observed. The Court indicates that even if criminal defendants have attorneys who are vigorously representing them, defendants cannot receive a fair trial if they are IST. Of course, as noted earlier, defendants may choose not to participate in their defense, leaving virtually all trial-related decisions to their attorney. That, however, is a choice made by the defendant and, under the CST standard, courts will respect that choice if the defendant made it with at least a basic understanding of the proceedings and with the capacity to consult with his or her attorney if the defendant so desired. Public confidence and trust in the judicial system, and the right to a fair trial, however, are seriously undermined if defendants who are no more than a shell of a person during their trial are convicted.

As for the basic CST test itself, *Pate v. Robinson* (1966) does not add a lot. It does establish that if a judge has a *bona fide doubt* about a defendant's CST, the judge must raise the issue sua sponte if the defense has not already done so. Thus, the judge must be vigilant in monitoring the defendant's CST. Because the severity and impact of mental disorders can vary over time, even if a judge is convinced that the defendant is CST at the beginning of the trial, the judge must *remain alert* for any indication that the defendant's mental status has changed during the trial in such a way that the initial CST finding may no longer be appropriate.

Although not firmly established by *Robinson*, the "bona fide doubt" standard may also be the test that should be applied by a trial judge evaluating a motion from the defense for a CST evaluation. But how demanding a standard is this, and how is it determined? A test often used in conjunction with criminal trials is the "probable cause" criterion, which, for example, is the standard regarding the level of evidence generally necessary for a judge to issue a search warrant.[8] This typically means that the information presented must be sufficiently trustworthy to lead a reasonably intelligent and prudent person to a given belief.[9] It is perhaps notable that the Court did not employ this well-known test, but rather used the arguably broader "bona fide doubt" standard, which suggests that any genuine reason to doubt a defendant's CST should trigger a CST review and determination.[10]

In addition, the Court established that it is not just the defendant's courtroom demeanor and behavior that are decisive; the trial judge must also consider anything that he or she knows about the defendant's past mental health history that might be germane. In other words, a relatively *broad range of information* must be taken into account. One might ask why this past history would be relevant when the CST test focuses on the defendant's present mental status. There are at least three possible reasons underlying this expanded focus. First, a defendant's trial demeanor and behavior are often not a very reliable means for ascertaining a defendant's CST as the demands characteristic of the courtroom inhibit expressive behavior in general, while the carefully circumscribed nature of trial proceedings limits a defendant's interactions with others and exposure to stimuli that might reveal any impairments the defendant is currently experiencing. Second, in a typical criminal trial, particularly if the defendant is represented by an attorney and does not take the stand, the judge will have very limited interactions with and few opportunities to closely observe the defendant.[11] Third, contrary to general public perception, mental disorders do not necessarily result in agitated or violent behavior, but may instead effectively "shut down" a person. Thus, a defendant with a mental disorder may sit compliantly in the courtroom but have little perception or understanding of surrounding events, or may lack the ability to communicate with others, including the defendant's attorney. A trial judge may be hard-pressed to detect this type of impairment, notwithstanding that it effectively leaves the defendant IST.

The dissenting opinion in *Pate v. Robinson* (1966) does raise, albeit indirectly, an important point. The effects and manifestations of a mental disorder often fluctuate over time, notwithstanding the common tendency to perceive them as static. As a result, the trial judge should continuously monitor the defendant's mental status, particularly during a relatively lengthy trial as events may occur within or outside the courtroom that trigger or exacerbate psychiatric symptoms that impair the defendant's CST. This responsibility poses a significant challenge for trial judges who typically have many other ongoing responsibilities both in conjunction with and outside the trial. In addition, they are generally cognizant that suspending and thereby lengthening the proceedings for multiple evaluations of a defendant's CST can impose a significant burden on the individuals involved or interested in the trial, including the attorneys, witnesses (lay and expert), jurors, and any victims of a crime, as well as often extending the incarceration of a defendant who at this point has not been convicted of any crime.

Drope v. Missouri (1975)

Factual and Procedural Foundation

The third, and final, declaration of the USSC regarding the substantive standard governing CST determinations was the product of its review of a Missouri case in which James Drope was charged with raping his wife. Drope's wife was called as the prosecution's first witness. She testified that Drope and four of his acquaintances, working together, had raped her. On cross-examination, she further testified that she had initially told Drope's attorney that she believed her husband was sick and needed psychiatric care and, as a result, signed a statement that she did not want her husband to be prosecuted for his actions. She further noted that when Drope did not get his way or was worried, he would "roll down the stairs." She added, however, that she changed her mind about not prosecuting her husband when he tried to choke her to death just before the trial began.

Also introduced into evidence at Drope's trial was a pretrial psychiatric report generated at the request of Drope's attorney, which described Drope as "markedly agitated and upset" and said that he "had difficulty . . . participating" in the evaluation, "a difficult time relating," and "was markedly circumstantial and irrelevant in his speech," although there was no sign of delusions, hallucinations, obsessions, compulsions, phobias, or other psychoses. Drope was diagnosed as having a sociopathic personality disorder, borderline mental deficiency, and a chronic anxiety reaction with depression. In the terminology of that era, he was antisocial, neurotic, and depressed, but not psychotic.

During the trial, Drope shot himself in the stomach and was hospitalized. His attorney, in response, moved for a mistrial, but the motion was denied. When Drope's attorney complained about the difficulty of proceeding without his client being present, the trial judge responded that this difficulty was caused by his client and ruled that the client's absence was voluntary. Following the conclusion of the trial, a jury found the defendant guilty and Drope was sentenced to life in prison. The defendant subsequently filed a motion to vacate the conviction and sentence, arguing that his constitutional rights had been violated when a psychiatric examination of him prior to trial was not ordered by the trial judge and when the trial was completed in his absence. As part of the hearing on this motion, Drope called two psychiatrists as witnesses.

One testified there was reasonable cause to believe that a person who attempted to commit suicide in the middle of a trial might not be CST, while the other testified that such an individual was at least in need of a psychiatric evaluation to determine his mental condition. Nonetheless, the defendant's motion was denied.

The Court's Ruling in Drope

On appeal, the USSC, in a unanimous ruling, reversed Drope's conviction, although it allowed the state to retry the defendant if it so desired. Rather than focus on whether Drope's absence following his suicide attempt was voluntary, the Court addressed his CST. The Court began its analysis by noting the lengthy history of the CST requirement in criminal trials and—somewhat ironically in lieu of the facts of this case—noted that some have viewed this requirement "as a by-product of the ban against trials in absentia" as both sets of defendants—those who are physically absent and those who are present but IST—do not have an effective opportunity to defend themselves.

The Court then pointed out that the test for CST is distinct from an assessment of the defendant's mental and emotional condition in general. As it did in *Drope*, the Court emphasized that CST is not a psychiatric question per se, but is rather one that addresses whether defendants are experiencing a mental disorder that impacts their ability to receive a fair trial—that is, whether they can they understand the proceedings and work with their attorney.

However, the Court also emphasized the difficulty of making this determination in light of the uncertainty of mental disorder diagnoses and the "tentativeness" of related professional judgments. Backing away a bit from *Pate v. Robinson*, the Court further noted that trial judges must depend to some extent on the trial attorneys to bring CST issues into focus, thereby suggesting that it is generally defense counsel who should initially raise a red flag regarding defendants' CST.

Nevertheless, the Court determined that, based on the psychiatric reports and the concerns expressed by the defendant's attorney, there was a sufficient basis, even before the trial began, for the trial judge to order a CST examination of Drope. Because the defendant's attorney is generally the one in closest contact with the defendant, the Court established that if this attorney questions defendant's CST, that should "unquestion-ably" be a factor the trial judge considers when deciding whether to order a CST evaluation. The Court pointed out that an early resolution of the CST issue serves the interests of fairness and sound judicial ad-ministration, and supported issuing these orders on a relatively routine basis when a bona fide CST question arises.

In Drope's case, the Court found there was virtually no justification for not ordering an evaluation of his CST in light of the information uncovered during the trial, including the testimony regarding the de-fendant's history of pronounced irrational behavior, his suicide attempt during the trial, and his wife's testimony regarding Drope's attempt to choke her to death just before the trial when she "had hesitated about pressing the prosecution" and his "fate depended in large measure on [her] indulgence." This information, in conjunction with the informa-tion available prior to trial, "created a sufficient doubt" of Drope's CST and necessitated further inquiry into the matter by the presiding judge. As in *Pate v. Robinson*, the Court emphasized that a defendant's trial demeanor is not the only factor to consider in determining whether to probe a defendant's CST; evidence of a defendant's previous irrational behavior and any prior medical opinion on CST are also relevant. Any one of these factors, the Court pointed out, may in some circumstances be sufficient to require an assessment of the defendant's CST.

The Court further explained that the defendant's attempted suicide was relevant not just because it suggested "a rather substantial degree of mental instability," but also because his resulting absence denied the trial judge and defense counsel an opportunity to further observe and gauge his demeanor in the context of the trial, including whether he was "able to cooperate with his attorney and to understand the nature and object of the proceedings against him." The Court asserted that it was clear that this was a bona fide suicide attempt as a self-inflicted wound near vital organs, as in Drope's case, did not suggest malingering or manipulation.

Finally, the Court again recognized the variability over time of mental disorders and emphasized that a determination of CST at the start of a trial does not rule out the possibility that a defendant may become IST during the trial. Thus, if subsequent developments emerge that call a defendant's CST in question, the trial should be suspended at that point until an evaluation can be conducted.

Analysis of Drope

The Supreme Court in *Drope* reiterated its views that (a) CST is a foundational element necessary to ensure a criminal defendant receives a fair and just trial; (b) it is the trial judge's responsibility to be proactive in looking for indications that a defendant may be IST, and should not simply wait for defense counsel to raise the issue; (c) a range of information sources should be considered in weighing whether to suspend proceedings so that a CST evaluation can be conducted; and (d) a CST determination is not a once-and-done matter and thus trial judges need to remain alert during the trial for possible changes in the defendant's mental status that call for another evaluation.

At the same time, the Court recognized how challenging these determinations are for trial judges because (a) the impact of many mental disorders varies over time and in response to events of which a trial judge may be unaware; (b) the signals of an impairment may be very difficult to detect for the judge, who must remain impartial, juggle many responsibilities, and maintain decorum during the trial, all of which limit the judge's interactions with the defendant and opportunities to observe first-hand possible impairments; and (c) criminal defendants may be tempted to fake (that is, malinger) symptoms of a mental disorder or otherwise falsely raise concerns about their CST in the hope that this will delay the proceedings and enable them to avoid an unfavorable verdict, even though this is generally a relatively misguided hope.

As for the CST determinations themselves, the standard articulated in *Drope*, because it is mandated by the US Constitution, continues to be the baseline that must be employed in American criminal trials. Each state, however, is free to adopt a test providing criminal defendants appearing in its courts with greater protection. Missouri, like other states, has arguably chosen to do so, with its statutory test reading: "No person who as a result of mental disease or defect lacks capacity to understand the proceedings against him or to *assist in his own defense* shall be tried . . . so long as the incapacity endures."[12]

While the first part of this test differs little from the understanding prong set forth in *Dusky*, there is a subtle, but arguably important distinction made in the second part of the Missouri standard.[13] Instead of just requiring that defendants be capable of "consulting" with their attorney as established by *Dusky*, Missouri states that defendants must be able to "assist" their attorney.[14] This suggests they must not only be able to consult or communicate with their attorney, but must also be capable of the more active role of assisting or working with their attorney. Although the Court in *Drope* does not specifically embrace this standard, it is worth noting that the Court began its ruling by stating that it has long been accepted that a defendant cannot be tried if "he lacks the capacity to understand the nature and object of the proceedings against him, to consult with counsel, *and to assist in preparing his defense*"—a statement that suggests that the Court supports this more expansive requirement although it did not explicitly amend the test it set forth in *Dusky*.[15]

What if the defendant is not being represented by an attorney and is appearing before the court pro se? Why did the Court not establish a distinct standard for this scenario? It can be argued that to ensure a fair and just trial, the requisite mental status for a defendant appearing pro se should be much higher considering these defendants must devise their own trial strategy, understand how to attack the prosecutor's and introduce their own evidence, know how to maneuver within the rules of the court, including preserving issues for appeal, and make a myriad of decisions on the fly while rapidly processing a host of information. One likely explanation for why this scenario was not addressed is that the Court typically tackles only the issues placed before it by the parties of a given case, and in *Drope*, as in *Dusky* and *Robinson*, the defendant had been represented by counsel. It is very difficult to anticipate all possible permutations of a hypothetical case, and thus the Court is generally hesitant to reach beyond the specifics of the case before it, which can be fully described by the parties as they have direct knowledge of the pertinent details. In addition, the Court generally "paints with a broad brush" as the more finely it parses its ruling, the more difficult it becomes for lower courts and future litigants to apply it.

The Court may also have wanted to avoid sending a signal that the mental status of a criminal defendant is less important and relevant when the defendant is represented by an attorney. It is, after all, the defendant's life and liberty that are at stake. Model legal representation is built on a series of exchanges between the defendant and the attorney and is not a set of unilateral decisions made by an attorney without input from the defendant. To embrace the latter scenario is to degrade the input of the defendant who has much more at stake and typically has superior insights into the events associated with the criminal charge. The right of defendants, including defendants with a mental disorder, to be active participants in their criminal defense is much too important for it to be negated, both from the defendant's perspective and from that of society even when represented by an attorney.

Impact of Drope

What was the long-term impact of *Drope*? First, the Court established *three factors for trial judges to consider* when determining whether a defendant's CST should be evaluated.

1. HISTORY OF IRRATIONAL BEHAVIOR. As it did in *Pate v. Robinson*, the Supreme Court in *Drope* directs trial judges to examine whether the defendant has a history of irrational behavior. Such a history necessitates further inquiry even if there are no apparent current indications that the defendant might be IST. This retrospective analysis is incorporated because CST is such an important issue and because trial judges may miss indications of IST at trial due to their relatively restricted ability to observe the defendant. In Drope's case, a history of irrational behavior was suggested by his (a) trying to choke his wife on the eve of the trial even though she was going to withdraw her support for his prosecution; and (b) throwing himself down flights of steps when he didn't get his way. It is also worth noting that the Court did not require that evidence of a serious mental illness be associated with this history as Drope's reports did not include findings of a concurrent psychosis such as delusions or hallucinations. This expanded focus hearkens back to the Supreme Court's suggestion in *Dusky* that a diagnosis of a serious mental illness is not a precondition for evaluating a defendant's CST. Just as it is enough, for example, that the defendant has difficulty participating in or relating to the events of the trial, or is circumstantial and irrelevant in his or her speech, so a history of irrational behavior will similarly suffice for a CST evaluation.

2. DEMEANOR AT TRIAL. Arguably, the defendant's demeanor at trial is the factor most directly relevant to the CST question. In *Drope*, however, it was defendant's absence for a substantial portion of the trial

while hospitalized that may have led the Court to place greater weight on the other two factors as his absence prevented the trial judge from observing Drope's demeanor for much of the trial.

3. ANY PRIOR MEDICAL OPINION. Any previous medical opinion regarding the defendant's CST can enhance trial judges' understanding of a defendant's mental health history; enable them not to rely exclusively on their trial observations of the defendant, which may be skewed or incomplete; and provide additional observations of the defendant at different times and under different circumstances, including, when possible, events analogous to those unfolding at or during the trial.

Implications of Drope

A second set of long-term take-aways that emanated from *Drope* was the guidance it provided regarding *the approach that should be employed* to ascertain whether a defendant is CST.

1. THE TRIAL JUDGE MUST REMAIN VIGILANT. *Drope* underscores the importance of the trial judge remaining vigilant during the trial for indications the defendant may be IST, particularly as mental disorders are not static in their manifestations and their impact may evolve over time.

2. THE CST HEARING CAN BE HELD SUA SPONTE. *Drope* further establishes that trial judges should be prepared to conduct a hearing on their own motion (that is, sua sponte) to determine whether a defendant is CST, and should not wait for the defense to initiate this inquiry. This rule further underscores the importance of ascertaining whether a defendant is CST.

3. STATES CAN MAKE ESTABLISHING IST EASIER. *Drope* also indicates that the Court will not preclude a state from employing a more demanding test to establish a defendant's CST;[16] nor does it prevent a state from utilizing a relatively relaxed standard for requiring a CST evaluation, such as Missouri's "reasonable cause to believe" criteria.[17] This latitude reinforces the inference that the Court believes that it is better to err on the side of caution with regard to a defendant's CST and to resolve this issue at a relatively early point in the trial to avoid

compromising the integrity of the trial and to conserve precious trial resources that might be wasted if the defendant is only later determined to have been IST and necessitate a mistrial.

4. CST PROCEDURES MAY VARY. Fourth, in noting that *Pate v. Robinson* did not "prescribe a general standard with respect to the nature or quantum of evidence necessary to require" a CST evaluation,[18] *Drope* leaves open the possibility that CST procedures may vary with the legal context. The Court would later affirm that CST procedures are governed by the due process clause of the US Constitution,[19] which has been read to permit criminal trial procedures to vary in general depending on the nature of the proceeding. Thus, more relaxed procedural requirements can be employed for a traffic violation than for a death penalty case. This suggests that variations in CST-related procedures may also be acceptable depending on the nature of the criminal charge and potential punishment, with more relaxed CST procedures permissible when defendants face a relatively minor criminal charge, such as a misdemeanor. On the other hand, it can be argued that any criminal conviction is a serious matter for the defendant involved, with significant associated consequences, and that no defendant should be subject to conviction if unable to participate in his or her defense. Nonetheless, the Supreme Court seems sensitive to the limited nature of judicial resources and appears to be generally receptive to different allocations of these resources for CST determinations, depending on the severity of the criminal charges involved.

5. THE BASIC STANDARD HAS NOT CHANGED. Finally, it is worth noting that the CST standard originally adopted in 1960 by the USSC in *Dusky* has basically remained *unchanged over the years*, although *Pate v. Robinson* and *Drope v. Missouri* implicitly recognize that states can afford greater protection to a criminal defendant's right to be CST.

Why has it remained unchanged? Does the Court believe it got it right the first time? Consider that the Court in *Dusky* did not discuss or cite its own research into and justification for the test it embraced, but simply adopted the test suggested by the US solicitor general, who is an appointed officer of the Justice Department (thus, a member of the executive branch who reports to the US attorney general). The solicitor general is not a neutral party but rather represents the federal government in cases accepted for review by the Supreme Court, although the solicitor general tends to be quite well known to and respected by the members of the Court because of the nature of this role. This, however, raises the question of whether this issue has been sufficiently explored by the Court.

But perhaps the Court has not delved deeper into this issue for practical reasons. Given that the articulated test and basic approach did not apparently necessitate a massive change in the status quo, have not triggered strenuous objections over the years, seem to work relatively well in practice, and are sufficiently amorphous to give trial judges considerable leeway in handling cases in which CST may be an issue, the Court may have been essentially saying, "If it ain't broke, don't fix it." Of particular relevance is that by pragmatically assigning the primary CST decision-making authority to the trial judges presiding over these cases, by embracing a standard that these judges could readily understand and apply, and by affording them considerable latitude and discretion in resolving CST issues, the Court arguably satisfied its most important audience regarding these rulings—namely, the trial judges making these determinations.

The Current Standard

The upshot of *Dusky*, *Pate*, and *Drope* is that the USSC established that criminal defendants have a federal constitutional right to be CST. This right is found in the guarantee of a fair trial under the due process clause of the Fourteenth Amendment of the US Constitution, which in turn is intended to promote fundamental fairness in criminal proceedings.

By linking the CST requirement to the US Constitution, the Court has established the minimum CST standard that can be employed in criminal proceedings in both federal and state courts. This means it is a foundational requirement and ensures a relatively uniform standard across the country. States can make it easier to establish that a criminal defendant is IST, but not more difficult. As will be discussed, the USSC has not similarly ruled that the federal Constitution assures criminal defendants a right to an insanity defense, thereby leaving states free to widely modify and even reject this defense if they are so inclined.

Key Aspects of the CST Test

As for the controlling test for CST, there are a few points worth emphasizing.

Present Mental Capacity

Assessments of criminal defendants' CST should focus on their present not their past mental ability or capacity. Whereas an insanity defense examines defendants' mental state at the time of the alleged crime, CST addresses defendants' mental status at the time of their trial.

Capacity, Not Willingness

CST focuses on defendants' mental ability or capacity, not their willingness to exercise their mental functions. Defendants can choose to ignore what is transpiring in the courtroom or to not communicate with their attorney, but neither will lead to a finding of IST. Alternatively, defendants may be trying very hard to understand or communicate, but if they lack the basic necessary ability or capacity, they will be deemed IST.

Functional Test

Note that the Supreme Court's CST test makes no reference to mental illness, mental disorder, mental state or status, or psychiatric diagnosis. Assigning a psychiatric label to a defendant is not per se relevant.[20] As set forth by the Supreme Court, CST is a functional test, and the question is whether a defendant has the requisite ability or capacity to understand and communicate, not whether the defendant is experiencing a psychiatric condition. Including such a label in a mental health professional's report may help to explain why the defendant lacks the requisite ability or capacity to understand or communicate, and the presiding judge may refer to that label in explaining his or her determination, but the presence or absence of such a label should not be a decisive factor. Indeed, defendants may be diagnosed as having a severe mental disorder with psychotic symptoms, for example, and still be found CST if the disorder does not impair their ability to understand the proceedings and communicate with counsel. This "functional" focus ensures that CST will remain a legal question to be answered by the judge, or in a few states a jury, and not a psychiatric question to be resolved by a mental health professional.[21]

Factual and Rational Understanding

Keep in mind that the Supreme Court distinguished between a factual and rational understanding of the criminal proceedings and dictated that a defendant must possess both types of understanding. It is not enough for defendants to have a *factual understanding* of the proceedings and, for example, be able to recite the charges and potential penalties they face, comprehend what the judge, jury, prosecutor, and defense attorney basically do, and be able to parrot back the definitions of key concepts such as sworn testimony, presumption of innocence, and burden of proof. Defendants must also have a *rational understanding* of the proceedings, including, for example, knowing how a trial works in general, the nature of the typical interactions between the key players, and the likely impact of basic trial-related events and what can change or shape them. Defendants must also not be delusional. For example, they must not hold idiosyncratic beliefs about key elements of the trial that are contradicted by reality, such as the belief that all the key players are working together in a conspiracy against them.

Reasonable Degree of Understanding

Defendants do not have to have an extensive understanding of trial-related terms and concepts and how trials operate, but they do need to possess a reasonable degree of understanding. That is, defendants must possess a sufficient level of understanding to generally realize what is at stake, how trials work, and how verdicts are reached, free of delusions and gross misperceptions. This understanding does not have to be pre-existing, however. It will suffice that someone taught them the necessary basic information at the time of the trial, provided they can retain this information during the trial.

Consult with Attorney

Defendants must be able to use this understanding in a meaningful way and be capable of participating in their defense. In other words, defendants must have, at a minimum, the ability to consult with their attorney. Use of the term "consult" suggests defendants must be capable of more than just talking to their attorney, but must also be able to ask and answer questions. Note that the states are free to expand this requirement. Some, like Missouri and Virginia, have done just this and require that defendants be able to *assist their attorney*, a stipulation that suggests an even more active role with defendants capable of engaging in give-and-take discussions and collaborating with their attorney on a relatively ongoing basis.[22] California takes this a step further and requires that defendants be able to assist their attorney *in a rational manner*.[23] None of these standards should be taken to indicate that defendants must be capable of conducting their own defense. Not only does doing so require a level of expertise that few defendants possess or can readily acquire, but this degree of expertise is also why the Supreme Court has ruled that criminal defendants have a right to an attorney.[24] Rather, what the standards seek to ensure is that defendants be able to meaningfully interact with their attorney so that a fair and just trial can occur.

Assessment of CST and Relevant Capacities

Even though the CST standard has been formulated so that it is a decision to be made by the trial judge or, in a few states, a jury, these decision-makers are typically eager to obtain input from mental health professionals who have met with and evaluated the defendant outside the courtroom, generated a report with their findings, and, if requested, provided expert testimony at trial. To help mental health experts formulate their findings, various clinical instruments have been constructed to probe whether a defendant is CST. Perhaps the most widely used is the MacArthur Competence Assessment Tool—Criminal Adjudication (MacCAT-CA). However, there are several such instruments, each with respective strengths and limitations as described in various reviews.[25]

Regardless of which, if any, instrument is employed, there are eight key capacities an evaluator will generally examine when assessing a criminal defendant's CST. It is worth emphasizing that this is an illustrative and not an exclusive or exhaustive list. Furthermore, no single capacity is determinative, meaning that a defendant can lack a number of these capacities and still be found CST. What follows is simply a set of capacities evaluators generally explore when making their determinations, with their ultimate determination based on an overall analysis of whether the defendant meets the CST standard. It is also important to emphasize again that this is not necessarily a one-time only determination and that a request to reassess a defendant found CST may be made later. In addition, efforts can be made to inform and educate defendants initially perceived to be IST to see if they can attain the necessary capacity, with such efforts sometimes made by the evaluators themselves during their assessments.

Can Understand the Current Legal Situation

Defendants will typically be asked to state and explain the charges they face; key issues associated with these charges; likely related trial procedures; potential defenses that might be raised; possible pleas, verdicts, and penalties; and likely outcomes and an appraisal of their chances, with this last factor providing insight into a defendant's rational understanding of the proceedings.

Can Understand and Can Disclose Relevant Facts

Defendants will be assessed to determine whether they are oriented with regard to time and place (for example, do they know where they are, why they are here, what date and day of the week it is, and who the president is) and whether they can describe what they were doing at the time of the alleged crime, identify likely witnesses, and articulate possible alibis, excuses, or justifications. Evaluators, however, may avoid addressing key facts of the case lest they be viewed by defendants as judging them or be asked to testify at trial regarding what the defendant said about the alleged crime.

Can Understand the Roles of the Trial Participants

Do defendants know what their attorney, the prosecutor, the judge, a jury, a testifying witness, the evaluator, and a defendant in general do, both individually and as they interact with one another?

Can Relate to Counsel

Defendants will be examined to explore whether they can communicate effectively with their attorney, comprehend counsel's instructions and advice, make decisions after receiving counsel's input and advice, maintain a collaborative relationship with and trust their attorney, and help counsel plan their legal strategy.

Can Follow Witness Testimony

Defendants will be evaluated to ascertain whether they can track witness testimony for contradictions and errors it may contain, and point them out to their attorney.

Can Testify Relevantly and Tolerate Cross-Examination

Defendants will be probed to determine whether they can manage the stress and pressure associated with providing testimony; understand and reply to the types of questions they are likely to face (or will instead, for example, go off on tangents); understand and follow directions from the judge; remain calm and collected on the witness stand (or will instead lose composure or become volatile, mute, or withdrawn); follow and understand a line of questioning; and testify in a self-interested manner.

Can Tolerate the Stress of Trial and Awaiting Trial

Defendants will be studied to see if they can refrain from irrational, disruptive, or unmanageable behavior during the trial; are likely to interrupt witnesses, counsel, or the judge; or will decompensate (in other words, deteriorate mentally or otherwise fall apart) before or during the trial.

Can Protect Themselves

Defendants will be assessed to learn whether they can employ available legal safeguards, including the right to remain silent; will act consistently with their best interests (or will instead subjugate their interests to those of others or otherwise fail to promote their own interests); will follow events and act in a self-interested manner (or will instead be out of touch with the events in which they are immersed or engage in self-destructive behavior); and speak up on their own behalf (or will instead be passive or withdrawn).

Criticisms of the CST Doctrine

Although not as controversial as the insanity defense, the CST doctrine has been criticized.[26] Those who are focused on holding individuals accountable for their criminal behavior may view an IST finding as essentially allowing these defendants to avoid responsibility for their criminal wrong-doing. A finding of IST, however, does not exonerate a defendant or constitute an acquittal; nor does it typically result in a dismissal of the criminal charges. As will be discussed, the State is permitted to retain custody of the IST defendant for a reasonable period of time while it attempts—usually successfully—to restore the defendant's CST. During this time the criminal trial proceedings are usually simply suspended. If the defendant's CST is restored, the trial will then either resume at the point where it was suspended or, if a substantial period has elapsed, a new trial will be ordered. Even if the defendant's CST cannot be restored within a reasonable period of time, this does not necessarily mean the defendant is immediately released free and clear back into the community. The State at this point can initiate civil commitment proceedings and, if the standard for commitment is met, involuntarily hospitalize the defendant or impose outpatient commitment (that is, mandatory mental health treatment while the individual resides in the community).[27]

Objections may also be voiced by those with a direct interest in the trial. For the victims of the crime, as well as the defendant's family members and friends, the suspension of trial proceedings to restore the defendant's CST prevents them from obtaining closure in these cases and may extend or even exacerbate their emotional distress. In addition, individuals participating in or wanting to be present during the trial must return to the courtroom at a later time when proceedings resume, which may be an inconvenience or disruption for them. Finally, memories may fade during this gap in time, impeding the ability of witnesses to give accurate and full testimony, as well as hindering the ability of juries and judges to issue fair and just verdicts based on their recollection of the evidence previously presented.

At the other end of the spectrum are those who view the CST process as unfair to defendants. They may argue that the CST test is too stringent and provides inadequate protection for the many criminal defendants who have a marginal mental capacity. These defendants, it is contended, are unfairly forced to stand trial when they are little more than passive observers of proceedings they do not understand in a meaningful fashion. Complaints may also be raised about IST defendants who have not been convicted of any crime having to remain in State custody for what may be a relatively lengthy period of time while efforts are made to restore their CST, which in some cases may exceed the time they would have been incarcerated if convicted.

Another criticism notes that relatively stringent criteria must be met to involuntarily hospitalize someone who is not a criminal defendant (typically there must be a showing that the individual is a danger to him- or herself or to others or is unable to provide for his or her own basic needs), but for an IST defendant to be involuntarily hospitalized, all that must be shown is that the defendant is IST. In addition, IST defendants are increasingly likely to remain or be placed in a correctional setting while efforts are made to restore their CST.[28] Such a restrictive and non-therapeutic setting is virtually never used to treat someone who has been involuntarily hospitalized pursuant to civil commitment criteria, notwithstanding that the treatment provided may be similar. Furthermore, the criteria for forcibly medicating IST defendants over their objection, as will be discussed, may be more relaxed than for individuals hospitalized pursuant to civil commitment proceedings.

Alternative Approaches to CST

Perhaps because CST proceedings have not received much attention or perhaps because of a general satisfaction with the status quo, there has been limited discussion of alternative ways to handle these cases. Nevertheless, some suggestions have been made.[29]

Waiver of the Right to Be CST

Some may argue that defendants should be able to waive their right to be CST, much as they can waive other rights including the right to a trial, particularly if they are only marginally incompetent and are represented by counsel. Since IST findings can result in defendants' prolonged detention in State custody for evaluation and then restoration of CST without an initial finding of guilt, they might be better off if they waived their right to be CST. Even if found guilty, they at least begin serving their sentence immediately with an eye on eventual release, rather than languishing for a relatively lengthy period with no credit for the time spent applied to their sentence while attempts are made to evaluate or restore their CST.[30] Defense counsel will typically manage the trial anyway and may not need to rely on the defendant to access needed information.

It can be countered that it is contradictory to assert that defendants who have been found IST can knowingly and intelligently waive their right to be CST. It might be added that it is a "poor spectacle" to try defendants who are IST—that such trials reflect badly on the courts and the criminal justice system. In addition, there is no way of knowing whether counsel has access to all needed information if counsel is unable to fully consult with the person who is typically best positioned to provide this information, namely, the defendant. Plus, an IST finding generally represents only a relatively brief interlude in the proceedings, and defendants are typically restored to CST. Finally, trial judges will be disinclined to risk granting such a waiver and expending the time and effort needed to conduct the trial, only to have the verdict reversed on appeal when a higher court rules the CST waiver was improperly granted.

Enhanced Disclosure Requirements Imposed on Prosecutor

Another possibility is to allow the trial to proceed uninterrupted notwithstanding that the defendant has been found IST, but with special procedures implemented to compensate for the defendant's IST. For example, the prosecution could be directed to fully disclose to the defense all relevant evidence within its possession. Ordinarily the prosecutor has considerable latitude regarding what evidence it will introduce at trial.[31] This full disclosure may give the defense access to evidence of which it is unaware and thereby compensate for its potentially reduced ability to generate its own evidence as a result of the defendant's IST (as when IST defendants are unable to remember or describe what they were doing at the time of the alleged crime, for example).

Higher Burden of Proof

Another option is to allow the trial to proceed uninterrupted but impose a higher burden of proof on the prosecution than the usual "beyond a reasonable doubt" standard to compensate for IST defendants' diminished ability to defend themselves.

Require Corroborating Witnesses

Alternatively, the prosecutor could be required to produce a corroborating witness for each element of the crime with which the defendant is charged, once again mandating that the prosecution do more since IST defendants are able to do less in conjunction with their defense.

Amended Jury Instructions

Another possibility would be to issue standard instructions that direct judges or juries to consider the diminished capacity of IST defendants to mount a defense when reaching their verdict, although this can be a double-edged sword in that they may perceive criminal defendants with a mental disorder, and thus IST defendants, to be more culpable and a greater threat to society.

Although all of these options may have some merit, each one also has the disadvantage of carving out a unique and distinct procedural path for IST defendants, one that may be seen in retrospect as either unduly favoring or disfavoring them. These options may also raise unexpected issues or generate results that undercut the guarantees of a fair and just trial. Because the weight of opinion seems to favor the status quo, there seems to be little existing impetus to adopt such modifications.

Conclusion

Despite being a foundation of American jurisprudence, the CST doctrine (unlike the insanity defense) has received surprisingly little attention. Nevertheless, the CST of a criminal defendant is often questioned and evaluated, with forensic mental health examinations playing a pivotal role in these determinations. While there is a series of elements and guidelines for trial judges and forensic mental health evaluators to consider and apply, the CST of criminal defendants remains an issue largely resolved on a case-by-case basis. At the same time, as the following chapter will discuss, greater attention has been given to adopting standard procedures to be employed when making CST determinations.

5

Procedural Aspects of Competence to Stand Trial Determinations

Today we decide only that one State's practice does not violate the Constitution; the more challenging task of crafting appropriate procedures for safeguarding incompetents' liberty interests is entrusted to the "laboratory" of the States . . . in the first instance.
—Justice Sandra Day O'Connor, Concurring Opinion, *Cruzan v. Director, Missouri Department of Health* (1990, 292)

While the US Supreme Court (USSC) established the general approach and the basic test for competence to stand trial (CST) determinations with its rulings in *Dusky*, *Robinson*, and *Drope*, it was only when it issued a pair of decisions in the 1990s that the Court addressed specific procedural elements governing these determinations. A CST determination is effectively a trial-within-a-trial, but its unique nature and potentially significant outcome raised procedural questions for which there were few clear precedents.

Just as it is noteworthy that the USSC did not address the CST standard until 1960 when it decided *Dusky* and then set out only very basic and "judge-friendly" parameters for the governing test, it is also striking that the procedural aspects of CST determinations did not receive attention from the USSC until the 1990s and that here again the Court adopted a very restrained approach in its examination and oversight of state laws governing these proceedings. This late date and the considerable deference afforded these procedural rules suggest that the Court is relatively comfortable with how these matters are typically managed and content to leave them primarily in the hands of the trial judges presiding over these cases and the legislatures adopting the procedures that govern these cases in general.[1] As a result, CST hearings continue to be resolved in a fairly informal manner, which can vary considerably from court to court, with the trial judge given considerable latitude in managing a CST determination, and the various states free, for the most part, to make procedural adjustments where deemed necessary.

Nonetheless, it is likely that many of the same factors that ultimately drove the Court to address the CST standard, similarly led the Court to review at least some procedural aspects of CST determinations and may pave the way for additional examinations of these procedures in the future. Such factors, which have been discussed in earlier chapters, include a growing awareness of mental disorders in general, including their impact and prevalence; the frequency of these disorders among criminal defendants and the growing number of cases where CST is an issue; the relatively unique nature of the procedures used to determine CST; the potentially disruptive impact of CST proceedings; and the pivotal impact a CST ruling can have.

Medina v. California (1992)

Factual and Procedural Foundation

The first of the two cases focused on CST procedures involved Teofilo Medina Jr., who was alleged to have stolen a gun and gone on a month-long crime spree that included a series of hold-ups in which three people were killed. After his attorneys questioned Medina's CST, the trial judge granted their motion for a hearing, resulting in a six-day hearing in which six experts who had evaluated Medina provided testimony. Although most of them thought Medina was experiencing paranoid schizophrenia,[2] their findings varied widely. The hearing was interrupted by Medina's verbal and physical outbursts, including his overturning counsel's table.

Under California law, which governed these proceedings, if the defense raised the CST issue, the burden was on the defense to show by a preponderance of the evidence that the defendant was IST. In other words, California law presumed that a defendant was CST, and so it was up to the defense to show that the defendant was more likely than not IST (by 51 percent or more of the evidence), and if the evidence was evenly split, the ruling had to be that the defendant is CST. Although not at issue in this case, California employs a relatively unique approach wherein a jury can be assembled to decide just the CST question (Texas does as well, but most states leave this issue to the trial judge to decide). A jury found Medina to be CST. After a new jury was then assembled to address the criminal charges filed against Medina,[3] a trial was conducted during which Medina raised an insanity defense. This jury rejected the insanity defense and found Medina guilty on three counts of first-degree murder and issued a death sentence. On appeal, Medina argued that placing the burden of proof on him to show he was IST violated his right to due process.

The Court's Ruling in Medina

The USSC ultimately ruled that a state can place the burden of proof on defendants to show they are IST. The Court began by rejecting a test that would essentially have balanced the defendant's interests in how this question is resolved against the government's interests. Instead, it determined that with regard to criminal trials, the defendant is already guaranteed specific procedural protections under the Bill of Rights found in the US Constitution, such as the right to an attorney. Beyond these protections—in a position that is now widely accepted and played out later in *Indiana v. Edwards*, discussed below—the Court noted that because dealing with crime is the special business of the states and because the procedures employed in criminal justice proceedings reflect considered judgments by state legislatures, the Court must undertake a narrower inquiry when examining these procedures and apply a presumption that they meet the requirements of the federal Constitution. As a result, a distinct test must be used when reviewing a state criminal trial procedure: namely, does it offend some principle of justice so rooted in tradition and the conscience of our people as to be ranked fundamental? If not, the procedure will be upheld.

Regarding Medina's appeal, notwithstanding that in a criminal trial it is the prosecution that typically has the burden of proof to introduce evidence establishing that all the elements of a crime are met before a guilty verdict can ensue, the Court determined that placing the IST burden of proof on the defendant is permissible. The Court asserted that there existed no settled tradition on this matter, as early English common law was either silent or ambiguous about who must carry the CST burden of proof, both nineteenth-century English cases and twentieth-century American cases were inconsistent on this issue, and contemporary practice is split with some states placing the burden on prosecutors to show defendants are CST and others, like California, placing the burden on defendants to show they are IST.[4]

Because there was no relevant history to serve as a guide, the Court turned to whether California's allocation of the burden of proof was fundamentally unfair to defendants. In its analysis, the Court noted that this allocation affects only a relatively small number of cases—namely, those in which the evidence is in equipoise (that is, equally balanced between CST and IST). Furthermore, this allocation was considered to have a far less significant impact than assigning the burden of proof in general to defendants at trial where the determination of guilt hangs in the balance. In addition, if the CST determination is inaccurate, the Court contended that the defendant's attorney is still there to protect the defendant, and even if the defendant is unable to assist his or her attorney, counsel is well positioned to raise the CST issue again at a later time.

The defense had argued that because psychiatry is an inexact science, it was unfair and thus a violation of due process to force defendants to bear the risk of an erroneous CST finding (in other words, because of this risk, the evidentiary burden should be shifted so that defendants are presumed IST until shown to be competent). The Court acknowledged its prior rulings recognized that "[t]he subtleties and nuances of psychiatric diagnosis render certainties virtually beyond reach in most situations" because "[p]sychiatric diagnosis . . . is to a large extent based on medical 'impressions' drawn from subjective analysis and filtered through the experience of the diagnostician."[5] The Court responded, however, that the due process clause does not require every possible step be taken to eliminate the possibility that an innocent person will be convicted and thus it is enough that defendants are given a reasonable opportunity to demonstrate they are not CST. The Court added that those cases in which the burden of proof is placed on the State generally reflect concerns about lawless behavior by the police or prosecutors, which was not the case here.

A concurring opinion was issued by Justice Sandra Day O'Connor. The first woman appointed to the USSC, O'Connor frequently espoused the maxim that trial procedures should generally be developed and tested within the "laboratory of the states"; in other words, states, rather than the federal government, should serve as laboratories for new social and economic experiments impacting society and be granted considerable leeway when they conduct these experiments. She also noted that an advantage of placing the burden on defendants to show they are IST is that it gives them an incentive to cooperate with evaluators during psychiatric examinations and to supply all relevant information, including making family and friends available for related interviews.

The dissenting opinion, in contrast, argued that the CST burden of proof question was not just a procedural matter, but a substantive, foundational issue because defendants must be CST before they can exercise their other trial rights (such as the right to counsel, the right not to incriminate oneself, the right to question witnesses). Moreover, the dissent maintained a defendant who is IST is "not really present at trial."[6] The dissent contended that assigning this burden to defendants who may be IST limits the accuracy of determinations of guilt and raises concerns about both the fairness of and the "appearance" of unfairness in these proceedings, which will undermine confidence in the criminal justice system. The dissent also asserted that defense attorneys are not in the best position to appraise a defendant's CST since the defendant is typically in the custody of the State at the time (that is, in jail or prison before and during the trial), and thus it is the State that has the greatest opportunity to observe a defendant's behavior. Furthermore, the dissent added, defense counsel generally does not have the psychiatric expertise needed to discern if a defendant lacks CST, and if defense counsel takes the stand to testify that the defendant is IST, such testimony will likely be discounted as biased and could be considered unethical if the defendant does not want to be found IST.

Analysis of Medina

One question raised by Medina is whether the procedures associated with CST determinations are indeed best left to the states to determine for themselves or whether being CST is so foundational to the right of a defendant to receive a fair trial that there is a need for a uniform approach, one perhaps that requires that close cases favor the defendant and result in an IST ruling. Your response may depend on whether you think it is better for marginally competent defendants to be found CST or IST. It may also rest on how much you think the outcome will be affected if the trial is permitted to continue when a defendant is marginally CST, as well as how much impact you think such scenarios have on our perceptions of and faith in the judicial system. Another guiding factor might be how accurate, imprecise, or uncertain you think mental health evaluations of a defendant's CST are likely to be. Furthermore, do you believe mistakes in evaluations are more likely to lead to a CST or an IST determination? Finally, is research that has found that when an insanity defense is raised assigning the burden of proof to either the prosecution or the defense has a significant impact on the verdict,[7] germane to the assignment of the burden of proof with regard to CST?

Cooper v. Oklahoma (1996)

Factual and Procedural Foundation

Four years later, the USSC reviewed another case that focused on the evidentiary standard in CST cases. Bryan Keith Cooper was charged with the brutal killing of an eighty-six-year-old man during a burglary in Oklahoma. Under state law, a criminal defendant was presumed to be CST unless the defendant proved that he or she was IST *by clear and convincing evidence*; that is, a more demanding requirement was imposed than the preponderance of the evidence standard used in California[8] and reviewed by the USSC in *Medina*.

Cooper's CST received significant attention both before and during his trial, with a judge on five separate occasions considering whether Cooper had the ability to understand the charges against him and assist defense counsel. The first three arose prior to Cooper's trial. Initially, based on the opinion of a clinical psychologist employed by the state, Cooper was found IST and committed to a state mental health facility for treatment. Upon his release from this hospital three months later, another hearing was held at which two state-employed psychologists testified but expressed conflicting opinions regarding Cooper's CST; at that point, the judge ruled that Cooper was CST. A week before Cooper's scheduled trial, his lead attorney raised the issue a third time, advising the judge that Cooper was behaving oddly and was refusing to communicate with him. Nonetheless, the judge declined to revisit his earlier ruling that Cooper was CST.

On the first day of the trial, Cooper's bizarre behavior resulted in the judge addressing Cooper's CST a fourth time. Cooper refused to change out of his prison overalls for the trial because the clothes he was offered were "burning" him, and in the courtroom he talked to himself and an imaginary "spirit" who, Cooper claimed, gave him counsel. A competency hearing was held at which the judge observed the defendant and heard testimony from several lay witnesses, a third clinical psychologist who concluded Cooper was presently IST, and the defendant himself. Cooper testified that he thought his lead defense attorney wanted to kill him. Indeed, every time this attorney approached Cooper in the "witness enclave" where he was seated, Cooper would stand up and move as far away from his attorney as he could. At one point, when Cooper's attorney continued to approach him instead of backing off as in the past, Cooper fell backward over the railing that enclosed the witness enclave, landing head-first on the marble floor. The trial judge, although voicing uncertainty and noting his view that Cooper was not normal, once again determined Cooper was CST, ruling that he had not met his burden of proving his incompetency by clear and convincing evidence.

During the ensuing trial, Cooper did not communicate with or sit near defense counsel, remained in prison overalls for most of the proceedings, crouched in a fetal position, and talked to himself. After Cooper was found guilty, but prior to sentencing, defense counsel moved for a mistrial or a renewed investigation into Cooper's CST. These motions were denied, and Cooper was sentenced to death.

On appeal, the defense challenged Oklahoma's placing the burden of proof on defendants to show that they are IST by clear and convincing evidence. A lower court reviewing the case ruled, after cautioning it can be difficult to determine whether defendants are malingering, that the Oklahoma standard was justified because of the inexactness and uncertainty of CST determinations, because the State has a great interest in assuring its citizens thorough and speedy trials, and because truly IST defendants can prove they are IST with "relative ease" through their attorneys and experts.[9]

The Court's Ruling in Cooper

The USSC in reviewing Oklahoma's approach applied the test previously adopted in *Medina*: namely, does the procedural requirement offend some principle of justice so rooted in the traditions and conscience of our people as to be considered fundamental?

Unlike in *Medina*, here the Court pointed out that there was no historical precedent for the use of the clear and convincing standard in this context, with English common law and older American cases uniformly using a preponderance of the evidence standard. The Court further reasoned that "[c]ontemporary practice demonstrates that the vast majority of jurisdictions remain persuaded that the heightened standard of proof imposed on the accused in Oklahoma is not necessary to vindicate the State's interest in prompt and orderly disposition of criminal cases";[10] in fact, only three states other than Oklahoma employed it, and a number of states even went so far as to require the prosecutor to prove that the defendant is CST once the issue was raised. The Court determined that "[t]he near-uniform application of a standard that is more protective of the defendant's rights than Oklahoma's clear and convincing evidence rule supports our conclusion that the heightened [Oklahoma] standard offends a principle of justice that is deeply 'rooted in the traditions and conscience of our people.'"[11]

The Court then turned to whether Oklahoma's approach was fundamentally fair in practice. The Court began by noting that the function of a standard of proof is to establish the degree of confidence society thinks factfinders should have in the correctness of their decision, and that rather than jealously guard an incompetent criminal defendant's fundamental right not to stand trial, Oklahoma's requirement that the defendant prove incompetence by clear and convincing evidence imposed a significant risk of an erroneous determination that the defendant is CST. The Court asserted that, unlike the California approach that was addressed in *Medina* and impacts only those few defendants for whom the evidence is in equipoise, the Oklahoma approach affected a much larger number of defendants—namely, not only those for whom the evidence is in equipoise, but also those who have shown it is more likely than not that they are IST but have not necessarily shown it to a clear and convincing level.

The Court added that the consequences of a mistake regarding the defendant's CST are "dire" as IST defendants may be unable to exercise other rights essential to receive a fair trial, including the "profound" choice of whether to plead guilty, whether to take the witness stand and thereby waive their right to remain silent, whether to waive the right to a jury, and whether to waive the right to cross-examine witnesses, as well as compromising their ability to make the "myriad" smaller decisions associated with deciding the course of their defense. In contrast, the Court found that the injury to the State of an error in the opposite direction—incorrectly finding a defendant to be IST—was "modest" because the error can be corrected at a later hearing and because the State can detain the defendant for a reasonable period to see if the defendant can attain CST. The Court acknowledged that the "inexactness and uncertainty" that characterizes CST proceedings may make it difficult to discern whether a defendant is IST or simply malingering, but it "presume[d] . . . that it is unusual for even the most artful malingerer to feign incompetence successfully for a period of time while under professional care."[12] The Court added that "the difficulty of ascertaining where the truth lies" did not justify Oklahoma's elevated standard of proof, which "does not decrease the risk of error, but simply reallocates that risk between the parties" when CST is at issue.[13] The Court concluded that it could "perceive no sound basis for allocating to the criminal defendant the large share of the risk," as "the defendant's fundamental right to be tried only while competent outweighs the State's interest in the efficient operation of its criminal justice system."[14] The Court, in a unanimous opinion, struck down Oklahoma's approach.

Other CST Procedures That Might Be Contested

As discussed, the USSC affords states a fair amount of latitude in constructing procedures that underlie determinations of a criminal defendant's CST, but draws the line when these procedures create too great of an imbalance and can significantly undercut the defendant's right to a fair trial. Beyond *Medina* and *Cooper*, the USSC has had little to say about the procedures pertaining to CST determinations, although—as will be discussed—the Court has issued a pair of important rulings pertaining to efforts to restore to competence a defendant found IST. Nevertheless, the rulings in *Medina* and *Cooper* provide a basis for extrapolating how the Court might address other CST-related procedures.

Right to a Jury Trial

With the exception of a few states such as California and Texas, the CST determination is made by a judge and not a jury.[15] Does denying defendants access to a jury to determine their CST offend some principle of justice so rooted in the traditions and conscience of our people as to be ranked fundamental?

A criminal defendant's fundamental right to a jury trial can be traced back to the Magna Carta; jury trials themselves were institutionalized in England during the seventeenth century. The right to a jury trial in general is guaranteed in both the body of the US Constitution and the Sixth Amendment of the Bill of Rights, and it is embraced by the constitution of every state in the Union.[16] On the other hand, the right to a jury trial does not exist when the defendant is charged with a "petty" crime, which includes any crime for which the authorized maximum penalty is not more than six months.[17]

Among the arguments for recognizing defendants' right to have a jury determine their CST is that this is a pivotal aspect of the criminal trial, since the proceedings are not to continue if the defendant is IST. Just as defendants are entitled to have a jury of their peers determine their guilt or innocence, so, too—it can be asserted—they should be entitled to have a jury of their peers determine whether they are CST. It can also be contended that a CST determination is basically a societal determination, particularly insofar as the USSC in *Dusky* established that these determinations are to be based on a "functional" test, and thus a jury—as a representative of society—is the appropriate body to make these determinations. In addition, a CST determination could benefit from the group deliberation associated with jury decision-making, ostensibly diminishing the effect of individual biases regarding, for example, mental disorders, enhancing the incorporation of a range of community viewpoints, avoiding the institutional biases judges may hold, including the pressure to move trials along swiftly, and promoting a "common sense" based decision.

Typically, however, the CST issue arises following a motion (that is, after a request for a ruling by one of the parties or after the trial judge has raised the matter sua sponte), with motions typically decided by the trial judge, not a jury. In addition, assembling a jury to address CST interjects additional delay and expense, which can be magnified if, as sometimes happens, the defendant's CST is called into question on multiple occasions and a new jury has to be assembled each time. It might also be countered that jurors lack the skills or expertise to resolve the unique issues associated with a CST determination, and that community members may be more likely to employ widespread stereotypes and prejudices regarding mental disorders, their impact, and the general behavior of individuals and criminal defendants who are experiencing a mental disorder.

If defendants have a right to have their CST determined by a jury, should a unanimous decision by the jurors be required or will a majority vote suffice, as is permitted in some states for jury trials in general?[18] Should a separate "CST jury" be assembled so that its determination is not influenced by information previously received during the trial and, conversely, so that the information received during the CST hearing does not influence the final verdict of the "ultimate jury"?[19] If a defendant's CST is called into question on multiple occasions during the criminal proceedings, should a new "CST jury" be required on each occasion so that it is not biased by the evidence presented on earlier occasions? Because CST is based on a "functional" test, should traditional rules of evidence be waived or modified regarding the information presented to a "CST jury"?

Alternatively, because of the widely held prejudice toward and stereotypes about individuals with a mental disorder within the communities from which juries are drawn, and because of jurors' general lack of knowledge and understanding regarding mental disorders and their impact, does the imposition of a jury as the entity determining whether a defendant is CST, rather than the trial judge, offend some fundamental principle of justice rooted in the traditions and consciences of our people, which, in turn, would call for a ruling that the use of juries in this context is unconstitutional? Is it better public policy to have CST decisions made by the trial judge than by a jury?

Formality of the CST Hearing

In some jurisdictions, the hearing to determine whether a criminal defendant is CST may be a relatively formal affair, employing procedures and evidentiary rules much like those used in the criminal trial itself. Such a hearing can take several days and involve sworn testimony from a series of qualified witnesses—both lay and expert—subject to direct and cross-examination; the filing of expert reports and other documents pursuant to the rules of evidence; and the interjection of objections and motions ruled upon by the presiding judge. In other jurisdictions, the hearing may be relatively informal and brief, with the judge requesting information from various parties and deciding largely on his or her own what information to consider and what weight to give it.[20] Which of these approaches is best for resolving a criminal defendant's CST? Is it necessary or appropriate to conduct a CST hearing with the same level of formality and rules employed for criminal trials in general to ensure these proceedings do not offend a principle of fundamental justice, or is an equally or more valid determination likely when an informal approach is used? Are certain procedural components necessary, but not others, and, if so, which ones?

As the USSC has acknowledged, determining a defendant's CST is difficult.[21] These determinations may lack a firm scientific foundation; rely heavily on observations—which are themselves not particularly rigorous or extensive—of the defendant's demeanor, body language, interactive style, and nonverbal cues; and may be based on judgments that cannot be readily articulated and explained. Are CST determinations especially subject to human bias? Are formal or informal procedures required to ensure the proceedings do not offend "a principle of fundamental justice"?[22]

Presiding Judge

Typically, the judge presiding over the criminal trial will also conduct any requested CST hearing and determine whether the defendant is CST. The main exception to this norm is when a motion to assess the defendant's CST is filed prior to the commencement of the trial, particularly if a judge has not yet been assigned to manage the trial.

If the CST hearing is conducted by the trial judge, however, the judge may have previously received trial-related information that could bias his or her CST determination. Similarly, during the CST hearing the trial judge may hear information that could bias his or her determination of whether the defendant is guilty of the charged crime. Although judges, like juries, are expected to compartmentalize the evidence they receive and apply it only to the issue for which it is introduced, there is always a danger of leakage. At the same time, employing one judge for the CST determination and another for the trial itself adds expense and delay to the proceedings, particularly if there are multiple occasions on which a defendant's CST must be determined and different judges are used each time. In addition, relevant contextual information may be lost with this compartmentalization. Requiring separate judges for the CST hearing and the trial per se is likely to be particularly problematic in a jurisdiction where a limited number of judges are available to fill these roles.

The guarantee of a fair and unbiased judge is one of the preeminent principles of justice. Is the potential for bias sufficient to necessitate that a different judge presides over the CST determination? Alternatively, must the same judge preside over both the CST hearing and the trial in general in order to enhance his or her opportunity to observe and communicate with the defendant over a longer time frame? What role, if any, should added expense and delay play in resolving this issue?

Rules of Evidence

What evidence is relevant to a CST determination and what information, if any, should be excluded? Judges (and jurors in those states that assign this decision to a jury) may rely on a wide range of information coming from diverse sources in reaching their CST decisions, including their own observations of the defendant in the courtroom. This information gathering may not always strictly adhere to the rules of evidence, which are supposed to establish what information cannot be considered during criminal (and civil) proceedings because it is viewed, among other concerns, as too unreliable, speculative, or prejudicial. Strict adherence to the rules of evidence, however, may result in the exclusion of information that judges or jurors want to know about or consider important in making their decision. Is adhering to or disregarding the rules of evidence likely to offend a "principle of fundamental justice" during a CST hearing? Should a separate set of evidentiary rules govern CST hearings?[23]

Expert versus Lay Witnesses

Judges presiding over CST hearings will typically receive mental status evaluation reports regarding the defendant prepared by mental health professionals serving as an expert witness, which may be accompanied by sworn testimony from the professional. One of the key distinctions between expert witnesses and lay witnesses is that the latter can testify only as to what they directly observed, while expert witnesses are permitted to make inferences and offer their opinions or conclusions about facts placed in evidence, including the observations of other individuals. As discussed, a judge may find making a CST determination to be particularly challenging and welcome a report and testimony from an expert witness. However, as also noted, in articulating the applicable standard in *Dusky*, the USSC seems to have indicated that a CST determination is not a medical question, but a functional test, and thereby seems to have placed great weight on lay observations and conclusions, including those of the presiding judge.

What if a state adopts a rule that excludes lay testimony—such as testimony by friends, family members, or jail inmates regarding the defendant's behavior, ability to understand surrounding events, communicate with others, and follow directions—from CST hearings because it is considered too unreliable, uninformed, speculative, or biased? Alternatively, what if a state adopts a rule that excludes from CST hearings expert testimony—such as a psychiatric diagnosis by a mental health professional—because it is considered likely to be given undue weight and is not directly relevant to the functional test that is at the heart of a CST determination? Would either of these rules deny judges presiding over CST hearings access to relevant and helpful information, undercut their ability to accurately discern when defendants are IST, and thereby offend "a principle of fundamental justice"?

Limiting Which Professionals Can Report and Testify

Should certain credentials be required of professionals before they can submit an evaluation report or provide expert testimony at a CST hearing, thereby excluding all professionals who lack these credentials? Traditionally, CST reports and testimony were generated by and limited to psychiatrists and other licensed physicians, in part because they dominated the delivery of mental health services. In recent years, however, a wide range of other mental health professionals have entered the field, including psychologists, clinical social workers, advanced practice psychiatric nurses, licensed professional counselors, and marriage and family therapists, with clinical social workers accounting for as much as 65 percent of all mental health services.[24]

Alternatively, how critical is it that these professionals have extensive mental health training? Other than psychiatrists, physicians typically have limited training and experience with mental disorders, yet they may generate CST reports and testimony, often because they tend to be highly regarded or have extensive experience as expert witnesses in general or because they have been the defendant's treating physician, know the defendant relatively well, and have a baseline with which to compare the defendant's current behavior, interactions with others, or cognitive functioning.[25] Should professionals providing CST evaluations be required to have received specialized training germane to conducting forensic mental health evaluations in general or CST evaluations in particular, as well as in generating related reports and testimony?[26]

There is also considerable competition among these various disciplines as they jockey for recognition, respect, and a right to deliver and be reimbursed for various mental health services, including forensic reports and expert testimony. Plus, in some parts of the country, particularly rural communities, and in some institutional settings, such as jails, the availability of certain providers, particularly psychiatrists, may be quite limited. Although their expertise overlaps to a degree, distinctions can be drawn among these professional groups, with some viewed as having greater expertise in certain areas. It can also be argued that professionals' expertise increases the longer they practice their specialty, or is enhanced by certain types of education, training, or experience. It can further be contended that providing CST evaluations are particularly challenging since they require a distinct expertise, and that it is critically important that the mental health professionals providing these evaluations be fully qualified to do so. At the same time, there are few clear indicators regarding which discipline or which individuals within a profession are best qualified to address a defendant's CST.[27]

What if a state or a court adopts a rule limiting who can provide CST reports or testimony to those individuals who are members of a given profession, have acquired specified experience, or have completed a given training program?[28] Would such a rule offend a "principle of fundamental justice," particularly if a criminal defendant is unable to procure the report or testimony of an expert who meets these requirements when seeking to establish the defendant is IST? What if one reason for the dearth of available qualified experts is that a state has set the fees for their services so low that professionals with these qualifications are generally unwilling to accept these appointments, while other mental health professionals who tend to receive lower fees for their services in general are willing?[29]

Conversely, does it offend a "principle of fundamental justice" if the appointed expert lacks the qualifications or training necessary to ensure CST evaluations, reports, and testimony are sufficiently well done to safeguard their validity and reliability? It can be argued these functions require unique skills and knowledge and necessitate that professionals obtain specialized related instruction and training. For example, does attending a single five-day program about forensic evaluations in general, with a day devoted to CST evaluations and reports, provide the needed expertise? Should there be a continuing education requirement for these experts? Should an initial internship, where a candidate works under the supervision of an experienced evaluator, be mandatory? Should a written or performance test be required? Should there be an annual review of the professional's performance by an independent, experienced forensic evaluator or team of evaluators? Should a license or certification be required, and, if so, what entity should oversee licensure/certification and what requirements should be imposed to obtain and maintain licensure/certification?[30] Should an independent body be charged with adopting guidelines for the education and training necessary to qualify a professional to conduct these evaluations?[31]

Finally, who should be allowed to select a qualified expert to conduct a CST evaluation and provide a related report or testimony? Should this selection be made solely by the trial judge? If so, should the defense or the prosecution be allowed to provide recommendations or preferences to the judge? Should this selection be made by the defendant/the defendant's attorney? By the prosecutor? Should more than one or all of the above be allowed to select an expert, followed by a "battle of the experts" at the CST hearing?[32] Should any trial participant have the right to object to or veto the selection of an expert as biased, unqualified, too expensive, or on some other grounds? Should the appointment be made by an independent entity?

Location of the Evaluation

Following a successful motion to have their CST evaluated, defendants were traditionally ordered to report to either a psychiatric facility or a hospital with a psychiatric unit (incarcerated defendants would be transported to this facility), where they would remain until the evaluation was completed or, as in more recent practice, for a maximum period of time (for example, thirty days), although this period could be extended pursuant to a court order. Such facilities were considered the best environment for assessing defendants as they provided around-the-clock observation over an extended time, thereby enhancing detection of malingering; could readily administer needed treatment or emergency care; and provided a safe and secure environment. Moreover, if the defendant was found IST, this would typically be the facility to which he or she was committed for restorative services, thereby enhancing continuity of care and the likelihood that the defendant received those services needed to restore CST.

In recent years, however, many of these facilities have closed for various reasons, including cost savings and concerns that they are not optimal placements for treating mental disorders. Among those facilities still in operation, their beds have become a scarce commodity for which there is considerable demand, and a considerable amount of time can pass before a defendant can be admitted for a CST evaluation.[33] In addition, placements in these beds can be very expensive and potentially preclude the admission of someone who is experiencing a psychiatric crisis. Having defendants receive community-based CST evaluations is now generally seen as the preferred option.[34] As a result, CST evaluations of criminal defendants are now ordered on an outpatient basis (that is, in the community rather than within a psychiatric unit or facility) whenever possible in most jurisdictions.[35]

However, for those defendants who have not been previously released into the community either on bail or their own recognizance, orders for an outpatient evaluation do not necessarily translate into greater freedom for them because these evaluations are increasingly being conducted in the jail or prison where the defendant is currently incarcerated. Continued incarceration following arrest may occur for defendants who are denied bail because they committed a violent crime or are deemed a flight risk, but it may also occur if they are unable to raise the funds needed to post bail. Although it might be argued that a CST evaluation conducted while the defendant is incarcerated provides a useful opportunity for a close and continuous observation of the defendant, furnishes an enhanced level of safety and security, is a cheaper alternative, and avoids the need to transport the defendant to a psychiatric facility, it is also increasingly recognized that jail and prison settings can induce, sustain, or enhance a mental disorder, particularly among inmates whose mental health is relatively fragile, and even trigger or exacerbate a defendant's IST.[36]

In addition, although there may be a maximum length of time initially set for the evaluation, extensions of the initial CST evaluation order tend to be readily granted, which, in turn, can increase, sometimes substantially, the time that a defendant who is being evaluated—and who has not thus far been convicted of a crime—can be incarcerated.[37] Moreover, although the USSC has established that under the US Constitution jails and prisons must provide health care, including mental health services, to inmates,[38] these services tend to be limited, and a CST evaluation order does not necessarily ensure adequate mental health treatment.

Does placing a criminal defendant for whom a CST evaluation has been ordered in a correctional setting, or extending the time he or she is incarcerated to complete this evaluation, offend a "principle of fundamental justice"?[39]

Factors That Can Complicate a CST Evaluation

There are three especially tricky issues that may arise in conjunction with a CST determination.

Impact of Medication

At the time the CST evaluation is ordered, many criminal defendants are experiencing a mental disorder for which medication may be or has already been prescribed. The question may arise whether the CST assessment should focus on the defendant's "natural" (that is, nonmedicated) state. The medication a defendant is receiving or might receive may cloud this assessment, and thus, it could be argued, defendants should not be receiving any medication at the time of the evaluation. In addition, some of the medications used to treat mental disorders can have significant side-effects. What if it is these side-effects that are causing the defendant to be IST, when the defendant might be CST without the medication?

The general rule, however, is that it is not relevant why or how defendants attained their current mental state. The only issue, as set forth in *Dusky*, is what impact defendants' current mental state has on their ability to understand the proceedings and consult with their attorney. Thus, the judge will not consider whether a defendant would be IST or CST if taken off the medications he or she is currently receiving. The sole focus will be the defendant's current functional state, and the fact that a defendant is or is not medicated is irrelevant.[40] It should also be noted that there would be significant ethical and legal concerns raised if a defendant's needed medications were denied or suspended. In addition, many previously administered medications can linger in the blood system for a lengthy period, making a "natural" assessment difficult in any case.

Impact of Developmental Factors, Intellectual Ability, or Age

In attempting to understand the strengths and limitations of their clients, many mental health providers have for some time employed various categories, often referred to as *developmental stages*, to assess a client's progress toward becoming a fully functioning and actualized adult. Different developmental factors have been identified, including those that pertain to a person's *cognitive development* (such as Piaget's sensorimotor, pre-operational, concrete operational, and formal operational stages);[41] *psychosocial development* (such as Erikson's stages of trust, autonomy, initiative, industry, identity, intimacy, generativity, and ego integrity);[42] or *moral development* (such as Kohlberg's stages of preconventional, conventional, and postconventional moral reasoning).[43] Regardless of their specific focus, these approaches tend to share the notion that individuals who fall into a "less-developed" stage are impeded in their ability to effectively interact with others and accurately perceive the world around them. Furthermore, various instruments have been devised to determine within which stage an individual falls.[44] Similarly, tests that assess an individual's intelligence level are often used by mental health professionals to determine if an individual has an intellectual limitation or disability.[45]

These assessments of developmental progress or intellectual ability could be used as indicators of whether criminal defendants are CST. They might provide a relatively objective measure of a related impairment and ostensibly make CST evaluations less subjective and increase confidence in the conclusions reached. Although the developmental factors described above are not typically incorporated into CST assessment instruments per se, other instruments have been constructed to evaluate a defendant's "developmental immaturity,"[46] although they are employed primarily in conjunction with the assessment of the CST of juveniles,[47] with some states having identified "immaturity" as a basis for finding a juvenile IST.[48]

It can also be argued that the age of minors provides a proxy for their development and maturity, and could be used as an indicator of how well they understand the criminal proceedings and whether they are capable of communicating with their attorney. Since 1899, there have been separate juvenile courts in the United States that employ an approach for alleged juvenile offenders that is distinct from that used for adult defendants, based on the premise that the youth and lack of maturity of juveniles make them less capable of understanding criminal proceedings and participating in their own defense, as well as less culpable for any crimes they committed.[49] It can similarly be argued that the age of relatively young individuals charged with criminal activity should be incorporated in an assessment of their CST.

Age, intelligence level, and developmental factors, however, have not been accepted as per se tests for CST and do not by themselves provide a sufficient basis for a finding of IST. The perspective has generally been that these measures do not relate directly to CST and are not sufficiently valid and reliable to be used exclusively for a CST assessment. In addition, it is argued that the functional capacities of individuals of a given age, intelligence level, or developmental stage vary considerably. An exception might be made for defendants who are very young (for instance, age of four), have a severe intellectual disability, or fall within the lowest developmental stage, but even then, because a CST determination is considered a functional test, courts will generally take this information only as a factor to be considered and probe further to ascertain whether these defendants have adaptive skills that enable them to function at a higher level and thereby render them CST. The general rule is that age, intellectual level, and developmental level alone do not provide a sufficient basis for a finding of IST.

Amnesia

Amnesia—the total or partial loss of memory for an event or a series of events—can be caused by brain injury, a disease or other underlying medical condition, drug or alcohol use, or psychological trauma, and it poses a particularly thorny issue for courts assessing a criminal defendant's CST.[50] It is not unusual for an individual to suffer amnesia following a violent incident, particularly if a head injury is involved. This amnesia can be anterograde (meaning that the individual is unable to learn and retain new information and thus cannot remember events that followed the trauma for a period of time), retrograde (in which case the individual is unable to recall previously learned information and thus cannot remember events that preceded the trauma), or both. Claims of retrograde amnesia are frequently the focus of CST disputes, with as many as one-third of defendants accused of a violent crime claiming amnesia regarding events surrounding the time of the crime; indeed, 25 to 40 percent of defendants found guilty of homicide make such claims, although they are also made in a wide range of cases.

To the extent that a defendant cannot remember events occurring around the time of the crime, which could include extenuating circumstances that justify (as in self-defense) or excuse (as in duress) what otherwise would be considered criminal behavior or might provide an alibi (for example, that the defendant was somewhere else at the time), amnesia puts defendants at a considerable disadvantage at trial as they cannot take the stand to testify as to what happened and cannot assist counsel in constructing their defense, including helping to defuse potentially damaging evidence (such as raising points to be used in cross-examining the prosecution's witnesses). However, such claims can also be quite convenient for defendants, who can thereby effectively avoid interrogation and cross-examination at trial regarding events at the time of the crime. It has been estimated that at least 20 percent of all instances of claimed amnesia by criminal defendants involve malingering.

Virtually every American court that has addressed the issue has ruled that, assuming the defendant is otherwise CST, amnesia is *not an automatic bar to prosecution*. These rulings tend to be based in part on the assertion that being able to remember events at the time of the crime is not required for a defendant to receive a fair trial, and because a claim of amnesia, including its presence and impact, is extremely difficult to assess, as well as because of concerns about possible malingering.

In recent years, however, courts have split on whether amnesia can at least be part of a CST determination. Those courts refusing to even consider a defendant's amnesia in determining CST tend to rely on four main arguments: (1) trials in general are imperfect venues, where everyone suffers from lost or unavailable evidence, and memory is ephemeral for all; (2) defendants may feign amnesia; (3) the criminal justice system will be unable to function if amnesia is recognized as a basis for an IST finding, resulting in defendants not being held accountable for their crimes; and (4) defendants do not have to rely on their memories for evidence as they have alternative means of generating needed information.

Those courts concluding defendants' amnesia should be part of a fact-specific, case-by-case inquiry into CST contend that (a) like any other major mental abnormality, amnesia should be taken seriously and that amnesia is more than just a defendant suffering from a poor ability to remember things; (b) there are tests (such as Symptom Validity Testing [SVT] and Structured Inventory of Malingered Symptomatology

[SIMS]) that can be administered to assess whether defendants are malingering when they claim amnesia for events at the time of the crime; (c) criminal defendants with amnesia for these events will not necessarily walk away from their crimes as better treatment techniques that can help them regain lost memories and restore their CST are being developed; and (d) possible alternative means of generating needed information and evidence are not necessarily sufficiently adequate, which, in turn, raises the question of whether defendants' rights to a fair trial and due process are violated if amnesia is not taken into account.

Six factors have frequently been identified as relevant when a fact-based, case-by-case determination of the impact of amnesia on a defendant's CST is conducted. They include (1) the impact of defendants' amnesia on their ability to consult or assist their attorney, (2) the impact of the amnesia on their ability to testify on their own behalf, (3) the extent to which they can reconstruct what happened from other evidence, (4) the extent to which the prosecution has assisted the defendant in this reconstruction (that is, has the prosecutor shared all relevant information within the prosecutor's possession), (5) the strength of the prosecution's case, and (6) the likely availability of an alibi or another defense or mitigating claim if the defendant was not experiencing amnesia.[51]

Evaluator's Report

Mental health professionals who agree to evaluate a defendant's CST typically prefer to meet with the defendant at the evaluator's office. If the defendant is incarcerated and such a meeting can be arranged, the defendant will be transported to a secure room at the evaluator's office by police officers or jail or prison personnel, who will then wait outside the room until the interview is completed, and then return the defendant to the correctional facility. Evaluators may meet with defendants at the jail or prison where they are being detained if transport is unavailable, a defendant is unwilling or unable to be transported because of mental state or physical condition, or the defendant is deemed dangerous or a flight risk, although this tends to not be an ideal location for an evaluation.

As discussed earlier, in addition to interviewing the defendant and administering any appropriate tests, evaluators will generally review any relevant records and attempt to interview other individuals who may have insights into the defendant's mental status.[52] After acquiring this information, evaluators generally place their findings and conclusions in a report prepared for the court or the party that secured their services.[53]

There are six basic issues that generally must be addressed in conjunction with a CST evaluation and should be incorporated in the evaluator's report. The first two pertain to *the CST test* set forth by the USSC in *Dusky*. Namely, does the defendant have the present capacity/ability to *understand the criminal proceedings* in which he or she is involved and to *consult with/assist his or her attorney*? Any additional criteria imposed as a matter of state law will also need to be applied and discussed.[54]

A third issue, imposed by several states and relevant in general, is whether a defendant who is determined to be IST *will need treatment*, and, if so, the likely nature of that treatment and where it can best be delivered (that is, on an outpatient or inpatient basis).[55] Because the state is generally given an opportunity to restore a defendant's CST, this information will help guide judges in deciding where to place the defendant for related services.

Fourth, as suggested by *Jackson v. Indiana* (1972) and discussed below, if the defendant is determined to be IST, the report should indicate the *likelihood that the defendant's CST can be restored*.[56] For example, if the defendant has a severe intellectual disability that is unlikely to improve over time, the evaluator can recommend that the court release the defendant rather than order restorative services that are unlikely to change the defendant's mental status. This information will also help judges make subsequent placement decisions.

Fifth, if the evaluator concludes that the defendant is CST or likely to be found CST, but believes the defendant's CST is marginal and could deteriorate, the evaluator should advise the judge on *accommodations* that can be made during the trial to enhance the defendant's ability to understand the proceedings and assist his or her attorney, or to help prevent deterioration of this ability. For example, the evaluator might recommend that the courtroom be arranged so that no one is sitting directly behind a defendant experiencing symptoms of paranoia (for example, by letting the defendant sit with his or her back to a wall), or that frequent breaks be taken in the proceedings or as requested by the defense to enable the defendant to better process the proceedings and not misunderstand or be overwhelmed by them.

Finally, evaluators should include *any qualifications* to their opinion that the judge should keep in mind. For example, if the defendant is CST primarily because of the medications he or she is taking, the evaluator should alert the judge as to what to look for—such as changes in behavior or attention—if for some reason the medications are discontinued or changed, thereby indicating that the defendant may no longer be CST. Similarly, evaluators should provide the judge with possible indicators that the stress of the trial is causing the defendant to decompensate and perhaps become IST, necessitating a new CST evaluation.

Under the Fifth Amendment,[57] as well as state law in some jurisdictions,[58] the evaluator should also *omit* from the CST report any statements made by the defendant regarding events that occurred at the time of the offense.[59] This is because CST evaluations should focus on defendants' present ability to understand the proceedings and work with their attorney, not their past mental capacity, which is irrelevant to a CST determination. Including information pertaining to what occurred at the time of the offense—particularly if it indicates that the defendant committed a crime—can determine the outcome of the trial and violate a defendant's Fifth Amendment privilege against self-incrimination. Some evaluators may be tempted to ask about the alleged crime, particularly if it is a relatively notorious case, and some defendants may spontaneously want to talk about it, in part because they see this interview as an opportunity to establish their innocence or justify their actions. The inclusion of this information in the evaluator's report, however, is highly prejudicial, and if presented to the court, may lead to a mistrial. Furthermore, if such information is included, future defendants may, upon the recommendation of their attorneys, be less forthcoming during their evaluations. To enhance the accuracy of these reports and CST determinations in general, it is critical that the discussions between defendants and CST evaluators be full and frank. If defendants inadvertently raise this information, evaluators should not incorporate it in their reports or subsequent testimony.[60]

It is also worth noting that typically copies of the report generated in response to a *court-ordered* CST evaluation will be supplied not only to the trial judge, but also to the prosecutor and defense counsel. Unlike an initial insanity evaluation report obtained by the defense, to which typically only the defense has access unless the defendant formally raises an insanity defense,[61] a court-ordered CST evaluation is germane to both the prosecution and the defense, as well as the presiding judge, and *all are generally entitled to a copy*. Redactions based on assertions of confidentiality or an attorney-client or patient-therapist privilege, or because the report contains prejudicial or otherwise objectionable information, are typically not available.

Notwithstanding that many, if not all, of the participants may be eager to resume and complete the trial proceedings, evaluators in some jurisdictions are not under any obligation to complete their CST evaluation and report their findings within a *specified time period*. In some extreme instances, it may take months for them to complete their assessment. The rationale for not setting a deadline on this process is that evaluators may want to meet with and assess the defendant on multiple occasions; need to acquire additional sources of information that are not readily available; and require an extended period to digest and analyze the information obtained, reach a considered conclusion, and generate a full and responsive report. In addition, evaluators may sometimes be very busy, unanticipated events or demands on their time may arise, or they may just be especially deliberate or cautious in general or regarding a specific case.

The question may arise whether taking a lengthy period of time to generate a CST report at some point offends a "principle of fundamental justice," particularly if the defendant, who has not yet been convicted of a crime, is languishing in jail or is experiencing a mental disorder. Such concerns have triggered the filing of motions and lawsuits asserting that there was an improper failure to complete these evaluations in a timely fashion.[62] Some jurisdictions, in response to these concerns, have adopted guiding language stating when a report must be completed, for example, that it must be submitted "promptly" after the completion of the evaluation,[63] or that it must be completed within a given maximum period of time.[64]

Conclusion

The procedures associated with a legal determination of a defendant's CST, as well as the absence of such procedures, can be outcome-determinative. To the extent that society prefers one type of verdict over another, it can be a relatively simple matter to interject or omit procedural hoops to enhance the likelihood of a favored outcome in most instances. Procedural hurdles are also sometimes instituted because society wants a high level of certainty before a certain outcome is obtained either because of the serious or long-lasting consequences that may result or because the nature of the applicable evidence is typically so uncertain or imprecise that we are hesitant to impose an adverse outcome on someone based on such evidence.

Procedural components can be particularly dispositive regarding CST determinations. Historically, IST findings have been disfavored because of their perceived potential to deny society the opportunity to hold offenders accountable for their crimes and to give victims the satisfaction of seeing justice done. In addition, considerable uncertainty has traditionally been associated with these findings because of our amorphous understanding of mental disorders and their impact on human behavior. Such factors likely explain at least in part why CST determinations were traditionally handled informally by the presiding trial judge. With few procedural checks in place, these judges had considerable discretion to move trials forward based on a finding that the defendant was CST. As our understanding of mental impairments and their impact increased, along with a recognition of the widespread adverse stereotypes and biases concerning individuals with a mental disorder and of the mistreatment of individuals with a mental disorder in general, unease with such an informal process began to emerge. However, defendants with a mental disorder remained a relatively disfavored class, and this informal process was often simply replaced by a more formal one that still made CST determinations relatively likely. The Supreme Court has taken some cautious steps to examine these procedures and ensure a more balanced assessment, although a range of possible procedural challenges remain unaddressed.

As discussed, forensic evaluators must incorporate and address the governing standard in their CST reports, as well as recognize and work within the bounds of the procedures governing CST determinations. As briefly noted above, but examined in greater detail in the following chapter, a key aspect of these reports and an important procedural component of CST determinations is what happens to the defendant after the CST hearing.

6

Dispositions after the Competence to Stand Trial Hearing

As in the story of the blind men and the elephant, understanding the impact of mental disorders is a challenging undertaking made more difficult by the multifaceted and diverse nature of mental disorders and the numerous misconceptions, stereotypes, and biases related to them. Attempting broad generalizations based on a single or even a few cases will typically result in a skewed picture that provides a poor fit when applied across the board. This challenge extends to determinations of whether the competency of a defendant found IST has been restored and what steps can be taken to facilitate restoration.

Post-CST Hearing Dispositions

Criminal proceedings are generally *suspended* while a competence to stand trial (CST) evaluation is conducted, although trial attorneys can sometimes file various motions with the court in the interim, such as a request to suppress the proposed introduction of evidence on the grounds that it is inadmissible. For the most part, however, the trial is simply placed on hold and does not resume unless and until the defendant is found to be CST.

If the defendant is eventually *found to be CST*, the trial proceedings will typically resume where they left off when the CST evaluation was ordered. Sometimes, however, the judge may order a retrial, particularly if a lengthy break in the proceedings resulted or the trial is especially complex, in which case jurors or the judge may have difficulty remembering previously presented opening arguments, testimony, or evidence, which, in turn, may compromise the accuracy and fairness of any resulting verdict. Regardless of whether the trial is simply continued or a new trial ordered, the judge must remain vigilant during subsequent proceedings for additional indications that a defendant may be IST. If a bona fide doubt of the defendant's CST arises, the judge must once again suspend the proceedings to determine whether the defendant is CST.[1]

If the defendant is *found to be IST*, the trial proceedings will generally continue to be suspended while the State is given an opportunity to try to restore the defendant's CST. Although it happens relatively infrequently, the prosecutor will *drop the charges* against the defendant in some instances, primarily when the defendant is charged with a minor crime or the prosecutor concludes that the defendant's CST is unlikely to be restored within a reasonable period of time.[2]

If the charges are not dropped, the trial judge will usually order the IST defendant into treatment, where an effort will be made to restore his or her CST. Historically, IST defendants were placed primarily in *psychiatric facilities*. Today, placements in these facilities are relatively expensive and scarce, which results in long delays before an incarcerated defendant can be transferred to one, although lawsuits have been filed challenging these delays.[3] These placements, particularly if lengthy, can also significantly disrupt defendants' lives as they are often relocated far from their homes and any available support network. A loss of an existing job or housing and in some instances a decrease in adaptive skills can also be a consequence of long-term residence in a psychiatric institution. It is now widely accepted that *outpatient community treatment* is generally preferable for an individual with a mental disorder—including disorders associated with an IST finding—if a danger of self-harm or harm to others is not likely to be associated with such a placement. Much as they do in the CST evaluations discussed previously, trial judges today will typically order that IST defendants be treated on an outpatient basis unless it is determined hospitalization is necessary because either a more intensive treatment is needed or, more often, defendants are deemed to pose a flight risk or considered to be at risk of harming themselves or others if placed in the community.[4]

Increasingly, however, and again much as in CST evaluations, restorative CST services are provided within *a correctional facility*.[5] Justifications for this placement may include that it is simply an extension of where the defendant is currently housed, thereby providing a certain level of continuity and eliminating the costs and risks associated with transporting the defendant to another setting; that restorative services can be commenced immediately rather than waiting, sometimes for a considerable period of time, for space to become available in a more expensive psychiatric facility or an outpatient program in the community; and that it provides greater security for the community. Detention in a jail setting, however, is arguably an inappropriate environment for someone with a mental disorder and has the potential to exacerbate rather than successfully address any underlying mental disorder.[6] Furthermore, jail officials may not want this population housed within their facility since (a) mental health treatment is neither their primary mission nor an area of expertise in correctional facilities; (b) these inmates can be relatively expensive to treat, particularly because of the medications typically required, and can thereby pose a significant challenge for a correctional facility's assigned budget; and (c) they can be difficult to manage, sometimes because they are disruptive or dangerous, but more often because they are relatively likely to be victimized by others or are at significant risk of harming themselves, which necessitates increased staff allocations to provide needed supervision.

Like criminal defendants in general, who have few champions, this population has few advocates lobbying on their behalf for better care and placements. While defense attorneys might be expected to protest the extended placement of IST detainees—who have not been convicted of a crime—in a correctional setting, these attorneys may feel that they have done their part by facilitating an outcome that defers what they perceive as their client's likely conviction and sentence, even though the IST finding results in the defendant's (continued) placement in a jail setting and typically only delays an expected guilty verdict.

In addition, mental health systems generally do not want IST detainees, in part because of the expense of caring for them, which includes heightened security requirements; in part because they may be a more challenging population to manage; and in part because of the paucity of psychiatric beds in general, and the fact that those that are available need to be devoted to patients who face a more immediate psychiatric crisis and potential harm than this population. Because the correctional system has generally become the system that "can't say no" and because placement there is typically the cheapest, most secure, and most convenient, and given that this is often where the defendant was housed prior to the IST determination, defendants are often placed in correctional facilities after an IST determination is issued.

After placement, a periodic *reporting requirement* is imposed on whoever has custody or supervision of the IST defendant.[7] Typically, they must also notify the court immediately if the defendant becomes CST so the criminal proceedings can resume as soon as feasible.[8] They must also notify the court if they conclude that the defendant is unlikely to be restored to CST within the foreseeable future, although perhaps because this is harder to establish and perhaps because it is seen as a less pressing issue, there may not be a mandate to report this immediately or within a prescribed period of time. In some jurisdictions, if the defendant is charged with a misdemeanor and is not restored to CST within a relatively short period of time (for example, forty-five days), this scenario must also be reported to the court and will serve as a precursor to the defendant's release, presumably because these defendants could not have been kept in custody much longer had they been convicted of the underlying criminal charges.[9] In general, though, a CST *hearing must be held periodically* (for example, in Virginia, every six months for adults[10] and every three months for juveniles[11]) to ascertain whether the defendant continues to be IST and whether, pursuant to *Jackson v. Indiana* (1972), discussed below, the defendant can be restored to CST within a reasonable period of time. These steps are intended to ensure that such defendants are not detained indefinitely or become "lost" in the system.

Jackson v. Indiana (1972)

Factual and Procedural Foundation

The USSC ruling driving the requirement that criminal defendants found IST and held in custody for restorative services must have their status checked periodically was established in a case involving Theon Jackson. Jackson was accused of separately robbing two women in Indiana, stealing the one woman's purse, which was estimated to be worth $4, and taking $5 from the other woman. Age twenty-seven at the time of the robberies, Jackson was described by the USSC as "a mentally defective deaf mute with a mental level of a pre-school child," who "cannot read, write, or otherwise communicate except through limited sign language."[12]

At a CST hearing, the two psychiatrists appointed to examine Jackson jointly submitted a written report and each provided testimony. They concluded that Jackson's "almost non-existent communication skill, together with his lack of hearing and his mental deficiency, left him unable to understand the nature of the charges against him or to participate in his defense,"[13] and that his prognosis for improvement was dim. There was additional testimony that Indiana had no facility that could help someone with Jackson's impairments gain minimal communication skills. Nevertheless, after finding the defendant IST, the trial judge "ordered [Jackson] committed to the Indiana Department of Mental Health until such time as that Department should certify to the court that 'the defendant is sane.'"[14] On appeal, the defense argued this amounted to a "life sentence" for Jackson, in spite of his not having been convicted of a crime. The State responded that this did not represent an indeterminate sentence as Jackson's placement would continue only until he recovered and that it was the inexact nature of psychiatric predictions of the course of mental disorders that was the reason for this arrangement.

The Court's Ruling in Jackson

In response, the USSC unanimously ruled that "Indiana cannot constitutionally commit [Jackson] for an indefinite period simply on account of his incompetency to stand trial on the charges filed against him,"[15] and reversed the trial court order. In reaching its decision, the USSC determined that Indiana's arrangement violated both the equal protection clause and the due process clause of the US Constitution.

The equal protection clause guarantees that no individual shall be denied the same rights and protection of the laws as are enjoyed by others in similar conditions and circumstances. The Court observed that IST detainees in Indiana were being handled differently than both individuals who had been involuntary hospitalized pursuant to civil commitment laws and prisoners involuntarily hospitalized for mental health treatment at the end of their prison sentence. For these two groups, the criteria for hospitalization were more demanding and the release criteria less stringent; in contrast, it was easier to involuntarily hospitalize defendants found IST and more difficult for them to obtain their subsequent release. The practical effect of this distinction, the Court determined, was that the involuntary hospitalization of IST detainees was permanent, while this was not the case for the two other groups of similarly situated individuals. The Court added that it had not been shown that IST detainees were inherently in need of custodial care or detention or that their hospitalization for treatment was always appropriate, and that the mere filing of criminal charges against them could not justify this practice. The Court concluded that the State could not subject this population to more relaxed hospitalization and more stringent release standards than employed for those not charged with an offense.

As for due process, the Court noted that "[t]he practice of automatic commitment with release conditioned solely upon attainment of competence has been decried on both policy and constitutional grounds." It continued: "One source of this criticism . . . undoubtedly [comes from] the empirical data available which tend to show that many defendants committed before trial are never tried, and that those defendants committed pursuant to ordinary civil proceedings are, on the average, released sooner than defendants automatically committed solely on account of their incapacity to stand trial."[16] The Court contended that "due process requires that the nature and duration of commitment bear some reasonable relation to the purpose for which the individual is committed" and that "Jackson was not afforded any 'formal commitment proceedings addressed to [his] ability to function in society,' or to society's interest in his restraint, or to the State's ability to aid him in attaining competency through custodial care or compulsory treatment."[17]

In determining the proper response, the Court employed a "reasonableness" standard and embraced the approach employed within the federal judicial system. Namely, it ruled that an IST defendant "cannot be held more than the reasonable period of time necessary to determine whether there is a substantial probability that he will attain that capacity [to stand trial] in the foreseeable future."[18] After this, "the State must either institute the customary civil commitment proceeding that would be required to commit indefinitely any other citizen, or release the defendant."[19] The Court refrained from specifying the maximum amount of time IST defendants can be held in custody as part of an effort to restore their CST, most likely in order to afford states some flexibility in these matters, but it also pointed out that Jackson had already been held for three-and-a-half years on a record showing he was unlikely to ever be CST.

Analysis of Jackson

The bottom line in *Jackson* is that criminal defendants found to be IST can be held in custody only for a "reasonable period of time" in an effort to restore their CST. After that, if the defendant is likely to remain incompetent for the foreseeable future, the defendant must be (a) released, (b) civilly committed (the process used to involuntarily hospitalize someone with a mental illness), or (c) civilly certified (the process used to involuntarily hospitalize someone with an intellectual disability).[20] Although not widely available in 1972, today there is a fourth option: namely, an effort can be made to civilly commit the defendant as a sexually violent predator.

In response, some states have set a maximum of six to eighteen months for the administration of restorative services, after which one of the four options listed above must ensue. Other states use the maximum sentence for the charged crime as the ceiling on how long IST defendants can be held.[21] It is questionable, however, particularly under the tougher sentencing regimes imposed in most states near the end of the twentieth century, whether the "reasonable period of time" standard imposed by *Jackson* is met when the maximum sentence is decades in duration and most clinicians acknowledge they will know within a matter of months whether someone is likely to regain CST.[22] Most states set no limits on the duration and leave it to the trial judge's discretion, with only periodic review mandated.[23]

In recent years, some states have expanded their criteria for civil commitment,[24] ostensibly making it easier to civilly commit an individual found IST. Should that shorten the period of time that a state can hold an IST defendant since the alternative of civil commitment is ostensibly more available? Moreover, should the fact that the length of stay following civil commitment, one of the primary comparison models in *Jackson*, has dramatically decreased similarly reduce the length of time an IST defendant can be held for restorative services?[25] With the median length of stay for someone civilly committed now being around thirty days, is the six- to eighteen-month maximum period for the restoration of an IST defendant to CST by some states reasonable? What justification is there for holding an IST defendant for restorative services for the maximum sentence that the defendant faces, as is permitted in some states?

On the flip side—and keeping in mind that even if the defendant is civilly committed, this commitment typically extends the period of time the defendant is held in custody only by a matter of months, if not weeks—does this potential relatively quick release of the nonrestorable IST defendant back into the community adequately protect public safety or provide a sense of justice being done to any victims of these crimes? It is perhaps no surprise that some states have rushed to embrace, when applicable, the fourth nonrestorable IST dispositional option, namely, civil commitment as a sexually violent predator, since these individuals will often be held in custody for a very lengthy period.[26] Is this a "reasonable" option for nonrestorable IST defendants who have been charged with but not convicted of a sexual offense?

The fact that IST defendants can still be held in State custody for a relatively lengthy time has some important implications for the judge, the prosecutor, and the defense attorney in a criminal trial. All of them can request a CST evaluation, and arguably all have a responsibility to do so if they suspect the defendant is IST in order to ensure that the defendant is afforded a fair trial. At the same time, inappropriate considerations may sometimes drive these requests. For example, prosecutors with a weak case may perceive an IST finding as a viable substitute for a conviction as it ensures that defendants perceived to be dangerous will remain in State custody for a relatively extended period of time and perhaps even be housed within a correctional facility. Furthermore, during this time prosecutors may be able to discover additional evidence that will enhance the likelihood of their obtaining a conviction. Defense attorneys, on the other hand, may be so focused on avoiding a conviction for their client, particularly if they see the defendant's case as weak, that they readily embrace the IST disposition, failing to take into account that their client may end up spending more time in State custody than if he or she had simply been convicted, and may be placed in a setting no different from where the client would have been housed if convicted. Finally, trial judges who, like prosecutors, are concerned about public safety or, like defense attorneys, are concerned about wrongful convictions may also welcome the IST alternative. In addition, all three may see IST dispositions as a means to bypass or shorten trials and thereby reduce the crushing caseloads they all frequently experience.

There are two other issues to consider here. First, under the Sixth Amendment, a criminal defendant is entitled to a speedy trial.[27] Is this right violated when IST defendants are held for a relatively lengthy period while the State administers restorative services? The speedy trial guarantee is designed to ensure, in part, that convictions are not based on "stale" evidence, a concern that would seem to come into play here. Second, what should happen to the charges defendants faced if it is determined that they cannot be restored to CST? Often the charges will be dropped, but there are instances when prosecutors refrain from doing so—particularly if a very serious crime is involved or the prosecutor thinks the defendant is malingering—in case the defendant unexpectedly improves, thereby permitting them to reinstitute criminal proceedings. Is it proper to leave criminal charges hanging over the head of IST defendants who have been found to be nonrestorable?

Refusal of Treatment

As discussed, states and the federal government are "on the clock" with regard to their efforts to restore the CST of criminal defendants, which may result in relatively intrusive treatment modalities being employed to speed restoration. In other words, the approach chosen may be one that is thought likely to work in a reasonably short period of time, which generally translates into the administration of psychotropic medications.[28]

Such medications were first introduced in the late 1940s.[29] At the time, they were viewed as a revolution, if not a miracle. The number of individuals needing hospitalization for a mental disorder dropped dramatically in the United States, from over 500,000 to under 50,000; hospital stays of individuals with a serious mental illness markedly shortened from years, if not decades, to days or a few weeks; and treatment could be delivered in the community rather than in a psychiatric facility.[30] Such medications often minimize and in some cases eliminate psychiatric symptoms, although when used to treat a severe mental illness, they are generally not seen as a "cure" because they cannot be permanently discontinued. These medications significantly reduce relapses (that is, the reoccurrence of symptoms), and the intervals between relapses are generally longer. Their use also greatly lessens the fear and anxiety often experienced by the family and friends of individuals with a mental disorder.

At the same time, the effectiveness of these medications varies considerably from person to person, with some individuals benefiting little and some actually getting worse on a given medication.[31] Furthermore, because the symptoms of a mental illness can be difficult to categorize, individuals may be misdiagnosed and given the wrong medication. These drugs are also sometimes administered for nontreatment purposes, such as an effort to make individuals more manageable, not necessarily better.

In addition, most of these medications have a wide range of possible toxic effects. The so-called "first generation" of these medications could induce side effects such as dystonic reactions (uncontrollable muscle spasms, tongue protrusions, grimacing); akathisia (agitation, the inability to remain still); Parkinsonism (drooling, muscle stiffness, shuffling gait, tremors); drowsiness, weakness, or dizziness; low blood pressure; dry mouth; blurred vision; the loss of sexual desire; apathy or depression; constipation or diarrhea; and tardive dyskinesia (an irreversible condition, involving involuntary tongue sweeps from side to side, the opening and closing of the mouth, jaw movements in all directions, and stiff, jerky movements of the fingers, arms, and legs). This last effect occurred in roughly 15 to 20 percent of patients who received this class of medications for more than six months.

Beginning in the 1990s, a new class of medications referred to as "second generation" or "atypical" antipsychotics was introduced for the treatment of schizophrenia, a mental illness often found among IST defendants. These medications are generally, although not always, more effective, have fewer side effects, and may leave patients displaying more emotional interest and expression. However, they often induce their own set of metabolic side effects, particularly obesity and diabetes, and tend to be much more expensive, although they have come to be the predominant medication employed.

Regardless of which class of medications is employed, a substantial percentage of recipients, given the choice, discontinue them because they find them ineffective or the side effects intolerable, or for other reasons such as their "mind-altering" effects or a perception that they are an intrusion into their privacy. Of these recipients, 75 percent discontinue the first-generation medications and 64–82 percent discontinue the second-generation medications within eighteen months. Indeed, the American Psychiatric Association has noted:

Side effects of medications are a crucial aspect of treatment because they often determine medication choice and are a primary reason for medication discontinuation. Side effects complicate and undermine antipsychotic treatment in various ways. The side effects themselves may cause or worsen symptoms associated with schizophrenia, including negative, positive, and cognitive symptoms and agitation. In addition, these side effects may contribute to risk for other medical disorders. Finally, these side effects often are subjectively difficult to tolerate and may affect the patient's quality of life and willingness to take the medication.[32]

In light of the mix of benefits and risks associated with these medications, another issue that arises in conjunction with the State's efforts to restore the competency of IST defendants is the right of these defendants to refuse treatment and the State's ability to override such refusals.[33] Until the 1950s, there was little that could be done to successfully treat mental disorders in general and restore IST defendants in particular. In addition, IST defendants—much like individuals with a mental disorder in general—were afforded few rights, and their care and treatment received little scrutiny. Their treatment preferences, as a result, were largely disregarded, and their criminal trials typically proceeded unabated, with the few found to be IST simply diverted to the mental health system and institutionalized indefinitely.

More recently, as discussed, the right of defendants to be CST has been established and limits have been placed on the dispositions employed. At the same time, as also discussed, a range of treatments, particularly psychotropic medications, has become widely available. Until the 1970s, consistent with prior practice, people held in custody, including IST defendants and individuals civilly committed, generally could be forcibly treated with these medications over their objection. They were deemed to have automatically lost a number of rights of self-determination (such as the right to leave, the right to contract, the right to vote, and so on) as a result of their detention, and were considered to be presumptively incompetent to make medical decisions for themselves; similarly, the concept that they had a right to reject treatment gained little traction.

Today, however, following a number of judicial rulings, it is widely recognized that institutionalized persons in general have a right to refuse treatment.[34] Because the recognition of this right has generally arisen in conjunction with the proposed involuntary administration of psychotropic medications, its application to other forms of treatment, such as psychotherapy, is unclear, although this is rarely an issue with regard to IST defendants, given that the predominant choice of treatment for them is psychotropic medications because of their greater likelihood to work quickly.

The value of a right to refuse treatment has been vigorously debated.[35] The identified benefits of such a right include: (a) increased patient participation in and commitment to treatment, (b) lowered dosages of medication, which reduce side effects, (c) a reduction of polypharmacy (the simultaneous use of multiple drugs to treat a condition), decreasing complications from the largely untested interactions of these medications, (d) more frequent changes in medication to see if a more effective or less noxious result can be obtained, and (e) diminished delegations of authority among treatment professionals, with the professionals with the greatest expertise more directly involved in the administration of these medications.

The identified costs of a right to refuse medication include: (a) relatively lengthy delays in the administration of medication because negotiations with the patient must first occur in an attempt to obtain the patient's consent and, if the patient cannot be persuaded, then court hearings must be held in an effort to obtain an order to treat the patient over his or her objection; (b) the mental status of untreated patients may deteriorate, although most of them are ultimately medicated or remedicated with no general increase in violence and disruption noted in the interim; (c) medical and nursing staff complain that their work is made more onerous; and (d) additional costs are incurred as a result of having to prepare for and participate in hearings to obtain a court order to provide treatment over objection.

The right of institutionalized persons to refuse psychotropic medications has not, however, been recognized as an "absolute" right by the courts; rather, it is one that must be balanced against the interests of the State. This, in turn, suggests that this balance may vary depending on the weight of the State's interests in the context in which treatment is being proposed. Most of the early cases focused on patients who had been involuntarily hospitalized and did not address criminal defendants, which left unanswered what weight should be given to the State's interests in adjudicating criminal offenses when the treatment over objection of an IST defendant is proposed.

Sell v. United States (2003)

FACTUAL AND PROCEDURAL FOUNDATION

The USSC ultimately resolved this question in *Sell v. United States* (2003). Charles Thomas Sell, once a practicing dentist, had what the USSC described as "a long and unfortunate history of mental illness." Ultimately, he was charged under US law with submitting fictitious insurance claims to obtain payment for dental services he purportedly provided. A few months later a new indictment was issued, charging Sell with attempting to murder the FBI agent who arrested him and a former employee who planned to testify against him in the fraud case. The fraud and the attempted murder charges were joined together into a single trial.

Following an evaluation, a federal magistrate initially found Sell CST. At a subsequent hearing to revoke his bail, however, Sell was described as "totally out of control," it was concluded that his condition had worsened, his bail was revoked, and he was incarcerated. Roughly a year later, Sell asked the magistrate to reconsider his CST. Sell was sent to a US medical center for federal prisoners in Missouri for examination, and the magistrate subsequently found Sell was now IST. The magistrate ordered Sell hospitalized for up to four months to determine whether there was "a substantial probability" he could attain CST. After two months, the medical staff recommended that Sell take antipsychotic medication, but Sell refused to do so. The staff then sought a court order to treat Sell over his objection.

What followed was a range of expert opinions and court orders. A reviewing psychiatrist concluded that Sell was mentally ill and that, although he was not a danger while imprisoned, he would be dangerous if allowed back into the community because of his threats and delusions; the psychiatrist also noted that he needed medication to become CST. The medical center where Sell was housed noted differences of professional opinion as to the proper classification and treatment for Sell but asserted that Sell's "pervasive belief" that he was being targeted by various governmental officials made him a potential safety risk if allowed back into the community and concluded that antipsychotic medication was the intervention most likely to ameliorate Sell's symptoms.

At the next judicial hearing, there was testimony that Sell had approached a nurse at the medical center and indicated he was in love with her, criticized her for having nothing to do with him, and said he could not help his "inappropriate behavior." The magistrate ruled that the evidence showed that Sell was a danger to himself and others; that antipsychotic medication was the only way to make him less dangerous; that the benefits of the drugs outweighed their risks; and that these medications were the only way to render Sell CST. The magistrate then issued an order authorizing the involuntary administration of antipsychotic drugs.

A federal district court judge, reviewing the magistrate's order, determined that Sell was not dangerous within an institutional setting, but upheld the medication order because medication presented the only viable hope of restoring Sell's CST and concluded that this order was necessary to serve the government's compelling interest in obtaining an adjudication of Sell's guilt or innocence. The US Eighth Circuit Court of Appeals found, on appeal, that Sell was not dangerous in any setting, but could nevertheless be medicated over his objection because of the government's essential interest in bringing the defendant to trial.

THE COURT'S RULING IN *SELL*

In examining the Eighth Circuit's ruling, the USSC acknowledged that bringing an individual accused of a "serious crime" to trial constituted an important governmental interest because the government is seeking thereby to protect society through its application of the criminal law. The Court did not define what constituted a "serious crime," but it did state that this criterion could encompass property crimes in addition to crimes against a person.[36]

Nevertheless, the Court noted that the Fifth Amendment of the US Constitution states that the government may not deprive any person of liberty without due process of law.[37] Although prior cases had established that the government may involuntarily medicate criminal defendants if they pose a danger to themselves or others,[38] the Court pointed out that these cases also indicated that when such medication is proposed solely to restore a defendant's CST, permission is rarely granted and only under very specific circumstances—namely, when the treatment is (a) medically appropriate, (b) substantially unlikely to have side effects that may undermine the fairness of the trial, and, (c) taking into account less intrusive alternatives, significantly necessary to further important governmental trial-related interests.

Furthermore, these medications could render a trial unfair, the Court declared, if they (a) significantly interfere with the defendant's ability to assist or communicate with his or her attorney, (b) sedate the defendant, (c) prevent the defendant's rapid reaction to trial developments, or (d) diminish the defendant's ability to express emotions in the courtroom. Thus, a reviewing court must specifically find that administration of the medication is "substantially unlikely" to have these or other side effects that will make the trial unfair. The Court added that it must also be shown that the administration of the proposed medication is "substantially likely" to render the defendant CST, that its administration is in the defendant's "best medical interest" in light of his or her medical condition, and that any alternative, less intrusive treatments are unlikely to achieve substantially the same results.

Even though the Court had previously established that treatment over objection could be administered based on a defendant's dangerousness or because the refusal to take a proposed medication puts the defendant's health "gravely at risk," the Court established that alternative means should be pursued first and that a judge who is asked to administer medication over objection to an IST criminal defendant should initially ask whether these alternatives have been pursued and, if not, ask why they have not been pursued.

With regard to Sell, the Court found that both the medical center where Sell was residing and the presiding magistrate approved his involuntary medication substantially because Sell posed a risk of danger to others—a determination the Court found support for within the record. Even though the two reviewing courts relied on different grounds, the Court suggested that the dangerousness issue had clouded their analysis and should have been given greater and more specific consideration. The Court further concluded that insufficient attention had been given to whether trial-related side effects were likely to ensue from the proposed medication and whether there was sufficient justification for forcing medication on CST grounds alone. As a result, the Court reversed the initial order to treat Sell over objection, although it permitted the government to refile its request for forcible medication based on Sell's current condition pursuant to the guidelines the Court had set forth.

ANALYSIS OF *SELL*

Following the issuance of the USSC ruling, there was considerable concern among prosecutors and ancillary treatment professionals that the *Sell* framework would make it more difficult to override the refusal of IST criminal defendants to take prescribed medications and thereby restore their CST. There was even concern it might change CST determinations in general.

Arguably, the basic framework articulated by the Court in *Sell* was not earth-shaking, at least not to health-care providers.[39] It basically set forth what was considered good medical decision-making by then; the criteria being: is the proposed treatment medically appropriate, what are its benefits and risks, do its benefits generally outweigh its risks, and is there a less intrusive alternative that can essentially achieve the same result?

There are, however, at least two aspects of this basic framework that were relatively unique. First, the Court effectively stated that—much like CST determinations themselves—treatment over objection is not a purely medical determination but also a legal decision. As a result, health-care providers and the judges reviewing proposed treatment plans must also take into account the context in which this proposal is being made—namely, CST determinations—and the key accompanying legal questions. Specifically, they must address whether the proposed treatment will undermine the fairness of the trial (that is, this is an additional potential risk of the treatment that must be weighed) and whether it is significantly necessary to further an important governmental trial-related interest (thus, it reformulates the calculus to be used in weighing the benefits of the treatment and any less restrictive alternatives). It is not enough that a health-care provider concludes that the proposed treatment will improve a defendant's medical condition. Although this is still a necessary first step in the analysis, it is not the end of the analysis. Because the proposed treatment may impact the right of criminal defendants to make trial decisions for themselves (that is, it may affect their autonomy) and their right to receive a fair trial, these additional considerations must also be taken into account.[40]

Second, by spelling out these details, the Court effectively mandated that treatment professionals and reviewing judges systematically consider these issues and document their analysis. This is a level of specification that had not previously been required and that ostensibly subjects these determinations to greater scrutiny upon examination and review and could increase the likelihood of successful appeals when medication over objection is ordered.

In addition to its articulation of the applicable framework, three of the four possible side effects the USSC specifically directed trial judges and treating professionals to consider had for the most part not been previously established by the Court as germane to CST determinations. The four considerations, as discussed, are will the medication (1) significantly interfere with the defendant's ability to assist or communicate with his or her attorney, (2) sedate the defendant, (3) prevent rapid reaction by the defendant to trial developments, or (4) diminish the defendant's ability to express emotions in the courtroom? The first, of course, is a basic reiteration of the *Dusky* CST standard, although it indicates that what is required is more than just the defendant's ability to "consult" or "communicate" with (that is, talk or pass notes to) an attorney, but also the capacity to engage in the more active role of "assisting" the attorney (such as providing the attorney with suggestions or leads).

The other three, however, were not discussed in *Dusky* or its progeny. All three are essentially focused on the sedating aspect of many psychotropic medications. As a result of their mental disorder, IST defendants are often agitated, distracted, or prone to acting out. While the medications prescribed for them are frequently intended to diminish such behavior and while they may considerably ameliorate such symptoms, the Court's ruling means that trial judges must not overlook the fact that these medications may sedate defendants to such an extent that their cognitive awareness of and responsiveness to the trial proceedings are diminished—an aspect often overlooked in the past. Compared to the defendant whose relatively out-of-control courtroom behavior often provides the impetus for an initial IST determination, the now-tranquil defendant may appear to be in control of his or her thoughts and actions, but what the Court's ruling should remind trial judges is that a quiet, well-behaved defendant is not necessarily a CST defendant. In addition, the Court's focus also calls attention to the fact that major depression is a severely debilitating mental disorder often found among criminal defendants and that just because defendants are not "acting out," their ability to follow and understand the proceedings and participate in their own defense may be severely impaired by this condition. Defendants who are withdrawn and disengaged as the result of a mental disorder can be just as IST as criminal defendants who are swearing, acting in a belligerent manner, or otherwise interrupting the proceedings.

Although the *Sell* framework arguably necessitates a more rigorous approach when assessing requests to treat IST defendants over their objection, there is little indication it has posed an insurmountable barrier or even a significant impediment for mental health professionals seeking such orders or trial judges reviewing these requests.[41] There may have been a small degree of inconvenience initially insofar as *Sell* required a greater consideration of related issues and germane documentation, but because this was not a "game-changer," there has been little to suggest trial judges and treatment professionals have been unable to readily adapt.[42]

At the same time, with many IST defendants now receiving restorative services in a correctional setting, government officials may be less inclined to seek an override of the treatment refusals of IST defendants in general. Because IST defendants are no longer tying up scarce, expensive, and critically needed psychiatric beds, and because the general public may be relatively comfortable with this arrangement, given that the IST defendants are being detained in a secure environment, there may be little motivation to vigorously push for the restoration of IST defendants and the resumption of trial proceedings. In addition, the prosecution may welcome this outcome if the likelihood of obtaining a conviction is questionable, while conversely, the defense may embrace it if a conviction is likely. Indeed, considering that the verdict in a criminal trial is often uncertain, both sides may simultaneously find this option attractive in a given case, thereby further reducing pressure for the administration of treatment over objection to an IST defendant. Furthermore, the government officials involved may rationalize this arrangement as justified since treatment was offered and refused. At some point, however, this arrangement should run afoul of the *Jackson* requirement that an IST defendant can be held in custody to administer restorative services only for a reasonable period of time, as well as the more specific time frames instituted in many states in response to *Jackson*, although, as discussed, if the defendant faces serious criminal charges, this authorized detention may be relatively lengthy in duration.[43]

Jared Lee Loughner

The proceedings involving Jared Lee Loughner provide an example of the post-*Sell* approach to overriding the objections to treatment of an IST defendant.[44] As described earlier, Loughner stood accused of shooting and killing six people, including Chief US District Court Judge John Roll and a nine-year-old bystander, and injuring thirteen others, including the target of the attack, Congresswoman Gabrielle (Gabby) Giffords, at a political event in 2011 in Tucson, Arizona. After his arrest, Loughner was placed in a nonmedical correctional facility, diagnosed with paranoid schizophrenia, and found IST. After he refused treatment, efforts to obtain a court order to involuntarily medicate him commenced.[45] Initially, the Ninth Circuit, on appeal, ruled that Loughner could not be treated as his right to refuse antipsychotic medications trumped the government's interest in restoring his CST in order to bring him to trial.[46]

A few weeks later, however, the court reversed itself when it determined that Loughner's condition had deteriorated and he now posed a danger to himself and others.[47] Staff at the facility where Loughner was housed stated that after discontinuing the medication he had previously accepted, he kept himself awake for fifty hours straight, refused to eat and lost nine pounds even though he was already thin, paced and walked in circles until he developed sores on his foot but refused to take antibiotics to treat a resulting infection, and was placed on suicide watch.[48] Although it was acknowledged that the medication Loughner subsequently received may have contributed to the "flat, expressionless affect" he then displayed in court,[49] nevertheless, in August of 2012, Loughner was determined to be CST and pled guilty to nineteen counts of murder and attempted murder. Three months later he was sentenced to spend the rest of his life in federal prison with no eligibility for parole.[50] It was reported that he "showed little emotion as he listened to a succession of victims" testifying at the hearing, and that he told the judge "that he did not want to speak at the hearing."[51]

Conclusion

Recent years have seen a continuing, albeit still sporadic, reexamination of the fairness of CST dispositions. While it may be argued that defendants whose CST is questionable, much like criminal defendants with a mental disorder in general, still face an uphill battle, at least practices and procedures are now in place to ensure that the issue is not pervasively ignored or that raising the question is not essentially futile. As part of this progression, the USSC's rulings in *Jackson* and *Sell* set a ceiling on how long IST defendants can be held by the State in order to ostensibly restore their CST, established that these defendants have a right to refuse the administration of medication proposed to facilitate this restoration, and specified the criteria that must be met if the State seeks to administer this medication over a defendant's objection. Although various aspects of these issues may seem complex, multifaceted, and difficult to understand, a framework has gradually emerged over time that enables the parties involved in this process to systematically resolve these issues in a relatively fair and just manner. As will now be addressed, a reexamination of the impact of mental disorders on various other trial-related competency issues, and the related procedures to determine the relevant presence or absence of competence, has also emerged in recent years.

7

Other Criminal Trial–Related Competency Issues

Miranda *Waivers/Confessions, Waiver of Counsel, Guilty Pleas, and Competence to Testify*

Because most forensic evaluations focus on a defendant's CST, this determination receives the bulk of attention from commentators, but it is not the only competency issue that may arise during a criminal trial. Although much of what has been discussed regarding CST assessments applies to these other competency evaluations as well—including the general nature of forensic evaluations, the appropriate sources and means of obtaining relevant information, and the application or "translation" of a forensic evaluation to a legal question—nevertheless, the focus and the underlying test should differ because distinct functional capabilities are being examined in conjunction with these other issues. It must be acknowledged up front, however, that judges tend not to make fine distinctions in reaching these determinations and often rely on a CST-type approach and evaluation.

These other criminal trial–related competency issues include criminal defendants' competence to confess to a crime, which encompasses their competence to waive their right to remain silent; their competence to plead guilty and thereby waive their right to a trial; their competence to appear before a judge pro se (that is, without an attorney) and thereby waive their right to legal counsel; and their competence, as well as that of any witness, to testify. Other issues pertaining to criminal defendants' mental status, which will be addressed in later chapters, are whether a defendant had the requisite actus reus and mens rea at the time of the crime, as well as the insanity defense and variations of this defense.

Potential Impacts of Mental Disorders on a Defendant's Competence

Before addressing these other competency issues, it may be useful to consider seven potential impacts of mental disorders (by no means an all-inclusive list) and how they might be relevant to these issues.[1]

1. THE MENTAL DISORDER IMPAIRS THE DEFENDANT'S ABILITY TO UNDERSTAND WHAT HE OR SHE IS BEING TOLD. The inability to adequately process information input may result in defendants not understanding the *Miranda* warnings given to them at the time of their arrest, which may cause them to not realize or recall that they have a right to remain silent and a right to an attorney. They may instead think, for example, that they have to immediately answer affirmatively anything police officers and prosecutors ask them, including whether they committed the crime. Additionally, their mental disorder may cause them to feel overwhelmed by the pressure of the moment or leave them unable to act in their own self-interest, leading them to confess to a crime just to escape this anxiety-inducing situation. They may similarly fail to understand the warnings given them before they enter a guilty plea or waive their right to counsel. If they take the stand, they may misunderstand the questions asked or fail to appreciate that they must answer questions truthfully.

2. THE MENTAL DISORDER IMPAIRS THE DEFENDANT'S ABILITY TO COMMUNICATE. The inability to adequately process information may result in defendants failing to express their confusion or ask for clarification regarding their situation, the criminal events in question, their rights, or the questions they are being asked. Even if they understand the questions posed, they may not be able to articulate intelligible answers, or their answers may be misunderstood and perhaps used against them. For example, they may respond that they understand their *Miranda* rights when they do not. They may think they are invoking their right to an attorney and want the questioning of an arresting officer to stop, when their response seems to express to the arresting officer just the opposite. They may believe they have indicated they want an attorney to represent them at trial, when the judge understands them to be indicating they want to proceed pro se. If they take the stand, they may think their testimony explains why they are not guilty, while the jury or

the judge views these statements as highly incriminating. Additionally, mental disorders may render defendants mute, preventing them from providing relevant alibis or explanations, excuses, or justifications for their behavior.

3. THE MENTAL DISORDER IMPAIRS THE DEFENDANT'S MEMORY. Defendants' short-term or long-term memory may be impaired. An impairment of the former can limit their capacity to communicate with others, including police officers and attorneys, since they cannot remember what they have just been told or asked. A disruption of long-term memory can cause confusion, uncertainty, and sometimes partial or total amnesia regarding prior events, which in turn may cause defendants to misreport or be unable to explain what occurred at the time of the crime, including inaccurately indicating that they were involved in the crime. Such a disruption can also undercut their ability to generate what otherwise would have been a viable alibi, a plausible explanation of the events surrounding the crime (they were an innocent bystander), an acceptable justification for their actions (acting in self-defense), or a legally-accepted excuse for their behavior (they were experiencing an epileptic episode). Moreover, an impairment of memory can also impact defendants' competence to confess, to plead guilty, and to testify, as well as their ability to receive a fair trial in general.

4. THE MENTAL DISORDER IMPAIRS THE DEFENDANT'S JUDGMENT. An impairment of defendants' judgment may undercut their capacity to fully or accurately appreciate the consequences of their actions and decisions, as well as recognize what is in their best interests and act accordingly. These defendants may overestimate their ability to avoid responsibility for their actions or underestimate their ability to be treated fairly and justly. The former may lead them to take excessive chances or make outlandish claims that have little chance of bearing fruit, while the latter may result in defendants being overly passive and unduly resigning themselves to an adverse fate. Defendants may fail to accurately perceive the consequences of a confession and the value of the right to remain silent, mistakenly thinking—as a child might—that all will be forgiven if they readily confess to committing a crime. They may misunderstand the consequences of entering a guilty plea, focusing instead on the short-term relief gained by ending an investigation or trial, while failing to recognize that this may result in a lengthy jail sentence. Defen-

dants may waive their right to counsel because they mistakenly believe that they can conduct their defense better than an attorney and fail to appreciate how difficult this will be.

5. THE MENTAL DISORDER IMPAIRS THE DEFENDANT'S ABILITY TO REFLECT AND PLAN. An impaired ability to reflect and plan diminishes defendants' capacity to act rationally. These defendants may blurt out something without contemplating its meaning and impact. Their actions may be relatively random without purpose or direction. An internal pressure to speak or act may override warnings that the person has a right to remain silent, leading to unwise and sometimes inaccurate confessions; trigger unwarranted guilty pleas contrary to the advice of counsel; precipitate a failure to appreciate the difficulty and peril of acting as one's own attorney; undercut the ability to participate in and formulate one's defense; or result in counsel's advice being disregarded.

6. THE MENTAL DISORDER IMPAIRS THE DEFENDANT'S SPEECH OR ACTIONS. A psychiatric impairment can erode criminal defendants' ability to act freely or speak accurately and effectively. For example, a desire to be punished stemming from a mental disorder may lead defendants to falsely confess to a crime or fail to provide exonerating evidence to an arresting police officer or counsel. Defendants with a mental disorder may view a news account of a crime and experience impulses or hear voices telling them that they are responsible for the crime even though they had nothing to do with it. Similarly, they may feel compelled to confess or plead guilty to a crime they did not commit because their mental disorder drives them to engage in self-injurious behavior. Defendants may waive their right to an attorney because their paranoia prevents them from trusting or relying on others. An inability to adequately articulate their thoughts may lead to trial testimony that fails to exonerate them of criminal responsibility.

7. THE MENTAL DISORDER IMPAIRS THE DEFENDANT'S PERCEPTIONS OF REALITY. A mental disorder can cloud and distort how criminal defendants perceive surrounding events. They may falsely believe that it was their thoughts or past behavior that somehow triggered criminal actions by another, and thus they inaccurately perceive themselves as responsible for these actions and confess or plead guilty to the crime. Alternatively, they may confess or plead guilty to a crime or

provide false incriminating testimony because they believe that a prison cannot hold them or because they think they will be rescued miraculously. They may waive their right to counsel because they believe the prosecutor and defense counsel are working together in an effort to obtain their conviction. They may testify falsely because they think they are accountable to some imagined higher authority that is dictating what they say.

There are many ways in which a mental disorder can impact the competency of a defendant to confess, plead guilty, waive counsel and self-represent, or testify. Although a lack of competence in these domains can greatly distort the judicial process and result in unfair, unjust verdicts, they have received only limited attention from the judiciary. What follows is a description of how the judiciary has responded when it has addressed these issues.

Competence to Confess

Of the various competence issues discussed here, defendants' competence to waive their right to remain silent and confess is the one most frequently raised. Does the criminal justice system like confessions? Absolutely. Obtaining confessions in which suspects state that they committed the crime makes life much easier for law enforcement officials, prosecutors, and judges. It eliminates the need for further investigations, simplifies efforts to prosecute defendants, streamlines related trial proceedings, and makes reaching verdicts much easier. Indeed, one can argue that the criminal justice system is dependent on confessions insofar as the system, which is already stretched thin, might collapse without them.[2] In addition, sometimes a confession is the lone direct evidence accessible because only the defendant was present when the crime was committed or no other witness is available to testify. Without a confession, the prosecution may be forced to rely on circumstantial evidence to make its argument, almost always a more difficult case to establish.

Indeed, confessions have most likely always played a pivotal role in criminal prosecutions, with limits placed only relatively recently on how confessions are acquired. For example, at one point in English history, accused individuals would be stretched out on the ground with more and more weight placed on their chest until they confessed.[3] Needless to say, a very high confession rate was obtained using this method, or at least the need to continue the investigation further was eliminated.

Why were limits placed on these and similar efforts to obtain confessions? It is generally agreed that if you exert enough pressure on someone (for example, torture them), an individual will confess to almost anything. Such confessions, however, do not necessarily provide an accurate depiction of what happened. Plus, fairness and justice are keys for a judicial system to be widely accepted and respected, with fairly obtained and accurate verdicts its hallmark. Coerced confessions are not considered sufficiently trustworthy and are inconsistent with the respect for human dignity expected of civilized societies and their court systems.

The standard applied in American courts, almost from their inception, has been that a criminal confession must be *voluntary*. In applying this standard, courts initially examined whether a confession was *trustworthy*—in other words, whether you could rely on the truthfulness of what was said. This, in turn, led to an examination of whether the confession was obtained in a way that tainted its trustworthiness. If a confession was coerced, and thus not given voluntarily, it was considered to be not trustworthy and not admissible into evidence.[4]

For a long time, however, courts largely deferred to the police and the techniques they used in conducting their criminal investigations, with the primary exception occurring when it could be shown that blatant physical or psychological abuse had been employed. Then, and only then, did the courts throw out a subsequent confession.

During the 1960s and 1970s, however, when many governmental actions were being questioned, courts began to look more closely at law enforcement activities in general, and police-generated confessions in particular. The US Supreme Court began to put limits on police activities and to recognize the corresponding rights of criminal defendants.

Miranda v. Arizona *(1966)*

THE COURT'S RULING IN *MIRANDA*

In 1966, the US Supreme Court (USSC) issued its landmark ruling in *Miranda v. Arizona* regarding the confessions of criminal defendants and established a new standard for determining their admissibility into evidence. The Court held that under the Fifth Amendment of the US Constitution, the introduction into evidence of a forced confession to a crime can deprive defendants of their right to due process.[5] The Court specifically focused on *custodial interrogations* conducted by law enforcement officials. A custodial interrogation occurs when law enforcement officials have arrested criminal suspects or placed them in circumstances that would lead a reasonable person to believe they are not free to leave. Under such circumstances, the Court ruled, defendants must be advised of their rights under the Fifth Amendment, including their right to remain silent.

This ruling ultimately led law enforcement officials to read to suspects in police custody a relatively standardized set of warnings, their so-called *Miranda rights*. A failure to read these rights precludes the admission into evidence at trial any confession subsequently obtained. The typical warning states that (a) you have the right to remain silent and not answer questions, (b) anything you say can be used against you in a court of law, (c) you have the right to have an attorney present before and during questioning and to consult with this attorney before answering any questions, and (d) if you cannot afford an attorney, you have the right to have one appointed for you at public expense before any questioning occurs.

At the same time, the Court noted that defendants are free to *waive* these rights, although such waivers must be *knowing, voluntary, and intelligent*. This ruling expanded the prior focus on whether a confession was "voluntary" to also encompass whether the waiver of the right to remain silent was "knowing" and "intelligent."

In addition—and this gave the ruling particular weight—the Court applied what is known as the *fruit of the poisonous tree* doctrine to this context.[6] Under this doctrine, not only is an improperly obtained confession inadmissible as evidence, but so is all evidence discovered as a result of the improperly obtained confession. For example, if an improperly obtained confession enabled the police to find the murder weapon and, upon testing, it was determined the defendant's fingerprints were on the weapon, the weapon and the fingerprints would also be inadmissible as evidence, unless, the Court added, the State can establish that the evidence would have been found by means independent of the confession. As a result, pivotal evidence amassed by law enforcement officials can be excluded from a defendant's trial if an improperly obtained confession was the sole basis for the discovery of this information, thereby considerably weakening the State's case against the defendant.

Thus, the relevant legal principles regarding confessions obtained from criminal suspects in the custody of law enforcement officials or other "state actors" are that (a) a forced confession constitutes a violation of the due process clause, and (b) an improperly obtained waiver of the privilege to remain silent is a violation of the Fifth Amendment.[7] Under either criteria, a resulting confession will be ruled inadmissible as evidence at the defendant's trial.

IMPACT OF *MIRANDA*

There was a great uproar at the time *Miranda* was issued. It was asserted these restrictions would cripple law enforcement efforts as confessions would never be forthcoming once criminal suspects' *Miranda* rights were read to them. Subsequent research, however, has shown that the reading of these rights has had little impact on the rate at which confessions are obtained.[8] For one thing, criminal suspects have a tendency to ignore or not fully understand the *Miranda* warnings. It is also the case that more subtle pressures are just as effective as blatant force in encouraging a suspect to confess. And suspects themselves have various overriding reasons for speaking—including a need to talk about what happened, a hope that they will be given credit for being forthright, or a belief that their explanation of what happened will absolve them of criminal responsibility. These factors may outweigh any concern by the suspect that the likelihood of a criminal conviction will be enhanced as a result of their statement to law enforcement authorities.

Regardless of its broader impact, the question remained how the Court's ruling in *Miranda* should be applied to suspects with a mental disorder. The initial interpretation of the *Miranda* requirement that a confession be "voluntary" was virtually the same as under the "voluntary" rule employed prior to *Miranda*: namely, courts examined whether coercion led to the confession and the waiver of the right to remain silent. If coercion was present, the defendant's behavior was deemed involuntary, and the confession was thrown out regardless of the source of the coercion. Thus, even if it was a suspect's mental disorder that "coerced" the confession, the general view was that the confession was involuntary under these circumstances and thus inadmissible. In 1986, however, the USSC rejected this approach.

Colorado v. Connelly *(1986)*

FACTUAL AND PROCEDURAL FOUNDATION

In an unusual turn of events, the defendant, Francis Connelly, had flown from Boston to Denver in August of 1983, gone downtown, approached a police officer, and—without any prompting—said that he had murdered someone and wanted to talk about it. Unsurprisingly, the officer thought this was strange behavior, but nevertheless immediately advised Connelly of his right to remain silent and his other *Miranda* rights. Connelly said he understood, but still wanted to talk about the murder. In response to the officer's questions, Connelly denied he had been drinking or taking drugs, although he acknowledged he had been a patient in several psychiatric facilities in the past. The officer again told Connelly he was under no obligation to say anything, but Connelly said he wanted to talk to the officer because his conscience had been bothering him. As far as the officer could tell, Connelly appeared to understand what he was doing.

A short time later, a homicide detective arrived, and Connelly was again advised of his *Miranda* rights. Connelly then told the detective that he had come from Boston to confess to murdering Mary Ann Junta, a young girl, whom he had killed in Denver the previous November. Connelly was taken to police headquarters where a search of police records revealed that the body of an unidentified female had been found in April. Connelly openly gave a detailed account to the detective and a police sergeant and readily agreed to take them to the scene of the killing. Under Connelly's direction, they proceeded to the location of the crime, where Connelly pointed out where the murder occurred. The detective later claimed that throughout these events she perceived no indication that Connelly was suffering from any kind of mental illness.

Connelly was held overnight, but the following morning, during an interview with someone from the public defender's office, he became visibly disoriented, began giving confused answers to questions, and for the first time stated that "voices" had told him to come to Denver and that he was obeying these voices in confessing. Before his trial could begin, Connelly was sent to a state hospital for evaluation and found to be IST. After six months of hospitalization and treatment, however, he was determined to be CST, and the trial commenced thereafter.

At a preliminary hearing, the defense attempted to suppress all of Connelly's statements to the police as involuntary. A psychiatrist from the state hospital testified Connelly was suffering from chronic schizophrenia and was in a psychotic state at least as far back as the day before he confessed to the police. Connelly told the psychiatrist he had been following the "voice of God," which instructed him to withdraw money from a bank, buy an airplane ticket, and fly from Boston to Denver. Upon his arrival, the voice became stronger and told Connelly either to confess to the killing or commit suicide. The psychiatrist further testified that in his expert opinion Connelly was experiencing "command hallucinations" and that although this condition did not significantly impair Connelly's cognitive abilities or result in his not understanding the police officers when they told him he did not have to speak, it did interfere with his ability to make free and rational choices. While admitting that the "voices" could just be Connelly's interpretation of his own guilt, the psychiatrist was of the opinion that it was Connelly's psychosis that had motivated his confession.

In response, the trial court ruled that even though the police had done nothing wrong or coercive in obtaining Connelly's confession, his statements had to be excluded because they were "involuntary"; that is, because Connelly's mental illness destroyed his volition and compelled him to confess, his statements were not a product of his "free will." In addition, the court ruled that Connelly's illness vitiated his attempted waiver of his *Miranda* rights. The Colorado Supreme Court affirmed the ruling of the trial court.

THE COURT'S RULING IN *CONNELLY*

The USSC, however, embraced a different approach after it accepted the case for review. The Court asserted that the Fifth Amendment is concerned only about inappropriate police behavior and does not protect criminal defendants from coercion emanating from other sources, including mental illness or a third party (such as a family member). Therefore, as long as the police acted appropriately and did not coerce the suspect, then a confession is admissible even if a mental disorder "forced" the defendant to confess. Otherwise, the Court reasoned, courts would have to engage in far-ranging inquiries into what motivated defendants to speak or act as they did in giving their confession.

At the same time, the Court did indicate one avenue by which a defendant's mental disorder could be relevant when challenging the admissibility of a confession. If the defendant's psychiatric condition left the defendant particularly susceptible to coercive techniques by the police, and the police knowingly took advantage of this susceptibility, then the confession may be inadmissible. This test might be met, for example, when criminal suspects known to be claustrophobic are left alone in a small, isolated jail cell for an extended period of time after being told they are going to remain there until "we get to the bottom of this."

With regard to Connelly, however, the Court determined that the officer did not observe any signs that the defendant was blatantly psychotic and simply adhered to good police practice in their interactions. Thus, because the officer did not know Connelly was experiencing a mental illness or take advantage of his condition, Connelly's confession was properly obtained.

Three members of the Court disagreed. Justice Brennan in his dissenting opinion argued that prior cases had focused on whether the confession was voluntary, not on police misconduct. He contended that all forms of involuntary confessions are antithetical to due process and that free will is a matter of constitutional importance and a key to respecting human dignity. Ensuring that free will was exercised, he continued, is necessary to establish the reliability of the statement given, and the reliability of the evidence introduced at trial is a fundamental concern of the criminal justice system. Finally, he asserted that even under the majority's approach, this confession should have been ruled inadmissible as the police knew about the defendant's psychiatric history, and thus knew about Connelly's mental illness and took advantage of it in securing his confession.

ANALYSIS OF CONNELLY

What led the majority to adopt the position it did? On the one hand, it may seem like Connelly knew what he was doing in that he was able to book and take a flight on a plane, seek out and recognize the uniform of a police officer, coherently explain to the officer what he wanted to do, and then direct the police unassisted to where an unidentified female victim's body had been previously found. However, as someone who apparently used to live in Denver, he might have heard or read about and remembered news accounts regarding this unsolved murder, which probably would have received a lot of local publicity. As a result of his mental disorder, he could have become obsessed with this crime and ultimately have incorporated it into his delusional state. Someone with schizophrenia, for example, may seem to be managing day-to-day matters relatively well, while still being caught up in a distorted perception of reality, which leads the individual to engage in irrational, bizarre, and counterproductive behavior.

As for the legal framework adopted by the USSC, one might attribute it to the different eras in which *Miranda* and *Connelly* were issued. As noted, *Miranda* was decided in 1966 by what is commonly referred to as the Warren Court, when a majority of the justices on the Court were concerned about overreaching on the part of law enforcement and saw a need to protect civil liberties, including the protections afforded criminal defendants. When *Connelly* was decided twenty years later, Chief Justice Warren was no longer a member of the Court, his place having been taken by Chief Justice Rehnquist, and a majority of the Court held more conservative views regarding criminal justice issues, and were more supportive of law enforcement officers and less sympathetic to criminal defendants.

Alternatively, the USSC may have adopted the same strategy in *Connelly* as it employed in *Dusky* when it established the CST standard. As discussed, the Court in *Dusky* rejected a medically oriented test in favor of a functional standard that could be readily employed by judges and jurors, arguably so they would not have to delve into concepts and terminology pertaining to mental disorders, and thereby avoided an especially "foggy" domain with which even mental health experts struggle.

The ruling in *Connelly* similarly spares judicial decision-makers from having to routinely assess the impact of mental disorders on defendants' thoughts and behavior in conjunction with their confessions, in particular their ability to exercise free will. This type of assessment would be especially difficult in this context in that it would not target a defendant's current competence (the focus of CST evaluations, for example), but rather the defendant's competence at that point in the past when the defendant waived his or her right to remain silent and provided a confession. Retrospective evaluations of the effects of mental disorders generally tend to be more challenging and subject to greater variation. Indeed, the retrospective evaluations of defendants' mental state in conjunction with the insanity defense may be one of the reasons why this defense has traditionally been disfavored. Although not expressed by the USSC in *Connelly*, concerns about this kind of analysis may have underlay its decision to focus on the behavior of the law enforcement officials involved and not the defendants' mental state at the time of the confession.

Another possible explanation for the *Connelly* ruling was the difficulty of finding a "bright line" test that could be employed to govern the approach endorsed by the Colorado courts. As discussed, mental disorders come in "all shapes and sizes." Even for a given diagnosis, the associated symptoms can fluctuate considerably over time and vary enormously across individuals. Establishing when a defendant's confession should be considered to be the product of his or her free will and when it should be determined to be the result of the defendant's mental disorder would be quite challenging. For defendants with a severe mental disorder who are in the midst of a psychotic episode it may seem readily apparent that it was the mental disorder driving their behavior, but for many other defendants with a mental disorder, such as a major depressive disorder, this can be a daunting undertaking that is difficult to resolve with the kind of consistency expected of a governing legal standard. The appropriateness of police behavior may be easier to judge as there may be a greater consensus as to what constitutes police coercion.[9]

Most commentators, however, appraise the *Connelly* ruling according to what they see as the goal of the Fifth Amendment. Those who think it is intended to ensure the reliability of confessions so that the criminal justice system reaches fair and just outcomes would disallow as inherently unreliable confessions that are influenced by or the product of a mental disorder. They would be joined by those who believe in general that enhanced protections should be afforded to individuals who are vulnerable to self-injurious behavior as a result of their mental disorder.

At the other end of the spectrum are those who think that the Fifth Amendment—and the Bill of Rights in general—is designed to curb overreaching and abuses by the State and its law enforcement agents, and thus confessions should be disallowed only if these agents engaged in coercive or improper behavior while obtaining a confession. They would be joined by those worried about "handcuffing" the police with an expansive or variable application of a criminal suspect's *Miranda* rights, as well as those who believe that assessing the impact of mental disorders on criminal suspects' behavior is a morass the courts should largely avoid. A question you might ask is whether these views would recede if the "fruit of the poisonous tree" doctrine was diminished so that a ruling that a confession is inadmissible did not play such a pivotal role in limiting criminal prosecutions.

Current Focus

Today, the first question asked in reviewing the confession or other self-incriminating statements of a suspect with a mental disorder is whether the requisite *Miranda* warnings were given, although this inquiry is the starting place for examining confessions obtained from all suspects in police custody.[10] For suspects with a mental disorder, however, a relatively distinct analysis is then applied to resolve whether they adequately understood their right to remain silent, with *Connelly* establishing that any waiver of this right must be "knowingly, voluntarily, and intelligently" given.

With regard to whether defendants "knowingly" waived their *Miranda* rights, the issue is not whether they understood all the implications and consequences of this waiver. The courts generally just look to see whether they roughly knew where they were and what they were doing. Most defendants with a mental disorder will meet this requirement, although some who are very disoriented as to their current "time and place" as a result of their disorder may be deemed incompetent to waive their *Miranda* rights under this criterion.

With regard to whether defendants "voluntarily" waived their *Miranda* rights, the courts—pursuant to *Connelly*—will examine only whether the confession was the result of police coercion. If police coercion is not present, then even if suspects confessed, for example, only because they heard the voice of their deceased mother telling them to do so, the waiver is still valid. One exception, as discussed above, is if the police knew of a defendant's mental disorder and manipulated the situation to take advantage of this vulnerability in obtaining the confession, then the confession will be deemed inadmissible.[11]

With regard to whether defendants "intelligently" waived their *Miranda* rights, the courts will not examine whether the confession was a smart decision. It usually is not. The question is simply whether a defendant was able to exercise his or her mind/intelligence in making this decision. Although *Connelly* effectively removed the possibility of using a defendant's mental disorder as a basis for excluding a confession under the "voluntary" waiver prong, the "intelligent" waiver prong remains somewhat applicable. If it can be established that the defendant's mental disorder was so debilitating that the defendant could not exercise his or her mind at a very basic, fundamental level—one that would enable the defendant to weigh at least somewhat the advantages and disadvantages, the risks and benefits, of waiving his or her *Miranda* rights and making an incriminating statement—a court may disallow a confession on this basis. Such individuals, however, would have to be so impaired that it is questionable whether they would even have the ability to effectively and reliably communicate a confession under these circumstances.

Although defendants with a mental disorder have tried to argue that one of these three prongs was not met in their case, the argument is difficult to pursue successfully because the bar to establish incompetence is set very high.

Procedures for Determining Whether a Criminal Defendant Is Competent to Confess

While the USSC has addressed the procedures for determining defendants' CST, it has not issued any rulings regarding the constitutionality of the procedures employed to resolve whether criminal defendants were mentally competent at the time they waived their right to remain silent and confessed to a crime or made other incriminating statements. By focusing on whether the behavior of the law enforcement officers who obtained the confession was lawful (that is, did the officer coerce or otherwise unduly force the defendant to confess?), the USSC in *Connelly* effectively marginalized constitutional questions pertaining to the procedures used to assess a defendant's mental state at the time the confession was obtained.

Nonetheless, as described above, defendants' mental state at the time of the incriminating statement may become relevant if it is asserted that law enforcement officials took advantage of the defendant's mental state in obtaining this statement.[12] Furthermore, as the USSC noted in *Connelly*, states can impose additional requirements beyond those established by the US Constitution when scrutinizing the admissibility of confessions, including that they cannot be "forced" by or be the product of a mental disorder.

Although motions that a confession should be thrown out because it was the product of or tainted by a defendant's mental disorder are not frequent, states have had to devise procedures to address such questions when they do arise. For example, the Virginia Supreme Court has ruled that in determining the validity of a defendant's waiver of the right to remain silent, Virginia courts are to consider the "totality of the circumstances" under which the waiver was given.[13] Among the factors identified that may be relevant, but not necessarily dispositive, are the defendant's mental illness and intellectual disability at the time.[14] If the prosecution indicates that the defendant's confession or other incriminating statements will be introduced into evidence at trial, the defendant may submit in response a motion to suppress (that is, keep out) the information on this basis.

Although Virginia law, for one, does not specify a procedure for evaluating the defendant's mental state at the time of the confession, courts often simply exercise their inherent authority to order an evaluation of the defendant and appoint an independent mental health evaluator, sometimes after consulting with the parties and permitting them to agree on who should fill this role. The evaluator is expected to focus on the defendant's mental state at the time the incriminating statements were made and may review any record of the interrogation (such as an audio or video recording). Evaluators are expected to address (a) any mental disorder–related susceptibility to coercion that might induce incriminating statements (whether a law enforcement official took advantage of this susceptibility will be an issue for the attorneys to address at trial); and (b) defendants' understanding of their *Miranda* rights as read to them by law enforcement officials and their competency at the time to waive these rights.[15] Like all forensic mental health evaluations, evaluators should avoid stating an opinion on the "ultimate issue," namely, whether a defendant was competent to waive his or her *Miranda* rights and provide a confession or other incriminating statements. The defendant's mental status at the time the statements were made is only one of several possible factors related to this determination under the "totality of the circumstances" standard, and this determination is for the trial judge to make. The admissibility of the incriminating statements into evidence will then be decided by the judge at a pretrial suppression hearing.

Competence to Plead Guilty

Whether a defendant is competent to enter a guilty plea is another criminal trial-related competency issue that might arise. Guilty pleas, like confessions, play a central role in the criminal justice system, with 90–95 percent of criminal trials resolved by a plea bargain.[16] When defendants enter a guilty plea, they forego their right to a trial and waive a number of related constitutional rights, including their Fifth Amendment privilege against self-incrimination and their Sixth Amendment rights to a trial and to call and confront witnesses.

Needless to say, entering a guilty plea represents a major decision on the part of the defendant. Because of its significance, a court may closely scrutinize the plea. However, a number of factors weigh against such an in-depth examination, including the large volume of cases judges must process, the relatively informal nature of the procedure whereby guilty pleas are entered, and the relatively short time such hearings last, which limits a judge's opportunity to examine the defendant's competence. Furthermore, neither the prosecutor nor the defense attorney is typically motivated to challenge a defendant's competence at this stage; the prosecutor is generally quite pleased to obtain a conviction and bring the matter to a prompt close, while the defense, which enters the plea, has little reason to challenge this outcome unless the defendant is acting contrary to the advice of counsel. Only if the trial judge has a specific reason for questioning the defendant's competence as the guilty plea is submitted will the defendant's competence be closely assessed.

Because entering a guilty plea is such a decisive moment in a trial and has such significant and relatively irreversible ramifications for defendants, most states do mandate that trial judges ask defendants a series of questions at the time a guilty plea is submitted to ensure defendants have a basic understanding of what they are doing and that they are doing this voluntarily. However, these questions tend to be delivered in a relatively rapid, rote-like manner, are not terribly penetrating, and require defendants to give little more than simple yes-or-no answers, which provide judges with little insight into the mental state of the defendant at the time.

Thus, there have been few cases where a defendant's competence to plead guilty has been called into question. One that generated attention in recent years involved former US Senator Larry Craig from Idaho. Craig, who was rated as the third most conservative member of the Senate at the time, was arrested in 2007 in a Minneapolis airport bathroom as part of an undercover gay sex sting. Perhaps hoping to avoid publicity, he quickly entered a guilty plea. He later attempted to rescind the guilty plea, claiming he entered it only as a result of the stress he was experiencing due to related media inquiries into his sexuality. The motion to rescind was denied, and this ruling was upheld on appeal.[17]

Some questions were also raised about the competence to enter a guilty plea of Ted Kaczynski, a.k.a. the Unabomber, who later claimed the submission of his plea was involuntary in that he entered it only because his request to represent himself was denied and his attorneys were insisting, against his wishes, on presenting evidence of his serious mental illness (schizophrenia) at trial. Kaczynski's plea was purportedly motivated in part by his fear that evidence of his experiencing a serious mental illness would undercut the credibility of his manifesto, in which he proclaimed that modern technology was eroding human freedoms. Kaczynski's subsequent motion to rescind his guilty plea was denied by a split panel of the US Ninth Circuit Court of Appeals.[18]

When determining the competence of defendants to plead guilty, the test employed by the USSC is whether the plea is "intelligent and voluntary."[19] Thus, it incorporates two of the three criteria used to examine the competence of defendants to waive their *Miranda* rights and provide a confession that can be entered into evidence; the *Miranda* "knowingly" criterion is not employed, perhaps simply as a matter of historical accident. However, competence to plead guilty involves a context that is distinct from that associated with a defendant's competence to waive *Miranda* rights, so the functional abilities assessed will also be somewhat different.

For the "intelligent" element, all that is required is for defendants to have a basic understanding of what they are doing—namely, do they understand (a) the essence of the charged offense, defenses that would otherwise be available, and possible penalties they may incur as a result of their guilty plea, and (b) that a guilty plea waives several constitutional rights to which they would otherwise be entitled.

When examining whether the guilty plea was "voluntary," the test requires actual voluntariness; that is, that the plea is truly voluntary. Thus, the meaning of "voluntary" here is different than it is when assessing the voluntariness of defendants' waiver of their *Miranda* rights; for competence to enter a guilty plea, possible coercion by a law enforcement official is not the sole focus. Internal compulsion, such as that caused by a mental disorder, can suffice to establish that a defendant is incompetent to enter a guilty plea. Thus, incompetence to enter a guilty plea can be established by the presence of (a) coercion or similar force utilized by a law enforcement official, (b) coercion from a third party (that is, someone other than a law enforcement official, including a defendant's spouse, family member, acquaintance, or enemy), or (c) internal compulsion, such as may result from a mental disorder. If a defendant's guilty plea is not voluntary, regardless of the source that "forced" the plea, the defendant is not competent to plead guilty.

Godinez v. Moran *(1993)*

FACTUAL AND PROCEDURAL FOUNDATION

The Ninth Circuit and other circuits of the US Court of Appeals at one point embraced a more demanding standard for establishing a defendant's competence to enter a guilty plea than the one that is required for defendants to be found CST. For those incorrectly found to be CST, they contended that the defendants are still protected by (a) the subsequent trial, in which their attorneys can vigorously advocate on behalf of them, (b) the criminal justice system's independent incorporation of elements designed to ensure that criminal trials are fair and just, and (c) the fact that defendants' attorneys or even the trial judge can raise the CST issue again later during the trial and have the matter reconsidered. In contrast, these courts asserted, if defendants are wrongly found to be competent to plead guilty, their trial is now over with no subsequent protections available to them. Thus, these courts determined that the competence of criminal defendants to plead guilty should be examined more closely than their CST, with the Ninth Circuit ruling that the test should be whether a defendant has the capacity to make a "reasoned choice" among alternatives.[20]

THE COURT'S RULING IN *GODINEZ*

A majority of the USSC, however, rejected this position in *Godinez v. Moran* (1993) and determined that the competence to plead guilty test is subsumed within the CST test. The Court refused to make the distinction made by the Ninth Circuit and others and effectively said that for this purpose competency is competency. In other words, under the US Constitution, defendants found to be CST should also be considered to be competent to plead guilty. The Court declared that both determinations address a potential loss of similar trial-related rights, including the right to a trial and the right to confront one's accusers.

The two justices who dissented argued that a guilty plea may be the product of a severe mental illness or medications that leave the defendant numb to, confused by, or unaware of what is at stake. This, in turn, may result in defendants' providing monosyllabic yes-or-no answers to routine and relatively superficial questions from the trial judge, which fail to adequately probe their competence. These justices further contended that CST and competence to plead guilty reflect different contexts; namely, CST addresses only defendants' competence to assist their attorney, while defendants found competent to plead guilty forego both their attorney's assistance and their right to a trial. Thus, they argued, due process should require the use of different standards when evaluating one as opposed to the other.

IMPACT OF *GODINEZ*

Nonetheless, because of the Court's ruling in *Godinez*, a trial judge may rely on an evaluation and determination establishing that a defendant is CST as a sufficient basis for concluding that the defendant is also competent to plead guilty, with separate evaluations of the two issues not required. Thus, it is important that attorneys who represent defendants for whom a CST evaluation is ordered ask the mental health professional conducting the examination to specifically evaluate their clients' competence to plead guilty as well, as they may not get another chance to have this aspect of their clients' trial-related competence evaluated. Mental health professionals, in turn, when asked to evaluate a defendant's competence, should recognize the potentially distinct capacities associated with the two determinations and be prepared to report that a defendant is CST but not competent to plead guilty and, thereby, avoid a miscarriage of justice.

Procedures for Determining Whether a Criminal Defendant Is Competent to Plead Guilty

Usually when defendants enter a guilty plea, the trial judge will ask them a series of questions to ensure that they understand what they are doing, including the consequences of their plea. In as much as formal requests to evaluate a defendant's competence to enter a guilty plea are raised relatively infrequently, the nature of the questions posed to the defendant as part of this exchange is important in that the answers given in response can provide a rough indicator of whether the defendant is competent to plead guilty and waive the right to trial.

The Virginia Supreme Court, for example, has suggested a series of questions that trial judges should ask defendants pleading guilty.[21] They include: Do you fully understand the charges against you? Do you understand what the prosecutor must prove before you may be found guilty? Do you understand the maximum punishment you may receive? Have you had enough time to discuss with your attorney possible defenses to the charges filed? Are you satisfied with the work of your attorney? Did you decide for yourself to plead guilty? Are you entering your plea freely and voluntarily? Has anyone connected with your arrest or prosecution threatened or forced you to plead guilty? Do you understand that by pleading guilty you are waiving your right to a trial by a jury? Your right not to incriminate yourself? Your right to cross-examine witnesses? Your right to defend yourself? Your right to appeal? Are you in fact guilty?

Note, however, that all of these questions can be answered with a simple yes or no, which provides virtually no insight into the defendant's thought processes or understanding of the concepts involved. Indeed, in practice these questions tend to be asked in rapid-fire fashion, with the defendant's answers being nothing more than a series of monosyllabic responses (yes . . . yes . . . yes . . . yes). Typically, it is only if a defendant's answer to one of the questions is contrary to the expected response that the judge will ask the defendant any follow-up questions; even then, however, the reason for the follow-up question is usually not to assess the defendant's competence to plead guilty but rather because such an answer can be grounds for a reversal on appeal, which no trial judge wants. If a severe sentence is likely to ensue, particularly in a death penalty case, a trial judge may question the defendant more closely since the stakes are higher, the case is more likely to be followed by the media and the community, and there is a greater likelihood of appeal, although again the focus tends not to be the defendant's mental status.

It should also be noted that although some of these questions probe whether anyone coerced or forced the defendant to plead guilty (that is, whether the guilty plea is being entered voluntarily under *Godinez*), there are no questions that seek to ascertain whether the defendant is experiencing a mental disorder that may be influencing his or her guilty plea. At the same time, even if the judge is inclined to pursue such a line of questioning, it is worth asking whether a judge is adequately trained to do so in open court and whether the defendant is likely to respond candidly in this setting. Indeed, it is likely that most judges would prefer to avoid having to proceed down this path altogether.

Another context in which competence to enter a plea might be questioned is when a defendant seeks to enter, in those jurisdictions that authorize it, a plea of not guilty by reason of insanity or a plea of guilty but mentally ill (GBMI). With these pleas defendants are indicating that they experienced a mental disorder in the past (that is, at the time of the offense), which raises the distinct possibility that they may be currently experiencing the effects of a mental disorder. In addition, as will be discussed, defendants frequently misunderstand the consequences of an insanity or GBMI verdict.

Thus, the New York legislature, for one, has established a series of questions the trial judge must ask a defendant before accepting an insanity plea, including do you understand (a) the nature of the charge and the consequences of your plea, (b) that you have a right to plead not guilty, (c) that you have a right to be tried by a jury and the right to assistance of counsel, (d) that you are waiving your right to a trial, (e) that if you enter an insanity plea, the court will ask you questions about the offense,[22] and (f) that if accepted, this plea is the equivalent of an insanity verdict.[23] The court must address the defendant personally in open court, determine that the plea is "voluntary, knowingly made, and not the result of force, threats, or promises," and be satisfied that the defendant understands the proceedings, has sufficient capacity to assist in his or her own defense, and understands the consequences of an insanity plea.[24] In addition, before the plea can be accepted by the judge, the prosecution must detail the evidence in its possession pertaining to the charges against the defendant and attest to the court that it is satisfied that the insanity defense would be established at trial by a preponderance of the evidence.[25] In turn, the defendant's attorney must vouch that in his or her opinion the defendant is CST and understands the consequences of an insanity plea, and detail the psychiatric evidence that would be used to establish the insanity defense.[26] The court can also conduct a hearing to explore these issues more fully before accepting the plea.[27]

Perhaps reflecting how few challenges to a defendant's competence to plead guilty there are, most court systems do not have in place a separate scheme for evaluating a defendant's competence to plead guilty. If the question does arise, it will typically be raised at the arraignment, where defendants initially enter their guilty or not guilty plea. If the trial judge questions a defendant's competence to enter a plea voluntarily and intelligently, the judge may simply order a CST evaluation and employ the approach associated with such an evaluation.

If a judge finds the defendant incompetent to plead guilty, one of two procedural options is typically employed. First, the judge may enter a not guilty plea on behalf of the defendant and allow the trial to begin. One might question this approach, however, given that in *Godinez* the USSC essentially said that competence to plead guilty is the equivalent of CST, and thus, conversely, if a defendant is incompetent to submit a plea, it would seem that under *Godinez* the defendant must also be IST and the trial should not begin until it is affirmatively established the defendant is CST. Arguably the better option is for the judge to suspend the proceedings once the defendant is found to be incompetent to enter a plea and order the defendant into treatment until the defendant's competence to enter a plea is restored, just as the judge would if the defendant had been found IST.

Competence to Waive the Right to Counsel

Criminal defendants have a right to be represented by an attorney under the Sixth and Fourteenth Amendments of the US Constitution. The Sixth Amendment states: "In all criminal prosecutions, the accused shall enjoy the right . . . to have the Assistance of Counsel for his defense."[28] Although this provision gave criminal defendants a right to counsel when facing prosecution in a federal court, it was not until 1963 that the USSC determined that the Fourteenth Amendment extended this right to prosecutions of serious crimes in state courts as well,[29] with serious crimes subsequently interpreted to include any crime that could result in incarceration.[30] These provisions further ensure that if the defendant cannot afford an attorney, one will be provided for the defendant at government expense.[31]

At the same time, as with many constitutional rights (although, as discussed, notably not the right to be CST), defendants can waive their right to an attorney and represent themselves in a criminal proceeding (that is, appear pro se), provided they are not unduly disruptive in doing so.[32] There are many reasons why defendants sometimes waive their right to counsel and represent themselves. They may not fully understand or appreciate what attorneys do and can accomplish. They may distrust attorneys in general. They may be dissatisfied with their attorney's performance thus far. They may have an agenda of their own—including a political motive—that they want to pursue at trial, and either their attorney will not cooperate, or they fear their attorney will not cooperate. They may overestimate their ability to represent themselves. They may be paranoid about the legal system and believe, for example, that their attorney is working in cahoots with the prosecution. These various reasons may, however, reflect the impact of a mental disorder.

When defendants express their desire to represent themselves, the question is not whether they will do a good job of representing themselves; arguably, few defendants will do as good a job as an attorney would, and many are likely to do a poor job of representing themselves. The issue for the trial judge to consider is whether the defendant adequately understands the implications of waiving the right to counsel. In other words, is the defendant competent to waive his or her right to counsel? If competent, then defendants are entitled to represent themselves, although the trial judge will often appoint an attorney to be present and "shadow" the proceedings so that defendants who change their mind about self-representation can turn to the attorney for consultation or permit the attorney to take over the reins without the judge having to order a mistrial. In the case of John Mohammad, a.k.a. the Beltway Sniper, the defendant made his own opening statement, which enabled him to express some personal viewpoints he felt it was important to convey, but soon allowed an appointed "shadow" attorney to represent him for the remainder of the trial.[33]

There have been other well-publicized cases in which a defendant opted for self-representation, but questions were subsequently raised about the defendant's competence to waive the right to counsel. As discussed earlier, Ted Kaczynski, a.k.a. the Unabomber, sought to represent himself.[34] Colin Ferguson, a.k.a. the Long Island Rail Road Shooter, fired his counsel on the eve of trial and represented himself in a performance that news reporters at the trial described as bizarre and surreal.[35] Zacarias Moussaoui, a.k.a. the Twentieth 9/11 Hijacker, was found competent to waive his right to counsel, then used a pretrial hearing to present a fifty-minute diatribe calling for the "destruction of America," and during the trial insulted and derided the judge and claimed that he, Moussaoui, was part of another Al-Qaeda plot. Moussaoui was ultimately convicted and given a life sentence.[36]

Clearly, a defendant's decision to self-represent is an important one. A criminal trial and its associated procedures and maneuvers are very complex. Defendants representing themselves must know more than just how to put together a trial defense, although that alone is quite challenging. They must know, for example, when and how to plea bargain; determine whether to request a jury trial and, if they do, know how best to select a jury; anticipate the prosecution's trial strategy, identify their own strategy, decide what points they will emphasize, and how to successfully make those points; understand what it means to make a motion, when and how to do so, and how to respond to a motion made by the prosecution; know how to compose and present opening and closing arguments; know how to discover relevant information and get it admitted into evidence; know when and how to object to and argue against the admission of evidence the prosecution seeks to introduce; know how to obtain the assistance of an expert witness, along with knowing what makes someone qualified to testify as an expert and how to examine or cross-examine an expert; know how to call and examine witnesses in general, as well as how to cross-examine the prosecution's witnesses; know how to prepare jury instructions if it is a jury trial; and know how to preserve issues for appeal and how to pursue an appeal if needed. The challenge of these tasks is magnified by the fact that decisions must be made under the stress of trial and during the rapid developments that often mark the course of a trial. For a defendant who is incarcerated at the time, the difficulty of conducting the trial is compounded even more.

Applicable Standards

The test employed for ascertaining whether defendants are competent to waive their right to counsel is whether the waiver is knowingly, voluntarily, and intelligently made[37]—the same terms used to judge the competence of defendants to waive their *Miranda* rights and make a confession, and a test that closely parallels the standard for ascertaining a defendant's competence to plead guilty. It can be argued that a higher level of competence should be required for a defendant to waive his or her right to counsel than for a defendant to be determined CST, given that defendants incorrectly determined to be CST generally still have their attorney to assist them at trial and to question their CST again later in the trial, whereas defendants found competent to waive their right to counsel conduct their trial without the assistance of counsel.

In *Godinez v. Moran* (1993), discussed above, the USSC was unwilling to make this fine a distinction in determining a defendant's competence to waive the right to counsel. The Court rejected the argument that a higher level of "knowing" was needed for this waiver than for CST and overruled the Ninth Circuit's use of a "rational choice" test for this determination. The Court determined that this waiver was no different from a defendant's waiver of other constitutional rights, in essence, saying again that "competence is competence" regardless of the context. Thus, the Court ruled that the competence of defendants to waive their right to an attorney was subsumed within the CST standard, and that if a defendant has been found to be CST, there is no constitutional requirement that it be further established that the defendant is also competent to waive the right to counsel. A dissenting opinion asserted that CST addresses only a defendant's ability to assist his or her attorney; acting as one's own attorney necessitates a higher level of competence and a more stringent test.

It is worth noting that—here as well—states are free under the US Constitution to adopt a more stringent and protective test when examining whether criminal defendants are competent to waive their right to the assistance of an attorney, as well as whether they are competent to represent themselves. For example, California trial judges must assess whether defendants have adequate ability to lawyer their case, or at least can recognize any deficiencies that will impair their ability to self-represent.[38] In contrast, in Virginia a defendant's ability to self-represent is to be considered, but the defendant's competence to self-represent need not be explicitly established.[39]

Procedures for Determining Whether a Criminal Defendant Is Competent to Waive the Right to Counsel

States are also free to adopt their own procedures for determining whether defendants are competent to waive their right to an attorney and self-represent, although few have done so, perhaps because of the infrequency with which this question arises and the USSC's directive that this issue can be subsumed within a CST evaluation. In Virginia, for example, no statutory proceeding has been established for evaluating a defendant's competence to waive the right to an attorney. As may happen in conjunction with a competence to plead guilty determination, a trial judge asked to appraise a defendant's competence to waive the right to an attorney may simply order a CST evaluation pursuant to the court's inherent authority to take those steps necessary to conduct a fair and just trial. In California, in a slight variation, once a "doubt" as to the defendant's CST has been declared by the trial judge, the judge cannot address a defendant's request to self-represent unless and until the defendant has been deemed CST.[40]

A mental health professional evaluating a defendant's competence to waive the right to an attorney and self-represent should examine the defendant's understanding of (a) the right to counsel, and (b) the consequences if this right is waived, as well as whether the defendant is waiving this right voluntarily. In addition, just as was the case regarding defendants' competence to plead guilty discussed above, mental health professionals conducting CST evaluations should recognize that their assessment may also be used to establish whether a defendant is competent to waive the right to an attorney, and thus they should specifically address this issue in their evaluation and incorporate any related findings in their report if there is an indication this issue may arise.

Issues regarding defendants' competence to waive their right to an attorney typically will be addressed at a pretrial hearing, although on occasion defendants will attempt to "fire" their attorney midway through the trial. At this hearing the judge will determine the validity of a defendant's waiver and should caution the defendant regarding the hazards of self-representation. If the waiver is accepted, the judge may order the presence throughout the trial of a "stand-by" counsel who is prepared to assume the role of defendant's attorney should the defendant change his or her mind or if the defendant's mental state deteriorates and/or his or her behavior becomes disruptive to the point that a fair and just trial cannot be conducted.

Competence to Self-Represent

Indiana v. Edwards *(2008)*

In *Indiana v. Edwards* (2008), the USSC ruled on the related matter of a defendant's competence to self-represent. After Ahmad Edwards was discovered trying to steal a pair of shoes from a department store, drew a gun, fired at a store security officer, and wounded a bystander, he was arrested and charged with attempted murder as well as a series of lesser offenses.

Five months later, Edwards's court-appointed attorney asked for a psychiatric evaluation of the defendant. The judge ultimately found Edwards IST and committed him to a state hospital. Seven months after hospitalization, doctors determined Edwards had improved to the point that he was now CST. Several months later, Edwards's lawyer asked for another psychiatric evaluation. Following another hearing, the judge determined that although Edwards suffered from mental illness, he was CST. After another seven months, but still before trial, Edwards's counsel sought yet another psychiatric evaluation. The judge held a third hearing at which expert testimony was provided and determined that Edwards was now IST and recommitted him to the state hospital. Eight months after that, the hospital reported Edwards's condition had improved and he was now CST.

One year later, Edwards's trial began. Just before trial, however, Edwards requested that he be allowed to represent himself. He also asked for a continuance, which he said he needed to proceed pro se. The judge refused Edwards's request for a continuance, so Edwards had his attorney represent him at trial. At the close of the trial, a jury convicted him of criminal recklessness and theft, but failed to reach a verdict on the charges of attempted murder and battery.

The prosecutor decided to retry Edwards on the attempted murder and battery charges. Just before the retrial, Edwards once again stated that he wanted to represent himself. Referring to the lengthy record of psychiatric reports, the judge noted Edwards still suffered from schizophrenia and concluded he was CST but not competent to represent himself. At the retrial, Edwards was again represented by counsel and the jury in this trial convicted him on both of the remaining charges. On appeal, Edwards argued that the trial court's refusal to let him represent himself deprived him of his constitutional right to self-representation.

The USSC began its review of this case by observing that ordinarily an attorney cannot be forced on a criminal defendant. It also noted, however, that the right of self-representation is not absolute and can be denied if the defendant is disorderly, disruptive, or disrespectful. It further determined that its ruling in *Godinez* did not apply here as this case focused on a defendant's competence to represent himself, not a defendant's competence to waive the right to counsel.

The Court also observed that the defendant's mental condition in this case fell in the "gray area" between the constitutional requirement set forth in *Dusky* for being CST and the somewhat higher standard that measures a defendant's capacity to conduct trial proceedings. Thus, a defendant's mental status may satisfy the test in *Dusky* but the defendant may still be unable to carry out the tasks associated with conducting a trial. As a result, the Court concluded, a different standard is needed to assess a defendant's competence to conduct a trial.

In determining this standard, the Court emphasized that mental illness is not a "unitary concept," but rather varies in degree, can change over time, and can interfere with an individual's functioning at different times in different ways, with the history of Edwards's case illustrating "the complexity of the problem." The Court also expressed its concern that allowing a defendant who lacks the mental capacity to self-represent to do so can create a humiliating spectacle; can undercut the most basic of the Constitution's criminal law objectives, namely, ensuring a fair trial; and does not affirm the dignity that is purportedly associated with allowing a defendant to represent oneself. Finally, the Court contended that trials must not only be fair, but must also appear to be fair to those who observe them, and a trial will not appear to be fair when the self-representing defendant lacks the capacity to do so. In support of its position, the Court cited a ruling it issued over fifty years earlier in which it said: "No trial can be fair that leaves the defense to a man who is insane, unaided by counsel, and who by reason of his mental condition stands helpless and alone before the court."[41]

Although the *Dusky* standard can sometimes prevent such aberrations, the Court reasoned that it will not always suffice in light of the different capacities needed to proceed to trial without counsel, and that a more fine-tuned test may be required. Accordingly, the Court ruled that "the Constitution permits States to insist upon representation by counsel for those [CST] under *Dusky* but who still suffer from severe mental illness to the point where they are not competent to conduct trial proceedings by themselves."[42] The Court refrained from adopting a specific standard, but it did conclude that to ensure a fair trial, it may be appropriate to permit trial judges to make this determination as they may be best positioned to assess whether defendants are experiencing a severe mental illness that leaves them incompetent to represent themselves.

The two justices who dissented objected to what they characterized as the majority's paternalistic approach. They argued that the majority's approach permits a state to strip a defendant with a mental illness of the right to self-represent if the trial judge merely concludes that the trial will be unfair to the defendant as a result, but contended that this inappropriately overrides defendants' right to make their own case at trial—a right long understood as essential to a fair trial. They took the position that a defendant who is mentally ill but CST and who knowingly and voluntarily elects to proceed pro se does receive a fair trial that comports with the Fourteenth Amendment and due process, and that the right to proceed pro se should be protected even if doing so may be detrimental to the defendant's case. They asserted that it is wrong to selectively disregard rights as the majority was doing, and added that the real dignity at stake here is the supreme human dignity of being the master of one's fate and making decisions for oneself. Furthermore, they viewed the majority's holding as "extraordinarily vague" in that it did not establish a standard for assessing the competence to self-represent. The dissent maintained that the trial judges charged with making this determination "will have every incentive to make their lives easier" by avoiding "the painful necessity of deciphering" the defendant's words and actions and will instead simply appoint "knowledgeable and literate counsel." The dissent further noted that the majority's ruling did not even have the advantage of being "politically correct" as it carved out individuals with a mental illness from all other defendants who want to appear pro se, treating them differently and, in the dissent's view, unfairly.

ANALYSIS OF *EDWARDS*

This case is noteworthy in that for the first time the USSC made the presence of a mental disorder a factor to be directly considered in ascertaining a criminal defendant's competence at trial. Beginning with *Dusky*, the USSC seemed to have been scrupulously avoiding explicitly incorporating the presence or absence of a mental disorder and its impact on a defendant's thinking and behavior in its tests for assessing the trial-related competence of criminal defendants. Instead, the Court employed functional standards that could be readily applied by judges and jurors who are not experts on mental disorders and their impact. Although mental health professionals are routinely employed to evaluate the trial-related competencies of criminal defendants, their reports and testimony have been expected not to focus on psychiatric diagnoses and assessments, but to be "translated" to address specified trial-related functions that defendants are expected to be capable of carrying out if they are to be considered competent. Thus, the final decision has been left to the presiding judge (or in some cases a jury) and is not to be made by the mental health professional. However, as the dissent points out, *Indiana v. Edwards* (2008) for the first time embraces a competency analysis that specifically examines whether a defendant has a mental disorder and, if so, what impact it is expected to have on the defendant's capacity to adequately self-represent. Insofar as this is now a diagnostic question rather than a functional test, the mental health professional assumes a much more pivotal role in these determinations.

A second unique feature of this case is its focus on the future competence of criminal defendants. Prior USSC rulings regarding competency evaluations addressed criminal defendants' past or present functional capacity. *Edwards*—with its attention to how well defendants will be able to represent themselves at trial—necessitates a prospective analysis regarding defendants' future capacity. This is a much more challenging determination as it is generally harder to anticipate and assess future human conduct, particularly when attempting to project the relatively unpredictable behavior of an individual with a mental disorder. What further complicates this analysis is that a much wider range of actions, behavior, and decisions are subsumed within the broad-ranging evaluation of a defendant's competence to conduct a trial than when evaluating a defendant's competence to enter a guilty plea, to waive one's *Miranda* rights, or to waive the right to counsel.

A third noteworthy aspect is that in *Edwards* the USSC affords trial judges extensive discretion in determining the competence of defendants to represent themselves. In prior competence-related rulings the USSC had established specific standards to which trial judges were expected to strictly adhere, perhaps because of a fear that allowing judges to decide competence on a case-by-case basis would introduce too much variation, inconsistency, and bias, and not sufficiently protect the rights of criminal defendants, particularly those with a mental disorder. It may be that these rulings occurred during an era when there was some concern about the professionalism of trial judges, the stereotypes that might influence them, and the few checks that curbed their authority. It was also an era when the vulnerability and exploitation of individuals with a mental disorder were increasingly being recognized. In contrast, the USSC in *Edwards* may have concluded that the variations in the manifestations and impact of mental disorders required that the appraisal of a criminal defendant's trial-related competence be assigned to a neutral party with extensive experience and understanding of trial procedures and activities, as well as the capacities needed to perform them, and someone who has an opportunity to dispassionately observe the defendant, namely, the trial judge. Needless to say, someone who has great respect for and faith in trial judges, which tended to be the case among the members of the Court when *Edwards* was decided, would be expected to endorse such a position.[43]

A final consideration is whether the ruling in *Indiana v. Edwards* (2008) will at some point impact or trigger a reanalysis of any of the prior rulings regarding trial-related competency and the standards employed. For example, the USSC might ultimately reject its ruling in *Godinez v. Moran* (1993) that effectively held that competency is competency is competency, and devise separate tests and standards for the various trial-related competencies. Alternatively, the USSC could instead abandon its effort to craft different approaches for these various competencies and move instead toward a "one-test-fits-all" approach that interjects a greater role for trial judges as the gate-keeper for these matters. Or the USSC might instead conclude that these determinations are beyond the ken of judges and jurors and designate a greater role for mental health experts in resolving these controversies. Or the USSC might even decide that these are matters best left to the states to determine through their legislatures and courts and empower them to establish their own standards, rules, and procedures for doing so.

Competence to Testify

A final criminal trial–related competency issue that may be raised is whether a witness, including the defendant, is competent to testify. This competence is considered critical if courts are to fulfill their truth-seeking role. All individuals who provide testimony during a trial are required to take an oath that the testimony they are providing is truthful. If a witness is not competent to testify, the offered testimony may not be accurate, which in turn can skew verdicts and the judicial process.

There are various capacities that a witness must possess to provide reliable testimony and that can be diminished by a mental disorder. For example, a witness must be able to observe events accurately, but a mental disorder can distort these observations. A witness must be able to recall these observations, but a mental disorder can alter or impede related memories. Witnesses must be able to communicate their observations in the courtroom, but a mental disorder can adversely affect their efforts to communicate with others, with speech rendered imprecise or garbled, if forthcoming at all. Further, witnesses must be able to intelligently frame answers to questions asked of them in the courtroom, but a mental disorder can hinder their ability to do so. A witness must understand the oath to speak truthfully and adhere to that oath, but a mental disorder may cloud, warp, or override that understanding and result in a failure to adhere to this duty in full or in part.

Applicable Standards

It should be noted, however, that the law typically sets no minimum age to serve as a witness.[44] If a young child can testify, the basic competency standard is obviously relatively low. If a witness has a general ability to observe and recall events, can answer questions and provide testimony in a generally coherent manner, and can promise relatively reliably to provide truthful testimony, the witness will typically be deemed competent to provide testimony.

Because of the Fifth Amendment right to remain silent, a criminal defendant is not required to provide testimony. If the defendant waives this right, however, and does provide testimony, the same competency criteria that apply to witnesses in general will apply to the defendant. Because of the negative perceptions many individuals, including jurors and judges, have about individuals with a mental disorder, if the defendant is represented by an attorney and the defendant has a mental disorder that is likely to be apparent during the course of his or her testimony, the defendant's attorney may prefer that the defendant not testify. At the same time, such defendants may be eager to have their "day in court" and testify, in which case a dispute with their attorney over whether they should take the stand could ensue. Indeed, this is sometimes the reason for defendants "firing" their attorney and seeking to appear before the court pro se.

Neither the USSC nor state courts in general have articulated a standard to be employed when ascertaining whether a witness has the requisite mental competence to provide testimony. Trial judges generally retain the discretion, albeit exercised infrequently, to exclude a witness who lacks the requisite mental capacity to testify.[45] With regard to criminal defendants, if they are CST, they will generally be considered competent to provide testimony, notwithstanding that the functional capacities assessed in conjunction with the *Dusky* CST standard arguably have little connection to the capacities needed to be found competent to testify.

Furthermore, it can be argued that the standard should be higher for establishing the competence of a criminal defendant to testify than for CST, as defendants incorrectly found to be CST can still rely upon their attorneys to represent them. With regard to competence to testify, in contrast, under the adversarial system employed in American courts the judge or jury can base their decisions only on what they hear at trial and if they are given inaccurate information, they may well decide a case incorrectly. Nonetheless, under the *Godinez* competency-is-competency approach, and the *Edwards* leave-it-to-the-trial-judge-to-decide approach, it is probably relatively unlikely that a standard more demanding than the *Dusky* CST test will be imposed to assess a defendant's competence to testify.

Procedures for Determining Whether a Criminal Defendant Is Competent to Testify

With the USSC silent on the matter, the states are relatively free to establish their own procedures to determine a prospective witness's competence to testify, including that of the criminal defendant, although they may also choose not to do so. In general, separate procedures for evaluating this competence have not been established. Such an evaluation will generally be triggered after the prosecution or the defense calls a witness to the stand and the other side objects to the proposed testimony. Trial judges, likely invoking their inherent authority to do so, may order the equivalent of a CST evaluation, particularly if the challenged witness is the defendant, but direct the evaluator to address instead the proposed witness' competence to testify.[46] Alternatively, if the proposed witness is a child and one of the parties objects that the child lacks the competence to testify, the judge may order a sidebar or take the child into the judge's chambers, interact with the child in the presence of the attorneys, and based on this interaction, determine whether the child is competent to testify.[47] A similar approach may be employed for an adult witness whose competence to testify is challenged.

Conclusion

Unraveling and deciphering all of the criminal trial–related competency threads can be a challenge. Until relatively recently, the USSC seemed to embrace a competency-is-competency approach that avoided making fine distinctions in evaluating the different trial-related competencies, notwithstanding that they arguably address different functional capacities. In part, this approach may have reflected the Court's initial uncertainty regarding the nature and impact of mental disorders on criminal defendants' behavior and cognition, and a reluctance to plunge too deeply into these murky waters. Ironically, as our understanding of mental disorders grows, we begin to appreciate even more our limited ability to predict their effects. This, in turn, may have further encouraged the Court to refrain from articulating detailed constitutional principles and standards in this realm, and to defer instead to the observations and expertise of trial judges and the mental health professionals who can provide these judges with individualized evaluations of the competency of the criminal defendants involved.

As described in the following chapters, a similar reluctance may explain the largely "hands-off" approach the USSC has taken to the various states' approaches to the insanity defense—arguably the most challenging and generally the most notorious set of mental health–related criminal cases. At the same time, as society's awareness of and understanding of the impact of mental disorders on criminal defendants continues to grow, the USSC and other courts may at some point shed some of their reluctance to intervene in these matters and become more willing to establish guiding principles and rules.

The Insanity Defense

If you did a general survey asking respondents to describe defendants who have raised the insanity defense, chances are pretty good that their depiction would resemble or incorporate one of the following, at least until the next seemingly inexplicable crime occurred.

CHARLES ("CHARLIE") MANSON: a wild-eyed cult leader who during the summer of 1969 directed a series of killings in Southern California ostensibly to trigger an impending apocalypse; the spree included the invasion of the home of the well-known movie director Roman Polanski and resulted in the death of his eight-months pregnant wife, actress Sharon Tate.

DAVID BERKOWITZ: responsible for a series of murders, in which all the victims were women, in the 1970s in New York City, mostly in Central Park; in a bizarre and chilling letter left at the scene of one of the attacks, addressed to an officer who was part of a task force organized to catch him, and subsequently leaked to the press, Berkowitz referred to himself as the "Son of Sam," which quickly became how he was identified in the ongoing media frenzy.

MARK DAVID CHAPMAN: a born-again Christian who had been an obsessed fan of John Lennon, but came to resent him after Lennon said The Beatles "were more popular than Jesus"; in 1980, Chapman shot and killed Lennon as he and Yoko Ono walked by Chapman outside the entrance to the Central Park West building in Manhattan where they lived on their way home from a recording session; Chapman remained at the scene of the shooting reading his copy of J. D. Salinger's *Catcher in the Rye* until police officers arrived and arrested him.

JOHN HINCKLEY JR.: attempted to assassinate US President Ronald Reagan in 1981 as Reagan left a conference at a hotel in Washington, DC, in an effort to impress a famous actress with whom he was obsessed.

JEFFREY DAHMER: killed seventeen young men in Milwaukee between 1978 and 1991, luring most of them to his apartment, and then drugging and sexually assaulting them before murdering them; following his arrest, decaying bodies in acid vats, severed heads in a refrigerator, and an altar of candles and human skulls were discovered in his apartment.

ANDREA YATES: in 2001 methodically drowned her five children, ranging in ages from six months to seven years, one by one in a bathtub at their home in a Houston suburb after her husband left for work; she had experienced a severe case of recurrent postpartum depression following each of the last two births; after killing the fifth child, she called 911 and her husband; when interrogated shortly afterward by a police officer, she explained she had drowned the children to save them from damnation for her failure to raise them properly.

LEE BOYD MALVO: the younger of the so-called Beltway Snipers, who in the fall of 2002 paralyzed the Washington, DC, area for three weeks, as they seemingly at random killed ten people and injured three others; Malvo, at the age of fourteen, had been taken under the wing of John Allen Muhammed, a former member of the US Army, who systematically controlled and indoctrinated Malvo to help him execute a grandiose ransom scheme that he believed would enable him to establish an independent nation; three years later, he and Malvo, now age seventeen, would take turns firing a high-powered rifle through a small hole bored into the lid of the trunk of Muhammed's car, while the other kept lookout from the steering wheel so that they could drive away quickly and undetected from the scenes of their shootings.

* * *

These notorious cases were closely watched and have shaped the public's perception of the insanity defense, its iterations, and mental disorders in general. They have also guided the debate regarding the insanity defense and related calls for its reform or abolition, even though they were more the exception than the norm for how these cases proceed.

As noted earlier, individuals with a mental disorder tend to be no more violent than the general population, with the possible exception of when a mental illness and substance abuse co-occur. In addition, defendants who raise an insanity defense are a highly diverse group of individuals, whom society, including the criminal justice system, struggles to systematically address. Evaluations of these defendants tend to be the "Sex, Drugs, and

Rock-n-Roll" of forensic mental health professionals' work since they receive a great deal of attention and scrutiny. In this and other ways, such cases are very different from those in which questions are raised about a defendant's CST or any of the other trial-related competency determinations, although the overarching challenge of appraising the impact of a mental disorder on a defendant's cognition and behavior remains.

Opinions regarding insanity defendants tend to gravitate to one of two poles. Some are relatively sympathetic toward these individuals, seeing their lives—through no fault of their own—turned upside down by mental disorders that leave them at times unable to control or direct their actions (see Andrea Yates). Those who embrace this view are likely to believe these defendants should be absolved of criminal responsibility, or at least not punished as harshly, for actions resulting from their mental disorder. At the other end of the spectrum are those who are repulsed and enraged by these defendants; they see them as more threatening and dangerous than criminal defendants in general. Those who embrace this perspective are likely to assert that these defendants should not only be held criminally responsible, but also be more readily convicted and severely punished. Trying to reconcile these two divergent views when attempting to adopt and implement relevant laws, rules, and procedures has long flummoxed the criminal justice system.

Early History of the Insanity Defense

The claim that impaired mental status should absolve an individual of legal responsibility for committing a criminal act is not a new concept. Indeed, it has existed since the very first legal codes were established, with the various articulations of this concept paralleling current applications of the defense.[1]

The insanity defense can be initially traced to the sixth century BCE, when Hebrew scripture likened the behavior of an individual with a mental disorder to that of a child. Both were considered amoral in that they were unable to weigh the moral implications and consequences of their behavior, and thus it was argued that just as we do not punish a young child for actions that would be considered criminal if committed by an adult, similarly, we should not punish an individual with a serious mental disorder.[2]

Two centuries later, Aristotle wrote: "The incontinent man acts with appetite, but not with choice." He described mental illness as an inherent craving, an uncontrollable drive, and saw people with a mental disorder as beast-like.[3]

The early Roman view was that individuals should not be held responsible for criminal behavior if they did not intend to commit a specific harmful act; without intent, the person was not seen as morally blameworthy.[4]

Pursuant to the Code of Justinian, a summation of all Roman law sponsored by the Byzantine Emperor Justinian I and completed circa 529 CE, insane individuals were distinguished from children. Accordingly, "[A child] is excused by the innocence of his intentions, [the insane] by the fact of his misfortune." Thus, insane individuals were absolved of responsibility not because of their innocence (as Hebrew scripture suggested), but because of their lack of insight and moral development. Such individuals were considered to be driven by their mental illness and perceived to be engaging in behavior that they did not cause and thus were not responsible for.[5]

These various articulations all shared a certain degree of sympathy for individuals with a mental disorder and a willingness to excuse their criminal acts. Essentially, they considered the criminal acts of an individual with a mental disorder to be the result of (a) a lack of insight (like a child), (b) a lack of control (like a beast), (c) a lack of intent, or (d) the mental disorder, per se.

Early History of the Insanity Defense in England

The insanity defense also has a lengthy history in England, where the concepts described above were adopted and refined.[6] Primarily, however, English courts tended to focus on either the cognitive or the volitional impairment of the defendant.

In 1200 CE, an English court first used the phrase "wild beast" to describe a criminal defendant with a mental disorder. During this era, however, the defendant who was insane at the time of the crime could be pardoned only by the ruling king or queen, rather than acquitted by a judge, as is currently the case. The first recorded case of outright acquittal by a judge in England was in 1505.

The insanity doctrine was developed more fully in 1724 in *Rex v. Arnold*. This case involved a known "madman" who killed a nobleman. It was determined he had experienced a delusion that "bewitched him" and "totally deprived him of his understanding and memory." It was also found that "[he] doth not know what he is doing, no more than an infant, brute, or wild beast." The focus became whether defendants could distinguish between doing good and evil, as well as understand what they did.[7]

In 1769, William Blackstone, perhaps the most famous English legal scholar of all time and author of *Commentaries on the Laws of England*, a four-volume treatise designed to provide a complete overview of English law, wrote with regard to the insanity defense: "Where there is no discernment, there is no choice; and where there is no choice, there can be no act of the will."[8]

In 1800, in a closely watched case, James Hadfield (sometimes spelled "Hatfield") was placed on trial following his attempted assassination of George III, the king of England.[9] Hadfield had fired a shot at the king as the king and queen were standing for the playing of the national anthem in their box at the Royal Theatre. Hadfield was a former British soldier who had been severely injured in battle when struck eight times on the head by a sabre and then captured by the French. After eventually returning to England, he came to believe the Second Coming of Jesus would be advanced if he was killed by the British government. He thus resolved to attempt to assassinate the king and thereby bring about his own execution. At his trial, Hadfield entered a plea of insanity. The test employed required that it be established that the defendant's action was the offspring of a delusion.[10] After two surgeons and a physician testified that his delusions were the result of his earlier head injuries, Hadfield was acquitted by reason of insanity. At that time in England, however, the disposition of defendants acquitted by reason of insanity was uncertain. Fearing that Hadfield might be released, Parliament quickly passed the Criminal Lunatics Act of 1800 to provide for the indefinite detention of insanity acquittees. Hadfield was subsequently placed for the rest of his life in Bethlem Royal Hospital, which later became Bethlehem Hospital (or Bedlam, as it was more widely known).

Forty years later, Edward Oxford was the first of eight people who tried to assassinate Queen Victoria, who ruled over England at the time. At his trial, an insanity defense was raised, along with testimony that

Oxford had always seemed of unsound mind.[11] Furthermore, both his father and grandfather were alcoholics and had exhibited signs of mental illness. This probably carried considerable weight with the jury as alcohol and heredity were widely viewed as causal factors of insanity at the time. Under the insanity test employed, defendants were to be acquitted if they could not resist the impulse to commit a crime because of a mental disorder.[12] The jury found Oxford to be not guilty by reason of insanity and acquitted him accordingly. He was sent to the Bethlehem Hospital, where he remained for the next twenty-four years and was described as a model patient. Queen Victoria was certain that Oxford had been sane at the time of the crime, which explains in part why she was so outraged at the verdict issued in the following case.

Daniel M'Naghten

Until 1843, no appellate court in England (or the United States) had stated the governing standard for the insanity defense. That changed with the Daniel M'Naghten case, probably still the most well-known insanity case ever decided. It also marked the emergence of the use of the science of human behavior in criminal proceedings, which coincided with the 1838 publication of *A Treatise on the Medical Jurisprudence of Insanity* by Isaac Ray, an American physician and one of the founders of the discipline of forensic psychiatry. This publication served as an authoritative text in the field for many years.

M'Naghten, a Scottish woodcutter (or woodturner, depending on the account), was born in 1813 and ran a successful business in Glasgow from 1835 until he sold it in December of 1840. Over time his political views became increasingly radical, and in 1842 he complained to those around him that he was being persecuted by the Tories, the political party then in power, and followed by their spies. Believing him to be deluded, no one took him seriously. In 1843, he traveled to London, where he attempted to shoot Sir Robert Peel, then prime minister and the leader of the Tories, at close range from behind, but instead shot Edward Drummond, Peel's private secretary, whom M'Naghten mistook for Peel. Drummond died five days later.

Appearing in court the morning after the shooting, M'Naghten made the following statement:

The Tories in my native city have compelled me to do this. They follow and persecute me wherever I go, and have entirely destroyed my peace of mind. . . . I cannot sleep at night in consequence of the course they pursue towards me. . . . They have accused me of crimes of which I am not guilty; they do everything in their power to harass and persecute me; in fact they wish to murder me.[13]

This was effectively M'Naghten's only statement as he did not testify at his trial. M'Naghten was defended by some of the highest profile attorneys in England at the time, perhaps, it has been suggested, because they opposed the Tories, or perhaps, it has also been contended, because of an emerging general interest in the interface between law and medicine and its potential impact on the use of the insanity defense in the criminal justice system. At the beginning of the trial, M'Naghten was asked to plead guilty or not guilty, to which he responded, "I was driven to desperation by persecution." When pressed further, he is reported to have said, "I am guilty of firing," which was registered as a not guilty plea. At trial, both sides agreed that M'Naghten suffered from monomania and delusions of persecution. The prosecution argued that despite his "partial insanity," M'Naghten could distinguish right from wrong and knew he was committing a crime. Defense counsel, quoting extensively from Isaac Ray, contended that M'Naghten's delusions led to a breakdown of his moral sense and self-control, which left him no longer a responsible being. The defense also called a series of medical experts who testified that M'Naghten's delusions had deprived him of control over his actions. The bench directed the jury to focus on whether the defendant (a) knew that what he was doing was wicked and wrong, and (b) was capable of distinguishing right and wrong. The jury found M'Naghten not guilty by reason of insanity.

The public was outraged at the verdict, as was Queen Victoria, who had been the target of three assassination attempts by then. The verdict generated the following cynical response from *The Times*, the leading newspaper in England:

> Ye people of England exult and be glad
> For ye're now at the will of the merciless mad
> Why say ye that but three authorities reign

Crown, Commons and Lords?—You omit the insane.
They're a privileged class whom no statute controls,
And their murderous charter exists in their souls.
Do they wish to spill blood—they have only to play
A few pranks—get asylum'd a month and a day
Then Heigh! to escape from the mad doctor's keys
And to pistol or stab whomsoever they please.[14]

Two days after the verdict, Queen Victoria called on the House of Lords to review the legal test for insanity that had been employed. The House of Lords determined the trial court had basically gotten the test right.

However, it may have been a relatively easy case for the jury to decide. The Crown (that is, the prosecution) did not present any expert testimony to rebut the defendant's six experts. After hearing the defendant's experts, the presiding judge asked the prosecutor if he had any counter medical evidence to offer, and, if he did not, he would have to stop the trial. After the prosecutor said he did not, the trial was essentially over. The prosecutor gave a short summary and told the jury that he could not press for a verdict but that it was up to the jury to decide. The judge told the jury that the medical evidence was all on one side and that a review of the evidence was unnecessary, although it was still up to the jury to decide whether the defendant could distinguish between right and wrong. The judge asked the jury if it required more information, to which the foreman of the jury said no. Without retiring, the jury informally and briefly huddled in the courtroom, and then the foreman announced the jury's verdict of not guilty by reason of insanity.

After the trial, M'Naghten was transferred to Bethlehem Hospital, where members of the public could take tours to see the "lunatics" for a penny. M'Naghten spent twenty-one years there, after which he was transferred to the newly opened Broadmoor Asylum for the Criminally Insane, where he died a year later at the age of fifty-two of apparent heart failure.

Main Threads of the Insanity Defense

The three primary threads that predominated in the various articulations of the insanity defense discussed thus far and that continue to resonate today are defendants' purported (a) lack of insight, (b) lack of intent, or (c) lack of control as a result of their mental disorder. Each necessitates a somewhat different focus, approach, and applicable standard.

When an insanity test targets criminal defendants' purported *lack of insight* at the time of the criminal act, the general inference is that to qualify for the defense the thoughts and behavior of the defendant must be child-like as a result of a mental disorder. In other words, this test focuses on defendants' impulsivity and inability to anticipate the consequences of their actions, with the question asked being whether they lack the cognitive understanding of their actions and their impact usually found in adults (that is, they lack the requisite *cognitive capacity*). If their resulting behavior is comparable to that of a child, this analogy tends to envelop their actions in an air of innocence and generates a relatively sympathetic portrait. It also suggests that, like a child, with proper treatment, care, and guidance they can develop needed insights into and change their behavior, and perhaps someday safely return to the community.[15]

Perhaps the least sympathetic characterization enveloped by an insanity test is when it focuses on criminal defendants' *lack of intent*, meaning that the commission of their criminal act was the result of their mental disorder, with the inference being such defendants lacked the *moral capacity* typically found in adults. These defendants are portrayed as (a) amoral in that they do not have a moral compass or appreciate the wrongfulness of their actions; (b) automatons, whose robot-like actions are directed by an "outside" or "higher" power; or (c) highly devious and calculating, unbounded by the conscience that curbs antisocial behavior in most humans. This test tends to portray qualifying defendants as unsympathetic and frightening in that they are perceived to be relatively immune to efforts to change their thoughts and behavior and likely to repeat their criminal activities in the future.[16]

A middle ground, associated with the third set of insanity tests, examines criminal defendants' supposed *lack of control* over their behavior due to their mental disorder, the inference being that they are like a wild beast, driven by primitive, irresistible impulses (that is, they lack *volitional capacity*). On the one hand, they may be seen as quite frightening in that their fury and rage can be set off by relatively trivial and irrelevant circumstances, making them seem quite unpredictable and destructive. There may, however, also be a certain level of sympathy for them insofar as their behavior, like that of a wild animal, is considered to be driven by primitive instincts beyond their control. Views tend to be similarly split regarding their rehabilitation, with some seeing these base instincts always lurking beneath the surface and capable of being unexpectedly triggered at any moment, while others see these individuals as redeemable and, like wild animals, malleable—that is, as individuals who can be successfully guided to temper their instincts and learn to successfully interact with others provided they are kept away from what has triggered their outbursts in the past.[17]

A question that should always be asked is how apt these various perspectives and analogies are. Some might argue that mental disorders comprise a unique category that necessitates a distinct framework when addressing defendants who committed criminal acts as the result of their mental disorder. Others might contend that a suitable approach would be equivalent to what the US Supreme Court (USSC) embraced in *Indiana v. Edwards* (2008) for determining a defendant's competency to self-represent, which essentially leaves decision-making to the discretion of trial judges who have the best opportunity to observe and interact with these defendants. Aided by mental health evaluations, trial judges thus decide each case on its own merits, with few, if any, preestablished principles. Still others may contend that when judges try to ascertain defendants' responsibility for criminal behavior, attempts to parse out the nature of mental disorders and their impact on human behavior are largely futile, will inevitably generate inconsistent and unjust results, and invite manipulation by defendants seeking to avoid responsibility for their actions. On the basis of this reasoning, proponents argue the insanity defense should be abolished.

In the midst of this continuing debate, the following questions remain: (a) What is the most appropriate test for assessing whether a defendant is not guilty by reason of insanity (NGRI)? (b) What are the relevant criteria that should be incorporated in this test and why? and (c) Should the insanity test be jettisoned entirely or does it represent something to which defendants should be entitled to ensure fair and just verdicts?

Current Insanity Defense Doctrine

Under the adversarial system embraced in the United States today, the State, through its criminal prosecutor, has the burden to prove each and every element of a crime beyond a reasonable doubt before it can convict a defendant and impose punishment. The law recognizes two defenses criminal defendants can raise that would entitle them to avoid a criminal conviction even though the prosecution has met its burden of proof.

The first is known as the *justification defense*, pursuant to which defendants effectively acknowledge that they did the acts with which they are charged, but maintain that they had a legally recognized good reason for their actions that absolves them of criminal responsibility. In other words, their actions are not and should not be considered morally wrong and worthy of punishment. This is usually behavior society is willing to see emulated because it benefits society in some way or upholds highly valued principles. Examples include acting in self-defense or in the defense of another or one's property, or acting out of necessity (such as when an emergency arises).

The second is known as the *excuse defense*, which is behavior the law allows because it is not deemed morally blameworthy, usually because there is some extenuating circumstance that leads to the conclusion that the defendant was not responsible for his or her actions. The focus of this defense is the defendant, rather than the defendant's actions. Defendants generally acknowledge that they committed the criminal act but assert that at the time of the act they did not know that they had committed this act or could not help themselves. In the end, the law understands why the defendants acted this way and excuses their behavior, although it is behavior that society does not want others to emulate. Examples include actions that were the product of duress, occurred while the defendant was involuntarily intoxicated, or happened when the defendant was unconscious, such as sleepwalking. The insanity defense is typically assigned to this category.

Rationale for the Insanity Defense

The insanity defense may be the most contentious issue that can be raised during a criminal trial. The rationale for it is generally built upon three premises.

First, it is generally agreed that the criminal justice system should punish only *bad acts*. An action is considered to be "bad" only if it was the product of a defendant's *free will.*

Second, society does not want to punish *morally blameless* people, such as young children or individuals who are acting to defend themselves or their family, who are under the control of someone who is threatening them or their loved ones with harm, or who are subject to some malfunctioning organ, such as the brain, where the malfunction is not self-induced. If the individual is morally blameless, the consensus is the person should not be punished.

Third, unlike CST, criminal responsibility focuses on the defendant's *mental state at the time of the offense.* The law examines defendants' thought-processes at the time of the crime, including whether they were so impaired by a mental disorder that they were not criminally responsible.

If these three premises are met—leading to a finding that a criminal defendant was so impaired by a mental disorder at the time of the offense that he or she was not criminally responsible—then the law should *excuse* the behavior and the individual who committed it.

Opposition to the Insanity Defense

As noted, throughout history and continuing today, there has been considerable opposition to the insanity defense. Several criticisms of it have been voiced.

First, opponents object to letting criminal behavior go unpunished. As part of an "eye-for-an-eye" approach, they contend that those who are responsible for a crime generally must be punished for that crime. Anything less, they further assert, undercuts the deterrent effect of the criminal law in that it sends a message that criminals will not routinely and reliably be punished for their criminal acts, which in turn will encourage more lawless behavior. In addition, they contend that this particular defendant will not be deterred from engaging in future criminal behavior since he or she will not learn that "crime does not pay." Moreover, because the defendant will not be incarcerated, he or she will not be prevented from committing future criminal acts during this time period and the criminal justice system will not have an opportunity to rehabilitate the individual.

A second argument is that another purpose of the criminal justice system is to "compensate" victims of criminal behavior by providing them with a sense of satisfaction and relief that the person who harmed them has been held responsible and punished for his or her actions. When defendants are found to be NGRI, it is contended, their victims cannot attain this sense of moral equilibrium.

Third, there is a wide-spread suspicion that these defendants are "faking" their mental disorder or its effect on their behavior. This concern is particularly likely to arise when a defendant does not have a significant preceding history of a mental disorder, or the disorder has not resulted in similar criminal behavior in the past. As discussed, mental disorders are difficult to assess in general, and it can be even more difficult to determine what impact, if any, a mental disorder had on a person's behavior at some point in the past. Although a well-trained evaluator is always alert for the possibility of malingering, claiming that a mental disorder caused the criminal behavior can be a very convenient way for a defendant to avoid criminal responsibility. Opponents of the insanity defense often believe that many of these defendants are faking their mental disorder or its impact and that attempts to determine malingering are too unreliable to justify the substantial "costs" associated with failing to hold them accountable for their criminal behavior.

A fourth concern is that even if these defendants were experiencing a mental disorder at the time of the offense, they still knew at some level what they were doing or could have done something to avoid or prevent the criminal act. In other words, the impairment was not sufficient to totally destroy their cognitive or volitional capacity, and these defendants simply did not try hard enough to resist the effects of their mental disorder. Alternatively, it is contended that they were aware of the impact their mental disorder tended to have, knew this impact was particularly likely to occur under certain circumstances, and yet knowingly entered a situation where such circumstances were likely to arise. The assertion is also sometimes made that they failed to employ available precautionary measures that could have prevented these events from unfolding, such as taking prescribed medications, not ingesting alcohol or other drugs, or avoiding individuals with whom they had a history of emotional and perhaps violent encounters.

Another criticism argues that assessing mental disorders and their impact on behavior takes the courts and forensic mental health evaluators into such a grey diagnostic domain that there is not sufficient certainty and accuracy associated with these findings to ensure the administration of justice. Courts in general have resisted admitting purported scientific evidence if it is insufficiently valid and reliable, lacks standardized procedures, or is viewed as prejudicial because a jury will give it undue weight. Such evidence is viewed as undercutting the truth-seeking role of the courts and faith in the integrity of the judicial system. For example, in recent years courts have been reluctant to admit the results of polygraph (lie-detector) exams into evidence because of such concerns.[18] Opponents of the insanity defense argue that because the assessments of mental disorders and their impact are insufficiently valid and reliable, the procedures for their evaluation are insufficiently standardized, and the testimony of mental health forensic evaluators is given undue weight, the insanity defense should not be recognized.

Opponents of the insanity defense may also be driven by a more visceral reaction to these defendants. Criminals in general are often seen as acting within relatively understandable and predictable, albeit objectionable, parameters, and thus can be deterred or at least avoided if appropriate measures or steps are taken. Criminals who raise the insanity defense, in contrast, are often viewed as irrational, unpredictable, and uncontrollable individuals who cannot be deterred or avoided, and who may strike anyplace or at any time, with anyone a potential victim. Thus, they may be perceived as more frightening than criminals in general, with the prospect of their being released back into the community considered particularly alarming.

Opponents of the insanity defense also note that the USSC—as will be discussed—has not recognized the insanity defense to be a fundamental component of the due process to which criminal defendants are entitled under the US Constitution.[19] Thus, a state is free to define the insanity defense narrowly, to not recognize the defense, or to abolish it entirely if it currently exists in that jurisdiction. Indeed, four states have abolished the defense: Idaho, Kansas, Montana, and Utah. In addition, there have been legislative efforts to limit the use of mental health experts' testimony in conjunction with these proceedings, although, as will be discussed, the USSC in *Clark* also established that such evidence cannot be excluded entirely if the defense asserts that the defendant's criminal actions can be attributed to a mental disorder.

Myths about the Insanity Defense

At the same time, it should be recognized that this opposition to the insanity defense is often driven by fear and uncertainty, leading to a series of myths about the defense.[20]

The first myth is that the insanity defense is overused, usually by defendants with nothing to lose. However, it is pled relatively infrequently, as it is raised in only one out of a hundred felony cases nationwide, and as low as one in a thousand cases in some states, even though as many as 7 percent of pretrial defendants are experiencing a major mental disorder. Furthermore, it is not very successful when it is raised, since only one of every four cases in which the defense is invoked leads to an NGRI acquittal.

The second myth, driven by media headlines, is that it is used primarily in murder cases. However, only about one out of three cases in which the defense is pursued address the death of a victim.

The third myth is that an insanity defense poses no risk for the defendant. However, defendants who raise it unsuccessfully receive longer sentences on average than comparable defendants who did not (after controlling for the nature of the offense and the demographic characteristics of the defendant).

The fourth myth is that insanity acquittees are quickly released back into the community following their trial. However, these acquittees are held in custody—albeit in a non-penal setting—for an extended period until the State deems it safe for them to return to the community. In one study, only 15 percent of insanity acquittees had been released after eight years, 35 percent were in full custody, and 47 percent were still subject to partial custody. Plus, the more serious the crime, the longer the acquittee tends to be retained in custody.

The fifth myth is that insanity acquittees spend less time in custody than defendants convicted of the same offense. However, they tend to spend twice the amount of time in custody as defendants charged with comparable crimes who were convicted.

The sixth myth is that defendants who plead insanity are usually faking their symptoms. As discussed, the diagnosis and evaluation of mental disorders are indeed challenging, but these defendants usually have a significant psychiatric history, and there is usually a significant concord between their clinical evaluations and the verdicts they receive.

The seventh myth is that most insanity trials feature a "battle of the experts" in which the prosecution and the defense each submit the reports and testimony of their own mental health experts, whose positions are polar opposites of one another. In most trials, however, the two sides stipulate to (that is, agree on) the mental status of the defendant.

The eighth and final myth is that defense attorneys use the insanity defense solely to "beat the rap" and thereby enable defendants to walk out of the courtroom without incurring any consequences. As noted, however, this defense tends not to be very successful; nor is it particularly beneficial for the defendant. Instead, it is often raised to explore and explain the underlying issues of the trial and in the hope that evidence regarding the defendant's mental disorder will be taken into account as a mitigating factor at sentencing, although there is little indication that this is a frequent outcome either.

The Insanity Tests Used Today

In those American jurisdictions that recognize an insanity defense, one of five variations of the insanity test tends to be utilized. It should be noted, however, that there is little indication that the wording of the test has much impact on the outcome of these trials. The more pivotal aspect, as discussed below, seems to be who is assigned the burden of proof, with roughly two-thirds of the states placing the burden on the defendant, who usually must show insanity by a preponderance of the evidence, although the federal government imposes the more demanding clear and convincing evidentiary standard.[21]

The M'Naghten Test

The first three standards discussed here are considered the classic tests because they have been employed for a considerable length of time. The first is derived almost directly from and often employs the same terminology as the *M'Naghten* case decided in England in 1843 and, unsurprisingly, is often referred to as the *M'Naghten test*. Sometimes described as a *cognitive* or "cognitive incapacity" *test*, it asks whether the defendant—at the time of the crime—was suffering from a "mental disease or defect" that resulted in a "defect in reason" that caused the defendant not to know either (a) the nature and quality of the act, or (b) that the act was wrong. In other words, did the defendant, as a result of a mental disorder, not know what he or she was doing at the time of the crime or that what he or she was doing was wrong? Examples used to demonstrate when this test is satisfied include the defendant thought (a) the gun was a banana; (b) the bullet fired from the gun would bounce off the victim because the victim was Superman; (c) it was a grapefruit the defendant was squeezing, not someone's neck; or (d) the victim was a demon or an alien, and thus the defendant did not think that he or she was killing a human being.

One complaint about this test is that it requires the factfinder, whether it be the judge or a jury, to essentially "get inside the head" of the defendant and understand the thinking of someone with a mental disorder, which is a complex and very difficult, perhaps impossible, undertaking. Another complaint is that defendants' cognitive processes may be intact (that is, they knew what they were doing), but their free will was overpowered by their mental disorder, and they effectively lost control of their behavior. Others would say it is less convoluted to just ask whether the mental disorder caused the defendant's behavior. Nonetheless, about half the states use some variation of the *M'Naghten* test, although Arizona and Texas, for example, employ only its second half, which requires that defendants show that because of their mental disorder they did not know that their actions were wrong.

The Irresistible Impulse Test

The second test is often referred to as the *irresistible impulse test*. This is a *volitional test* and attempts to address at least some of the identified shortcomings of the *M'Naghten* test. The cognitive capacity of the defendant is largely irrelevant under this approach, which focuses instead on whether, as a result of a "mental disease or defect," the defendant did not possess a will sufficient to restrain the impulse arising from his or her mental disorder. This is sometimes referred to as the "police officer at the elbow test" in that it effectively asks whether the influence of the mental disorder was so great that the defendant would have committed the criminal act even if apprehension was certain.

A complaint about this test is that it is very difficult to distinguish between an inability to resist and a decision not to resist, with some suggesting it is like trying to distinguish between sunset and dusk. Others complain that many mental disorders do not involve an "impulse," yet the defendant's behavior could still be the result of a mental disorder (such as a major depressive disorder that "paralyzes" self-control), which causes them to lack the requisite volition or free will. Still others contend that the cognitive element remains relevant and that a lack of cognitive capacity should be part of the insanity test. For example, defendants may not have experienced an irresistible impulse generated by a mental disorder but may still have mischaracterized or misunderstood events to such an extent as a result of their disorder that they should not be held responsible for ensuing criminal acts. A related argument is that the volitional analysis under the irresistible impulse test is irrelevant or misguided because most defendants whose criminal actions can and should be attributed to their mental disorder meet the requirements of the cognitive test.

The Product Test

The third test is typically designated the *product test*. More straightforward than the other tests, it simply asks whether a defendant's behavior was a "product" of his or her "mental disease or defect." It was crafted as an alternative to the *M'Naghten* and irresistible impulse tests, which were seen as too restrictive or too complex, or faulted for effectively placing these decisions in the hands of the forensic mental health professionals who evaluate these defendants. Much like the *Dusky* test for CST, the product test attempts to establish a straightforward and relatively basic standard that can be readily applied by judges and juries who do not have mental health expertise.

The product test was first employed by New Hampshire in 1870 and continues to be the governing standard there. As discussed in the next chapter, it was also employed in Washington, DC, beginning in 1954, when it was adopted by the District of Columbia Circuit of the US Court of Appeals in *Durham v. United States* (1954) in a ruling authored by the well-respected jurist David L. Bazelon. In his ruling, Judge Bazelon emphasized that insanity determinations should not be left to mental health expert witnesses who focus on the presence or absence of various psychiatric symptoms. Rather, they should be made by the jury (or the trial judge if the defendant did not request a jury). That is, Bazelon concluded that these decisions fell within the scope of a jury's traditional function to determine moral responsibility and if a defendant's acts "stem from and are the product" of a mental disorder, moral blame does not attach and the defendant should therefore not be found criminally responsible for his or her actions. A series of subsequent appellate rulings tried to clarify the use of this standard, including another ruling authored by Bazelon in *Washington v. United States* (1967). Controversy, however, continued to surround the *Durham rule*, and in *United States v. Brawner* (1972), Bazelon and the DC Circuit abandoned it, replacing it with the formulation devised by the American Law Institute, discussed below, which had been adopted by a majority of the other federal circuit courts.[22]

One of the criticisms levied at the product test is that it does not provide definitions of "product" or "mental disease or defect," and thus determinations under it are seen as lacking sufficient guidance and are viewed by many as being too wide open and variable. Ironically, it has also been criticized for effectively leaving the decisions in these cases in the hands of the evaluating mental health professionals, who inevitably offer their opinions regarding the impact of a mental disorder on a defendant's behavior, with no offsetting factual determination made available to the judge or jury under this standard that can serve as a basis for questioning the evaluator's opinion. Furthermore, the standard has been criticized as subject to misuse, given that someone with an antisocial personality disorder, for example, who feels no moral compunction to adhere to the law and society's other rules as a product of his or her disorder might qualify for this defense, even though most would say such individuals should not be entitled to an insanity defense acquittal.

The ALI/MPC Test

Because of the uncertainty and confusion created by these three "classic" tests for insanity, a national group of experts was assembled by the American Law Institute (ALI) in 1962 and asked to devise a rational and consistent test based on current scientific principles that could be incorporated in the ALI's Model Penal Code (MPC), an influential guide for legislators, judges, and other individuals interested in reforming their jurisdiction's criminal laws. The test they generated contains both a cognitive prong and a volitional prong. Widely referred to as either the *Model Penal Code test* or the *ALI/MPC test*, it states that a defendant should be found NGRI if the defendant, as a result of a mental disease or defect,[23] lacked *substantial capacity* either to (a) *appreciate* the *criminality* (or *wrongfulness*) of his or her conduct, or (b) *conform* his or her conduct to the requirements of the law. This standard introduced five significant changes.

First, it introduced the *substantial capacity* modifier. Previous insanity tests had essentially adopted an "all-or-nothing" approach with regard to the impact or effect of a mental disorder on the defendant's behavior. The ALI/MPC approach views the influence of mental disorders on individuals and their behavior as occurring on a continuum in which virtually no one is completely out of touch with reality (for example, they can still distinguish day from night) or has absolutely no control over their behavior (for instance, they can still scratch an itch). Instead, under the ALI/MPC standard, the law excuses criminal acts when the defendant, as a result of a mental disorder, lacked "substantial" cognitive or volitional capacity, a determination left to the factfinder.

Second, this test replaced the terms "know" or "knew" with *appreciate*. While the *M'Naghten* test focuses on the defendant's ability to *know* right from wrong, proponents of the ALI/MPC approach assert that this is an impractical requirement because it is difficult to establish when someone does or does not "know" something. The better question, they assert, is to ask whether the defendant could "appreciate" that what he or she was doing was wrong or a crime.

Third, the ALI/MPC model rejected the "right from wrong" criterion, which was viewed as too broad and undefined. In its place, jurisdictions are directed under the ALI/MPC standard to employ either the term *criminality* or *wrongfulness*, depending on the approach preferred in that jurisdiction. Thus, the insanity test in some jurisdictions focuses on whether the defendant knew (or perhaps appreciated, depending on the language adopted) that what he or she was doing was *against the law*. For these jurisdictions, use of the term "criminality" was suggested instead, as in: Did the defendant know (appreciate) the criminality of his or her conduct? Other jurisdictions target whether the defendant knew/appreciated that what he or she was doing was *morally wrong*. For these jurisdictions, the term "wrongfulness" was recommended, as in: Did the defendant know (appreciate) the wrongfulness of his or her conduct?

Fourth, the ALI/MPC approach substituted capacity to *conform* one's conduct in place of the phrase "irresistible impulse." This more contemporary terminology was considered to better reflect the more frequent impact of a mental disorder on a defendant and the defendant's behavior. As discussed above, some mental disorders can have a substantial impact on a person without creating an irresistible impulse. The phrase "irresistible impulse" suggests a short-term, overpowering effect, rather than the more typical chronic condition that weighs heavily on an individual. The ALI/MPC approach attempts to encompass the latter by asking whether the defendant had the capacity to "conform" his or her conduct to the requirements of the law.

Finally, the test *eliminated the nature and quality of the act prong* found in the *M'Naghten* standard, as in: Did the defendant know the nature and quality of his or her act? This "cognitive incapacity" test was perhaps seen as insufficiently connected with the defendant's behavior at the time of the crime to provide the necessary assessment of his or her responsibility for the behavior. The bottom line is that the ALI/MPC approach *incorporates* the essence of the so-called irresistible impulse test (that is, volitional incapacity) and the "knew that the act was wrong" prong from the *M'Naghten* test (that is, moral incapacity), albeit with slightly different language, and *eliminates* the "knew the nature and quality of the act" prong from the *M'Naghten* standard (that is, cognitive incapacity).

The ALI/MPC standard was initially very popular and adopted in about half of the fifty American states, until it was employed in the trial of John Hinckley Jr., who was found NGRI for his attempted assassination of President Ronald Reagan. Public reaction to this verdict was so negative that many states revisited their insanity tests, generally making them more restrictive, with a few states abolishing the defense altogether.[24]

The Federal Test

Another product of this public outrage was the federal *Insanity Defense Reform Act of 1984*. Previously, the federal courts were not required to employ the same insanity standard, with each circuit of the US Courts of Appeals free to adopt its own standard, although all but one had adopted the ALI/MPC standard. This changed with the passage of this law by Congress, which established a single standard for all federal courts. Although this legislation did not abolish the insanity defense in the federal judicial system, the goal was clearly to institute a stricter test to make the defense less available.[25] The resulting test reads:

> It is an affirmative defense to a prosecution under any Federal statute that, at the time of the commission of the acts constituting the offense, the defendant, as a result of a severe mental disease or defect, was unable to appreciate the nature and quality of the wrongfulness of his acts. Mental disease or defect does not otherwise constitute a defense.[26]

Four basic changes in the insanity defense test used in the federal courts resulted from this enactment.

First, the modifier *severe was added* to describe and limit the mental disorders that qualify for the insanity defense. In other words, defendants experiencing a mental disorder at the time of the crime that is not "severe" are not eligible for an insanity defense. This, of course, was intended to reduce, arguably rather dramatically, the number of defendants who can employ the insanity defense and to make it unavailable to defendants whose mental disorders are viewed as less severe, less debilitating. The term "severe" is not defined, but it is perhaps implicit that defendants who do not have a relatively significant and lengthy psychiatric history—including psychiatric hospitalizations on multiple occasions or at least pronounced symptoms confirmed by neutral observers over a period of time—will find it difficult to successfully pursue an insanity defense.

Second, this test *did not include a volitional prong* as found in the ALI/MPC and the irresistible impulse tests, suggesting that merely establishing that a defendant's behavior was "driven" by a mental disorder will not entitle the defendant to an insanity defense. The purpose here again no doubt was to reduce the availability of the insanity defense.

The third change brought back in effect the *cognitive incapacity prong* found in the *M'Naghten* test but eliminated by the ALI/MPC standard. However, the federal test couples it to the "moral incapacity prong" to actually make it harder to establish an insanity defense. Under the federal test, the defendant must have been "unable to appreciate the nature and quality of the wrongfulness of his acts." Unlike the *M'Naghten* test, pursuant to which defendants could qualify for the insanity defense if they could establish they lacked *either* the requisite cognitive capacity (that is, they did not know the nature and quality of their act) *or* moral capacity (that is, they did not know that the act was wrong), under the federal test they must establish that at the time of the crime they lacked *both*. The defendant's evidentiary burden is thereby increased.

The fourth change is that the *substantial capacity* modifier inserted by the ALI/MPC test was *dropped out*. Thus, it is not enough to establish a defendant lacked "substantial capacity" to appreciate the nature and quality of the wrongfulness of his or her acts. Under the federal test, defendants must establish that they were *unable* to appreciate the nature and quality of the wrongfulness of their acts. In other words, they must show they *completely lacked* this capacity.

Unsurprisingly, the main criticism lodged against the federal test is that it is too stringent and makes the insanity defense unavailable to many defendants who, because of their mental disorder, should not be held legally responsible for their criminal acts.

Clark v. Arizona (2006)

Notwithstanding all the attention given to the tests employed in conjunction with the insanity defense, the Supreme Court remained silent on the matter until it issued its ruling in *Clark v. Arizona* (2006), the USSC's first and thus far only direct examination of the insanity test. This was a case from Arizona that received almost no national attention until the USSC agreed to accept it for review.

Factual and Procedural Foundation

Eric Clark, the defendant, shot and killed a police officer when he was seventeen years old. Because of the nature of the offense (murder), he was tried as an adult. It was undisputed that he suffered from paranoid schizophrenia at the time and had demonstrated increasingly bizarre behavior for over a year before the shooting. Evidence was introduced that he thought the town where he lived—Flagstaff, Arizona—was populated with aliens, some of whom were impersonating governmental agents who were attempting to kill him. He further believed that bullets were the only way they could be stopped. In the early hours of June 21, 2000, Clark circled a residential block in his pickup truck with loud music blaring. After a police officer, responding to a complaint from someone who lived in the area, pulled Clark over, Clark shot the officer and ran away on foot. After being arrested, it took three years before Clark would be declared CST.

At his trial in 2003, an insanity defense and a mens rea defense were raised on Clark's behalf.[27] Arizona employed a relatively narrow insanity test that limited the availability of the defense to situations when the defendant was "afflicted with a mental disease or defect of such severity that the person did not know the criminal act was wrong." This not only excluded the key components of the irresistible impulse/volitional incapacity test, but limited what would otherwise be an adaption of the *M'Naghten* test to its right-from-wrong prong (that is, it incorporated the moral incapacity aspect), while eliminating the unable to understand the nature and consequences of their act prong (that is, it excluded the cognitive incapacity aspect).[28] As a procedural matter, Arizona also precluded defendants from using expert testimony to establish that the defendant lacked the requisite state of mind necessary for conviction, a key aspect of a mens rea defense.[29]

At trial, the defendant presented a psychiatrist's testimony that the defendant was suffering from paranoid schizophrenia with delusions about "aliens" when he killed the officer and was incapable of understanding right from wrong, and thus was legally insane at the time of the killing. In rebuttal, a psychiatrist for the prosecution testified that Clark's mental illness did not keep him from appreciating the wrongfulness of his conduct as shown by his actions before and after the shooting, including telling people he wanted to shoot police officers a few weeks before the crime, circling a residential block with music blaring as if to lure the police to intervene, evading the police after the shooting, and hiding the murder weapon. At the close of the trial, the prosecution argued that Clark's acts had been intentional, contending that the evidence showed he appreciated the wrongfulness of his actions. The defense argued that Clark thought he was luring an alien, not a police officer, at the time of the murder, and had been incapable of understanding the difference between right and wrong.

The trial judge rejected Clark's defense and found him guilty of first-degree murder and sentenced him to life in prison without any possibility of parole for twenty-five years.[30] On appeal, Clark argued that the provisions of Arizona's insanity test violated his due process rights in that, at a minimum, the test needed to incorporate both prongs of the *M'Naghten* test.

The Court's Ruling in Clark

The USSC in *Clark v. Arizona* (2006) ruled that such a limiting of the insanity defense does not violate defendants' right to due process because (a) there has been no historical deference to *M'Naghten* that would elevate its formula to the level of a fundamental principle, (b) there is wide variation in the insanity tests currently employed, including four states that do not offer an insanity defense at all, and (c) there is no particular formulation of the insanity test that establishes a due process baseline that other formulations must incorporate. The Court further noted that these variations are legitimate in light of the amount of flux and disagreement among legal and medical practitioners over conceptions of mental disorders and how they should be applied to excuse defendants from criminal responsibility. The Court concluded that, in light of this debate, it is appropriate to leave it to the prerogative of the states to formulate their insanity tests as they deem fit, just as the conceptualization and definitions of criminal offenses and defenses have traditionally been left to the discretion of the states.

Analysis of Clark

Insofar as the Court's ruling appears to have been driven by its perception that the concepts pertaining to mental disorders are in considerable "flux and disagreement" and by the uncertainty over how to apply them in this context, the Court seems to have considered it imprudent to attempt to formulate a binding standard when future developments might rapidly undercut the foundation for any prescribed standard. Accordingly, the Court may have perceived that the wiser course would be to leave the articulation of these tests to the "laboratory of the states," with their particular interest and expertise in devising and testing criminal laws and defenses suited to their respective populations.

The Court also indicated another pragmatic reason for its ruling. It was the Court's view that Arizona's focus on defendants' ability to know "right from wrong" in conjunction with an insanity defense did not preclude defendants from introducing evidence regarding their inability to know the nature and quality of their acts. The majority opinion implied that if a defendant lacked the latter, he or she would also be unable to distinguish right from wrong. Thus, in the Court's view, Arizona's formulation of the insanity test did not in effect substantially narrow the traditional *M'Naghten* articulation of the insanity defense.

Of course, one might ask, if Arizona's omission of the cognitive incapacity prong from its adoption of what otherwise would be the *M'Naghten* test is not critical, why have states ordinarily included both? Is it because no one really understands what the two prongs address or what their distinct impacts on insanity verdicts are? Is it because those who are responsible for adopting the insanity test for a given jurisdiction simply emulate what their predecessors ordained without understanding the implications? Is the majority opinion in *Clark* suggesting that the language used in the insanity test is not terribly discerning or dispositive, and that just as USSC Justice Potter Stewart said with regard to his threshold test for obscenity, "I know it when I see it,"[31] judges and juries deciding insanity cases are simply relying on an intuitive sense of what constitutes insanity, rather than on the wording of the insanity test they are supposed to apply? Or are these just relatively random verdicts driven by how sympathetic or frightening the defendant seems?

With regard to how defensible the Court's verdict in *Clark* is, opinions may vary depending on whether someone thinks (a) mental health evaluators and jurists are capable of reliably and consistently ascertaining whether the criteria for the insanity test have been met, (b) the verdict of NGRI is an appropriate outcome for a criminal trial, or (c) the dispositions that result if a defendant is found not guilty by reason of insanity sufficiently protect society, a topic that will be discussed in a later chapter.

Conclusion

Notwithstanding the lengthy, extensive, and controversial history of the insanity defense, there continues to be little consensus regarding what the relevant standard should be, although most agree that at least under some circumstances a defendant's mental status at the time of the crime is a factor that should be taken into account during subsequent criminal proceedings. This wide variation in approaches undoubtedly reflects the public's mixed emotions regarding mental disorders in general and the insanity defense in particular—an ambivalence compounded by the challenges associated with accurately evaluating a defendant's claim regarding the impact of a mental disorder on his or her behavior at the time of the crime. Perhaps reflecting this uncertainty, the USSC seems content to let each state decide for itself what test it will employ. As the next chapter will detail, this latitude has resulted in the deployment of a number of variations for addressing criminal responsibility and alternatives to the insanity defense when the mental disorder of the defendant may be relevant, as well as various associated judicial procedures, as courts and legislatures strive to find suitable resolutions for these cases.

9

Insanity Defense Variations and Alternatives for
Addressing the Criminal Responsibility of a
Defendant with a Mental Disorder

Believe half of what you see . . . and none of what you hear.
—Marvin Gaye, "I Heard It through the Grapevine" (1968)

On July 20, 2012, after dying his hair red, James Eagan Holmes, the
"Aurora Theater Shooter," opened fire in a Denver suburb at a sold-out
showing of the Batman movie *The Dark Knight Rises*. A report that was
quickly picked up by many media outlets and widely circulated claimed
Holmes told arresting officers that he was the Joker, Batman's evil arch-
enemy. It was a story that seemed to make some sense of this senseless
event, particularly when Holmes entered a plea of not guilty by reason
of insanity (NGRI) (ultimately, he was convicted of 24 counts of murder
and 140 counts of attempted murder). However, it was apparently not
true. No police officer claimed Holmes called himself the Joker (who
had green hair, not red hair), investigators heard no witness mention or
refer to the Joker, and there was no evidence indicating Holmes had a
Batman obsession. Indeed, Holmes later told a court-appointed psychiatrist he was surprised when inmates called him "the Joker."[1] In similar
fashion, myths and media headlines continue to confound efforts to formulate a coherent standard for and approach to the insanity defense.[2]

Insanity Defense Variations

As discussed previously, the US Supreme Court (USSC) has refrained
from declaring that a specific formulation of the insanity defense test
is required under the US Constitution.[3] In light of the Court's position
and with the insanity defense so controversial, it is unsurprising that, in
addition to the basic tests described earlier, there have been many variations in the approach employed. What follows is a brief description of

a number of these approaches, which reflect the wide range of perspectives regarding mental disorders and related criminal behavior that the insanity defense is expected to somehow encompass and address.

Loss of Will

In *Durham v. United States* (1954), Chief Judge Bazelon—perhaps the judge best known for attempting to systematically enhance the law's response to mental health issues—reflected on the pervasive unease regarding the predominant insanity tests employed at the time, namely, the *M'Naghten* test, the irresistible impulse test, and the product test. In *Durham*, the defendant, who was charged with housebreaking, had a long history of criminal behavior, mental illness, and insanity acquittals. His psychiatric diagnosis, however, was uncertain and variable, ranging from a psychosis to a psychopathic personality. Bazelon observed that none of the prevailing insanity tests provided a good fit for this case. Noting that mental illness is not an all-or-nothing condition, but that these tests treat it as such, he also asserted that the ability to tell "right-from-wrong" test was inadequate because cognition is only one aspect of the mind and individuals with a mental disorder may retain the ability to tell right from wrong, even though their emotions and impulses may be affected by their mental disorder. Similarly, he criticized the irresistible impulse test because, as a result of their mental disorder, defendants may be driven by their "brooding" but not be subject to an "impulse." Finally, Bazelon asserted that the product test was inadequate because not every mental disorder that affects a person's behavior should excuse criminal behavior.

Bazelon contended that the focus of the insanity test should not be defendants' psychiatric symptoms, but whether they *are deprived of or have lost power over their will*. Arguably, this iteration is broader than the irresistible impulse test and would encompass, for example, the effects of a major depressive disorder on a defendant. Perhaps reflecting the widespread unease with formulations that expand the reach of the insanity defense, this "loss of will" focus has gained little support.

Emotional Impairment/Moral Blameworthiness

Thirteen years later, Judge Bazelon seemingly backtracked on his position in *Durham* with his ruling in *Washington v. United States* (1967), in which he began by noting the reluctance of judges to grant insanity acquittals. He also pointed out that the "wild beast" test employed in the early eighteenth century could be readily applied by laypersons as it did not require the evaluation of a complex body of evidence; that is, jurors were presumed to know what it meant to be a wild beast. The shift to the "right from wrong" test, in contrast, required jurors to evaluate medical testimony in light of this standard, but then physicians complained this test resulted in too narrow an inquiry into defendants' mental condition and kept doctors from presenting important related medical data. The product test was introduced, Bazelon asserted, to remedy this latter problem by widening the range of permissible expert testimony so that jurors could consider all relevant scientific information. This effort, however, was also unsuccessful because this standard was viewed as too broad. Furthermore, its language did not coincide with the existing medical classifications that medical professionals tended to use, inappropriately, in insanity trials. So once again, the legal community modified the insanity standard, this time giving the applicable mental condition a legal definition explicitly independent of its medical meaning, while recognizing that there may be many reasons why individuals' "ability to control their behavior" is impaired. Unfortunately, Bazelon determined, jurors were thereby called upon to consider testimony governing the development, adaptation, and functioning of these controls on defendants' behavior, a daunting task.

In the case before Bazelon, the defendant had raised an insanity defense in response to charges of rape, robbery, and assault with a deadly weapon. Reviewing the trial record, Bazelon said he was "deeply troubled by the persistent use of labels and by the paucity of meaningful information presented to the jury." He noted that instead of the defendant's psychiatric history, the jury was given a "confusing mass of abstract philosophical discussion and fruitless disputation between lawyer and witness about legal and psychiatric labels and jargon." The focus, Bazelon asserted, ended up being whether the defendant had a passive-aggressive personality with an impulse to rape, effectively giving the jurors uninformative labels that distracted them from the facts of the case. Bazelon found the evidence that did exist suggested the defendant felt little empathy for others or guilt, and had little control over his desires and needs.

Bazelon had thought that his "loss of will" test would enable testifying mental health experts to employ familiar medical terms and not conclusory labels, but he found that under this test the emphasis was still, inappropriately, on labels. He argued that these experts should instead provide explanations of the relevant mental disorders, their dynamics, their development in a person, and how they affect the mental and emotional processes. The bottom line, he contended, should be whether defendants had an abnormal condition of the mind that substantially affected their mental or *emotional* processes and thereby substantially impaired their behavioral controls.

Bazelon believed that with this information in hand, juries should make the final determination regarding a defendant's insanity and decide for themselves whether the defendant is *blameworthy*. The judge's role, Bazelon continued, was to ensure that the relevant medical information was explained to the jury in a meaningful way, in terms that pertained to the defendant, and not as abstract concepts. The mental health expert, in Bazelon's view, should not testify regarding "product," "result," or "cause" (that is, whether a defendant's behavior was a product or the result of a mental disorder, or whether it was the cause of this behavior), although the expert can testify regarding whether a defendant suffered from a "mental disease or defect."

Bazelon's inclusion of an *emotional impairment* element was a new insanity test component. While it can be argued that this is indeed a significant aspect of many mental disorders, this focus has gained little traction in conjunction with the insanity test, perhaps again because of concerns that it would expand the scope of the defense. His directive that the factfinder should assess whether a defendant's insanity left the individual *morally blameworthy* was also a relatively novel emphasis. Although this concept is perhaps implicit in most formulations of the insanity defense, it too has not been widely embraced, perhaps because of fears that it would make the insanity defense verdict a moral rather than a legal determination, which would make most jurists uneasy as it raises issues arguably outside their expertise.

Deific Decree Defense

A few states, such as Washington and Colorado, have recognized some version of the so-called deific decree defense.[4] This doctrine wrestles with some of the thorny issues that arise when criminal law, in this instance the insanity defense, attempts to address religion and tenets of faith. This form of the insanity defense actually has a relatively lengthy history and can be dated back to a 1724 English trial, in which one of the jury instructions read:

> If [the defendant] was under the visitation of God, and could not distinguish between good and evil, and did not know what he did, though he committed the greatest offence, yet he could not be guilty of any offence against any law whatsoever; for guilt arises from the mind, and the wicked will and intention of the man.[5]

The first use of a deific decree defense in American jurisprudence is purported to be 1844, but it received national attention only in 1882, when it was invoked at the trial of Charles Guiteau following his assassination of James A. Garfield, the twentieth president of the United States.[6]

Some defendants who raise an insanity defense will testify they committed their criminal acts because they heard voices directing them to take these actions. Such testimony can provide a good fit for an insanity defense as the hearing of voices that no one else can hear is a well-recognized symptom of a severe mental disorder. Recall the case of *Colorado v. Connelly* (1986), in which the defendant asserted that voices told him to fly from Boston, Massachusetts, to Denver, Colorado, to confess to a murder.

This scenario, however, gets trickier when the defendant claims the voice was that of God or some other religious figure. Many religions have a lengthy tradition of individuals being directed by the voice of God to undertake some important task. To the adherents of these religions, the command of their deity is something that must be carried out virtually without question, even if the reasons for it are unclear or it involves criminal behavior. For them, hearing and obeying a divine command is not a symptom of a mental disorder, and asserting that it was the result of a mental disorder, as is required when raising an insanity defense, would be to disavow one's faith.

In the United States there has traditionally been a desire to not impose criminal punishment on those acting in accordance with their religious beliefs.[7] The inclination to excuse this behavior without requiring the defendant to resort to an insanity defense is perhaps what has led a few jurisdictions to embrace the deific decree defense, which parallels but is distinct from the insanity defense.

At the same time, ascertaining whether a defendant actually heard deific voices when the only evidence this occurred is the testimony of the defendant is a difficult task. For those looking to escape criminal punishment, it is very convenient to be able to assert they heard the voice of their deity and were following the deity's instructions when they committed the criminal act. Is this a sufficient basis to exonerate a defendant from criminal responsibility? Does this approach adequately address the harm suffered by the victims, as well as the need to ensure society's laws are followed and the community kept safe?

Furthermore, if a jurisdiction does recognize this defense, what happens to a defendant acquitted thereby? As will be discussed, insanity acquittees generally are not directly released back into the community but must undergo psychiatric hospitalization for a period of time—and for a serious crime this may be a very lengthy time period—until it is determined that it is safe to release the individual back into the community. Placing a defendant acquitted under a deific decree defense in a psychiatric facility could be considered inappropriate since it has not been established that the defendant is experiencing a psychiatric disorder, while placement in a jail or prison would be considered inappropriate since the defendant has not been convicted of a crime. The general public may be reluctant to allow the defendant to directly return to the community, but where else can this individual be placed?

Post-Traumatic Stress Disorder Defense

When *post-traumatic stress disorder* (PTSD) was first used as a foundation for an insanity defense in the wake of the relatively unpopular Vietnam War,[8] it was rarely successful.[9] Following the more broadly supported conflicts in Iraq and Afghanistan, along with society's increased recognition and understanding of this disorder's impact on thoughts and behavior, PTSD may now be enjoying a warmer welcome in conjunction with the insanity defense.

PTSD is a mental disorder that typically develops after an individual experiences a life-threatening or extremely traumatic event, including— but not limited to—exposure to war, threatened or actual physical assault, threatened or actual sexual violence, being kidnapped or taken hostage, a terrorist attack, torture, incarceration as a prisoner of war, natural or human-made disasters, and severe motor vehicle accidents.[10] Veterans of combat during military service are prime candidates for developing PTSD, and its pervasiveness in this population has received greater attention from mental health professionals, military officials, and society in general.[11] The prevalence of PTSD diagnoses in general has grown in recent years, which some attribute to the population's increasing exposure to violence or reports of violence, the wider impact of natural disasters, and the greater prevalence of traumatic events in general.[12]

PTSD can have long-term psychological and behavioral effects, such as a sensation of reliving the traumatic event, recurrent distressing dreams of the event, or intense physiological distress when exposed to internal or external cues that resemble an aspect of the event.[13] The sense of reliving the traumatic event, which can occur during nightmares or daytime flashbacks, is one of the most distressing PTSD symptoms reported. In the most severe cases, the mental images become so vivid that individuals start to behave as if they are back in that earlier situation where the trauma initially occurred. This experience is usually triggered by a sensory perception associated with the original trauma, such as a related sound or smell, and may last a few seconds or a few days. Indeed, individuals can be so vulnerable to this reoccurrence that even relatively unrelated or minor events may set this response in motion. Although individuals with PTSD may be cognizant that they are experiencing a flashback and conscious of their response, they may be unable to control their response.[14] Furthermore, their inability to manage their fear responses can impact their ability to react appropriately to environmental stimuli and they may overreact or respond violently to perceived threats, which may result in harm to another person and subsequent criminal charges.

When individuals commit crimes linked to their PTSD, opinions diverge on whether they should be held criminally responsible for their actions. Criminal culpability will vary depending on the jurisdiction's applicable insanity test and the nature and severity of the individual's PTSD.[15] One hurdle that defendants who attribute their criminal actions to PTSD must overcome is establishing that the PTSD constitutes the requisite mental disorder. As discussed, views differ on whether the insanity defense should be read broadly to encompass a wide range of mental disorders, including PTSD, or whether its availability should be curtailed or abolished from the legal system.

Typically the insanity defense is limited to psychotic disorders, a limitation intended to prevent defendants with a relatively minor psychological impairment from avoiding responsibility for their criminal behavior.[16] Insofar as the key features of a psychotic disorder are delusions, hallucinations, disorganized thinking, or grossly disorganized or abnormal motor behavior,[17] and because the mental impairment associated with a PTSD diagnosis often does not involve delusions or dissociation, most individuals with a PTSD diagnosis will be ineligible for the insanity defense.[18] Nevertheless, some of the symptoms associated with a diagnosis of PTSD may be viewed as constituting a psychotic disorder. For example, PTSD may result in a gross impairment in reality testing, especially when the disorder leads individuals to believe they are reliving a traumatic event or otherwise perceive their surrounding environment to be substantially different (and often more threatening) from that which actually exists. Consequently, individuals diagnosed with PTSD who experienced delusions or dissociative states may be able to meet the threshold requirement for the insanity defense.

In addition, not only has PTSD received more attention and validation as a mental disorder in recent years, but its origins are now established on a relatively reliable basis in that before the diagnosis can be assigned, there must be "exposure to one or more traumatic events."[19] Because defendants making this claim in conjunction with an insanity defense must generally show that they were exposed to or witnessed a life-threatening or other traumatic event in the past, which is often readily verifiable and thus provides a relatively objective means of providing a foundation for the claimed disorder, the concerns of some skeptics regarding these claims may thereby be abated.[20]

The fact that different versions of the insanity test are employed across jurisdictions has significant implications for defendants with PTSD who become embroiled in the criminal justice system as a result of their mental disorder. When individuals with PTSD psychologically relive a traumatic situation, they may be cognitively aware of their actions but be unable to control their behavior.[21] As a result, such individuals may be eligible for acquittal in a jurisdiction that has retained the volitional component of the insanity defense, but face conviction in a state that does not recognize this basis for an insanity defense.

Another key variable that influences whether a PTSD-based insanity defense is likely to succeed—one that also varies across jurisdictions and is discussed below—is the assignment of the evidentiary burden at trial (generically referred to as the "burden of proof"). All states place a "burden of production" on defendants to show sufficient evidence exists to permit them to initially raise an insanity defense.[22] Two-thirds of the states, however, also place on defendants the burden of persuasion (that is, what must be shown at trial to obtain the desired verdict). The evidentiary standard associated with the burden of persuasion is usually a preponderance-of-the-evidence standard. This means that supporting evidence, when weighed against evidence to the contrary, must be found to be more probably true than not. Hence, even if a diagnosis of PTSD is recognized as a valid foundation for the insanity defense in a given state and some evidence exists regarding the requisite linkage of the defendant's mental disorder to a cognitive or volitional impairment, states vary as to whether the prosecution or the defendant bears the subsequent burden of persuasion—a difference that can lead to dramatically different trial outcomes.[23]

As a result of these variations, the likelihood of PTSD constituting the requisite foundation for an insanity defense differs from jurisdiction to jurisdiction. Theoretically, however, at least in those states with a broadly formulated insanity standard, it should be possible for defendants to use a PTSD finding as the basis for an insanity defense. Nevertheless, PTSD has generally received only limited acceptance as a valid foundation for such a defense.

Battered Spouse/Battered Child Syndrome Defense

Battered spouse syndrome (BSS) has been defined as "a series of common characteristics that appear in [spouses] who are abused physically and psychologically over an extended period of time by the dominant . . . figure in their lives."[24] This syndrome can alter an individual's perception of the surrounding environment and cause this person to react unexpectedly to certain cues or events perceived to be threatening. Because BSS can alter perceptions of reality and induce related behavior accordingly, this diagnosis has been extensively studied and its application sought within criminal justice proceedings. Testimony related to this disorder has typically been presented at trial when a battered woman claims she injured or killed her spouse in self-defense.[25]

For example, in 1981, the Georgia Supreme Court determined the scientific foundation of BSS was sufficiently established to permit related expert testimony to be admitted into evidence to assist a jury evaluating a defense based on this syndrome.[26] In a 1997 ruling, the court added that evidence of BSS can be used to show "that the defendant had a mental state necessary for the [self-]defense . . . justification [even] though the actual threat of harm [to the defendant did] not immediately precede the homicide."[27]

In the 1997 appeal, the defendant had been convicted of voluntary manslaughter for shooting her husband. The defendant testified that her husband had not only "beat[en] her repeatedly" in the past, but had "held a gun to her head and threatened to kill her and abscond with her child."[28] She had called the police about a dozen times and left her husband twice. On the day of the shooting, her husband was upset that she had been out visiting friends, and subsequently struck her in the face and then continued to hit her. The Georgia Supreme Court determined that testimony regarding these incidents provided adequate evidence that the defendant had been psychologically traumatized by these beatings and lived in a fear-inducing environment. The court ruled that the jury should have been instructed on BSS and its implications for self-defense and that in the future a jury instruction should "be given in all battered person syndrome cases, when authorized by the evidence and requested by [the] defendant, to assist the jury in evaluating the battered person's defense of self-defense."[29]

The BSS defense received further support when the New Jersey Supreme Court reversed a conviction of reckless manslaughter after it held that BSS testimony is admissible on the issue of self-defense.[30] The court noted the prevalence of domestic violence in America (citing studies that report that over one million women are beaten in this country every year) and the increased attention BSS has received. A BSS expert at trial had explained the nature of the long-standing, deep-seated fear of severe bodily harm and isolation that results from being a battered spouse. The expert had been prepared to testify that the defendant, who had stabbed her husband with scissors after seven years in an abusive relationship, suffered from BSS and to explain how this affected her perception of her environment and shaped her behavior at the time of the stabbing. The New Jersey Supreme Court ultimately held that the expert's testimony could be relevant to a claim of self-defense and would have aided the jury "in determining whether, under the circumstances, a reasonable person would have believed there was imminent danger to her life."[31]

Perhaps the strongest indication that a defense has been accepted is when a state legislature passes a law formally recognizing it. The Ohio legislature did just that with regard to the BSS defense in establishing the following:

> If a defendant is charged with an offense involving the use of force against another and the defendant enters a plea to the charge of not guilty by reason of insanity, the defendant may introduce expert testimony of the "battered woman syndrome" and expert testimony that the defendant suffered from that syndrome as evidence to establish the requisite impairment of the defendant's reason, at the time of the commission of the offense, that is necessary for a finding that the defendant is not guilty by reason of insanity.[32]

A similar result can ensue when a defendant establishes that he or she was a battered child, with the alleged crime generally targeting a parent or guardian of the child. The *battered child syndrome* (BCS) was first identified in 1962 when a physician, Dr. C. Henry Kempe, and his colleagues published a research paper describing the syndrome and its causes.[33] Although related cases are relatively rare, there have been a few instances where the battered child syndrome has been raised as a defense.

In 1990, for example, expert testimony regarding BCS was admitted into evidence in a Washington state case.[34] At the age of seventeen, Andrew Janes shot and killed his mother's boyfriend as he walked in the door. His attorney introduced evidence that Janes had been physically and emotionally abused by his mother's live-in boyfriend for ten years, suffered PTSD as a result of this chronic and enduring abuse, and that this PTSD impaired his capacity to premeditate the killing of his mother's boyfriend. Although the trial court denied the defendant's request for an instruction to the jury to consider whether the defendant acted in self-defense, ruling that the physically and emotionally abusive events were too remote and insufficiently aggressive to justify such a defense, the trial judge did grant the defendant's request for a diminished capacity instruction (discussed more fully below), noting the acceptance of PTSD within the medical community.

The jury subsequently found Janes not guilty of first degree murder, although it did find him guilty of second degree murder, for which he received a reduced sentence of ten years imprisonment. The trial judge explained that the reduced sentence was given because the defendant had suffered a continuing course of physical abuse at the hands of the victim and his crime was in response to that abuse, and that his capacity to conform his conduct to the law was significantly impaired by his PTSD. In addition, because the defendant truly believed that killing the victim was the only way that he could stop the abuse he and his mother had experienced, he acted under duress and compulsion.[35]

The defense nonetheless appealed Janes's second-degree murder conviction and, in 1993, the Washington Supreme Court became the first appellate court in the nation to rule that expert testimony regarding BCS is generally admissible to aid defendants in proving that they acted in self-defense.[36] Although the trial judge had focused on what was characterized as the defendant's PTSD, the Washington Supreme Court addressed the defendant's state of mind in terms of BCS. The court began by noting that children accused of parricide have increasingly sought to introduce evidence of BCS in an effort to explain their actions.[37]

In ruling that evidence of BCS is admissible, the court extensively addressed the research regarding the causes and effects of BCS. It found that BCS "has come to describe both the physiological and psychological effects of a prolonged pattern of physical, emotional and sexual abuse," and that "child abuse is an extreme stressor that exceeds a child's capacity to cope with it or integrate it into their personality, their awareness, [and] their consciousness." The court also pointed out that one of the principal characteristics of the syndrome is hypervigilance, which leads the child to perceive danger in subtle changes in the parent's expressions or mannerisms, and results in the child constantly monitoring the environment, particularly the abuser, for those signals that suggest danger is imminent. A second characteristic of the syndrome, the court added, is "learned helplessness," a belief that all doors of escape are closed. The court also posited that BSS provides a close parallel to BCS, noted the court had already ruled that evidence of BSS was admissible and could find no reason to treat the two syndromes differently. Finally, the court concluded that evidence of BCS can help the trier of fact understand the sense of powerlessness, fear, and anxiety that permeate the battered child's world.

Ultimately, the court determined BCS met the requirements for admissibility because (a) it has achieved general acceptance in the relevant scientific community and (b) this evidence can assist the trier of fact to understand the evidence at trial or determine a fact in question. With this evidence in mind, the court ruled with regard to Janes that there may have been sufficient evidence that he believed he was in imminent danger of grievous bodily harm as to warrant a self-defense instruction to the jury. Because the necessary consideration of the effects of BCS on the defendant's perception of his situation had not been undertaken, the court ordered a retrial to determine whether the self-defense instruction should have been given.[38]

Perhaps the most prominent case in which the BCS defense was raised was the California trial of the brothers Lyle and Erik Menendez who were accused of killing their parents with shotgun blasts. This defense drew considerable skepticism nationwide and probably slowed the use of BCS as a foundation for the claim of self-defense in general.[39] The first trial of the Menendez brothers, broadcast on Court TV, in which the defense argued that the brothers had been psychologically and sexually abused by their parents, created a national frenzy when it ended in a hung jury on the charges of murder and manslaughter.[40] At the retrial, however, the trial judge ruled that the defense failed to introduce sufficient evidence to establish that the brothers had been sexually and psychologically abused by their father and that the killing of their parents was the result of duress and fear. After the judge instructed the jury accordingly, the jury in this instance convicted the brothers of murder, following which each was sentenced to life in prison.[41]

Urban Psychosis/Urban Survival Syndrome

Following the success of the BSS and PTSD defenses, attorneys have attempted to incorporate other "syndromes" into a similar defense.[42] One such effort involved what was characterized as *urban psychosis* or *urban survival syndrome* (USS).[43] In 1993, Damien Osby, an African American, killed Willie and Marcus Brooks in Fort Worth, Texas. According to the defendant, the two victims had repeatedly harassed and threatened him and his family. Osby claimed that he believed that the only way to escape serious harm or even death was to kill them first.

During the trial, the defense noted that Osby lived in an inner-city neighborhood with one of the highest violent crime rates in the country and argued that residents of this neighborhood quickly learned they were at great risk of being killed in its "war zone." Counsel further argued that as a result of the defendant's routine exposure to violence in this neighborhood, Osby had been conditioned to believe he needed to use lethal force to defend himself from these two men and, as a result, his actions were reasonable under the circumstances. Notwithstanding this defense, Osby was convicted of two counts of murder and sentenced to life in prison.[44]

In another case in which USS was raised as a defense, Torino Roosevelt Boney, also an African American, shot another man in the head in Washington, DC. At his trial in 1994, his attorney claimed that "poor urban areas foster a cycle of violence and despair among black men," conditioning them to respond with violence to the daily threats they encounter—a response so entrenched that ultimately "'a look, a bump or a glance [can] lead[] to extreme violence.'" Despite this argument, the jury convicted Boney as well.[45]

These USS cases illustrate that even when some support for a "syndrome" defense exists within the *DSM-5*, such a defense will not necessarily be successful. The *DSM-5* provides for a possible connection between urban violence and PTSD, for example, when it lists the traumatic events that must have been experienced before individuals may be assigned a diagnosis of PTSD. These include (a) experiencing, (b) witnessing another individual experience, or (c) learning that a close family member or close friend has experienced actual or threatened death, serious injury, or sexual violence.[46] Living in disadvantaged neighborhoods with high crime rates increases the likelihood that an individual will experience, witness, or learn of such violent and traumatic events.[47] According to proponents of the USS defense, the daily experience of racial segregation and violence found in many inner cities may cause a mental state—namely, USS—that is the equivalent of the mental state resulting from undergoing a traumatic combat experience.[48]

Nevertheless, the USS defense has gained little traction. Moreover, one commentator argues that the legal system should not encourage such defenses even though many inner-city defendants can meet the criteria for a PTSD diagnosis. She asserts that this defense perpetuates negative stereotypes about racial minorities and contends that efforts should be devoted instead to working to prevent these symptoms and the events that induce them from arising.[49]

The timing of the introduction of the USS defense to the legal system may also have impeded its success. When it was first presented to the courts in the 1990s, crime rates in the United States were rising, and national policy was focused on punishing and deterring crime. According to the United States Department of Justice, the rate of violent crimes (rape, robbery, aggravated assault, and homicide) reached an all-time high in the late 1980s and early 1990s, with urban crime a particular concern.[50] Hence, judges, juries, and the general public may not have been willing to embrace this new defense, which seemed to excuse and hold blameless the behavior resulting in urban crime. Much the same response has greeted similar efforts to reduce or escape criminal liability by attributing criminal behavior to defendants' immersion within other violent cultures, such as a "voodoo" defense or a "violent videogame" defense.[51]

Other Variations

As discussed below in conjunction with the temporary insanity defense, another iteration of the insanity defense is what may variously be referred to as the "rubber band," "psychological duress," or "defendant snapped" defense. Also addressed below in conjunction with the mens rea "defense" is the intoxication defense.

Other Issues and Trends Regarding the Criminal Responsibility of Defendants with a Mental Disorder

As indicated earlier, considerable attention has been given to the insanity defense in the United States, particularly following the attempted assassination of President Ronald Reagan by John Hinckley Jr., with most of the ensuing changes seeking to limit the availability of the defense. The following describes various approaches, beyond the insanity test itself, implemented to address and resolve the criminal responsibility of offenders with a mental disorder at the time of the crime.

Abolition of the Insanity Defense

The legislatures in four states—Idaho, Kansas, Montana, and Utah— have taken the most dramatic step and *abolished the insanity defense* entirely. However, as discussed below, Idaho, Montana, and Utah do permit a guilty but mentally ill verdict, while Kansas has authorized a "lack of mental state" defense (that is, a mens rea defense).[52] Indeed, the USSC has indicated that a state must allow evidence regarding the presence of mental illness at the time of the crime to be a factor in some manner in determining a defendant's verdict.[53] The Nevada legislature similarly abolished the insanity defense, only to have the Nevada Supreme Court strike down this legislation as being unconstitutional under both the United States Constitution and the Nevada Constitution, and thereby reinstate, the defense.[54] The state supreme courts in Idaho,[55] Kansas,[56] Montana,[57] and Utah,[58] however, have upheld the abolition of the insanity defense pursuant to their state constitutions.

Abolition of Mental Health Evidence

Some of the criticism of the insanity and related defenses has focused on the related expert reports and testimony provided by mental health professionals. The criticisms are varied but include arguments that these professionals are overly sympathetic to defendants; that their evaluations and conclusions lack scientific rigor, consistency, and validity; that their reports are cursory or filled with mental health jargon that is unresponsive to the legal question; or that the professionals are simply "hired guns."[59] Some jurisdictions, as a result, have considered *abolishing the introduction of mental health evidence* generated by mental health experts in conjunction with these defenses, thereby necessitating that these determinations be based solely on lay testimony.[60]

Shifting the Burden/Level of Proof

Some states and the federal government have responded by *shifting the burden of proof* or *changing the requisite level of proof* on the issue of insanity.[61] Rather than require the prosecution to establish that the defendant was sane at the time of the offense, they require that the defendant show that he or she was insane at the time. It has been found that this is the one procedural change that has a significant impact on the outcome of these trials. With regard to the standard of proof, the change typically implemented has been to require defendants to prove by clear and convincing evidence that they were insane at the time of the crime as opposed to requiring them to establish this only by a preponderance of the evidence.[62]

Guilty but Mentally Ill Verdict

Over twenty states now make a verdict of *guilty but mentally ill* (GBMI) available as an alternative to the insanity defense. A GBMI finding is not a "defense" because it cannot lead to a verdict that acquits a defendant of criminal responsibility (in contrast, an NGRI verdict does result in an acquittal). Instead, it enables the factfinder (that is, the judge or jury) to issue a guilty verdict, thereby providing society and any victims the satisfaction of knowing someone was held accountable for the crime, while ostensibly setting the foundation for a sentence reduction, as well as delivery of mental health services to the defendant, since the verdict acknowledges that the defendant was not fully responsible for the crime because the defendant's mental disorder impacted his or her thinking or behavior at the time.

Since the 1990s, however, sentences for crimes have generally been more firmly established with less flexibility afforded judges, making sentence reductions less available and even rendering this aspect of the GBMI verdict moot in some cases. The GBMI verdict is also supposed to assuage factfinders' concerns about what will happen to a defendant with a mental disorder following conviction. The expectation is that these defendants will receive a needed mental health placement, rather than be incarcerated in a correctional facility where they would be highly vulnerable and their mental disorder inadequately addressed, if not exacerbated.

In recent years, however, the dispositions dispensed pursuant to a GBMI verdict tend to be relatively indistinguishable from those that criminal defendants in general receive. GBMI inmates are typically initially placed in a correctional facility.[63] Although the early practice was to transfer them, like most inmates in need of mental health services, to a psychiatric facility on a relatively routine basis, these psychiatric beds have become relatively scarce and a precious commodity. In addition, correctional facilities are now constitutionally required to provide needed mental health services to inmates,[64] and although debate continues over the adequacy of these services, inmates with a mental disorder are increasingly likely to be treated within the correctional facility where they are currently housed rather than transferred to a psychiatric facility. As a result, to the extent that GBMI inmates are identified as being in need of mental health services, they, like other inmates, will often receive these services within a correctional facility and thus may serve out their sentence under circumstances virtually indistinguishable from other inmates.

Unsurprisingly, prosecutors tend to welcome this verdict as it tends to facilitate their ability to obtain criminal convictions by defusing sympathy toward or concern for the well-being of defendants who might otherwise obtain an acquittal or an NGRI verdict.

Diminished Capacity Defense

A similar variation is the *diminished capacity defense*. This defense acknowledges that the defendant broke the law but asserts that he or she should not be held fully criminally liable because at the time of the offense, the defendant was experiencing a mental disorder that diminished his or her mental capacity and that should be taken into account, even though the impairment was not sufficient to meet the requirements of an insanity defense. Much like the "temporary insanity" defense, discussed immediately below, the "diminished capacity" defense has tended to be misunderstood.[65] This defense can play out during either the guilt phase or the sentencing phase of a criminal trial. During the guilt phase, this defense generally asserts these defendants did not have the requisite intent necessary to convict them of a charged crime, even though they may be guilty of a lesser crime. Because of confusion about its scope and reach, this aspect of the diminished capacity defense tends to be referred to today as a "mens rea defense," which is also discussed below.[66] During the sentencing phase, the goal of defendants is also to establish that they deserve a reduced sentence as their mental disorder was at least partially responsible for their behavior, thereby reducing the culpability of the defendant and justifying a less severe punishment.

"Temporary" Insanity

The so-called *temporary insanity defense* is widely discussed by the media but legally speaking is basically a fiction since the law does not recognize it. This "defense" received considerable attention when it was widely cited as the basis for the acquittal of Lorena Bobbitt in a Virginia case that generated worldwide headlines. Bobbitt was accused of having cut off her sleeping husband's penis with a knife after he had cheated on her that evening. She testified that her husband had physically, emotionally, and sexually abused her and flaunted his unfaithfulness. Her lawyers argued that due to this abuse, she was suffering from clinical depression and PTSD and that her husband's constant abuse caused her to "snap." Expert witnesses testified that the abuse had been escalating and that she lived in constant fear of her husband. One expert testified that she experienced temporary insanity, which constituted an irresistible impulse. At the close of the trial, Bobbitt was found NGRI due to an irresistible impulse.[67]

Media headlines inaccurately referred to this as a successful temporary insanity or *psychological duress defense*, particularly when Bobbitt was released after a forty-five-day period of observation at a psychiatric facility with no apparent psychiatric impairment. However, this was actually an acquittal pursuant to the Virginia insanity standard (discussed in the next chapter). In the eyes of the law, the duration of the insanity is irrelevant. The question is whether the defendant was insane at the time of the offense. The defendant's mental status before or after the offense is technically irrelevant, although generally a mental disorder that seems conveniently to have only arisen at the time of the crime and to have just as suddenly disappeared afterward tends to be questioned and makes it difficult to obtain an insanity verdict. In Bobbitt's case, her counsel wisely focused on her preexisting psychological problems.

It is worth noting that some mental disorders do indeed feature a psychiatric crisis in which the individual's mental state significantly and dramatically changes, in what appears to be a *snapping of the mind* that is much like the snapping of a rubber band. To someone relatively unfamiliar with the individual, such a change may seem like a temporary insanity. Closer examination, however, will almost always reveal an extensive run-up to this "event," during which time the individual's mental state has considerably deteriorated, and is followed by a significant psychiatric impairment that lasts for an extended period after the event.

Actus Reus/Automatism or Unconsciousness "Defense"

Actus reus is the Latin phrase for "guilty act," which in combination with *mens rea*, Latin for "guilty mind," produces criminal liability. Although the actus reus element is not frequently considered in conjunction with mental disorders, if a defendant lacked the requisite actus reus needed for a criminal conviction because of his or her mental disorder, this may also absolve the defendant of criminal responsibility. For a criminal conviction to occur, the prosecution must establish that the defendant had both the necessary actus reus and the required mens rea (discussed below). In general, a person cannot be punished for simply thinking about a criminal act if the person does not act on this thought. To obtain a criminal conviction, the prosecutor must establish that the defendant took a material step toward carrying out the contemplated crime. For defendants who lacked control over their acts, a crime is not deemed to have occurred. Defendants' actions must be voluntary in the sense that they had conscious physical control over these actions. In other words, there must have been a "willed movement of a muscle."

The *automatism or unconsciousness defense* asserts that a criminal act has not been committed because the defendant did not have control over his or her acts, the defendant's actions were not thought-driven, or the defendant's acts were not voluntary. The classic example is when someone without warning pushes your arm so that it hits a third person. You cannot be convicted of assault because your action was not voluntary and you had no conscious control over it. There are four basic conditions somewhat akin to a mental disorder, albeit defined broadly, that may qualify for this defense.

The first is *epilepsy*. Epilepsy encompasses a spectrum of disorders wherein normal patterns of brain activity are disturbed, sometimes causing, among other things, unexpected behavior such as convulsions, muscle spasms, or loss of consciousness. The person's brain cells— outside the individual's conscious control—stimulate motor muscles and cause them to contract or extend, which in turn can result in involuntary behavior that harms another and would otherwise constitute criminal conduct. Although reports of criminal behavior associated with epilepsy-related violence are rare,[68] and related criminal convictions even rarer because of the automatism or unconsciousness defense, there have been reports of epilepsy-related criminal convictions. They occur primarily when individuals have prior knowledge of their epileptic condition and nevertheless engage in an activity (such as driving a car) that could harm others if an epileptic event ensued, with a conviction for criminal negligence or recklessness imposed when a crash, for example, occurred following such an event.[69]

A second possible qualifying condition is linked to *concussions*. The symptoms of a concussion can include confusion or feeling as if one is in a fog, with your behavior seemingly not your own, as well as amnesia. As a result of this brain injury, defendants may argue that their behavior was disconnected from their conscious control.[70]

The third condition is when defendants experience *dissociative fugue*, formerly referred to as a "fugue state" or a "psychogenic fugue," which is defined in the *DSM-5* as "apparently purposeful travel or bewildered wandering that is associated with amnesia for identity or for other important autobiographical information."[71] This dissociative state is marked by a person's sudden, unexpected travel away from home or customary place of work accompanied by amnesia for the person's past, identity confusion, or the assumption of a new identity; its onset is often caused by a traumatic or stressful life event.[72] Although this condition is not frequently raised as part of a defense, a California appellate court did rule that a trial court erred when it did not permit evidence to be introduced regarding the defendant's dissociative fugue state, leading the appellate court to reverse his battery conviction.[73]

The fourth condition is when a defendant commits a criminal act while *sleepwalking* or in another sleep-associated state. While recognized as the basis for a criminal defense in England and Canada, this defense has not been well-received in the United States.[74] Nevertheless, there has been a fair amount of interest in what is referred to as "sleepwalking violence," which has been defined as a violent act occurring during an episode of temporarily impaired consciousness caused by a sleep disorder.[75] Typically, there is no obvious motivation for the violent act, no precipitating event, and no existing psychopathology, and the individual generally does not recall the event when awakened. One case from 1878 involved a twenty-eight-year-old man with a long history of night terrors who fatally smashed his eighteen-month-old son against a wall in the middle of the night, but was acquitted of murder after he was found to be unconscious of the nature of his act by reason of somnambulism.[76] Some recent studies suggest that the number of cases of sleepwalking violence has increased with the introduction of various sleep medications, especially if ingested with alcohol.[77] Jurors and judges in these cases tend to struggle with how defendants can manage to walk, climb stairs, drive a vehicle, or engage in other motor activity, and yet be unaware of their violent actions, including not recognizing the face of a loved one, hearing the cry of the victim, or registering pain when they are injured during the episode. Similar arguments can be raised if a defendant commits a criminal act while in a hypnotic state,[78] although the influential Model Penal Code (MPC) explicitly states that "conduct during hypnosis or resulting from hypnotic suggestion" is not voluntary.[79]

It should be noted that the actus reus "defense" is also not a defense per se. Rather, it addresses the prosecutor's evidentiary burden of proving beyond a reasonable doubt each and every element of a charged crime, and thus it is distinguishable from the insanity "defense," which the defendant generally must both raise and establish. As a result, the actus reus "defense" offers a significant advantage to defendants. If the prosecution is unable to establish that a defendant had the requisite actus reus, the defendant must be acquitted and released, with no strings attached. In contrast, the insanity defense, while it excuses the defendant's behavior, permits the State to impose psychiatric observation and treatment on the defendant, often for an extended period (discussed in chapter 11).

Most states have not established any specific procedures for evaluating a defendant's actus reus, probably because the issue does not arise frequently. Trial judges may instead exercise their inherent authority to order defendants to undergo a psychiatric evaluation and employ the general procedures used for insanity evaluations (discussed in the next chapter). Because this issue addresses criminal responsibility as opposed to competency, the court will generally not employ the procedures used to evaluate a defendant's competency.

Insofar as the issue is raised, it is more likely to be raised in conjunction with an insanity defense, particularly if the jurisdiction employs an insanity test with a volitional prong (that is, a test that employs an irresistible impulse standard or something similar). If the jurisdiction does not incorporate a volitional prong in its insanity defense, then the defendant may simply assert that the prosecution has failed to meet its burden to establish the actus reus element of the charged crime.

Mens Rea "Defense"

In addition to the actus reus element, as noted, every crime also has a *mens rea*, or "intent," element, which focuses on the defendant's state of mind when the alleged criminal activity occurred. Pure accidents are not punishable under the criminal law. There must have been criminal intent for a conviction to occur. If the defendant recklessly caused harm (that is, pursued a course of action while consciously disregarding the substantial and unjustifiable risk it posed to others), there may be criminal liability, but if the defendant was acting as a reasonable person without criminal intent, criminal punishment generally cannot be imposed on the defendant just because something bad happened.

It should be noted that the *criminal* side of the law is distinct from its *civil* side. In civil actions, generally speaking, one person—the plaintiff—

brings a lawsuit against (sues) another person—the defendant—seeking to recover the damages unjustifiably caused by the defendant's actions; in these cases, it will usually suffice to show that the defendant was negligent (that is, did not take reasonable steps to prevent these damages from occurring), and it will not be necessary to show that the defendant specifically intended that this harm occur. In contrast, in a criminal case, it is the State—acting on behalf of the community—that is bringing the lawsuit (the criminal charge) against a person—the criminal defendant—and here it must be shown that the defendant intended that the harm occur or, for some crimes, acted recklessly.

The requisite level of intent associated with a criminal charge is established by a state's criminal code. The mens rea element for most crimes is satisfied if the prosecutor can show that an ordinary, reasonable person would have recognized that his or her act would or was likely to cause harm (a *general/objective mens rea*), regardless of whether or not the defendant did. This approach simplifies criminal trials since the prosecutor generally does not have to explore the mental state of the defendant at the time of the act.

Some crimes, however, particularly more serious crimes, require a showing of a *specific/subjective mens rea*. Here, the prosecutor must prove beyond a reasonable doubt that the defendant intended the harm or knew that harm was likely. Such crimes typically permit the State to punish a convicted defendant more severely and thus require a showing of a culpable level of intent or purpose on the part of the defendant.

Depending on the definition of a given crime, the specific/subjective mens rea element may require a state-of-mind showing of the defendant's intent, purpose, knowledge, recklessness, or, albeit rarely, negligence. Usually a pretty low level of "intentionality" is all that is required, as defendants do not need to have thought through their actions, anticipated all the steps needed to commit the crime, or recognized at the time the full consequences of their acts.

For example, the crime of first degree murder, generally considered to be the most egregious form of homicide, typically requires the prosecutor to show premeditation and deliberation on the part of the defendant to commit the murder (that is, specific intent), while the so-called lesser offense of manslaughter requires only a showing of general intent to commit an act prohibited by the law or recklessness, without the defendant necessarily having anticipated the specific events or results that transpired.[80]

If a charged crime has an *objective or general mens rea* element, evidence regarding a defendant's mental disorder is ordinarily not admissible into evidence because the focus of such charges is whether a "reasonable person" would have recognized the action would cause harm, not what the defendant perceived or intended. In contrast, if the crime includes a *specific or subjective mens rea* element, some states (although not all) will permit defendants to introduce evidence of a mental disorder to show that they either did not intend or did not know that harm would result.

The mens rea "defense" usually does not seek an outright acquittal, but rather represents an effort to reduce the grade or level of the crime of which the defendent is convicted, such as manslaughter instead of first degree murder or breaking and entering instead of burglary. This, in turn, reduces the severity of the punishment the defendant can receive, which often means a shorter sentence. Thus, the mens rea "defense" differs from the affirmative defense of insanity. The insanity defense provides an "excuse" that shields the defendant from criminal responsibility, although the State can still impose treatment upon the defendant following a "successful" insanity defense. In contrast, the mens rea "defense" simply asserts that the prosecution has failed to prove beyond a reasonable doubt an element of a charged crime. If the prosecutor fails to meet this burden, the defendant is acquitted of that charge and, if not convicted of any other charges, will be released, with no treatment obligations imposed following the conclusion of the trial. This mens rea "defense" is sometimes called a *diminished capacity* defense. Use of this phrase should, however, be avoided because it tends to be confused with "partial insanity" or "diminished responsibility," neither of which is recognized in conjunction with criminal law.

States differ on how the presence or absence of mens rea can be established at trial. While some states permit testimony from a mental health expert regarding a defendant's mens rea,[81] other states, including Arizona,[82] California,[83] Ohio,[84] and Virginia,[85] either do not permit or significantly reduce its use. The Federal Rules of Evidence, similar versions of which are employed by many states, also limits its use.[86] However, it should be recognized that if the defendant raises an insanity defense and introduces expert testimony to support this claim, this expert witness' evidence may "sneak in through the back door" to influence the factfinder's thinking regarding the mens rea element. In any case, it can still be used by the defense in conjunction with plea bargaining or sentencing to argue, respectively, for a reduced charge or a lesser sentence.

Supreme Court Rulings Regarding Variations and Alternatives to the Insanity Defense

Montana v. Egelhoff (1996)

FACTUAL AND PROCEDURAL FOUNDATION

The first USSC ruling to directly address mental health testimony and the mens rea element was *Montana v. Egelhoff*. In this case, law enforcement officials in Montana had found the defendant yelling obscenities in the back seat of a car that was stuck in a ditch along a highway. Next to him on the floor of the car lay a handgun with four loaded rounds and two empty casings. The defendant also had gunshot residue on his hands and his blood-alcohol level measured .36 over one hour later. In the front seat of the car were two men, each of whom had died of a single gunshot to the head. The three of them had been out drinking all night.

The defendant was charged with two counts of deliberate homicide. Montana law defines the crime as "purposely" or "knowingly" causing the death of another human being. The defense argued at trial that an unidentified fourth person must have committed the murders as defendant's extreme intoxication rendered him incapable of committing the murders and accounted for his inability to recall the events of that night. Pursuant to Montana law, the jury was instructed that it could not consider defendant's voluntary intoxication in determining whether the mental state ("purposely" or "knowingly") that was an element of the crime was established. The jury found the defendant guilty on both counts and the judge sentenced him to eighty-four years in prison.

The defendant appealed the conviction, arguing that excluding the evidence of defendant's voluntary intoxication as it pertained to the mens rea element denied him his right to due process. The Montana Supreme Court agreed and reversed the conviction. It concluded that the defendant had a due process right to present and have considered all relevant evidence that might rebut the State's evidence on the elements of the charged offense, and that the intoxication evidence was relevant to whether the defendant had acted "knowingly" and "purposely." With this evidence excluded, the court asserted, the State had been able to escape its burden of proving beyond a reasonable doubt every element necessary to establish the charged crime, and thus the defendant was denied his federal constitutional right to due process.

THE COURT'S RULING IN *EGELHOFF*

The State of Montana, in turn, appealed this judgment to the USSC. The Court began its ruling with a historical overview in which it noted the considerable variation among judges on whether a defendant's voluntary intoxication should be considered in a mens rea determination, with some asserting that voluntary intoxication can be used to defeat the State's assertion a defendant had the requisite specific intent (premeditation), and others contending that it should not be used as a basis for absolving a defendant of criminal responsibility and that, if anything, it should be a basis for punishing defendants more severely. The general societal view, the Court added, is that we all have a responsibility to stay sober if intoxication will jeopardize the lives and safety of others.

The Court ultimately concluded it was permissible for a state to hold defendants responsible for the consequences of their acts while intoxicated, and thus a state could bar evidence regarding a defendant's intoxication at the time of the crime. Based on its review of historical practice, the Court determined that common law courts had traditionally excluded this evidence and thus excluding it now did not violate a fundamental principle of justice under the US Constitution. Moreover, the Court found strong policy justifications for this exclusion: namely, that (a) a large number of violent crimes are committed by intoxicated offenders, and (b) disallowing this evidence may help deter this behavior. The Court also noted that defendants' right to a fair trial was not infringed by excluding this evidence as they do not have a constitutional right to introduce any and all evidence. A state, the Court continued, can limit the admission of some evidence if it has a "valid" reason for doing so, and these determinations should primarily be left to the states to make.

ANALYSIS OF *EGELHOFF*

A question raised by this ruling is whether the outcome would have been different if the defendant had instead been experiencing a mental disorder at the time of the crime, and Montana law prevented the defendant from introducing evidence of this disorder to show he had not acted "knowingly" and "purposely" with regard to the killings and thus lacked the requisite mens rea. The usual justification for treating the two distinctly is that intoxication is viewed as a voluntary choice, whereas a mental disorder is not. As for intoxication, the argument is that inebriated offenders voluntarily assumed the risk of ensuing criminal acts, while offenders with a mental disorder did not.[87]

There are, however, mental disorders in which the actions of the individual cause or contribute to the onset of the disorder or exacerbate associated symptoms, such as failing to take a prescribed medication. In addition, there are studies indicating that heritable, genetic factors play a significant factor in predisposing some to alcoholism; that many alcoholics have an inherent behavioral tendency called an "impulse trait" that leads them to overdrink; and that many alcoholics have a predisposing physiological makeup that results in their finding alcohol more "rewarding." Keeping these factors in mind, plus the power of addiction, advertising, and social peers, one might ask: Is the criminal justice system expecting some sort of extraordinary effort by alcoholics to refrain from ingesting alcohol, an extraordinary effort not expected of individuals with a mental disorder?

The dissent in *Egelhoff* argued that while a criminal defendant does not have an absolute right to present relevant evidence, the State must have a valid reason for precluding evidence that defendants want to present. Here the State excluded an entire category of evidence that could negate the prosecution's effort to establish the defendant's mens rea, which, the dissent contended, denied the defendant his opportunity for a fair trial as he could establish his mental state only circumstantially. Further, by excluding evidence that he was intoxicated at the time, the jury may have imputed to the defendant an unjustified degree of culpability. The dissent argued that this evidence was excluded solely to make it easier for the State to obtain criminal convictions.

Clark v. Arizona *(2006)*

FACTUAL AND PROCEDURAL FOUNDATION

Noted earlier for its holding regarding the insanity defense, the USSC ruling in *Clark v. Arizona* (2006) also contains a discussion pertaining to the mens rea element and related evidence regarding mental disorders. Under existing Arizona law, mental health experts could testify regarding a defendant's insanity defense, but could not address the defendant's mens rea. Much like the defendant in *Egelhoff*, the defendant in *Clark* argued that it was unconstitutional to preclude the defendant's use of expert testimony on this issue.

THE COURT'S RULING IN *CLARK*

In response, the Court, in a somewhat unusual scholarly exercise, declared that there are three categories of potentially relevant evidence in a criminal trial. First, there is what the Court deemed *observation evidence*. This category encompasses testimony from individuals who observed what the defendant did or heard what the defendant said. This type of evidence can be introduced at trial typically via a lay witness who was in the vicinity of the defendant at the time. Testimony may also be introduced to provide an expert's views regarding the defendant's behavioral characteristics, thereby confirming the observations of the lay witness.

The second category is what the Court characterized as *mental-disease evidence*. This evidence addresses whether the defendant suffered from a mental disorder that had certain features relevant to the criminal offense. Related testimony is generally provided by an expert witness, based on his or her examination and assessment of the defendant.

Third is what the Court described as *capacity evidence*. This testimony describes either the defendant's capacity for cognition or moral development in conjunction with an insanity defense, or whether the defendant had the requisite mens rea for a charged crime. It is also generally provided by an expert witness.

The USSC ruled that it was permissible for a state to channel the second and third categories of evidence exclusively to the insanity defense, which is what Arizona had done, and thereby exclude testimony from a "mens rea" expert regarding the typical behavior associated with a mental disorder, so long as the first category of evidence regarding whether the defendant had the requisite mens rea is allowed. In other words, a state can exclude evidence addressing whether defendants with a particular mental disorder will in general lack the required mens rea, and instead restrict the evidence to whether *this* defendant had the required mens rea, as demonstrated by the defendant's actions or words at the time of the offense. The Court reasoned that although defendants might want to use the former to establish that they likely did not have the required mens rea, a state can exclude relevant evidence if there is a good reason for doing so, as well as channel such evidence when appropriate.

The Court gave three reasons for why it is permissible for a state to channel the second and third categories of evidence exclusively to the insanity defense. First, the Court reasoned, just as states are entitled to limit the availability of the insanity defense by placing the corresponding burden of persuasion on the defendant, so too states should be free to limit the availability of the mens rea "defense." The Court noted that some categories of mental illness are controversial and that a diagnosis of a given mental disorder may mask an underlying ongoing debate among mental health professionals regarding the contours of the disorder. Thus, states are justified in being cautious about treating a psychiatric classification as an excuse for criminal behavior.

Second, the Court contended, because of the controversial character of some categories of mental illness, related evidence has the potential to mislead the factfinder. Even if a diagnosis is not controversial, the parties in a criminal proceeding may use the diagnosis as the basis for an unjustified inference. For example, the Court asserted that is very easy for a defendant to use a diagnosis of schizophrenia as a basis for sliding from a depiction of the defendant as "very different" into a determination that the defendant lacked the requisite mens rea at the time of the offense. In the Court's view, such unjustified inferences may result in distorted verdicts.

Third, the Court maintained that there is a danger of affording this evidence undue certainty, given that defendants' state of mind at the time of the offense is an inherently elusive concept. Psychiatric diagnoses, the Court continued, are designed to guide mental health treatment, not to establish a defendant's responsibility for a criminal offense. A state should be allowed to channel these categories of evidence in part because of the unreliability of expert judgments in general and in part because no one knows exactly what was on the defendant's mind at the time of the offense. An expert's opinion on the latter may be given un-justified authority by the factfinder.

Although stressing that mental health evidence must be allowed to play some role in these determinations, the Court concluded that a state has the option of channeling this evidence to either the insanity defense or the mens rea "defense," but does not necessarily have to permit it to be introduced for both purposes.

A four-member dissent criticized what it called the unworkable "re-structured evidentiary universe" of the majority opinion and the lack of convincing authority to support it. The dissent contended that the exclusion of this evidence denied the defendant a chance to introduce critical and reliable evidence regarding the mens rea issue. The dissent also asserted that observation evidence standing alone in this context makes little sense without mental health professionals being allowed to confirm and explain the account based on their experience with simi-lar individuals. For example, people with a mental disorder may play a radio loudly to drown out the voices they are hearing.[88]

Furthermore, the dissent noted that juries often address and handle a great deal of complex evidence. By excluding this mental health evidence, the majority was forcing them to decide guilt in a "fictional world" where they hear evidence regarding "undefined and unexplained" behaviors without the guidance provided by an enhanced understanding of mental illness. The dissent further argued that this mental health evidence was not inherently unreliable and that there was no bona fide rationale for restricting such evidence to issues pertaining to the insanity defense.

ANALYSIS OF CLARK

The majority's ruling in Clark reflects a continuing general skepticism regarding (a) the insanity defense and other mental health "defenses" in criminal proceedings, (b) the ability to reliably diagnose mental dis-orders and assess their impact on behavior, (c) the expertise of mental health professionals and their role in applying mental health concepts to criminal trial issues, and (d) the ability of jurors, as well as judges, to understand and use mental health evidence during criminal proceed-ings. As a result, Clark permits states to limit the role of (a) mental health evidence, (b) mental health experts, and (c) mental health "defenses" in these proceedings. Notwithstanding its acknowledgment that mental health information can be relevant in criminal proceedings, it is perhaps unsurprising that the USSC has generally refrained from wading deeply into the waters surrounding these issues.

Among the questions left unresolved by *Clark* is whether the Court would permit similar channeling to other aspects of the proceedings. For example, what if a state determined that mental health evidence and related expert testimony were too unreliable, uncertain, and prejudicial to permit their introduction during the guilt phase of a criminal trial, but instead, heeding the majority's warning in *Clark* that mental health evidence must be allowed to play some role in these determinations, channeled its introduction and consideration to the sentencing phase of criminal trials? Would that survive a due process challenge? What if a state channeled this information exclusively to GBMI determinations and precluded its use in conjunction with the insanity defense as well as the mens rea "defense"?

Conclusion

In light of the continuing controversy regarding what role, if any, the mental disorders of defendants should play in criminal trials in general and in determining defendants' criminal responsibility for their actions in particular, as well as the USSC's reluctance to interject itself deeply into the means used by the states to resolve these issues, it is unsurprising that a plethora of approaches for addressing and resolving the criminal responsibility of offenders with a mental disorder have been implemented. Furthermore, there is little indication that this diversity is going to diminish any time soon, although, as discussed in chapter 12, there does seem to be some support growing for the proposition that society is not well served by processing all offenders with a mental disorder through the criminal justice system and that these offenders, and the community, are sometimes better served by diverting them out of the criminal justice system and into the mental health system instead.

Indeed, notwithstanding that a few states have abolished the insanity defense per se, most states continue to make it available.[89] As a result, some defendants continue to be found NGRI. The question, which will now be addressed, is how should these proceedings be conducted. Once again, society's ambivalent feelings about mental disorders and related criminal behavior are a significant factor in shaping this process.

10

Procedural Aspects of Insanity Defense Determinations

Nothing fools you better than the lie you tell yourself.
—Teller, from the duo of Penn and Teller, American
magicians and entertainers

In addition to the numerous variations on the insanity test, states have adopted many different procedures for trying these cases, once again, largely because of the widespread uncertainty and disagreement over how to approach such cases. Unlike CST determinations, regarding which the USSC has issued rulings concerning associated procedural requirements, NGRI determinations and the procedures that guide them have been left primarily to the individual states to establish as they deem fit. As a result, these procedures can vary considerably from state to state. Because of the wide range in procedural approaches, and because the procedures employed within each state tend to be interlinked, space constraints dictate that the following discussion focus primarily on one such approach: namely, the NGRI procedures of Virginia, which employs an approach similar to that found in other states.

Virginia's Procedural Approach as an Example

Before turning to these procedures, it should be noted that Virginia's insanity test encompasses each of the three primary bases for establishing an insanity claim in the United States in that defendants can be found NGRI if, as the result of a mental disorder, they lacked the requisite cognitive, moral, or volitional capacity at the time of the crime. Unlike in some states, the governing test in Virginia was not enacted by the legislature, but is rather the product of a series of judicial rulings. The first of these, issued in 1881 by the Virginia Supreme Court, was followed by additional rulings that stretched across more than a hundred years and ultimately embraced all three bases for an insanity finding, thereby sparing Virginia legislators the difficult task of forging a consensus among themselves regarding the governing insanity test. The current test reads:

> The defendant will be found to be insane if at the time of the offense, as a result of mental disease or defect, the defendant: a) did not understand the nature, character, and consequences of his or her act, or b) was unable to distinguish right from wrong, or c) was unable to resist the impulse to commit the act.[1]

Ostensibly, the first prong of this test is somewhat more stringent than in other states in that the factors required to establish a defendant's cognitive incapacity are stated in the conjunctive rather than the disjunctive mode. In other words, to meet the requirements of the first prong, defendants must show a lack of understanding of the nature, character, *and* consequences of their actions. This may not have a significant impact on most verdicts since many defendants who lack one of these cognitive capacities will lack all three. However, the test does mean that the defense must be vigilant to ensure that evidence establishing all three cognitive incapacities is introduced during the trial. The wording of the other two prongs generally parallels the language found in other states that employ them, although instead of referring to an "irresistible impulse," the terminology used in Virginia is "unable to resist the impulse."[2]

In contrast, although the Virginia legislature has not set forth the test to be employed when defendants raise an insanity defense, it has established in some detail the following procedures for evaluating and adjudicating a proposed insanity defense.[3]

The Defense Controls Whether an NGRI Evaluation Will Be Conducted; Second Evaluations

Unlike a CST evaluation, for which the defense, the prosecutor, and/or the judge can enter the initial request for an evaluation, the initiating request for an NGRI evaluation must come from the defense. Like all criminal defenses, the decision to pursue an insanity defense is a strategic call left to the defendant, and thus only the defense can raise this issue. As discussed, some notorious defendants who might have met the requirements for an insanity defense (such as Ted Kaczynski) chose not to pursue it for various reasons.

On the other hand, there are at least three reasons why a defendant may request an NGRI evaluation even if an insanity defense is unlikely to be raised or be successful at trial.

First, the defendant, has sole access to this evaluator and the evaluator's findings unless and until the defendant (a) enters an insanity plea or (b) voluntarily shares these findings with the prosecutor,[4] at which point the prosecutor can contact the evaluator, as well as review and, if the prosecutor wishes, incorporate the evaluator's findings. But if neither of these actions occurs, the defense can effectively "bury" the evaluation, which is particularly likely if the information uncovered is unfavorable to the defendant.[5] If the defense does enter an insanity plea, then the prosecution can also have the defendant evaluated by its own expert or ask the court to appoint one to conduct a second evaluation, with which the defendant must cooperate.

Second, the defendant may seek an NGRI evaluation to discover mitigating or exonerating information unrelated to the insanity defense. During their investigation of the defendant's mental status and its impact at the time of the crime—which may include interviews with various relevant parties and a review of related documents—evaluators may gain important insights and uncover valuable evidence, some of which the defense may ultimately introduce at trial even if the defendant does not pursue an insanity defense. In addition, the evaluator may conclude that, although the defendant's mental disorder was insufficient to provide the necessary foundation for an insanity defense, the defendant lacked the requisite mens rea, or acted in self-defense or under duress. This may enable the defendant to avoid conviction or, at least, limit conviction to a lesser offense that imposes less severe penalties. Because the State may be required to pay for this evaluation if the defendant is indigent, this can be a valuable means of generating leads and gathering evidence for such a defendant.

Third, the defendant may seek an NGRI evaluation because the evaluator's report and the information uncovered by the evaluator may prove useful in conjunction with plea bargaining or sentencing. The prosecutor may be persuaded to drop the charges if the defendant's mental disorder was significantly linked to the criminal behavior, particularly if the charges are not too serious, the defendant agrees to obtain needed mental health treatment, or if other exonerating or mitigating information is uncovered. Alternatively, the prosecutor may agree to forego a more serious charge because, based on the evaluator's report, the prosecutor concludes that the defendant lacked the requisite intent or that an insanity or some other mental-status related defense might be successful. At sentencing, evidence regarding the defendant's mental state at the time of the crime may be introduced as a mitigating factor and enable the defendant to receive a reduced or suspended sentence or become eligible for parole at an earlier date.

At the same time, defendants may forego this evaluation even though there are indications they may be able to use it to successfully mount an insanity defense. Because of the stigma associated with mental disorders in general, and particularly when the disorder appears to be related to violent or repeated criminal behavior, an unsuccessful insanity defense may lead judges or juries to impose greater sanctions on a convicted defendant. Similarly, defendants may wish to avoid a defense that results in their being labeled as having a "mental disorder," as this may have adverse repercussions during incarceration or following release back into the community, as well as for their self-image. Indeed, fear of this label can be so great that some defendants prefer imprisonment over an insanity acquittal. An insanity acquittal also generally results in mandatory psychiatric hospitalization, often for an indefinite period that may exceed the length of time a defendant would have been incarcerated if convicted. Defendants may so dread psychiatric hospitalization, with its indefinite duration, that they decide an insanity acquittal is not in their best interest.

In Virginia, if a defendant does decide to pursue an insanity defense and plans to introduce expert testimony to support this defense, the defendant must provide the prosecution with written notice of his or her intent to do so at least sixty days before the trial.[6] In contrast, under the US Constitution, a defendant's CST can be raised at any time during the proceedings and without formal advance notice. Once notice of an insanity defense is given, as noted, the prosecution is then entitled to obtain its own evaluation of the defendant's sanity. The court will appoint one or more qualified mental health experts to perform such an evaluation, order the defendant to cooperate, and advise the defendant that a failure to cooperate can result in the exclusion of the defendant's expert evidence.[7]

Other states address this issue similarly. For example, in Texas, the defendant must file notice of his or her intent to raise an insanity defense at least twenty days before the date the case is set for trial, unless there is a pretrial hearing that precedes this twenty-day period. Then, the defense must provide notice at this hearing of its intention to offer evidence pursuant to an insanity defense.[8] A failure to provide this notice will result in the court excluding the defendant's insanity defense evidence at trial unless "the court finds that good cause exists for failure to give notice."[9] If the defendant does provide notice, the court may appoint one or more "disinterested experts" to examine the defendant and testify on the issue of insanity.[10] Furthermore, the court can issue an order compelling the defendant to submit to this examination, and if the defendant fails or refuses to submit to this examination, order the defendant into custody for a period not to exceed twenty-one days to enable this examination to be conducted.[11]

In New York, if the defense wants to introduce "psychiatric evidence" in conjunction with an insanity defense, the defense of "extreme emotional disturbance," or some other defense to which the defendant's mental state is relevant, the defense must provide written notice of its intention to introduce this evidence to the prosecution and the court before trial and within thirty days after entering a plea of not guilty, although the court can make an exception to this deadline if "good cause" is shown. After notice is filed, the prosecution can seek a court order directing the defendant to submit to an examination by a qualified psychiatrist or licensed psychologist chosen by the prosecution at a time and place designated by the psychiatrist or psychologist. If the court finds that the defendant has "willfully refused to cooperate fully" with this examination, the court may preclude the defense from introducing testimony by a psychiatrist or psychologist concerning the defendant's mental disorder at trial. If the defense has other evidence pertaining to its psychiatric defense, such evidence is still admissible, but the court will instruct the jury that the defendant did not submit to or cooperate fully with the court-ordered, pretrial psychiatric examination and that such failure may be considered by the jury in reaching its verdict.[12]

In another example, defendants in Iowa who intend to call an expert witness pursuant to an insanity defense must file written notice of the name of each such witness with the court and, upon such notice and an application by the prosecution, the court will order the examination of the defendant by a state-named expert.[13]

Obtaining an Expert for an Indigent Defendant

If, as often occurs, the defense lacks the funds to hire its own mental health expert to evaluate the defendant's sanity at the time of the crime, Virginia, as noted above, will pay for such an evaluation if the defendant can convince the trial judge that "there is probable cause to believe that the defendant's sanity will be a significant factor in his defense and that the defendant is financially unable to pay for expert assistance."[14] Usually this motion will be granted, but there are some drawbacks associated with this arrangement for the defendant.

First, under this provision the judge chooses the expert, not the defendant, and this may result in the appointment of an expert whom the defense might not have selected if given the choice. How the expert is selected varies from jurisdiction to jurisdiction in Virginia. Sometimes the local community mental health agency is tasked with providing the expert and designates someone who is already working with the agency as an employee or a consultant, or this agency may designate someone with whom its staff is familiar. Alternatively, judges may compile their own list of potential experts, possibly taking into account their performance in prior cases. Sometimes judges will ask the defense for recommendations and choose someone from the list the defense supplies if the court deems one of the nominees appropriately qualified. Occasionally, the judge will even ask the prosecution for its input on whom to appoint.

Second, the fee paid to the expert for this court-appointed evaluation is set by the legislature and the Virginia Supreme Court, with a maximum permitted fee of $500, plus mileage and a fee of $100 per day for any trial testimony.[15] This may not be much compensation in light of the expertise required and the effort and time typically needed to complete the task, with levels of reimbursement provided in other states. Highly qualified, conscientious experts, particularly those with a special expertise, may find Virginia's fee insufficient to persuade them to take time from their busy schedules to provide the requested evaluation. Some experts willing to accept this level of pay may do so because they are not in high demand for various reasons, including a lack of experience in conducting such evaluations.

These factors may result in defendants being assigned an expert the defense considers less than ideal. Balancing this out to a certain extent, the Virginia legislature does mandate the same appointment mechanism and fees if the prosecution requests its own mental health evaluation.[16]

Qualifications of the Evaluator

Each state is free to establish its own requirements as to who can provide an expert evaluation and testimony. Psychiatrists in good standing are generally authorized to provide NGRI evaluations and testimony. There is an ongoing debate, however, over which other mental health professionals (such as clinical psychologists and social workers) should also be deemed qualified to conduct these evaluations and provide related testimony. There has been a general push to allow at least some of these groups of professionals to supply NGRI evaluations and testimony because typically they (a) must meet their own licensure requirements within their respective states; (b) are generally authorized to provide a broad range of mental health evaluations and treatments;[17] (c) are more readily available, particularly in rural areas; (d) are less expensive; and (e) may supply a different perspective or expertise.

In Virginia, the state legislature has declared that the mental health expert appointed to conduct an insanity evaluation on behalf of an indigent defendant or the prosecution must be either a psychiatrist or a clinical psychologist. The legislature also requires that the psychiatrist or clinical psychologist

(i) has performed forensic examinations, (ii) has successfully completed forensic evaluation training recognized by the Commissioner of Behavioral Health and Developmental Services, (iii) has demonstrated to the Commissioner competence to perform forensic evaluations, and (iv) is included on a list of approved evaluators maintained by the Commissioner.[18]

These are the same qualifications set for evaluators of CST in Virginia.

Similarly, in Texas, only a psychiatrist or psychologist can be a court-appointed expert charged with examining the defendant and testifying regarding the defendant's insanity defense. In addition, he or she must be licensed in Texas, be board certified, have completed at least twenty-four hours of specialized forensic training relating to incompetency or insanity evaluations, have at least five years of experience in performing criminal forensic evaluations for courts, and have completed eight or more hours of continuing education relating to forensic evaluations in the preceding twelve months, although a psychiatrist or psychologist lacking these credentials can be appointed if "exigent circumstances" arise.[19]

In Virginia, if the mental health evaluator's fee is being paid by the defense or if the evaluator is being called as a witness by the prosecution, the trial judge will determine on a case-by-case basis—as with any other witness called to provide expert testimony—whether the evaluator has the requisite qualifications to provide expert testimony. Although the qualification requirements established for an indigent defendant's expert witness noted above carry considerable weight, other qualifications, such as membership in a professional group, may be deemed sufficient or necessary by the trial judge for a mental health evaluator to be qualified to serve as an expert witness regarding the defendant's insanity at the time of the crime.

States in general tend to afford trial judges considerable latitude and discretion in deciding whether to permit a mental health professional other than a psychiatrist to serve as an expert witness in an insanity trial. In Tennessee, for example, a court rule establishes that "the court may order the defendant to submit to a mental examination by a psychiatrist or other expert designated in the court order," with an accompanying advisory commission comment specifically clarifying that this rule "allows examination by other experts and not just a psychiatrist."[20]

Location of the Evaluation

Forensic evaluations, including insanity evaluations, were traditionally conducted at psychiatric facilities. The availability of these facilities, however, has dramatically decreased in recent years, and it has become imperative to reserve them for patients with the greatest need, particularly for crisis interventions. As a result, accessing these beds for forensic evaluations has become increasingly difficult, as well as expensive, with lengthy travel often needed to transport individuals to the beds that are available. For incarcerated criminal defendants, transportation must usually be provided by on-duty law enforcement officials, which is a costly and resource-draining arrangement.

Thus, states have increasingly allowed insanity defense-related evaluations to be conducted on an outpatient basis. These evaluations may be of shorter duration, easier to arrange, cheaper, and less intrusive than those involving placement within a psychiatric facility, as well as necessitating less travel. For defendants raising an insanity defense while in custody, such evaluations are increasingly conducted at the correctional facility where they are housed.

As discussed earlier, outpatient settings, including correctional facilities, are the norm for CST evaluations as well. However, the relatively short period of personal observation that mental health evaluators tend to have in these settings, compared to the "around the clock" observation in a psychiatric facility, has raised concern that these placements may result in a truncated or skewed "snapshot," which does not adequately demonstrate defendants' true mental state, including possible indicators of malingering. As for evaluations conducted in a correctional facility, there are additional concerns that the correctional environment, with its restrictions on behavior, may shape or bias the assessment. Nonetheless, the Virginia legislature, for one, has expressly established that

> [t]he [insanity] evaluation shall be performed on an outpatient basis, at a mental health facility or in jail, unless the court specifically finds that outpatient services are unavailable, or unless the results of the outpatient evaluation indicate that hospitalization of the defendant for further evaluation of his sanity at the time of the offense is necessary.[21]

Another concern that has arisen is that the duration of the NGRI evaluation is becoming unduly lengthy, much as it has for CST evaluations. Historically, defendants housed in large psychiatric facilities for these evaluations could get "lost in the shuffle" and forgotten—particularly as these placements tended to ensure that these defendants posed no danger to the community—even though such extended stays were problematic in that the defendants had not thus far been convicted of any crime.

Although placement in psychiatric facilities for these evaluations is no longer the norm, similar delays can occur today when defendants are evaluated on an outpatient basis, particularly when they are being held concurrently in a correctional facility while awaiting trial. Busy mental health evaluators may be slow in arranging initial observational visits with defendants or find it difficult to arrange such visits. In addition, they may deem it advisable to schedule follow-up sessions with the defendant to track possible changes over time or to confirm earlier observations, as well as arrange and conduct third-party interviews and obtain and review relevant records. They may also need time to reflect upon their observations, reach their conclusions, and generate associated reports. All of this may delay their determinations and the commencement of trial, which, in turn, may extend the time the defendant is incarcerated. Sometimes these delays occur because the defendant, third parties, and records are not readily available, but sometimes it may be because there is no institutional pressure to complete the task, such as the need to free up a psychiatric bed or begin the trial. Such delays may undercut a defendant's right to a speedy trial, but also be resented by the prosecutor and the judge who would like to move their caseloads along, although if the defendant is incarcerated during this time, they may be mollified knowing the defendant does not pose any danger to the community.

Lawsuits have been filed in response to concerns about such delays.[22] In addition, the Virginia legislature, for example, has established that defendants *hospitalized* for an NGRI evaluation cannot be hospitalized for more than thirty days.[23] It has not been established, however, that this cap applies as well to NGRI evaluations of incarcerated defendants. As a result, they, like defendants being evaluated for CST, may remain incarcerated for a lengthy and indefinite period while awaiting completion of the NGRI evaluation. One check on such delays that does exist under Virginia law is that trial judges are authorized to designate a time period within which the evaluator's report must be prepared, although the judge who is setting such a time period is also instructed to take into account the time necessary to obtain and evaluate needed information.[24]

In New York, after a psychiatric examination requested by the prosecution is concluded, the evaluator must "promptly" prepare a written report for the court.[25]

Information That Must Be Provided to the Evaluator

An evaluation is usually only as good as the information provided to the evaluator. Prosecutors and defense attorneys who are often very busy with their caseloads and other commitments may prefer that someone else generate the information evaluators need to do their job. They may also be reluctant to provide information to the evaluator because they may have favorable information presently unknown by their opponent and fear that providing it to the evaluator will result in their opponent gaining access to it. Defense attorneys, for example, will typically have greater access to information provided by the defendant and the friends and family of the defendant, while prosecutors have greater access to the law enforcement officials who conducted the relevant criminal investigation and their findings. Because justice can be compromised if defense counsel does not have access to critical information relevant to their case, the Fourteenth Amendment due process clause of the US Constitution requires that prosecutors share exculpatory evidence within their possession or control with the defense,[26] although a similar disclosure requirement does not apply to the defense.

As a result, it may be necessary for courts or legislatures to establish rules regarding which party must provide needed information to the evaluator. In Virginia, for example, the party making the motion for an evaluation is generally required to provide most of the information the evaluator needs, although the trial judge has the prerogative to order any other party deemed appropriate to provide relevant information. Because only defendants can initiate an insanity defense, if the defense has secured its own expert, it must provide, at least initially, all needed information to the evaluator. If the defendant is indigent and files a motion for the appointment of an evaluator at state expense, the defense is still charged with providing most of the relevant information to appointed evaluators. Such information includes, but is not limited to (a) a copy of the warrant or indictment, (b) the names and addresses of the prosecutor, defense counsel, and the judge who appointed the expert,

(c) information pertaining to the alleged crime, including statements made by the defendant to the police, and transcripts of any preliminary hearings, (d) a summary of the reasons for the evaluation request, (e) any available psychiatric, psychological, medical, or social records deemed relevant, and (f) a copy of the defendant's criminal record, to the extent it is available.[27]

This approach is different from that used in Virginia for CST evaluations, discussed earlier, in which the prosecutor provides most of the information to the evaluator. These divergent approaches may reflect the difference in focus of the two evaluations. A CST evaluation addresses a defendant's current mental status, while an NGRI evaluation examines the defendant's mental status at the time of the alleged offense. In as much as the defendant may currently be in the State's custody, it follows that the State may be best situated to provide the relevant information needed for a CST evaluation. In contrast, the defendant will generally not have been in the State's custody when the alleged offense occurred and thus the defense, with its greater access to the defendant and the friends and family of the defendant, may generally be better situated to provide the information required for the NGRI evaluation. Moreover, unlike the CST issue, the insanity defense is generally disfavored and not required under the federal Constitution, and so the Virginia legislature may have considered it appropriate to place the burden for providing this information initially on the defense.

The responsibilities are reversed when the expert is appointed pursuant to a request by the prosecution for an evaluation of the defendant following defendant's notice that he or she intends to pursue an insanity defense. Under this scenario, the prosecutor must supply the evaluator with the information listed above.[28]

A related question is whether the attorneys for the prosecution and the defense can be present at the evaluation, and, if they can, whether they can also ask the defendant questions at that time. New York, for example, has established that the defendant has a right to have his or her attorney present at evaluations requested by the prosecution, and that the prosecutor may be present as well, although both attorneys can only observe and cannot take an "active role" in the examination (that is, they cannot ask the defendant questions).[29]

Scope of the Expert's Assistance

Typically, an expert witness's primary obligation is to the party who hired or otherwise secured the expert's services, with their conversations and exchanges of information protected by the attorney-client privilege. Of course, any witness, including an expert witness, has an obligation to tell the truth when testifying or preparing reports submitted to the court, and a failure to meet this obligation can subject them to court-imposed sanctions for perjury. If the defendant does raise an insanity defense, usually the defense and the prosecution each secures its own experts, which then raises the specter of the so-called "battle of the experts" at trial.

If the defendant is indigent and must rely upon a court-appointed evaluator, an argument can be made that the evaluator's ultimate responsibility is to the court. Even under this scenario, however, pursuant to Virginia law, for example, the evaluator is effectively working for the defense as the evaluator's report "shall be sent solely to the attorney for the defendant and shall be deemed to be protected by the lawyer-client privilege."[30] If the defendant does not pursue an insanity defense or otherwise use the report at trial, the report and access to the evaluator's observations will remain in the sole possession of the defense and are unlikely to ever be disclosed. If the defense does decide to "(i) put in issue [defendant's] sanity at the time of the crime charged and (ii) to present testimony of an expert to support his claim on this issue at trial," written notice of this intent must be given to the prosecutor sixty days prior to the trial.[31] If the case involves a felony, the prosecutor must then be given a copy of the evaluator's report, the results of any other evaluation of the defendant's sanity at the time of the offense, and psychiatric, psychological, medical, or other records obtained during the course of any such evaluation.[32]

As for the expert's duties, ordinarily the expert will conduct an evaluation of the defendant, prepare a report based on this evaluation for the party that hired the expert, and be available to testify at trial regarding his or her findings if the party calls the expert to the stand. Although imposing basically the same duties, Texas authorizes a variation in the general approach by allowing the trial judge, once the defendant gives notice of an intent to raise an insanity defense, to appoint one or more "disinterested experts" to examine the defendant and testify on the insanity defense;[33] to submit a written report describing the procedures used in the examination and the examiner's observations and findings pertaining to the insanity defense to the court within thirty days of the order of examination; and to provide copies of the report to defense counsel and the prosecutor.[34]

Sometimes experts will also be asked to serve as consultants during the trial, providing relevant information or guidance to the attorney who hired them, typically with an additional fee provided for this assistance. Perhaps because of the limited funds available to indigent defendants, the legislature in Virginia has specified that this consulting role is the responsibility of an expert appointed by the court to assist the defendant and that "where appropriate" the expert will "assist in the development of an insanity defense."[35] For example, the expert may help defense counsel plot strategy for how best to present the insanity defense, including what points to raise and emphasize and in what order, what witnesses to call to establish these points, and how best to question these witnesses. In addition, the expert may assist counsel in identifying weaknesses in the testimony of opposing experts and other witnesses addressing the defendant's sanity called by the prosecution, as well as provide advice on how best to cross-examine them. This consulting role may require these experts to be present throughout the trial and to provide consultation outside the courtroom, both of which are relatively time-consuming tasks that evaluators may perceive as going beyond the typical responsibility of a forensic mental health evaluator and that constitute a considerable imposition on them, considering the fees they are being paid. As for why the Virginia legislature mandates this assistance, it may reflect its view that this type of assistance is vital to ensure that indigent defendants are able to reasonably pursue an insanity defense and receive a fair trial, given that defense counsel may not be well-versed in mental disorders and their impact, and related concepts and terminology, and may not otherwise able to secure this type of assistance.

Content of the Report

Typically in their report, evaluators will summarize their findings regarding the defendant's mental state at the time of the alleged crime and its impact on the defendant's behavior. Some evaluators will go into extensive detail, including a recitation of all individuals interviewed and documents reviewed, summaries of these interviews and documents, tests administered and their results, a description of the defendant's behavior and presentation, their conclusions, and a specification of what they relied on and why in reaching their conclusions. Other experts are much more succinct, sometimes arguing that the more information included the more confusing it becomes for their audience, and the more fodder it provides for opposing counsel to draw upon in mounting a cross-examination challenging their findings and conclusions. Of course, some evaluators simply conduct less extensive evaluations, relying almost exclusively on their interactions with the defendant, even if relatively limited.

In some instances, the evaluator will be asked to address both whether the requirements of the jurisdiction's insanity test were met and the defendant's CST (or other trial-related competencies). This may be done for the sake of efficiency. That is, if both issues have been or may be raised at the defendant's trial, relevant individuals, including the defendant, can be interviewed, documents reviewed, and an associated report generated a single time. Sometimes this is done as a cost-savings measure, especially if the evaluator's fee is discounted accordingly. In Virginia, for example, when a court-appointed expert is evaluating both the defendant's sanity at the time of the offense and the defendant's CST, the fee for the two evaluations done separately would be $500 and $400, respectively, but when done concurrently it is $750.[36]

However, there are some risks associated with this multitasking. These evaluations should be exploring different issues and applying distinct standards, which may be blurred or overlooked when addressed jointly. A determination regarding one may also inappropriately shape the conclusion reached on the other. In addition, if a defendant is found to be IST by the evaluator, any accompanying report regarding the defendant's sanity is questionable as the information provided by the defendant pertaining to this issue, a key aspect of this determination, should be suspect, assuming the defendant is able to address related events at all. As a result, in Texas, for example, an expert can be appointed to evaluate both a defendant's CST and the defendant's sanity at the time of the crime, but if so appointed must submit to the court separate written reports on the two topics; if the expert concludes the defendant is IST, he or she is not permitted to evaluate the defendant's sanity.[37]

Perhaps the most controversial issue regarding the content of an insanity, as well as a CST, report is whether evaluators should include their opinion regarding the "ultimate issue"—namely, whether the defendant's mental state at the time of the offense satisfied the requirements for the insanity defense. Typically, this would entail the evaluator reciting the legal standard and then identifying those aspects of their findings that led them to conclude the defendant's mental status did or did not meet the specific requirements of this standard.

The position of most scholars is that evaluators should not address the ultimate issue since this is the exclusive domain of the judge or jury, and incorporating an ultimate issue conclusion in their report or testimony is likely to unduly sway the ruling of the judge or the jury.[38] Because judges and jurors generally do not possess expertise regarding mental disorders and their impact and because these matters are often difficult to decide, these scholars contend that judges and jurors will consciously or unconsciously be persuaded by the ultimate issue opinion of the mental health "expert," even though the point of having a judge or jury decide an issue is to ensure community input into its resolution. Their argument is that a critical pillar of the criminal justice system will be undercut if judges and juries abdicate their decision-making role to the mental health expert. Indeed, the Federal Rules of Evidence, although not binding on state courts and while not prohibiting ultimate issue testimony in general, establishes that for a criminal case in a federal court "an expert witness must not state an opinion about whether the defendant did or did not have a mental state or condition that constitutes an element of the crime charged or of a defense. Those matters are for the trier of fact alone."[39]

Judges and jurors, on the other hand, may welcome this ultimate issue opinion, with some judges pressing for it if it is not readily forthcoming from the evaluator. They may assert that such judgments are largely beyond their expertise and that they need this input to maximize the likelihood of a just verdict.

As an example of one state's approach, a Virginia statute directs court-appointed evaluators to prepare a "full" report concerning defendant's sanity at the time of the offense, but does not indicate what a "full" report encompasses. The Virginia legislature, in general, provides little guidance regarding what specific content should be in these insanity evaluation reports. In an interesting twist, however, this legislation does direct these evaluators to include in their report "whether [the defendant] may have had a significant mental disease or defect which rendered him insane at the time of the offense."[40] This language seems to direct them to include in their report whether the defendant meets this standard, which is at most a step removed from addressing the ultimate issue.

Conclusion

While the USSC has left it to the states to devise their own procedures for resolving whether a defendant's mental state at the time of the offense satisfied the requirements of the jurisdiction's insanity test, forensic mental health evaluators play a key role here just as they do when courts address whether a defendant has a requisite trial-related competency such as CST.

As discussed, a key distinction between the procedures governing NGRI and CST evaluations is that an NGRI evaluation, at least initially, is generally under the exclusive control of the defendant and defendant's counsel and accessible only by them; any resulting findings are generally not shared with the prosecutor or the court unless the defendant takes the requisite formal steps to raise an insanity defense, which typically involves providing notice of this defense to the court and the prosecutor. Also, even if the defense is not pursued, the NGRI evaluation can serve as a valuable investigative tool for the defense. Another distinction between these two sets of evaluations is that the defendant's NGRI evaluator, whether a private hire or a court-appointed expert, may also serve as a consultant for the defense during the trial.

Among the ongoing controversies shared by both sets of evaluations is which professionals are qualified to conduct them and what fees they should be afforded if the defendant is indigent; where these evaluations can or should be conducted, particularly if they extend the incarceration of a defendant who has thus far not been convicted of any crime; who is responsible for providing specific types of information to the evaluator on a timely basis; and whether the expert can address the "ultimate issue" in any generated report for or testimony to the court.

If the defendant in the end is found to be NGRI, a separate but similarly thorny set of issues arises regarding the defendant's disposition. These are addressed in the following chapter.

11

Dispositions Following a Successful Insanity Defense and Risk Assessments

Only a fool knows everything. The wise know how little
they know.
—Author

Because a not guilty by reason of insanity (NGRI) verdict "excuses"—
rather than exonerates—defendants of criminal liability, the State has the
prerogative of retaining custody of these individuals following the completion of their trial to ensure that they receive treatment and do not pose
a danger to the community.[1] Each state employs its own procedures for
the post-trial disposition of insanity acquittees, but generally they include
an initial period of mandatory psychiatric hospitalization for observation
and evaluation, followed by a hearing to determine whether the individual
can be safely returned to the community. If it is determined that such a
return is safe, the individual is released. If it is determined that such a
return may not be safe, which is the more frequent finding at this stage,
the individual will typically either continue to be hospitalized or will be
placed on conditional release. The latter is akin to probation or parole in
that it allows these individuals to return to the community on at least a
part-time basis but under close supervision so that if they fail to adhere to
their treatment plan or other indications that they may pose a danger to
themselves or others arise, they can be readily rehospitalized.

Following an NGRI verdict in Virginia, for example, defendants are
placed in the temporary custody of the Department of Behavioral Health
and Developmental Services—the agency responsible for the delivery
of state-sponsored mental health services.[2] If charged with a relatively
serious crime, the defendant is placed in a secure psychiatric facility in
central Virginia, while those charged with a relatively minor crime are
typically placed in a less secure psychiatric facility at another location.
Upon placement, defendants are evaluated by a psychiatrist and a clini-

cal psychologist to determine their need for continued hospitalization; this evaluation must be completed within forty-five days.[3]

For as long as the insanity acquittee remains in the custody of the state, the court where the defendant was initially tried retains jurisdiction over the matter. This provides oversight of the process by the judge who presided over the trial, who ostensibly knows the individual's case well, and who is arguably best positioned to ensure the safety of the community should there be a proposal to release the insanity acquittee back into the community. Logistical challenges may arise, however, if this judge is located far away from the psychiatric facility where the acquittee is housed, as well as from the community where the acquittee may be placed.

Nonetheless, within the initial forty-five-day evaluation period a hearing must be held before this judge. Under Virginia law, this is a civil proceeding, which means the judge cannot impose any criminal sanctions on the acquittee. At the same time, it is generally acknowledged that the commitment laws pertaining to insanity acquittees cast a broader "net" than those governing civil commitment in general. In other words, it is easier for this judge to order an insanity acquittee's continued hospitalization. Following this hearing, the acquittee can be released, placed on conditional release, or committed (that is, hospitalized in a psychiatric facility) for an indefinite period, unless the insanity acquittee was initially charged with no more than a misdemeanor, in which case hospitalization can be only for a maximum of one year.[4] In Texas, in contrast, an insanity acquittee cannot be committed for a cumulative period that exceeds "the maximum term provided by law for the offense for which the acquitted person was tried," although after that period, the acquittee can be subjected to inpatient or outpatient treatment and supervision pursuant to a civil commitment proceeding.[5]

The initial expectation of most insanity acquittees is that they "caught a break" when they were found NGRI.[6] Thinking that they have avoided incarceration and will soon be released back into the community, they may see placement in a psychiatric facility as a relatively pleasant way to spend the interim. These expectations tend to be almost immediately dashed, however. Insanity acquittees typically go through periods of confusion regarding their status, frustration over the stringent restrictions placed on them, disillusionment with the notion that release will be shortly forthcoming, and ultimately fear that their confinement will never end.

Insanity acquittees quickly discover that they are housed in a secure facility, subject to strict regulation, expected to adhere to their treatment plan and the directives of staff, and constantly observed, leaving them with little privacy. They also learn that their treatment team is working for the court that assigned them there, not for them, and that they need to satisfy both the court and the treatment staff to obtain release. They may become upset when they feel they have done everything asked of them—including fully participating in treatment and behaving themselves—and yet their requests for release or at least conditional release are denied by the court and perhaps not even supported by their treatment team. Adding to their sense of disillusionment, frustration, and isolation, they may wonder why their attorney, who they feel must have the ability to secure their release, has not contacted them. Ultimately and painfully, the length of time they may be there sinks in.

At the same time, it should be recognized that the treatment staff at the facilities where the insanity acquittees are housed may also be struggling with their role. They have been trained as treatment providers, but in this setting, they are also expected to serve as social control agents, a role with which they may feel uncomfortable. They often feel torn between an allegiance to their client, whom they want to see progress and achieve freedom, and to the community, which they want to protect. Moreover, there are numerous barriers that limit their interactions with their clients, in part for their own safety and in part to ensure that they are not manipulated by their clients. Plus there is a lot of paperwork and supervision of their activities. Because of a need to avoid overcrowding at the facility, they may also feel pressured at times to recommend the release or conditional release of a client, but face significant adverse consequences if their recommendation proves ill-advised when their client "acts-out" in the community and harms someone, commits a crime, or fails to adhere to the conditions of release, including maintaining the prescribed treatment regimen.

Constitutional Framework Governing NGRI Dispositions

There is an ongoing tension between returning insanity acquittees who have not been convicted of a crime to the community and keeping the community safe from individuals who effectively admitted as part of their insanity defense that they committed a crime. This tension played out in the two US Supreme Court (USSC) rulings that provide the constitutional framework governing insanity acquittee dispositions. Unsurprisingly, states have tended to err on the side of caution and are often slow in returning insanity acquittees to the community. In recent years, however, census pressures and the costs of housing these individuals for extended periods have diminished some of this caution, although it tends to return following a widely-publicized adverse incident involving an insanity acquittee returned to the community.

Jones v. United States (1983)

FACTUAL AND PROCEDURAL FOUNDATION

Michael Jones was charged with shoplifting a jacket, a misdemeanor subject to a one-year maximum sentence. At his trial, Jones was found NGRI and, as a result, automatically committed to a psychiatric hospital, where he remained hospitalized for over a year (that is, longer than he could have been detained if he had been convicted of the crime with which he was charged). On appeal, his attorney argued that (a) the maximum length of time Jones could be committed for hospitalization as an insanity acquittee was the maximum sentence that could have been imposed on him at trial, and (b) an independent hearing immediately following the trial to establish that Jones was currently mentally ill and dangerous should have been held before hospitalization could be ordered.

THE COURT'S RULING IN JONES

In response, the USSC issued three primary rulings. First, the Court determined that an NGRI verdict is a sufficient basis for automatically committing these defendants to a treatment facility and that it is not necessary to independently determine that they are currently mentally ill and dangerous as would be required prior to involuntary hospitalization in conjunction with civil commitment. The Court concluded that a state can presume that an individual is sufficiently mentally ill and dangerous to justify commitment based solely on an NGRI verdict because (a) a state can assume insanity acquittees' mental illness is unchanged since the time of the crime even if a significant period of time may have passed since the crime occurred and even though they were subsequently found to be CST; and (b) the crime committed by insanity acquittees is sufficient to establish their current dangerousness, even if it was a relatively minor crime in which no one was harmed.

Second, the Court ruled that at subsequent hearings held to determine whether to continue insanity acquittees' commitment to a psychiatric facility, it is permissible to employ a standard of proof authorizing retention that is less demanding than the standard used for involuntary hospitalization (that is, civil commitment) proceedings in general. The USSC had previously established that for the latter at least a "clear and convincing evidence" standard must be used to reduce the likelihood of inappropriate hospitalizations and their associated curtailment of freedom.[7] But when judging whether insanity acquittees should remain hospitalized, the Court concluded it was permissible for a jurisdiction to employ the less demanding "preponderance of the evidence" standard, because insanity acquittees had acknowledged their mental illness and criminal behavior at their criminal trial. Thus, there was a lower risk of error at these subsequent hearings, which justified the less demanding evidentiary standard.

Third, the Court ruled that the length of hospitalization imposed on insanity acquittees can exceed the length of the maximum punishment for the underlying criminal charge an insanity acquittee faced. According to the Court, the permissible maximum length for involuntary hospitalization is governed by the purpose of the hospitalization. With insanity acquittees, the Court concluded, the commitment is for treatment, not punishment, and thus its length should not be dictated by the length of time they could be incarcerated for the charged crime.

ANALYSIS OF *JONES*

In examining the Court's reasoning in *Jones*, one might ask whether it makes sense to assume that the mental state of insanity acquittees remains unchanged from the time of the offense (the focus of the insanity defense) until the end of the trial. Keep in mind that months, even years may pass between these two events. The crime may not be immediately detected. A considerable period may pass while the crime is investigated. More time may lapse before the defendant is arrested and the trial commences, particularly if the defendant is identified as possibly IST, as often occurs in these cases. If so identified, time will then be spent evaluating the defendant's CST. If the defendant is determined to be IST, more time will be spent restoring the defendant's CST. Once CST, time will typically be needed for both the defense and the prosecution to obtain mental health evaluations pertaining to the defendant's insanity defense. Additional delays in beginning and completing the trial may arise for various reasons, including attorney and witness availability. Considering the fluctuations over time of the symptoms and manifestations of many mental disorders, as well as the fact that some may go into remission, is the assumption that the mental state of insanity acquittees remains the same from the time of the offense to the close of the trial a valid one?

In addition, insanity acquittees may have received treatment for their mental disorder in the interim, particularly if they have been deemed to be IST. Would not this alone be grounds for questioning the assumption that the manifestation and impact of their mental disorder remain unchanged? Furthermore, are the mental disorder and its impact that are needed for a successful insanity defense the same as the mental disorder and impact that must be present to justify involuntary hospitalization? Was the Court more likely driven by an appreciation that the various jurisdictions do not want to risk immediately returning insanity acquittees to the community following trial and should not be required to do so simply because they cannot establish the current presence of a sufficiently severe mental disorder? If so, should the Court have been forthright about this? Are community fears and public disapproval of immediate release sufficient justifications for the initial mandatory hospitalization of NGRI acquittees for further evaluation?

As for the evidentiary standard employed at post-verdict hearings to determine whether there is a sufficient basis to order the continued hospitalization of insanity acquittees, is it appropriate to permit states to employ the relatively relaxed "preponderance of the evidence" standard? This standard requires a state to establish only that it is more likely than not that the insanity acquittee meets the commitment standard (that is, that more than 50 percent of the evidence supports this verdict).[8] The precise wording of the commitment standard varies across jurisdictions, but the basic question asked is whether the individual is currently mentally ill and a danger to self or others.

Considering the uncertainty regarding diagnoses of mental disorders and predictions of future violence, is it appropriate to use such a low evidentiary standard at these commitment hearings? If judges or treatment staff at facilities where insanity acquittees are placed are hesitant for whatever reason to see an individual released back into the community, there are often grounds available for them to determine or recommend that continued hospitalization is appropriate. For example, frustration at being unable to obtain release may trigger a verbal outburst that can be construed as an indication of the individual's mental illness or dangerousness. A similar conclusion may be reached if medication is refused, notwithstanding that the refusal may be largely triggered by the side effects associated with the prescribed medication. Finally, insanity acquittees' prior acknowledgment of their mental illness at the time of the crime and criminal behavior may continue to provide a foundation for continued retention, notwithstanding the significant passage of time since the crime. Both the judge and the treatment staff frequently worry that they will be blamed if an insanity acquittee who is allowed back into the community commits a violent or otherwise criminal act, and as a result they tend to be relatively conservative in their release determinations.[9]

With regard to the Court permitting the length of hospitalization to exceed the maximum sentence insanity acquittees could have received for their charged crime, one might ask whether their commitment is truly for treatment alone, when they have essentially admitted that they engaged in what would otherwise be criminal behavior? As discussed above, there is considerable concern about releasing insanity acquittees back into the community, and this concern may well be an influential factor in deciding whether to grant this release. In light of the uncertainties regarding the treatment of mental disorders, should the maximum sentence at least be a factor to be considered when weighing conditional release? For example, should there be at least a presumption favoring conditional release after a period corresponding to the maximum sentence has passed? Is it relevant that most of these cases are the result of a plea bargain between the defense and the prosecution, but defendants are often not informed about or consider the possibility of extended hospitalization when they agree to the plea bargain? Their focus at this point tends to be that they are thereby avoiding (further) incarceration. Is it relevant that insanity acquittees' attorneys, who typically have limited experience with these types of cases, are also often unaware of this possible outcome? Is it relevant that both insanity acquittees and their attorneys do not realize the level of scrutiny and restrictions acquittees will generally experience following such a verdict?

IMPACT OF *JONES*

Regardless of all of these questions, the Court's ruling in *Jones* remains the governing standard today, although a state can implement procedures that are more favorable to insanity acquittees if it chooses to do so.

For example, a state can require that an independent hearing be held immediately after the insanity verdict to determine whether insanity acquittees currently meet the requirements for involuntary hospitalization (namely, that they are sufficiently mentally ill and dangerous). Because the insanity verdict remains relatively disfavored, however, states have been reluctant to do so. The concern has been that insanity acquittees who do not meet the commitment standard would appear to be able to walk directly out of the courthouse as a free person, notwithstanding that they just admitted to committing a crime. To avoid this possibility, an interim period of evaluation in a secure setting is generally imposed following NGRI verdicts.

Alternatively, at recommitment hearings states could employ a more stringent evidentiary standard, such as the "clear and convincing evidence" standard, before continued retention is authorized. This approach is attractive in those states where facilities dedicated to this population are overcrowded and financial constraints make their expansion an unappealing option. An initial period of mandatory hospitalization is thus assured, but extended retention becomes less likely.

As a third option, a state could tie the length of hospitalization to the maximum sentence the insanity acquittee might otherwise have served. Because of the census pressures noted above and because the insanity acquittees who would benefit from this mandatory release are generally those whose crimes were less egregious and whose earlier release would be less likely to raise public outcry and alarm, some states have implemented a permutation of this approach.[10]

Foucha v. Louisiana *(1992)*

FACTUAL AND PROCEDURAL FOUNDATION

It was not until its decision in *Foucha v. Louisiana* (1992) that the USSC put any substantial limits on the involuntary hospitalization of insanity acquittees. Terry Foucha, who had a history of drug and alcohol abuse, entered the home of a married couple in Louisiana brandishing a revolver, chased them out, and had begun stealing some of the home's contents when the police arrived. Attempting to flee, he fired his revolver in the direction of a police officer before being subdued and taken into custody. Charged with aggravated burglary and the illegal discharge of a firearm, Foucha was initially found IST, but was able to stand trial four months after the incident. During the trial, evidence was introduced that Foucha was experiencing a drug-induced psychosis at the time of the crime. At the close of the trial, Foucha was found NGRI and involuntarily hospitalized.

Four years later, at a hearing to determine whether Foucha should be released, staff at the hospital where Foucha had been placed recommended his discharge. Two examining physicians said his mental illness was in remission, but they acknowledged that he could be a danger to others in the future. Indeed, Foucha had been involved in several altercations at the facility. He had also been diagnosed as having an antisocial personality disorder, which was described as untreatable. Generally, such a diagnosis does not provide a sufficient basis for either an insanity defense or involuntary hospitalization; although classified as a mental disorder, it is not typically considered to be the requisite mental illness for these outcomes. Accordingly, the judge at the release hearing found Foucha was not mentally ill. However, he determined that he was enough of a danger to others to justify his continued hospitalization, and thus the judge refused to order his release.

THE COURT'S RULING IN FOUCHA

Upon appeal, the USSC held that following their initial commitment, insanity acquittees must be released unless they are *both* mentally ill and dangerous. The Court determined that continuing to hold an individual if both conditions are not present violates the due process and equal protection clauses. The Court's position was that criminal behavior should be addressed through the criminal justice system, and not via this mechanism. Therefore, dangerousness alone was insufficient to justify the continued retention of insanity acquittees, and Foucha was ordered released because the state had not argued that he was also currently mentally ill.

ANALYSIS OF FOUCHA

Still, a major question left unresolved by *Foucha* is whether a diagnosis of antisocial personality disorder (APD) can constitute the requisite "mental illness" needed to extend the hospitalization of an insanity acquittee. Louisiana had not argued such a diagnosis constitutes the requisite "mental illness," asserting instead that it could continue to hold Foucha simply because he was dangerous. Thus, the USSC did not address whether such a diagnosis can satisfy this requirement.

It should be noted that a few years later, the USSC ruled first in *Kansas v. Hendricks* (1997) and then in *Kansas v. Crane* (2002), that an APD diagnosis can satisfy the mental illness requirement needed to involuntarily commit a sexually violent predator, a line of cases that share some similarities with those involving insanity acquittees. In addition, the Virginia Supreme Court has ruled that drug addiction or alcoholism can qualify as the "mental illness" necessary to justify the retention of an insanity acquittee.[11] It reasoned that the legislature was not bound by the definitions of mental illness established by the medical profession, and thus could identify drug addiction and alcoholism as a qualifying "mental illness" needed for the continued hospitalization of insanity acquittees even if the medical profession does not consider either condition to be a "mental illness." At the same, the court remained silent on the question of whether APD qualifies as a "mental illness" for this purpose, even though this issue had been placed directly before the court.

There is considerable ambivalence about the APD diagnosis. Mental health professionals generally view it as a trait, rather than a condition, which is to say it tends to be a permanent feature of an individual that is unlikely to change over time and is relatively untreatable. Individuals with this diagnosis do tend to be dangerous, however, with some suggesting that 60 percent to 80 percent of all prison inmates could be assigned this diagnosis. As noted in *DSM-5*: "The essential feature of antisocial personality disorder is a pervasive pattern of disregard for, and violation of, the rights of others."[12]

Although it is a "mental disorder" under the rubric adopted by the American Psychiatric Association, APD generally does not meet the traditional definition of "mental illness" under involuntary hospitalization laws. Nevertheless, many people, including the judges presiding over these release hearings, are very reluctant to release insanity acquittees with this diagnosis back into the community, particularly if the precipitating event was a serious crime. At the same time, it is relatively unlikely that the diagnosis and outlook for these individuals are ever going to change, with the result that they may remain in custody for the rest of their lives, tying up expensive and scarce psychiatric beds while frustrating and exhausting treatment staff.

Another question is whether it makes sense that insanity acquittees who are drug addicts or alcoholics qualify for retention but not those with APD? Alternatively, should a mental illness that is "in remission"— that is, no symptoms of the mental illness are currently manifest—qualify as the requisite mental illness for retention? Are civilly committed sexually violent predators directly analogous to insanity acquittees? Both can be involuntarily hospitalized in a secure facility for an indefinite period, but should they be subject to the same retention criteria?

Post-Trial Procedures for NGRI Acquittees

Other than the requirement established by the USSC in *Foucha* that an insanity acquittee must be both mentally ill and dangerous for involuntary hospitalization to continue, the states remain generally free to process NGRI acquittees as they deem fit.

Many make four dispositions available. First, as approved in *Jones*, is *automatic hospitalization* following an insanity verdict to evaluate whether the insanity acquittee needs to remain hospitalized. Following this initial evaluation period, a hearing is then held. Based on the findings at this hearing, insanity acquittees can be *retained in a psychiatric facility*, approved for *conditional release* (although this option is not available in all jurisdictions), or granted *outright release*.

If the insanity acquittee is rehospitalized, review hearings will be held periodically to determine whether continued hospitalization is justified. If the acquittee is approved for conditional release, periodic review hearings will also be held to determine whether he or she is meeting the conditions of release. If not, the individual may be rehospitalized. If the conditions are being met, at some point the individual may be granted full release. If granted outright release, the insanity acquittee is generally not subject to further oversight by the State.

Each state tends to adopt slight variations on this process. To provide a more in-depth examination, the following discussion will focus on the procedures employed in Virginia.[13]

Temporary Custody/Initial Hospitalization

After the criminal trial, as noted earlier, insanity acquittees in Virginia are placed for a maximum of forty-five days in the temporary custody of the Department of Behavioral Health and Developmental Services (DBHDS).[14] Individuals charged with a more serious crime are typically placed at a secure psychiatric facility in Central Virginia, while those charged with less serious crimes may be placed at various other psychiatric facilities scattered across the state.

During this initial placement, the insanity acquittee is to be evaluated by at least one psychiatrist and one clinical psychologist, one of whom cannot be employed by the hospital where the insanity acquittee is confined. This arrangement is intended to counteract any institutional bias that may be present and influence the recommendation provided, such as a tendency to overhospitalize insanity acquittees to protect community safety or to fill hospital beds, or a tendency to release them too readily to reduce hospital census or to get rid of unruly patients.[15]

If either of these mental health professionals recommends conditional or unconditional release, the hospital and the local Community Services Board (CSB), which is the entity in Virginia responsible for the delivery of community mental health services, must jointly prepare a conditional release or discharge plan for the reviewing court's consideration. The hospital is involved in formulating this plan because at this point its staff is assumed to have the best relevant knowledge about the insanity acquittee, including his or her diagnosis, strengths, weaknesses, and potential risks. The CSB is involved because its staff is responsible for monitoring any insanity acquittees placed in the community in the region the CSB serves.

Copies of this jointly prepared plan are sent to the insanity acquittee's attorney, the State's attorney in the jurisdiction where the trial was held (that is, the prosecutor involved in the acquittee's trial or a colleague), and the CSB, thereby facilitating their respective abilities to participate in the subsequent court hearing. A copy is given to the insanity acquittee's attorney so that he or she can speak for and promote the interests of the insanity acquittee at the hearing; another copy is given to the State's attorney so he or she can speak on behalf of the community where the crime occurred and raise any concerns about public safety; and the CSB receives a copy because it will be responsible for monitoring the insanity acquittee if placed in the community and needs to know what the expectations are and be able to object if aspects of the proposed plan are deemed unfeasible or flawed.

The court where the criminal trial was held retains jurisdiction over these proceedings, is empowered to modify the proposed plan, and makes the final placement decision. This arrangement was made most likely because the State was unwilling to entrust the DBHDS with ultimate decision-making authority or subject it to the scrutiny and public attention that often accompany these decisions, when a multitude of factors beyond just what is treatment-appropriate may come into play. The belief may have been that a judge, as an independent representative of the community, would be better able to determine the appropriate placement. Because these judges presided over the original trial and heard the evidence introduced there, legislators may also have presumed that they would have valuable insights that should be incorporated when crafting the placement. Finally, the respect generally afforded the judiciary may have been seen as an important bulwark should criticism accompany the placement decision.

At the post-temporary custody hearing in Virginia, the judge has three options. The insanity acquittee can be (1) involuntarily hospitalized, (2) released conditionally, or (3) released without conditions. Insanity acquittees charged with a serious crime are almost never released without conditions at this first custody hearing. One noteworthy exception was Lorena Bobbitt, whose case, discussed earlier, generated considerable public sympathy and who had no prior criminal history or history of a mental disorder, did not exhibit indications of a mental disorder either at trial or during her temporary custody evaluation, gave no indications of being a future risk, and had a stable and reputable placement in the community awaiting her.

In most first custody hearings, however, the judge will decide between continued involuntary hospitalization and conditional release. The hearing generally focuses on the seriousness of the underlying crime and the insanity acquittee's perceived dangerousness. The seriousness of the individual's mental illness and its treatability are typically not factors unless they are intertwined with the individual's perceived dangerousness. These days most individuals with a mental illness are treated in the community, not in a psychiatric hospital, and the assumption is that nondangerous insanity acquittees can be treated in the same manner.

Involuntary Hospitalization

Following the initial forty-five-day evaluation placement, insanity acquittees will be hospitalized if they have a "mental illness or intellectual disability" and are "in need of hospitalization."[16] In making this determination, the court is to employ four criteria: (1) the extent of the individual's mental illness or intellectual disability, (2) the future danger posed by the individual to self or others, which in turn is based on whether he or she presents a "substantial risk of bodily harm in the foreseeable future," (3) the likelihood of successful outpatient treatment, and (4) "such other factors as the court deems relevant."[17] Even if the acquittee's mental illness is in remission, the individual can still be hospitalized if "the illness may, with reasonable probability, become active."

Obviously, these criteria afford the court a lot of flexibility. Even if the court decides that the insanity acquittee is not in need of inpatient hospitalization, the court can continue hospitalization if the judge determines that the individual will not receive needed treatment or habilitation on an outpatient basis. And, of course, being permitted to order hospitalization based on any other factor the court "deems relevant" provides the court with considerable discretion and largely shields this decision from challenge on appeal.

The key, however, is whether the insanity acquittee is perceived to be likely to represent a risk to others if placed in the community. Thus, the pivotal factor is whether the individual poses a "substantial risk of bodily harm in the foreseeable future." This aspect of the test indicates that not just any possible risk of bodily harm will suffice; the individual must pose a "substantial" risk. In addition, the risk must be of "bodily" harm, with a risk of "psychological" harm alone insufficient. Finally, the time span in which this risk is expected to arise is limited to the "foreseeable" future, with more extended time spans ostensibly excluded.

Beyond this, however, the test places virtually no limitations on the judge's discretion. As will be discussed, assessing the risk presented by an insanity acquittee is a tricky business, with many factors that could be considered. This test does not specify which factors should be weighed or excluded, or whether some should be weighed more heavily than others. This leeway may have been the legislature's way of saying that while the judge has to point to something specific—the judge cannot simply rely on a general sense of unease about the individual—but once the judge has done so, the legislature is fine with the judge erring on the side of keeping the community safe. Additionally, the legislature may have been indicating that it recognizes how difficult these determinations are and was willing to leave them primarily in the hands of the judges who have first-hand knowledge of these cases.

Review Process

Like all individuals whose freedom is curtailed by the government, insanity acquittees are entitled to various due process protections if involuntarily hospitalized, and this includes a right to periodic review of their continued need for hospitalization. In Virginia, the legislature distinguishes between felony and misdemeanor acquittees in establishing the parameters of this confinement and the associated review process.

If the most serious crime of which the insanity acquittee was acquitted is a misdemeanor, the individual can be hospitalized only for a maximum of one year, which corresponds to the maximum sentence a defendant can receive if convicted of a misdemeanor. After a year, these individuals must either be released outright or placed on conditional release. However, if the individual is placed on conditional release and violates one of the assigned conditions, the conditional release can be revoked and involuntary hospitalization reestablished, which could result in a cumulative series of hospitalizations that exceed one year in duration.

In contrast, insanity acquittees who have been acquitted of a felony can be hospitalized indefinitely. A review hearing that addresses whether they continue to need hospitalization must be held annually for the first five years and be conducted by the court that initially committed them; thereafter, a hearing before this court is required only every other year, although the insanity acquittee can petition the court for a hearing in the off-years. It should be noted that the State can petition for a review hearing at any time, thereby enabling treatment staff to facilitate the process of release or conditional release if they think one or the other is appropriate.[18] In general, as discussed earlier, the more serious the offense of which the individual was acquitted, the longer the insanity acquittee tends to remain in custody.

Conditional Release

The next step beyond involuntary hospitalization is conditional release. The criteria in Virginia for the conditional release of an insanity acquittee are: (a) the individual does not need inpatient hospitalization but does need outpatient treatment to prevent deterioration of their mental state, (b) appropriate outpatient supervision and treatment are reasonably available, (c) there is significant reason to believe that the individual will comply with the conditions imposed by the court, *and* (d) the individual's placement in the community does not create an undue risk to public safety.[19]

All four of these criteria must be satisfied before conditional release will be ordered. It is not enough that hospital staff have determined that hospitalization is no longer necessary or even beneficial. Indeed, they may conclude that placement in the community is now needed for further improvement of the insanity acquittee's condition and may even believe that continued hospitalization will be counterproductive. Nevertheless, if the three other criteria are not met, the individual cannot be granted conditional release. It is also worth noting that the second criterion—that appropriate outpatient supervision and treatment are reasonably available—is largely beyond the insanity acquittee's control as this is primarily a function of the community's willingness to fund and staff the needed number and type of related services.

Clearly these are a lot of hurdles for insanity acquittees to clear and a lot of reasons for courts to say no to a proposed community placement. The legislature likely adopted these criteria because once insanity acquittees are granted conditional release and placed in the community, they are less subject to supervision and control. One concern is that they may have feigned recovery and pose a continuing risk. Another is that they may discontinue their treatment, particularly prescribed medications, which could result in their mental state deteriorating and someone being harmed before intervention can occur. A third concern is that individuals who were previously victimized by the insanity acquittee, as well as the family and friends of these victims, may feel threatened or otherwise upset by the return of the acquittee to the community, particularly if it is unexpected. To address this latter concern, some states require that the court ordering an insanity acquittee's release or discharge on an outpatient basis notify any victim, or the guardian or close relative of the victim, of this upcoming change in status.[20]

IMPLEMENTATION OF CONDITIONAL RELEASE

Any approved conditional release plan in Virginia must be implemented by the local CSB, with the staff of this agency responsible for supervising the outpatient treatment of the insanity acquittee. The CSB must submit a semi-annual report to the court that ordered conditional release, in contrast to the annual reports that must be filed for hospitalized insanity acquittees. The greater frequency of these reports no doubt reflects the diminished control and supervision that can be exercised over these acquittees and the enhanced risk they are perceived to pose to the community.

The supervising court can revoke insanity acquittees' conditional release if they (a) violate one of the conditions of their release or (b) are no longer suited for conditional release, and (c) require inpatient hospitalization. In other words, the supervising court is again given wide latitude to act in that the conditional release can be revoked even if the acquittee has complied with all of the attached conditions, but the court determines the individual "is no longer suited" for this placement. A court should not revoke conditional release just because the judge thinks the community would be safer if the acquittee was hospitalized, something that could potentially be said about virtually all acquittees based on their previous criminal activity. Placement in a secure psychiatric facility, however, is a relatively scarce and expensive option that state officials need to reserve for those who truly need it. Nonetheless, if the judge can articulate a more specific basis for concluding that the acquittee should not be allowed to remain in the community, such as the individual is unable to secure a stable living arrangement or cannot find a job, this generally will suffice as a justification for revocation.

CONDITIONAL RELEASE PROCESS

Because conditional release imposes restrictions on the freedom of insanity acquittees, they are entitled to corresponding due process protections. Accordingly, a petition for modification or removal of a conditional release order can be filed with the supervising court by (a) the insanity acquittee on an annual basis, or (b) the CSB responsible for implementing the conditional release or an attorney representing the State at any time. Note that unlike the procedures associated with hospitalization orders, conditional release orders are not subject to automatic, periodic review hearings. This is perhaps because conditional release is not considered as intrusive or restrictive as involuntary hospitalization, and thus the need for periodic, formal hearings is not considered as vital. As a result, however, one of the designated parties must affirmatively request a change to the conditional release order or the status quo will continue indefinitely. Indeed, if there are no circumstances suggesting that the insanity acquittee now poses a risk, community members will generally be content with sustaining this relatively inexpensive option indefinitely as it ensures that the insanity acquittee will remain under supervision.

If a court hearing is requested, the insanity acquittee will be evaluated by one psychiatrist and one clinical psychologist, the same approach utilized in conjunction with the post–temporary custody hearing. If hospitalization is requested, the criteria described earlier in conjunction with involuntary hospitalization will be employed here as well. If the petition seeks the insanity acquittee's outright release and discontinuation of the previously attached conditions, the court is required to order this release if the acquittee no longer meets the criteria for either hospitalization or conditional release. However, before release will be ordered, a discharge plan must be prepared by the local CSB *and* the hospital where the acquittee was previously placed, thereby ensuring wider input into this plan, and this plan must then be approved by the supervising court. Ideally, this discharge plan will provide directions for the insanity acquittee in case future mental health issues arise, such as whom to contact for help.

Insanity Acquittee Risk Assessments

Protocols governing the disposition of insanity acquittees are designed primarily to ensure public safety and to prevent the premature release of an acquittee back into the community. Although addressing and enhancing the well-being of the acquittee are likely to be key factors in preventing relapses and adverse incidents, this well-being is arguably only a subsidiary issue in these dispositions. The focus of these complex protocols on public safety is a clear reflection of society's continuing discomfort with the insanity verdict and insanity acquittees in general.

Notwithstanding this pronounced public policy bias, the risk assessment of an insanity acquittee can be conducted in a systematic and scientific manner by a trained forensic mental health evaluator. Eight factors are commonly employed when assessing the future risk posed by an insanity acquittee.[21]

History of Aggression

The first factor typically examined, and one that resonates with the previously identified public policy concerns, is the acquittee's *history of aggression*. This requires a clinical assessment that draws heavily upon an account provided by the acquittee. However, because this self-report may be shaped by an acquittee's desire to avoid hospitalization or supervision in the community, which may result in the omission of less flattering details and events, forensic evaluators will typically seek out additional independent sources of related information. These may include reports compiled by law enforcement officials, court documents, school records, and accounts from family members or other individuals who know the acquittee well. If there is a history of aggression, the forensic evaluator will consider the age of onset, since the earlier the onset, the greater the likelihood of a continuing risk of aggression. The evaluator will also examine the frequency of aggressive events and any harm that resulted, and will attempt to determine if this aggression follows a pattern or cycle, with certain precipitants typically followed by an outburst. On the other hand, as the time since the last incident lengthens, the risk of future aggression is generally considered to recede.

Scores on a Psychopathy Scale

A second factor that may be considered is the acquittee's *actuarial scores on a psychopathy scale*. Psychopathy, sometimes referred to as "sociopathy" and now encompassed within the *DSM-5* diagnosis of antisocial personality disorder, is a psychological construct that describes an individual's antisocial behavior and chronic disregard for ethical principles.[22] It encompasses the characteristics of egocentricity, impulsivity, irresponsibility, shallow emotions, psychopathological lying, manipulativeness, violating social norms and rules, and lack of empathy, guilt, and remorse.[23] It is not a direct measure, but rather a predictor of an individual's level or likelihood of violence or dangerousness. The most frequently used measurement tool is the Hare Psychopathy Checklist—Revised (PCL-R), which has been found useful for identifying individuals at greater risk of criminal recidivism, although its use in this context has also been controversial.[24] While the base rate of psychopathy is low, some believe the predictive power of this test is high.

Substance Abuse

A third risk factor is the presence or history of *substance abuse,* which is derived from a clinical assessment of the acquittee by the forensic evaluator. In addition to examining the acquittee for indications of substance abuse or withdrawal symptoms, the acquittee's self-report will typically also be collected. However, in as much as self-reports about substance abuse are often unreliable as well, particularly if the insanity acquittee is currently hospitalized or closely supervised and without ready access to these substances or a culture that supports this abuse, the forensic evaluator will generally also explore other sources for this information, including accounts by family members or other individuals who know the acquittee well. The evaluator will be looking in part to determine if there is a pattern to this abuse or if there are likely precursors to its resumption. Substance abuse tends to be a particularly potent risk factor for this population, possibly the strongest, and may enhance the recidivism rate three-fold, so it tends to receive considerable attention.

Mental Illness

A fourth factor is the presence or history of *mental illness,* although some questions surround its application. As noted, the presence of a mental disorder at the time of the crime is a precondition for the insanity defense. However, the postulate that mental disorders cause or are significantly associated with criminal acts or violent behavior in general is quite controversial. As addressed earlier, most research indicates that individuals with a mental disorder are *not* more violent than people in general and, indeed, are more likely to be a victim of violence. The primary exception is when an individual with a mental disorder also engages in substance abuse, as these individuals do have a higher rate of violent behavior than the general population. This, of course, is why particularly close attention is given to whether there is an indication of current substance abuse or a history of such abuse when assessing the risk posed by an insanity acquittee. Further complicating risk assessments that focus on mental illness is the fact that the individual will often be receiving medication or other treatment designed to ameliorate the symptoms of a mental illness. As a result, the evaluator must often project what risks the insanity acquittee would pose if treatment is discontinued, which in turn requires the evaluator to anticipate the likelihood that treatment will be discontinued in the future and under what circumstances. This all requires considerable speculation. A more reliable indicator may be if the evaluator can ascertain an apparent link between the manifested symptoms of the individual's mental disorder and past incidents of aggression. If such a link can be established, then the evaluator can attempt to project whether those symptoms are likely to reappear and what might precipitate their reappearance.

Social Support System

A fifth factor assessed is the *social support system* available to the insanity acquittee. To the extent the individual has a stable place to live, healthy relationships with others, and employment, the future risk posed by the insanity acquittee tends to diminish. On the other hand, having to change residences frequently can make it difficult for an acquittee to maintain a constructive routine, including adherence to a treatment regime, and may induce stress that exacerbates the individual's psychiatric disorder or triggers outbursts and even violent behavior. In contrast, having a supportive and helpful social network, including relationship stability, can help the acquittee navigate the challenges of daily life and steer away from people, situations, and temptations that might induce relapse. Similarly, gainful employment can facilitate the acquittee's ability to be self-sustaining and independent, heighten self-respect and diminish discontent, and avoid hazardous situations.

Previous Failures

A sixth commonly identified risk factor for insanity acquittees is the individual's *previous failure when placed on conditional release*. Individuals' past behavior tends to be the best predictor of their future behavior. Thus, the evaluator will closely examine any previous placements in the community that ended in rehospitalization, attempt to identify what triggered a prior relapse, and seek to determine whether the same or similar factors await the acquittee if returned to the community. For example, is the individual likely to return to a dysfunctional relationship that played a role in getting the acquittee in trouble in the past or contributed to a failure to maintain a prescribed treatment regime? Is the acquittee returning to an old neighborhood where it will be difficult to obtain employment and prior acquaintances are likely to encourage substance abuse, an erratic lifestyle, or criminal behavior? Will the acquittee have difficulty obtaining needed mental health treatment on a timely basis because of a lack of transportation, an absence of encouragement from others to maintain treatment, a lack of mental health providers who have the needed expertise and are willing to accept the available payment for services, or for other recurring reasons?

Victim Access

A seventh factor for the evaluator to assess is whether the acquittee will have ready *access to a prior victim* following placement in the community. As discussed, patterns of behavior can be difficult to break. If there is a previous victim living nearby in the community where the acquittee will be placed, the evaluator should examine what precipitated the criminal behavior involving this victim in the past and whether those precipitants are likely to still be present. For example, were the victim and the acquittee involved in a sexual relationship that induced feelings of jealousy or rage on the part of the acquittee and, if so, might those feelings still exist or be readily rekindled? Was a family member, such as a parent or sibling, the victim of an attack by the acquittee? If that was the case, how likely is it that the acquittee will be dependent on that family member for housing or other support upon returning to the community? And further, if the acquittee's relationship with the victim was relatively dysfunctional, is their relationship likely to be resumed and, if this occurs, is it likely to trigger an outburst in the acquittee, psychological deterioration, or failure to adhere to his or her treatment plan? One of the challenges of assessing insanity acquittees while they are still hospitalized is that although the evaluator may observe positive and successful interactions with other individuals within this secure setting, these interactions may provide little indication of how they will act when reunited with individuals with whom they have a lengthy and oftentimes dysfunctional history and who may be uniquely likely to induce a relapse on the part of acquittees.

Demographic Characteristics

Various *demographic characteristics* are the eighth factor that a forensic evaluator is likely to consider. For example, it has long been established that young males pose the highest risk of violent and other criminal behavior. There is, of course, little that acquittees can do about their age and gender. Nonetheless, these characteristics may lead evaluators to be more cautious in recommending conditional release or discharge. Alternatively, they may consider how these characteristics may impact the likely success of a community placement and attempt to identify and recommend conditions of release that take them into account and minimize their impact. A particularly thorny issue is whether the race of acquittees should play a role in these assessments. Regarding any of these demographic characteristics, prevailing stereotypes and biases have the potential to inappropriately shape forensic evaluations and resulting recommendations. The training given to most forensic evaluators attempts to facilitate their ability to recognize potential stereotypes and biases and help them steer clear of them. This, of course, is much easier said than done, particularly when a mental disorder, which induces its own stereotypes and biases, is involved. Nevertheless, a competent evaluator will recognize that it is the mental disorder that has been determined to have played a significant role in the acquittee's criminal behavior, and to the extent that treatment of this disorder has progressed, these acquittees—regardless of their demographic characteristics—are entitled to a graduated reentry and opportunity to demonstrate they can successfully reintegrate themselves into the community.

Risk Assessment Instruments

These and other factors have been incorporated in various *risk assessment instruments* that can be employed in conjunction with insanity acquittee and other criminal justice proceedings (particularly sentencing, probation, parole, and sexually violent predator proceedings).[25] There is a lengthy, ongoing debate over the ability of these instruments, and of mental health experts, to *predict future violent behavior* in general. While an extensive discussion of this topic is beyond the scope of this volume and better reserved for a discussion on sentencing, particularly in conjunction with the death penalty, it is worth noting the following statement by a group of the leading scholars in the field: "Clinicians' involvement in violence prediction is extremely controversial. . . . There is no other area of the law in which expert testimony may exert so significant an impact. At the same time, . . . myriad factors limit clinicians' abilities in this area; many have questioned whether mental health professionals' predictions of violent behavior are sufficiently accurate to meet acceptable scientific or legal standards."[26] A relatively recent task force of the American Academy of Psychiatry and the Law reached a somewhat similar conclusion when it determined that "the use of structured assessment tools in risk assessment has increased in recent years, and their predictive validity has now been demonstrated in a range of settings. . . . The factors that affect risk in an individual case cannot always be captured by an instrument, however, and the . . . forensic roles of these techniques remain a subject of debate."[27]

This debate has been particularly pronounced with regard to proceedings about whether to release or conditionally release insanity acquittees *back into the community* since the determination must address both current mental illness and the risk of dangerousness, as well as balance the liberty interests of the insanity acquittee and the protection of society.[28] Previously, assessments of future dangerousness based on unguided clinical judgment purportedly gave greater weight to the protection of society and overclassified insanity acquittees as high risk.[29] In the past few decades, a number of structured risk assessment instruments have been developed, and although "researchers have consistently found that the use of structured risk assessments improves the accuracy of such decisions," it has also been demonstrated that these instruments "are rarely used in release decision-making," notwithstanding "revocation rates that range from 35 to 50 percent."[30] Work continues on developing risk assessment tools that have greater predictive validity in the hope that they will be more widely employed.[31]

Conclusion

Risk assessments in general, including those targeting insanity acquittees, can address only the probability of future events, not make guaranteed predictions. They are an attempt to identify factors that affect the likelihood of a particular outcome. When used to assess the likely success of a proposed placement for a given insanity acquittee, the relevant risk factors and the precision with which they can be determined will tend to vary as the conditions in the individual's life change, with estimates of risk being inevitably more accurate in the short term and when focused on a relatively limited question and predictable setting. Complicating these efforts is the fact that an acquittee's mental disorder may reemerge unexpectedly, evolve, or impact the individual's behavior in an unanticipated fashion. It is virtually impossible to predict with absolute certainty how a specific insanity acquittee will do when returned to the community, particularly over the long term. Although the forensic instruments used for these assessments continue to improve, forensic evaluators generally recognize the limitations of their assessments.

The problem, of course, is that courts and public officials, including prosecutors and other members of the criminal justice system, are responsible for helping to keep the community safe. As a result, they seek assurances that it is safe to return a given insanity acquittee to the community and are not pleased when evaluators equivocate or attach qualifications to their determinations. They are particularly displeased, however, when an evaluation that an insanity acquittee can be safely returned to the community proves incorrect. Nevertheless, the governing law mandates that a process must be in place that ultimately returns most insanity acquittees to the community. As discussed, finding the proper balance between this requirement and public safety is an ongoing challenge, as is establishing appropriate related procedures.

Such uncertainty, of course, is why society and the criminal justice system have long wrestled with how to respond to criminal defendants with a mental disorder. As the following, final chapter reiterates, frequent dissatisfaction with the status quo has resulted in continuing efforts to devise alternatives in the hope that they will produce better outcomes.

12

Alternatives and Closing Remarks

While fictional figures such as Sherlock Holmes are always able to see their way through the shroud that may envelop a criminal investigation and get to the "truth" of the matter, it should be clear by now that conducting a forensic evaluation is an incredibly challenging undertaking, with the administration of justice frequently hanging in the balance and numerous interested parties closely scrutinizing and often second-guessing and challenging these evaluations. As a result, this undertaking is not for the faint of heart and should always be accompanied with a dose of humility and reserve. When called upon as the "expert" in these cases, an evaluator may be tempted to assume an aura of supreme confidence and unassailability in attempting to "sell" his or her insights and findings to the factfinder, and perhaps the general public. It is essential, however, that forensic mental health evaluators meticulously consider and even second-guess their findings, as well as acknowledge the limitations of their craft both in general and with regard to the case before the court.

Alternatives to Traditional Criminal Justice Mental Health–Related Proceedings

In recognition of the fallibility of forensic mental health evaluations and the often controversial nature of the criminal justice procedures used to ascertain and address the competency, criminal responsibility, and dispositions of defendants with a mental disorder, it is important to note two options that many jurisdictions use to process these individuals without employing the traditional criminal justice system. Forensic mental health evaluators can provide important input here as well.

Diversion

An option that was once frequently employed, then became less available in the 1980s and 1990s, but that today is being used again more widely is the *diversion* of criminal offenders with a mental disorder out of the criminal justice system. The premise underlying this approach is that law enforcement officials responding to a crime who recognize the suspected offender has a mental disorder should *exercise discretion* and divert the individual to the mental health system, rather than arrest the person.

Typically, the law enforcement officials exercising this option start by establishing that the individual is not a continuing danger or at least would not be with appropriate services and treatment. Sometimes what is needed is to simply remove the individual from a situation that is triggering or exacerbating his or her mental disorder or to arrange for the individual to resume lapsed treatment such as medication. Diversion, however, is generally an option only when a relatively minor criminal offense occurred—usually, one that involves limited property damage—and when any individual harmed by the crime acquiesces in this diversion, which is more likely to be the case if a family member or an acquaintance was the victim.

Historically, responding law enforcement officials were readily able to exercise this type of discretion, in part because of the wide availability of psychiatric placements. During the 1980s and 1990s, however, as America and its criminal justice system embraced a "get tough on crime" philosophy, law enforcement agencies gravitated to a *broken window approach*, which asserted that the key to keeping communities safe and decreasing crime was to arrest individuals for even relatively minor infractions, thereby purportedly keeping offenders off the streets and preventing them from "graduating" to more serious crimes. This response also reflected the dwindling number of beds in psychiatric facilities, the fragmentation and unavailability of community mental health systems, and the limited insight of most law enforcement officials into mental disorders, the value of mental health services, and how to access the mental health system.[1]

More recently, it has come to be recognized that, especially when a mental disorder influenced their behavior, running relatively minor offenders through the criminal justice system does not tend to reduce crime and may even be counterproductive in that it often has a devastating effect on these individuals and their prospects in life.

In response, numerous jurisdictions have established *crisis intervention teams* (CITs). CIT is a model for community policing that brings together law enforcement officers, mental health providers, hospital emergency departments, and individuals with experience working with mental disorders and related criminal behavior. Sometimes the emphasis is on providing select members of the local law enforcement agency with mental health training, so that they can promptly assist officers in the field who have encountered a situation in which they believe a mental disorder played a significant role. Other times, there are designated mental health providers who have been trained to work with law enforcement officers and who are called to the scene when needed. In addition, in some situations, the law enforcement agency will call upon the local mental health system for information about an individual in the hope it will provide suggestions on how best to proceed, although this can raise confidentiality and privacy questions. Whatever the specific approach, the idea is that a person with mental health training can often better respond to and defuse these situations. Frequently, rather than arrest a suspected offender, this mental health "expert" may ascertain that both the suspected offender and the community are better served if the individual is instead diverted to the mental health system.[2]

Mental Health Courts

Another option increasingly appended to the judicial system is problem-solving or *mental health courts* (MHCs);[3] almost 350 of these courts are now operational in the United States.[4] Employed in California, Florida, New York, and other jurisdictions, MHCs typically try to divert nonviolent offenders with a mental disorder away from incarceration and into a judicially supervised mental health treatment regime instead. MHCs often apply the principles of *therapeutic jurisprudence*, a school of thought that has explored alternatives to the conventional criminal justice system approach. This school of thought recognizes that an offender's interactions with the criminal justice system can have anti-therapeutic consequences, and seeks to enhance the design of the criminal justice system to promote the psychological well-being of participants without sacrificing other societal values.[5]

MHCs seek to reduce the criminal behavior of offenders with a mental disorder by directly addressing the disorder associated with the illegal conduct. The general assumption is that there is a causal link between the disorder and the criminal behavior. Thus, these courts are limited to defendants with an identified mental disorder, although jurisdictions differ in how this eligibility requirement is defined. MHCs also commonly consider the type of offense committed when determining eligibility, with a quarter of them restricting participation to offenders with misdemeanor charges, although roughly half accept participants charged with felonies if the criminal behavior was nonviolent in nature.[6]

Many MHCs require an initial plea of guilty or *nolo contendere* (a plea wherein the defendant does not accept or deny responsibility for the charged crime but agrees to accept the corresponding punishment) from defendants as a condition of participation. This is done to better ensure that they acknowledge their responsibility for what occurred and their commitment to changing their behavior. At the beginning of the proceeding, however, attention may be given to the offenders' competence to participate in the proceedings and understand that participation is voluntary, part of an effort to ensure that they choose to enroll in the program knowingly and of their own accord.

While MHCs function on one level as criminal courts, they differ significantly from the norm in that they typically employ informal proceedings and a *nonadversarial team approach*, with the judge, the offender, and the defense and prosecuting attorneys assuming "cooperative" roles. Emphasis is often placed on negotiating and obtaining the defendant's agreement to a supervised program of community mental health treatment that typically requires the offender to take prescribed medications. Compliance is usually supervised by either dedicated court personnel or community mental health treatment professionals.

MHCs encourage adherence to treatment plans by offering incentives for compliance and imposing sanctions for noncompliance. Incentives range widely from simple praise by the judge at weekly status hearings to having the initial charges dropped or a conviction vacated after successful completion of the requirements established by the MHC.

Sanctions for noncompliance also vary considerably; they can include requiring that more mental health services be obtained, that the level of supervision be increased, and that participants be expelled from the program and placed in jail for the underlying crime. One of the purported strengths of the MHC system, and generally a prerequisite for these courts to function successfully, is the ability to forge and enhance linkages between the criminal justice system and the local community mental health system.[7]

Concerns, however, have also been expressed about the MHC system. For example, because it (a) does not attempt to process offenders as quickly as a traditional criminal court, (b) necessitates that additional services be made available to defendants, including supervision, and (c) requires extensive judicial involvement, this alternative can entail considerable expense. With state systems in general and court systems in particular often facing budgetary constraints, a significant issue is whether the initial and sustained funding needed for an MHC can be obtained. If it is, another dilemma is that this funding may be diverted from other needed programs, with the result that criminal defendants, including those with mental disorders, who are not placed in a MHC may receive even less attention and resources than the minimal levels they currently receive.

Some have also questioned whether these courts actually reduce recidivism, a pivotal issue in light of their expense. For example, although efforts are typically made to have offenders play a role in the proceedings and to have them engage in a dialogue with the judge, their involvement is still relatively limited or driven more by a desire to avoid sanctions than for self-improvement, with the result that important lessons may not be learned and retained. In addition, sometimes factors that are beyond the control of the offender may cause a relapse. Another concern is that given MHCs' tendency to limit participation to relatively high-functioning, treatment-compliant offenders—which may in part explain the purported successes they have achieved—MHCs may not benefit those offenders who have the greatest treatment needs and are the most vulnerable and likely to recidivate within the criminal justice system.

These courts may also find it difficult to identify needed community mental health treatment partners, particularly when the availability of these services is generally limited or costly, local mental health providers are unwilling to work with criminal offenders because they see them as more challenging or dangerous, or available services have previously proven ineffective for the individual appearing before the court. Concern has also been raised that the interjection of these courts may skew the local mental health service delivery system by placing a new and significant demand on its limited existing treatment resources, particularly if judges insist that MHC clients receive top priority. In addition, although MHCs may be more effective than traditional courts at encouraging treatment compliance, a substantial number of MHC clients still decline or fail to adhere to their mandated treatment program, or, as noted, adhere only superficially to their program to avoid the criminal sanctions they would otherwise incur, thereby failing to develop needed insights into the consequences of their criminal acts and that mental health treatment can prevent relapse and recidivism. Another fear is that as an appendage of the relatively regimented criminal justice system, MHCs may find it difficult to tolerate the sometimes slow, erratic, and uncertain course of treatment for mental disorders and make demands of offenders that are unrealistic or counterproductive.

Finally, studies indicate that input from the *victims* of the crime at MHC proceedings is quite limited. These victims may view MHCs as allowing offenders to escape responsibility for their actions, which, in turn, may undercut the *restorative function* of the criminal justice system and fail to repair the harm done to victims or mend prior relationships between victims and offenders.

Ultimately, the key questions regarding MHCs is whether they (a) provide a suitable and appropriate response to offenders with a mental disorder, (b) reduce recidivism and criminal activity in general, and (c) promote the well-being and recovery of these individuals, while also addressing the needs of the victims of these crimes and society in general.[8]

Closing Remarks

This text has delineated the many ways in which jurisdictions address and process criminal defendants with a mental disorder. A key for any response is a better understanding of mental disorders in general, their impact on behavior, particularly behavior associated with a possible criminal offense, and their cognitive and volitional effects, especially as they pertain to a criminal defendant's ability to receive a fair and just trial. While the high-profile cases described herein have often established the parameters of this system, they have also tended to skew rather than inform these efforts. Thus, even though it is important to be cognizant of these cases and the public's perception of them and associated stereotypes when attempting to craft an appropriate response, it is critical to dig deeper, in part because of the broad diversity of criminal defendants with a mental disorder who are immersed in the criminal justice system, but also to ensure that a fair and just approach is being employed.

In pursuit of these goals, this text has sought to provide an in-depth analysis of the various stages of criminal trials where the mental disorders of criminal defendants are a pivotal factor. It is hoped that readers have gained a greater understanding of key related issues, why they are addressed as they are, and the challenges and limitations of the prevalent responses. Attention has also been given to the central role played in these determinations by forensic mental health evaluators and their mental status evaluations, as well as the demanding nature of the task. Unlike Sherlock Holmes, they may not always "solve" every case brought before them, but they can greatly facilitate the fair and just resolution of these cases.

NOTES

INTRODUCTION

1 His name was reported in some accounts as Cho Sueng-Hui. For the report of the review panel convened by the governor of Virginia to investigate this event, see Virginia Tech Review Panel (2007).
2 Killer's Manifesto (2007).
3 Ziv (2014).
4 Jacobs, Filipov, and Wen (2013).
5 Preidt (2017).
6 Kessler et al. (2005a); Weiss (2005).
7 APA (2000).
8 Mental Health Early Intervention (2000).

CHAPTER 1. MENTAL DISORDERS AND CRIMINAL BEHAVIOR

1 A "mental disorder" has been defined as "a syndrome characterized by clinically significant disturbance in an individual's cognition, emotion regulation, or behavior that reflects a dysfunction in the psychological, biological, or developmental processes underlying mental functioning. Mental disorders are usually associated with significant distress or disability in social, occupational, or other important activities" (APA, 2013, 20).
2 The following material draws from previous publications by the author at Hafemeister, Garner, and Bath (2012), and Hafemeister and George (2012).
3 Chatterji, Alegria, and Takeuchi (2008); Kessler et al. (2005b); Preidt (2017); NIMH (2017a). Estimates vary somewhat depending on the methodology employed.
4 NIMH (2017a); Preidt (2017); SAMHSA (2014); Steenhuysen (2010). Although the terms "mental illness" and "mental disorder" are often used interchangeably, mental illness is generally viewed as a narrower category limited to "adults aged 18 or older . . . [with] a diagnosable mental, behavioral, or emotional disorder (excluding developmental and substance use disorders)" (SAMHSA, 2014).
5 NIMH (2017b); SAMHSA (2014).
6 SAMHSA (2008).
7 CDC (2011); Kessler et al. (2005a); SAMHSA (2008).
8 NIJ (2014).
9 NIMH (2017a).
10 NIMH (2017b).

11 Chatterji, Alegria, and Takeuchi (2008); NAMI (2007).
12 Colton and Manderscheid (2006); Manderscheid (2006); Trangle et al. (2010).
13 Walker, McGee, and Druss (2015).
14 Boyles (2009).
15 Chatterji, Alegria, and Takeuchi (2008); Walker, McGee, and Druss (2015).
16 Walker, McGee, and Druss (2015).
17 USDHHS (1999, 5). The US surgeon general, a position created by President Ulysses S. Grant in 1871, is considered to be the preeminent public health officer in the United States.
18 APA (2013, 21).
19 Wittchen et al. (2000).
20 USDHHS (1999, 17).
21 Kingdon, Sharma, and Hart (2004).
22 Council of State Governments (2002, xii).
23 Tyner (2015).
24 Dallas (2012); Hughes et al. (2012).
25 Maxwell (2009); Meltzer et al. (2013).
26 Mackler and Morrissey (2010, 56).
27 Mackler and Morrissey (2010, 3).
28 Dallas (2012).
29 Hafemeister and Vallas (2016).
30 Meltzer et al. (2013).
31 USDHHS (1999, 7).
32 Hiroeh et al. (2001).
33 Pescosolido et al. (1999).
34 IOM (2006).
35 Elbogen and Johnson (2009).
36 United Nations (2015). However, a vote on the Convention by the US Senate in 2012 fell six votes short of the two-thirds majority required for the treaty to be ratified by the United States (Helderman, 2012).
37 United Nations (2006, Art. 1).
38 Mental Health Early Intervention (2000).
39 Deane et al. (1999).
40 Menaster (2011); Teplin et al. (2005).
41 Council of State Governments (2002, xii).
42 Bernstein and Seltzer (2003, 145).
43 Bernstein and Seltzer (2003).
44 Kessler et al. (2005a).
45 Leonard (2014).
46 Radnofsky (2015).
47 Almquist and Dodd (2009, v).
48 Bernstein and Seltzer (2003, 143).
49 See Mackler and Morrissey (2010).

50 Hafemeister, Garner, and Bath (2012); Poythress et al. (2002b).

51 See SAMHSA (2006).

52 See SAMHSA (2006).

53 *Clark v. Arizona* (2006); Keedy (1917).

54 Melton et al. (2004, 234).

55 President's New Freedom Commission (2003).

56 President's New Freedom Commission (2003).

57 Harcourt (2007).

58 Human Rights Watch (2003).

59 Steadman et al. (2009).

60 APA (2000).

61 James and Glaze (2006, 12).

62 Kupers (1999).

63 See Almquist and Dodd (2009).

64 Mental Health America (2008).

65 The following is adapted from Slobogin et al. (2014).

66 Frank and Glied (2006); Pfeiffer (2007).

67 *Brown v. Plata* (2011).

68 USDHHS (1999).

69 Slobogin et al. (2014, 8, quoting Phillips et al. (2012, 12–13)).

70 Angell (2011). Angell also contends that this diagnostic process is further compli-
cated by the fact that "the boundaries of mental illness are being stretched for a
variety of reasons—to increase drug company sales, to enhance the income and
status of the psychiatry profession, and to get insurance coverage or disability
benefits for troubled families."

71 Slobogin et al. (2014).

72 For example, to receive a diagnosis of schizophrenia, the person must, for a
significant portion of a month, present delusions, hallucinations, or disorganized
speech (APA, 2013, 99).

73 APA (2013, 20).

74 Slobogin et al. (2014, 6).

75 Frances (2010).

76 APA (2013, 25).

77 APA (2013, 87).

78 NIMH (2015).

79 APA (2013, 102). See also NIMH (2015): schizophrenia affects about 1 percent of
US adults.

80 APA (2013, 625); CDC (2016).

81 APA (2013, 131).

82 Olfson, Blanco, and Marcus (2016).

83 APA (2013, 165).

84 APA (2013, 299).

85 APA (2013, 301).

86 See Perr (1991).

87 APA (2013, 265).

88 APA (2013, 287).

89 See Hafemeister and Stockey (2010).

90 APA (2013, 276).

91 APA (2013, 276).

92 APA (2013, 189).

93 APA (2013, 210).

94 APA (2013, 199).

95 APA (2013, 201).

96 APA (2013, 202).

97 APA (2013, 204).

98 APA (2013, 235). Although a person can have an obsession without a compulsion, or a compulsion without an obsession, most individuals with OCD have both (APA, 2013, 238).

99 APA (2013, 238).

100 APA (2013, 239).

101 APA (2013, 240).

102 APA (2013, 645).

103 APA (2013, 646).

104 APA (2013, 649).

105 The prevalence of paranoid personality disorder in the United States is estimated to be 2.3–4.4 percent (APA, 2013, 651).

106 APA (2013, 652).

107 The prevalence of schizoid personality disorder in the United States is estimated to be 3.1–4.9 percent (APA, 2013, 654).

108 APA (2013, 655).

109 The prevalence of schizotypal personality disorder in the United States has been found to be as high as 4.6 percent in one community sample (APA, 2013, 657).

110 APA (2013, 659).

111 APA (2013, 661). The twelve-month prevalence rate of antisocial personality disorder is estimated to be between 0.2 percent and 3.3 percent (APA, 2013, 661).

112 APA (2013, 663).

113 APA (2013, 664). The population prevalence of borderline personality disorder is estimated to be between 1.6 percent and 5.9 percent (APA, 2013, 665), and it is diagnosed predominantly in females, who account for about 75 percent of all instances (APA, 2013, 666).

114 APA (2013, 667).

115 APA (2013, 668). The population prevalence of histrionic personality disorder is estimated to be slightly less than 2 percent, with females more likely to be diagnosed with this disorder than males (APA, 2013, 668).

116 APA (2013, 669).

117 The prevalence of narcissistic personality disorder in the United States is estimated to be as high as 6.2 percent, with 50–75 percent of those with this diagnosis being male (APA, 2013, 671).

118 APA (2013, 672).

119 The prevalence of avoidant personality disorder in the United States is estimated to be about 2.4 percent, split evenly between males and females (APA, 2013, 674).

120 APA (2013, 675).

121 The prevalence of dependent personality disorder in the United States is estimated to be 0.6 percent and is diagnosed more frequently in females (APA, 2013, 677).

122 APA (2013, 678).

123 The prevalence of obsessive-compulsive personality disorder in the United States is estimated to be 2.1–7.9 percent, and is diagnosed about twice as often among males (APA, 2013, 681).

124 Personality disorders, however, are less likely to evolve and change.

CHAPTER 2. OVERVIEW OF FORENSIC MENTAL HEALTH ASSESSMENTS

1 In 1999, Dr. David Satcher, the US surgeon general at the time, wrote that "mental illness appears to result from the interaction of multiple genes that confer risk, and this risk is converted into illness by the interaction of genes with environmental factors" (USDHHS, 1999, 53).

2 APA (1994, xxi).

3 The content of this section is drawn in part from J. L. Snook III, personal communication, November 9, 2006. For an in-depth examination of forensic evaluations, see Melton et al. (2007); for professional guidelines, see AmPA (2013) or Glancy et al. (2015); for standards of practice, see Heilbrun et al. (2008).

4 Hagen (1997).

5 In Texas, for example, experts charged with examining a defendant and generating an opinion on whether the defendant is CST must submit their report to the court, the prosecutor, and the defendant's attorney no later than thirty days after the examination was ordered, although an extension can be obtained for "good cause" (Tex. Code Crim. Pro. Art. 46B.026 (2017)).

6 The *DSM-5* defines malingering as "the intentional reporting of symptoms for personal gain (e.g., money, time off work)" (APA, 2013, 326). This definition has been interpreted as encompassing "a condition . . . not attributable to a mental disorder, consisting of the intentional production of false or grossly exaggerated physical or psychological symptoms, motivated by external incentives," which can be further broken down into the categories of "pure malingering" (the feigning of a nonexistent disorder), "partial malingering" (the conscious exaggeration of currently existing symptoms), and "false imputation" (ascribing current symptoms to a cause the individual knows has no relation to the symptoms) (Glancy et al., 2015, S42).

7 It has been hypothesized that the rate of malingering is directly related to the strength of the incentive to malinger. In other words, the more there is to gain, the more likely it is that a person will malinger. Consistent with this hypothesis,

one study of defendants found incompetent to stand trial (IST) and sent to a state hospital for restoration, thereby delaying their criminal trial, found the rate of malingering to be double for IST defendants charged with murder or robbery (McDermott, Dualan, and Scott, 2013).

8 One such case, discussed in chapter 8, involved the conviction of Andrea Yates, which was overturned on appeal. A retrial was ordered after it was discovered that a forensic mental health evaluator had erred in his testimony at the initial trial.

9 The content of this section is drawn in part from J. L. Snook III, personal communication, November 9, 2006.

10 A review of related research found that estimates of malingering in competence to stand trial (CST) evaluations ranged from 8 percent to nearly 18 percent, while they reached almost 21 percent for defendants undergoing evaluations pertaining to criminal responsibility (McDermott, Dualan, and Scott, 2013).

11 Indeed, in Texas, an expert conducting a CST evaluation must document in his or her report to the court "that the expert explained to the defendant the purpose of the evaluation, the persons to whom a report on the evaluation is provided, and the limits on rules of confidentiality applying to the relationship between the expert and the defendant" (Tex. Code Crim. Pro. Art. 46B.025(a)(2) (2017)).

12 Under Texas law, however, "The expert's opinion on the defendant's [CST] may not be based solely on the defendant's refusal to communicate during the examination" (Tex. Code Crim. Pro. Art. 46B.025(a-1) (2017)).

13 In part because of the limited opportunities to interact with the defendant, the forensic evaluator may incorporate a structured forensic instrument into his or her evaluation. Available instruments include the MacArthur Competence Assessment Tool—Criminal Adjudication (MacCAT-CA), the Evaluation of Competency to Stand Trial—Revised (ECST-R), the Rogers Criminal Responsibility Assessment Scales (R-CRAS), the Historical Clinical Risk Management-20 (HCR-20), the Miller Forensic Assessment of Symptoms Test (M-FAST), the Personality Assessment Inventory (PAI), the Minnesota Multiphasic Personality Inventory (MMPI/MMPI-2), the Structured Interview of Reported Symptoms, 2nd edition (SIRS-2), the Structured Inventory of Malingered Symptomatology (SIMS), Symptom Validity Testing (SVT), and the Violence Risk Appraisal Guide (VRAG). For a discussion of such tools and their use, see Glancy et al. (2015); Melton et al. (2007, 59–62, 145–155, 254–257, 309–314; Rogers and Granacher (2011).

14 Glancy et al. (2015, S8): "Collateral sources of information, when available, are usually an important element of the forensic assessment."

15 New York, for example, has established that the defendant has a right to have his or her attorney present at follow-up insanity evaluations requested by the prosecution, and that the prosecutor may be present as well, although both attorneys can only observe and cannot take an "active role" in the examination (e.g., they cannot ask the defendant questions) (N.Y. Crim. Pro. L. § 250.10 (2017)).

16 For example, under the Federal Rules of Evidence, which govern federal but not state courts, it is established that "[i]n a criminal case, an expert witness must not

state an opinion about whether the defendant did or did not have a mental state
or condition that constitutes an element of the crime charged or of a defense.
Those matters are for the trier of fact alone" (FRE 704(b) (2017)). In all other contexts, however, "[a]n [expert witness's] opinion is not objectionable just because it
embraces an ultimate issue" (FRE 704(a) (2017)).

17   Melton et al. (2007, 600–605).

18   Melton et al. (2007, 62–67).

19   The content of this section is drawn in part from W. Stejskal, personal communication, August 26, 2004.

20   *United States v. Binion* (2005); *United States v. Greer* (1998).

21   Darani (2006, 128).

22   A somewhat similar but lengthier list of clinical factors suggestive of malingering
during forensic assessments generated by a task force of the American Academy
of Psychiatry and the Law can be found at Glancy et al. (2015).

23   The content of this section is drawn in part from W. Stejskal, personal communication, August 26, 2004.

24   With psychoses, for example, there may be a period of time— often referred to as the
"prodromal phase"—during which a person's thoughts, perceptions, behaviors, and
functioning change, even though he or she has not yet begun to experience psychotic
symptoms per se. These changes include the occurrence of depression, anxiety, social
isolation, and school or occupational failure (Larson, Walker, and Compton, 2011).

25   Available instruments include the Structured Interview of Reported Symptoms,
2nd edition (SIRS-2), the Structured Inventory of Malingered Symptomatology (SIMS), Symptom Validity Testing (SVT), the Miller Forensic Assessment
of Symptoms Test (M-FAST), the Personality Assessment Inventory (PAI), the
Minnesota Multiphasic Personality Inventory (MMPI/MMPI-2), and the Test of
Memory Malingering (TOMM). For a discussion of such tools and their use, see
Glancy et al. (2015, S43); Melton et al. (2007, 59–62); Rogers and Granacher (2011).

26   Feuerstein et al. (2005), cautioning, however, that such explanations may also
result in a defendant under-reporting symptoms indicative of a mental disorder.

27   *United States v. Binion* (2005), upholding a two-level enhancement of a defendant's sentence for obstruction of justice after a defendant filed a pro se motion
for a competence to stand trial evaluation, and evaluators at the medical facility
where he was transported for evaluation determined he was probably malingering
mental illness; *United States v. Greer* (1998), upholding a sentence enhancement
from 185 months to 210 months for a defendant's "intentional obstruction of justice" in conjunction with a determination of the defendant's competence to stand
trial, ruling that such enhancements will not unconstitutionally chill a defendant's
right to seek a competency hearing and that counsel should warn their clients that
such an enhancement may result if a court determines the defendant "willfully"
feigned incompetency to delay or avoid trial.

28   For example, it has been suggested that providing a warning "at the appropriate time and place" to a defendant that malingering during a forensic evaluation

can result in sentence enhancement "may give the evaluator more leverage in obtaining valid data," although it has also been cautioned that "once defendants learn that a confession of malingering [to an evaluator] can lead to an increased sentence, they are less likely to admit to malingering after a confrontation" (Knoll and Resnick, 1999, 625).

29 The content in this section is drawn in part from W. Stejskal, personal communication, August 26, 2004.

CHAPTER 3. UNDERPINNINGS OF THE COMPETENCE TO STAND TRIAL STANDARD

1 *Dusky v. United States* (1960); *Drope v. Missouri* (1975).
2 *Pate v. Robinson* (1966).
3 Cronin (2009); Poythress et al. (2002a, 50).
4 Hoge et al. (1992, 389); Poythress et al. (1994, 450).
5 For more information on this case, see Bardwell and Arrigo (2002); Kuby and Kunstler (1995).
6 For more information on this case, see Shields et al. (2007).
7 Possley (1998).
8 For more information on this case, see Johnson (2010).
9 *State v. Barzee* (2007).
10 *United States v. Mitchell* (2010).
11 For more information on this case, see DPIC (2017).
12 National Minimum Drinking Age Act (1984).
13 Grabowski, Campbell, and Morrisey (2004); Lawrence (2014). It has similarly been discussed whether physicians over a certain age should not be permitted to perform surgery unless they demonstrate their continued competence (Blasier, 2009).
14 The content of this section is drawn in part from Slobogin et al. (2014, 1037–1053).
15 For a description of catatonia, see APA (2013, 119–121).
16 With all of these tests, a determination of incompetence does not necessarily end the matter. For many legal decisions—although, as will be discussed, not CST—someone may be appointed to make the decision for the individual who has been found to be incompetent and questions may then arise regarding who this substitute decision-maker will be and how this person should make the decision.
17 Melton et al. (2007, 126).
18 See *Dusky v. United States* (1959); *Dusky v. United States* (1961).
19 *Dusky v. United States* (1960, 402–403).
20 *Gideon v. Wainwright* (1963).
21 *Dusky v. United States* (1959). Similar motions had been filed and granted in the federal district court where Dusky's trial was initially held and in conjunction with his appeal to the Eighth Circuit.
22 Appelbaum (1994, 3).
23 Appelbaum (1994, 4).
24 Torrey (1997).

25 The Spotlight Team (2016).

26 *Buckley v. Valeo* (1976).

27 Black and Spriggs (2008).

28 Something equivalent to an abbreviated mental status exam might also be used in conducting the associated evaluation. Such an approach can consist of as few as five steps: (1) listing three words the defendant is told to repeat and remember, (2) asking the defendant what day, month, and year it is today, (3) asking the defendant who you are and why you are here, (4) asking the defendant to count backward by three from one hundred, and (5) asking the defendant to repeat again the three words they were just asked to remember. The goal of this approach is to ascertain whether a defendant is generally oriented to time and place and has some recollection of events. This approach is still commonly used by forensic evaluators today as an initial mental health screen, although it will typically be followed by a series of questions designed to probe more deeply to ascertain whether the defendant meets the requisite legal test.

29 *Dusky v. United States* (1960, 403).

30 *Dusky v. United States* (1960, 402).

31 This issue will be discussed in chapter 7 in the section entitled "Competence to Self-Represent."

CHAPTER 4. REFINING AND APPLYING THE COMPETENCE TO STAND TRIAL STANDARD

1 The content of this section is drawn in part from Bonnie (1992).

2 Research has established that there is an association between traumatic brain injuries and the subsequent onset of a range of mental disorders (van Reekum, Cohen, and Wong, 2000; Schwarzbold et al., 2008). One of the first documented cases occurred in 1848 when Phineas Gage, a construction worker, had an iron bar go through his skull and seriously damage his frontal lobe, changing him—according to his doctor—from a responsible, socially well-adjusted person to someone who was profane, irreverent, negligent, and unable to take responsibility for his actions (Schwarzbold et al., 2008).

3 *Pate v. Robinson* (1966, 378).

4 *Pate v. Robinson* (1966, 384).

5 Justice Harlan, joined by Justice Black, wrote the dissenting opinion.

6 *Pate v. Robinson* (1966, 389).

7 *Pate v. Robinson* (1966, 391).

8 US Constitution, Amendment IV: "[N]o Warrants shall issue [for a search or seizure], but upon probable cause, supported by Oath or affirmation, and particularly describing the place to be searched, and the persons or things to be seized."

9 *Brinegar v. United States* (1949, 175).

10 California takes this a step further and requires trial judges to explore a defendant's CST if merely a "doubt" crosses the judge's mind regarding the defendant's competence (Cal. Penal Code § 1368(a) (2017)). The Texas legislature has similarly

established that the judge "is not required to have a bona fide doubt" about the defendant's CST; the threshold requirement for an informal CST inquiry in Texas "may consist solely of a representation from any credible source that the defendant may be incompetent" (Tex. Code Crim. Pro. Art. 46B.004 (2017)).

11 The upshot of having an attorney is that the attorney will manage the trial, and unless the defendant takes the stand (i.e., provides testimony under oath), the defendant may not speak or barely move while the judge is in the courtroom. In addition, defendants have a right not to take the stand and provide testimony (US Constitution, Amendment V) and often will not testify to avoid a cross-examination that might draw out potentially prejudicial past behavior or patterns of behavior that otherwise cannot be introduced into evidence.

12 Mo. Rev. Stat. § 552.020(1) (2017; emphasis added).

13 The pertinent language in *Dusky* reads: "whether [the defendant] has a rational as well as factual understanding of the proceedings against him" (1960, 402).

14 *Dusky* reads: "has sufficient present ability to *consult* with his lawyer with a reasonable degree of rational understanding" (1960, 402; emphasis added).

15 *Drope v. Missouri* (1975, 171; emphasis added).

16 For example, the current standard in Virginia for evaluating a defendant's CST is that the defendant "lacks substantial capacity to understand the proceedings against him or to assist his attorney in his own defense" (Va. Code § 19.2-169.1(A) (2017)).

17 In California proceedings, all that is required to raise the question of CST is for a "doubt [to] arise[ ] in the mind of the judge as to the mental competence of the defendant" (Cal. Penal Code § 1368(a) (2017)).

18 *Drope v. Missouri* (1975, 172).

19 See chapter 5.

20 California law, in contrast, does require a showing that a mental disorder or developmental disability in general was the cause of the defendant's incompetence to stand trial: "A person cannot be tried . . . while that person is mentally incompetent. A defendant is mentally incompetent . . . if, as a result of mental disorder or developmental disability, the defendant is unable to understand the nature of the criminal proceedings or to assist counsel in the conduct of a defense in a rational manner" (Cal. Penal Code § 1367(a) (2017)).

21 For example, a jury trial on CST is authorized in California upon the request of either the prosecution or the defense (Cal. Penal Code § 1369 (2017)), and in Texas upon the request of either the prosecution or the defense, or upon the motion of the court (Tex. Code Crim. Pro. Art. 46B.051 (2017)).

22 Mo. Rev. Stat. § 552.020(1) (2017); Va. Code § 19.2-169.1(A) (2017).

23 Cal. Penal Code § 1367(a) (2017).

24 *Buckley v. Valeo* (1976); *Gideon v. Wainwright* (1963).

25 Dawes, Palmer, and Jeste (2008); Fitch (2007); Grisso (2003); Nussbaum et al. (2007); Rogers et al. (2001).

26 For more information on this topic, see Miller (2003); Roesch and Golding (1979); Roesch and Golding (1980).

27 See, for example, provisions in New York (N.Y. Crim. Pro. L. §§ 730.50–.70 (2017)) and Texas (Tex. Code Crim. Pro. Arts. 46B.101–.107 (2017)).

28 See Cal. Penal Code § 1369.1 (2017), establishing that county jails can constitute a "treatment facility" for purposes of providing a placement to restore to competency a defendant found IST and can administer medically approved medication to defendants for this purpose; Tex. Code Crim. Pro. Art. 46B.0095, 46B.071 (2017), clarifying that a defendant found IST can be committed to a jail-based competency restoration program.

29 For additional information on this topic, see Miller (2003); Roesch and Golding (1979); Roesch and Golding (1980).

30 Some states, however, will deduct from a defendant's sentence the time spent in custody while efforts were made to restore the defendant's competency (see Cal. Penal Code § 1375.5 (2017)), and some states will deduct similarly the time spent waiting for a determination of competency (see Tex. Code Crim. Pro. Art. 46B.009 (2017)).

31 But see *Brady v. Maryland* (1963, 87): "We now hold that the suppression by the prosecution of evidence favorable to an accused upon request violates due process where the evidence is material either to guilt or to punishment, irrespective of the good faith or bad faith of the prosecution."

CHAPTER 5. PROCEDURAL ASPECTS OF COMPETENCE TO STAND TRIAL DETERMINATIONS

1 It also likely reflects not only the fact that it is an arduous, costly, and protracted endeavor to bring an appeal before the USSC, without any guarantee that the USSC will even take up the matter for review, but also the fact that a challenge to existing CST procedures would largely fall on the shoulders of criminal defendants, acting through their attorneys, whose resources tend to be severely limited.

2 It is perhaps worth noting that in conjunction with a habeas corpus appeal filed on Medina's behalf while he sat on death row, evidence was introduced that, much like Theodore Robinson (discussed in chapter 4), Medina suffered various head injuries as a child (*Medina v. Chappell*, 2015).

3 A second jury is typically used so that the information presented to the jury determining the defendant's CST, including evidence regarding the defendant's current mental status, will not "contaminate" or bias the trial verdict regarding the defendant's guilt or innocence.

4 Texas, for example, has similarly established that a defendant is presumed competent to stand trial and thus must be found to be CST unless proven incompetent by a preponderance of the evidence (Tex. Code Crim. Pro. Art. 46B.003 (2017)).

5 *Addington v. Texas* (1979, 430).

6 The dissenting opinion was written by Justice Harry Blackmun, and joined by Justice John Paul Stevens.

7 See chapter 9.

8 Cal. Penal Code § 1369(f) (2017).

9 *Cooper v. State* (1995).

10 *Cooper v. Oklahoma* (1996, 360).

11 *Cooper v. Oklahoma* (1996, 362).

12 *Cooper v. Oklahoma* (1996, 365).

13 *Cooper v. Oklahoma* (1996, 366).

14 *Cooper v. Oklahoma* (1996, 366, 367).

15 Cal. Penal Code § 1369 (2017); Tex. Code Crim. Pro. Art. 46B.051 (2017).

16 *Duncan v. Louisiana* (1968).

17 *Baldwin v. New York* (1970).

18 A jury must return a unanimous verdict on the CST issue in both California and Texas (Cal. Penal Code § 1369(f) (2017); Tex. Code Crim. Pro. Art. 46B.052 (2017)).

19 In Texas, for example, the CST jury must be different from the jury selected to determine the guilt or innocence of the defendant (Tex. Code Crim. Pro. Art. 46B.051 (2017)).

20 See, for example, California, where CST hearings have been designated as *civil* proceedings, meaning that the process employed will be somewhat different and more informal than that otherwise employed during the *criminal* proceeding (*People v. Lawley*, 2002; *People v. Pokovich*, 2006); and Texas, where the initial inquiry into whether a defendant is CST is specifically labeled as "informal" (Tex. Code Crim. Pro. Art. 46B.004(c) (2017)).

21 *Cooper v. Oklahoma* (1996); *Medina v. California* (1992).

22 In Texas it has been established that the defendant is entitled to representation by an attorney before any court-ordered competency evaluation and during any proceeding where this determination is made—a provision that suggests the gravity of the determination (Tex. Code Crim. Pro. Art. 46B.006 (2017)).

23 In Texas, the generally applicable Texas Rules of Evidence are to be employed during a competency hearing (Tex. Code Crim. Pro. Art. 46B.008 (2017)).

24 Slobogin et al. (2014).

25 Note, however, that in some states an expert involved in the treatment of the defendant may not be appointed to conduct a CST examination of the defendant (Tex. Code Crim. Pro. Art. 46B.021 (2017)).

26 In Texas, for example, the psychiatrist or psychologist conducting a CST exam must either be board certified or have completed at least twenty-four hours of specialized forensic training relating to incompetency or insanity evaluations and at least eight hours in the preceding year of continuing education related to forensic evaluations, although these requirements may be waived by the judge if "exigent circumstances" exist that require some other "specialized expertise" (Tex. Code Crim. Pro. Art. 46B.022(a) (2017)).

27 There have been a few efforts to empirically establish minimum necessary qualifications to conduct CST evaluations, although the results have tended to not be definitive. See, for example, Dawes, Palmer, and Jeste (2008); Skeem and Golding (1998).

28 For example, in Texas, CST evaluations can be conducted only by a physician or a psychologist (Tex. Code Crim. Pro. Art. 46B.022 (2017)).

29 For example, in New York, CST evaluators who are in private practice can receive only reasonable traveling expenses, $50 for each examination of a defendant, and $50 for each appearance at a court hearing or trial, but not more than $200 in fees for examinations and testimony in any one case (N.Y. Crim. Pro. L. § 730.20(7) (2017)), a fee level that many professionals may find insufficient.

30 For example, in New York, a court-ordered CST examination must be conducted by a physician who is either a diplomate of the American Board of Psychiatry and Neurology or is certified by the American Osteopathic Board of Neurology and Psychiatry, or is eligible to be certified by one of these boards, or by a "certified" psychologist (N.Y. Crim. Pro. L. §§ 730.10, 730.20 (2017)).

31 In California, this responsibility is assigned to the State Department of State Hospitals, with instructions provided on who should be represented on the "workgroup" responsible for devising these guidelines. However, "If there is no reasonably available expert [in a given case] who meets [these] guidelines or who has equivalent experience and skills, the court shall have the discretion to appoint an expert who does not meet [these] guidelines" (Cal. Penal Code § 1369 (2017)).

32 For example, in California, after the trial judge determines that a "doubt" exists as to a defendant's CST *and* the defendant or the defendant's attorney informs the court that the defendant is not seeking a finding of IST, an examination of the defendant's CST must nonetheless be conducted by two psychiatrists, two licensed psychologists, or a psychiatrist and a licensed psychologist, with one named by the defense and the other named by the prosecution (Cal. Penal Code § 1369 (2017)).

33 For example, a lawsuit settled in October of 2015 alleged that in Pennsylvania defendants with a severe mental illness sometimes languished for more than a year in jail before space could be found to admit them to a state psychiatric facility to restore their CST. A year after the settlement, delays were still prevalent, with an average wait time before transfer of 387 days (Brubaker, 2017).

34 See, for example, Fogel et al. (2013).

35 In New York, for example, "When the defendant is not in custody at the time a court issues an order of examination, . . . the court may direct that the examination be conducted on an out-patient basis" (N.Y. Crim. Pro. L. § 730.20(2) (2017)).

36 Hafemeister and George (2012); Shannon (2017).

37 In Texas, for example, although the expert charged with examining a defendant and generating an opinion on whether the defendant is CST must submit his or her report to the court, the prosecutor, and the defendant's attorney within thirty days after the examination was ordered, an extension can be obtained for "good cause" (Tex. Code Crim. Pro. Art. 46B.026 (2017)).

38 *Estelle v. Gamble* (1976).

39 See Shannon (2017, 865). Among the related cases discussed are: *Terry v. Hill* (2002); *Oregon Advocacy Center v. Mink* (2003); *Advocacy Center for the Elderly & Disabled v. Louisiana Department of Health & Hospitals* (2010); and *Trueblood v. Washington State Department of Social & Health Services* (2016).

40 While it is irrelevant to the CST determination per se that a defendant is or is not currently taking a medication, knowledge of the defendant's medication status and the impact of such medication can be useful information for the judge to have in that it can alert the judge as to its possible effect on a defendant's current CST and the possible change in mental status that may ensue should the medication be discontinued. Perhaps for this reason, an expert examining a defendant's CST in Texas is directed to consider whether the defendant is taking any medication, whether this medication is necessary to maintain the defendant's CST, and what effect, if any, it has on the defendant's appearance, demeanor, or ability to participate in the proceedings (Tex. Code Crim. Pro. Art. 46B.024 (2017)).

41 Piaget (2000).

42 Erikson (1950).

43 Kohlberg (1976).

44 See, for example, Domino and Affonso (1990).

45 Roid (2003).

46 See, for example, the Juvenile Adjudicative Competence Interview (Grisso, 2005), and the Fitness Interview Test—Revised (Roesch, Zapf, and Eaves, 2006).

47 Fogel et al. (2013, 180); Melton et al. (2007, 476).

48 See, for example, Fla. Stat. § 985.19(2) (2017).

49 Hafemeister (2004).

50 The content of this section is drawn in part from Tysse (2005); Tysse and Hafemeister (2006).

51 *Wilson v. United States* (1968).

52 Among the forensic assessment instruments focused specifically on a defendant's CST are the MacArthur Competence Assessment Tool—Criminal Adjudication; the Interdisciplinary Fitness Interview—Revised; the Fitness Interview Test (Revised Edition); the Evaluation of Competency to Stand Trial—Revised (ECST-R); and the METFORS Fitness Questionnaire (MFQ) (Glancy et al., 2015, S27). The law of the jurisdiction in which the evaluation is being conducted may also establish who must provide relevant information to the evaluator. See, for example, Tex. Code Crim. Pro. Art. 46B.021(d) (2017): the party making the motion for a CST evaluation or another party "as directed by the court."

53 Examples of CST reports can be found in Melton et al (2007, 607–620).

54 For example, the Texas legislature has established a relatively lengthy list of factors that are to be considered as part of a CST evaluation (Tex. Code Crim. Pro. Art. 46B.024 (2017)).

55 For example, in California, the expert must evaluate, in addition to the CST criteria, "whether or not treatment with antipsychotic medication is medically appropriate for the defendant and whether antipsychotic medication is likely to restore the defendant to mental competence[,] . . . whether the defendant has capacity to make decisions regarding antipsychotic medication and whether the defendant is a danger to self or others[,] . . . [and] the likely or potential side effects of the medication, the expected efficacy of the medication, possible alter-

native treatments, and whether it is medically appropriate to administer antipsychotic medication in the county jail" (Cal. Penal Code § 1369(a) (2017)). As will be discussed, this information anticipates post-disposition objections to treatment filed pursuant to *Sell v. United States* by a defendant found IST.

56 See, for example, Tex. Code Crim. Pro. Art. 46B.025(b) (2017).

57 See *Estelle v. Smith* (1981, 462); *People v. Jablonski* (2006, 120); *People v. Pokovich* (2006).

58 In New York, for example, "[A]ny statement made by [the defendant] for the purpose of the [CST] examination or treatment shall be inadmissible in evidence against [the defendant] in any criminal action on any issue other than that of [the defendant's] mental condition" (N.Y. Crim. Pro. L. § 730.20(6) (2017)).

59 It should be noted that in Texas, for example, an expert can be appointed to evaluate both a defendant's CST and the defendant's sanity at the time of the crime, but if so appointed must submit to the court separate written reports on the two topics; in addition, the expert may not evaluate the defendant's sanity if the expert is of the opinion that the defendant is IST (Tex. Code Crim. Pro. Art. 46C.103 (2017)).

60 One potential problem with evaluators audio- or video-recording their interviews with defendants, notwithstanding that these recordings may provide a valuable aid in refreshing evaluators' memories regarding interview sessions, is that the prosecution or the defense may want to obtain access to the recordings to augment their trial preparations and presentations. Evaluators should consider resisting sharing any such recordings on the grounds that they are protected by confidentiality or testimonial privilege.

61 The defense does have the option of privately securing the services of a mental health evaluator to assess the CST of a defendant. As in a defense-secured insanity evaluation, the defense can keep the results of this evaluation private unless it introduces its findings into evidence.

62 Brown (2016).

63 In New York, for example, the psychiatric examiner must "promptly" prepare an examination report and submit it to the court, with any hospital confinement for this purpose not to exceed thirty days, although an additional thirty-day period can be authorized if "necessary to complete the examination" (N.Y. Crim. Pro. L. § 730.20(4),(5) (2017)).

64 In Virginia, for example, "Upon completion of the evaluation [of a juvenile], the evaluator shall promptly and in no event exceeding 14 days after receipt of all required information submit the report in writing to the court and the attorneys of record" (Va. Code § 16.1-356(E) (2017)), although a similar deadline is not imposed for completion of the CST evaluation of adult criminal defendants.

CHAPTER 6. DISPOSITIONS AFTER THE COMPETENCE TO STAND TRIAL HEARING

1 Perhaps in recognition of the inconvenience and, on occasion, hardship that may arise from multiple suspensions of the trial proceedings to determine a defendant's

CST, in California when a competency hearing has already been held and the defendant was found to be CST, the trial judge does not have to suspend proceedings again unless "substantial evidence" has been presented showing a "substantial change of circumstances" or "new evidence" is introduced that casts serious doubt on the validity of the original finding (*People v. Jones*, 1997; *People v. Kaplan*, 2007).

2   See *Jackson v. Indiana* (1972), discussed below.

3   Shannon (2017, 871): "federal court decisions to date have repeatedly found due process violations in long delays between a state's determination of incompetency to stand trial and a transfer to a treatment facility for competency restoration services."

4   See, for example, Cal. Penal Code § 1370 (2017).

5   A California statute, for example, specifies that a "treatment facility" where services to restore a defendant's CST can be provided "includes a county jail" (Cal. Penal Code § 1369.1 (2017)).

6   Shannon (2017, 862), noting a Texas lawsuit filed in a federal court in 2016 alleging that "individuals with mental illness suffer needless deterioration of their mental health as they wait in jails, frequently in prolonged isolation for weeks and months before they receive [restoration treatment.] . . . Texas jails are not designed or administered to provide . . . competency restoration treatment for incompetent defendants."

7   In California, for example, a written report must be submitted to the court within ninety days of placement and at six-month intervals thereafter (Cal. Penal Code § 1370(b)(1) (2017)).

8   In some states, if the defendant is ultimately convicted and sentenced, the time he or she was held for restorative services will be deducted from the sentence (see Cal. Penal Code § 1375.5 (2017)), with some states also deducting the time detained while his or her CST was evaluated and the determination of competency reached (see Tex. Code Crim. Pro. Art. 46B.009 (2017)).

9   See, for example, Va. Code § 19.2-169.3(C) (2017).

10   Va. Code § 19.2-169.3(B) (2017). In California, a new CST hearing must be held every eighteen months, with a presumption of competence applied at this hearing (Cal. Penal Code § 1370(b)(4) (2017); *People v. Rells* (2000)).

11   Va. Code § 16.1-357(B) (2017). IST juveniles detained for restorative services may be checked on more often because the juvenile mental state is seen as more dynamic and more likely to fluctuate and because of concerns about the adverse impact on juveniles of an extended stay in custody.

12   *Jackson v. Indiana* (1972, 717).

13   *Jackson v. Indiana* (1972, 718).

14   *Jackson v. Indiana* (1972, 719).

15   *Jackson v. Indiana* (1972, 720).

16   *Jackson v. Indiana* (1972, 734).

17   *Jackson v. Indiana* (1972, 738).

18   *Jackson v. Indiana* (1972, 738).

19 *Jackson v. Indiana* (1972, 738).

20 There is considerable variation in what this process is called across the various states.

21 For examples of limits placed on the duration of detention of IST defendants, see Cal. Penal Code § 1370(c) (2017); N.Y. Crim. Pro. L. § 730.50(5) (2017); Tex. Code Crim. Pro. Art. 46B.0095 (2017).

22 In general, "The studies are relatively consistent in finding that the large majority of defendants referred for treatment are recommended as 'restored' within six months, and often earlier" (Melton et al. 2007, 162).

23 See Rosinia (2012, 689–690); Va. Code § 19.2-169.3 (2017).

24 Slobogin et al. (2014, 807).

25 Today the length of time a civilly committed individual is hospitalized is much shorter because (a) the shortage of and great demand for these beds necessitates a faster turnover of patients, (b) their considerable expense makes funding entities eager to quickly move patients out of these beds and into community alternatives, (c) the patients generally prefer to return to their community and to resume their lives as soon as possible, and (d) with much improved treatment regimes, particularly newer medications, patients can be stabilized and gotten back on their feet within a much shorter period of time.

26 Lave (2011).

27 US Constitution, Amendment VI: "In all criminal prosecutions, the accused shall enjoy the right to a speedy and public trial."

28 Zapf and Roesch (2011). Although not the focus here, because treatment providers working within the criminal justice system typically must adhere to a relatively fixed budget, the treatment chosen will also generally need to be cost-effective.

29 See Slobogin et al. (2014, 28).

30 Slobogin et al. (2014, 808–809).

31 See Gøtzsche, Young, and Crace (2015); Julien (2013).

32 APA (2010, 66–67).

33 Brooks (1987).

34 Slobogin et al. (2014, 1081–1126).

35 Brooks (1987).

36 Although the USSC has not resolved this issue, numerous lower courts have issued rulings on what constitutes a "serious crime" in this context. See *United States v. Evans* (2005); *United States v. Green* (2008); *United States v. Hernandez-Vasquez* (2008).

37 US Constitution, Amendment V: "No person shall . . . be deprived of life, liberty, or property, without due process of law."

38 *Riggins v. Nevada* (1992); *Washington v. Harper* (1990).

39 The framework asks whether the proposed treatment is (a) medically appropriate, (b) substantially unlikely to have side effects that may undermine the fairness of the trial, and, (c) taking into account less intrusive alternatives, significantly necessary to further important governmental trial-related interests. There were some legal commentators who argued that this medical framework was inappro-

priate for resolving a legal issue and that "the question courts should be deciding is whether administering involuntary antipsychotic medications is reasonable— that is, whether the government's interest in bringing the defendant to trial is important enough to justify the harms of involuntary antipsychotic medications" (Klein, 2009, 164).

40 For example, as will be discussed, a psychotropic medication may have a sedating effect on a defendant, making him or her very passive and unable to act in his or her best interests; unable to cognitively process subtle distinctions and nuances relevant to his or her trial-related decisions; or less capable of following and understanding the trial proceedings.

41 Klein (2009). For examples of early cases applying *Sell* where a request to treat over objection was refused, see *People v. O'Dell* (2005, 907); *Carter v. Superior Court* (2006).

42 Although considerable litigation over how to apply the *Sell* factors ensued, particularly at first as the various parties wrestled over their meaning, scope, and impact, jurisdictions have generally worked out how to process these cases, with the competence to stand trial of most IST defendants continuing to be ultimately restored (Cochrane et al., 2013; Morse, 2017; Moyer and Nakic, 2016; Wasser and Trueblood, 2015).

43 An issue also not addressed by *Sell* is the means by which medication may be administered to an IST defendant who is refusing treatment. In Texas, the use of "reasonable force" to administer court-ordered medication is authorized (Tex. Code Crim. Pro. Art. 46B.086 (2017)).

44 The criminal trials of Brian David Mitchell and Wanda Barzee for the kidnapping of Elizabeth Smart, discussed earlier, provide another widely publicized example in which treatment over objection to restore a defendant's CST played a pivotal role. See Johnson (2010).

45 Felthous (2012).

46 Quinn (2011).

47 Associated Press (2011).

48 Hartmann (2011).

49 For a discussion of the associated proceedings, including the various administrative hearings conducted at the facility where Loughner was held, and the subsequent rulings, see *United States v. Loughner* (2012); Williams (2012).

50 Turgal (2012).

51 Ball (2012).

CHAPTER 7. OTHER CRIMINAL TRIAL–RELATED COMPETENCY ISSUES

1 The reader should recognize that these impairments are also germane to CST determinations.

2 The exact prevalence of custodial confessions is unknown, although roughly 95 percent of all criminal convictions involve a guilty plea. See *Missouri v. Frye* (2012, 1407); Cohen and Reaves (2006). It can be argued that a guilty plea constitutes a

confession as the defendant typically admits in open court to acts that satisfy the elements of the charged crime, although it has been countered that plea bargains are not confessions as they do not generally involve detailed admissions of guilt, may not be given under oath, and are usually not supported by an extensive factual record, but rather are given to avoid the likelihood of a more severe sentence if the case went to trial (Garrett, 2016).

3 Slovenko (2002).

4 Inbau et al. (2013, 415). See, for example, *Bram v. United States* (1897): under the Fifth Amendment, a confession must be free and voluntary to be admissible into evidence; it cannot be extracted by any sort of threats, violence, or undue influence.

5 US Constitution, Amendment V: "nor shall [any person] be compelled in any criminal case to be a witness against himself, nor be deprived of life, liberty, or property, without due process of law."

6 The "fruit of the poisonous tree" doctrine was first articulated by the USSC in *Silverthorne Lumber Co. v. United States* (1920).

7 A "state actor" is a person who is acting on behalf of a governmental body, which subjects the actions of this person to the protections afforded under the US Constitution's Bill of Rights.

8 Leo (1996).

9 This task may have gotten easier in recent years as a number of jurisdictions have taken to routinely taping confessions—particularly for cases involving serious crimes such as homicide—to establish an absence of coercion, although questions may still arise regarding the conversations and police officer behavior that preceded the recording.

10 Although relatively rare thus far, a suspect's mental disorder may increasingly come into play in determining whether he or she was in the "custody" of a law enforcement official at the time of the incriminating statement, and thus entitled to receive *Miranda* warnings before questioning could proceed. This clearly occurs when a law enforcement official tells a defendant that he or she is under arrest. It can also occur, however, when a reasonable person believes that he or she is not free to leave/avoid police questioning, such as when placed in an interrogation room at the police station with a police officer standing in front of the door. It was generally assumed that what constituted "custody" involved relatively objective criteria (i.e., it was the same for everyone) and would not vary depending on the mental state of the defendant.

The USSC in *J. D. B. v. North Carolina* (2011), however, suggested that at some point the defendant's mental status may be relevant. In *JDB*, the Court ruled—on a 5–4 vote—that there are circumstances when a juvenile may be more likely to feel like he or she is within the custody of the police than an adult. In this case, a thirteen-year-old student was taken out of a classroom to a conference room where he was questioned by two officers and two school administrators for thirty to forty-five minutes without being given his *Miranda* warnings and then confessed to a crime. The Court ruled this constituted a custodial interrogation for someone of his age, even though it might not be for an adult, and thus the juvenile needed to have been read his *Miranda* rights for his confession to have been admissible. It can be argued that the mental disorder of some defendants similarly heightens their perceived sense of being in custody (for example, someone with claustrophobia placed in a small, windowless room) and this entitles them to *Miranda* warnings at an earlier stage of a law enforcement investigation, with a failure to do so barring any incriminating statement subsequently given.

11 See, for example, *United States v. Preston* (2014). For a discussion of instruments employed to evaluate the competency of a defendant to confess, see Melton et al. (2007, 171–173).

12 Although not the focus here, an evaluation of a defendant's mental state at the time of the confession may be introduced at trial to challenge the accuracy and reliability of the defendant's confession and associated statements.

13 *Bradshaw v. Commonwealth* (1984).

14 *Correll v. Commonwealth* (1987); *Terrell v. Commonwealth* (1991).

15 Although strictly speaking it is not part of an evaluation of a defendant's competence to waive his or her *Miranda* rights and provide incriminating statements, trial judges, in the interests of efficiency, may also order an evaluator to assess the *reliability* of these statements in light of any mental disorder defendants may have been experiencing at the time these statements were made.

16 *Missouri v. Frye* (2012, 1407); Cohen and Reaves (2006).

17 Pershing (2008); "Senator Pleaded Guilty" (2007).

18 *United States v. Kaczynski* (2001).

19 *Boykin v. Alabama* (1969, 242).

20 *Moran v. Godinez* (1992, 266–267).

21 Rules of Supreme Court of Virginia, Form 6 (2017).

22 The answers to such questions, as will be discussed, may be used to determine the dangerousness of the behavior in which the defendant engaged at the time of the offense and serve as the basis for a more restrictive post-verdict placement and process for the insanity acquittee to eventually obtain release.

23 N.Y. Crim. Pro. L. § 220.15(3) (2017).

24 N.Y. Crim. Pro. L. § 220.15(4) (2017).

25 N.Y. Crim. Pro. L. § 220.15(1) (2017).

26 N.Y. Crim. Pro. L. § 220.15(2) (2017).

27 N.Y. Crim. Pro. L. § 220.15(1) (2017).

28 US Constitution, Amendment VI.

29 *Gideon v. Wainwright* (1963).

30 *Argersinger v. Hamlin* (1972).

31 *Powell v. Alabama* (1932); *Johnson v. Zerbst* (1938).

32 *Faretta v. California* (1975).

33 Vries (2003).

34 Shields et al. (2007).

35 Bardwell and Arrigo (2002); Kuby and Kunstler (1995).

36 Lithwick (2002).
37 *Indiana v. Edwards* (2008).
38 *People v. Burnett* (1987).
39 *O'Dell v. Commonwealth* (1988).
40 *People v. Horton* (1995).
41 *Massey v. Moore* (1954, 108).
42 *Indiana v. Edwards* (2008, 178).
43 It might be noted that at one point in their careers many appellate judges were trial judges. In addition, they often extensively interact and are good friends with trial judges. Indeed, the brother of the author of the *Edwards* ruling—Justice Stephen Breyer—was a trial court judge at the time the case was decided.
44 However, some states direct trial judges to more closely examine the competence to testify of young children. See, for example, New York Criminal Procedure Law § 60.20(2) (2017).
45 Rule 601 of the Federal Rules of Evidence (2017), which governs federal courts but not state courts, does address "Competency to Testify in General" and states that "Every person is competent to be a witness unless these rules provide otherwise." The accompanying notes add: "No mental . . . qualifications for testifying as a witness are specified. Standards of mental capacity have proved elusive in actual application. A leading commentator observes that few witnesses are disqualified on that ground. . . . Discretion is regularly exercised in favor of allowing the testimony. A witness wholly without capacity is difficult to imagine. The question is one particularly suited to the jury as one of weight and credibility, subject to judicial authority to review the sufficiency of the evidence." At the same time, if it is apparent that a witness is significantly impaired (which arises primarily when a witness is clearly intoxicated or under the influence of drugs), the trial judge generally retains the right to exclude the witness (*United States v. Meerbeke*, 1976; *United States v. Harris*, 1976).
46 If a CST evaluation is simultaneously ordered for the defendant, the judge may simply order the evaluator to also address the defendant's competence to testify, or simply use the results from a CST evaluation to determine the defendant's competence to testify, notwithstanding its questionable fit.
47 Hafemeister (1996).

CHAPTER 8. THE INSANITY DEFENSE
1 Maeder (1985).
2 This approach, as will be discussed, resembles the "moral incapacity" aspect of the insanity defense sometimes employed in American courts.
3 Aristotle (1999 [350 BCE], Book III). This approach tends to fall within the "volitional incapacity" category, described below, used by some American courts in conjunction with the insanity defense.
4 This concept resonates with the "cognitive incapacity" prong articulated by the USSC in *Clark v. Arizona* (2006).
5 Today, this approach would probably fall within a "product of mental illness" test.

6 Williams (1955).

7 The former, in today's terminology would probably be referred to as a "moral incapacity" test, and the latter as a "cognitive incapacity" test.

8 This statement might be categorized today as embracing both a "cognitive incapacity" test and a "volitional incapacity" test.

9 *Hadfield's case* (1800).

10 In today's parlance, this test might be encompassed within the "product of mental illness" standard.

11 *Regina v. Oxford* (1840).

12 Today, this test would probably fall within the "volitional incapacity" standard.

13 Moriarty (2001, xv–xvi).

14 West and Walk (1977, 9).

15 A possible example from the vignettes described above is Andrea Yates, and perhaps Mark David Chapman, John Hinckley, and Lee Boyd Malvo.

16 Possible examples from the vignettes described above include David Berkowitz and Jeffrey Dahmer.

17 A possible example from the vignettes described above is Charles Manson as he is often pictured.

18 *United States v. Scheffer* (1998); Stroud (2015).

19 *Clark v. Arizona* (2006).

20 As described by Perlin (1994); Perlin (2017).

21 Iowa, for example, has established that "the defendant must prove by a preponderance of the evidence that the defendant at the time of the crime suffered from such a deranged condition of the mind as to render the defendant incapable of knowing the nature and quality of the act the defendant was committing or was incapable of distinguishing between right and wrong in relation to the act" (Iowa Code § 701.4 (2017)).

22 "Introduction: The Insanity Defense" (1973).

23 It should be noted that although the phrase "mental disease or defect" is still found in some articulations of these tests, this terminology has come to be disfavored and replaced by what is considered more appropriate language. Today, the phrase "mental disorder" is widely used in place of the phrase "mental disease or defect." (APA, 2013).

24 "From Daniel M'Naghten to John Hinckley" (2002).

25 As discussed in the next chapter, a number of procedural requirements governing the insanity defense were also instituted pursuant to this legislation to make it more difficult to obtain an insanity verdict, including placing the burden of proof on the defendant and requiring the defendant to show insanity by clear and convincing evidence (18 U.S.C. § 17(b) (2017)).

26 18 U.S.C. § 17 (2017).

27 As will be discussed in the next chapter, a mens rea defense is raised when it is claimed that the defendant did not have the requisite intent that is an element of at least one of the crimes with which the defendant is charged. To obtain a convic-

tion on a given charge, the prosecution must establish beyond a reasonable doubt that each and every element of the crime was present.

28 The insanity test used by the Arizona courts had initially included the cognitive incapacity prong as well, but the Arizona legislature deleted it in 1993.

29 This aspect of Arizona law, as well as the mens rea defense in general, will be discussed in the next chapter.

30 Arrillaga (2006).

31 *Jacobellis v. Ohio* (1964, 197).

CHAPTER 9. INSANITY DEFENSE VARIATIONS AND ALTERNATIVES FOR ADDRESSING THE CRIMINAL RESPONSIBILITY OF A DEFENDANT WITH A MENTAL DISORDER

1 Meyer (2015).

2 In an attempt to counter the usual public and media reaction following yet another mass murder, the headline of a recent newspaper article read, "Are Mass Murderers Insane? Usually Not, Researchers Say" (Carey, 2017).

3 *Clark v. Arizona* (2006).

4 *People v. Serravo* (1992); *State v. Crenshaw* (1983).

5 Belt (2015, 762, quoting from *Rex v. Arnold* (1724)).

6 Belt (2015).

7 This desire may have become less widespread in recent years as the result of terrorist attacks purportedly carried out as an act of faith.

8 In 1980, in response to pressure from groups representing veterans of the Vietnam War, the American Psychiatric Association (APA) added the diagnosis of PTSD to its third edition of the *Diagnostic and Statistical Manual of Mental Disorders* (*DSM-III*).

9 The content of this section is drawn in part from Hafemeister and Stockey (2010).

10 APA (2013, 274).

11 Hoge et al. (2004).

12 Kinchin (2007). PTSD, however, is not a new phenomenon, particularly among soldiers. Related disorders have existed, albeit under different names, from at least the time of the American Civil War, variously referred to as "soldier's heart," "railway spine," "shell shock," "war neurosis," "combat fatigue," and "battle shock." Nevertheless, it was not until the Korean and Vietnam conflicts that PTSD began to really gain the attention of mental health professionals and others (Kinchin, 2007).

13 APA (2013).

14 Garcia-Rill and Beecher-Monas (2001); Kinchin (2007).

15 Alternatively, in extreme cases, if individuals can establish an absence of control over their actions, PTSD defendants may be able to employ, as discussed below, an automatism defense. Although technically not the equivalent of an insanity defense, it can be employed when an individual had no conscious perception of what was occurring. The automatism defense may be appropriate when an individual suffers PTSD symptoms that include a physiological reaction to external or

internal cues or after experiencing a dissociative flashback episode and reenactment (Gover, 2008).

16 Bonnie et al. (2004).
17 APA (2013, 87–88).
18 Fradella (2007).
19 APA (2013, 274).
20 Gover (2008).
21 Kinchin (2007).
22 The *burden of proof* is the obligation to prove the assertions presented in a legal action. It can be broken into two components: the *burden of production* and the *burden of persuasion*. The burden of production usually lies with the party who initiated the proceedings and must be met to enable the case to go forward. The failure to do so will result in a legal action being summarily dismissed by the judge and will not, as a result, reach the fact finder (the jury or the judge if there is no jury) for a verdict. In contrast, the burden of persuasion focuses on who has the ultimate obligation to convince the fact finder that the stated facts are true and support a given outcome.
23 Bonnie et al. (2004).
24 *State v. Kelly* (1984, 371). The content of this section is drawn in part from Hafemeister and Stockey (2010).
25 Faigman (1986).
26 *Smith v. State* (1981). Another early appellate ruling addressing the admissibility of evidence pertaining to what was then referred to as *battered woman syndrome* came in *Ibn-Tamas v. United States* (1979).
27 *Smith v. State* (1997, 822).
28 *Smith v. State* (1997, 820).
29 *Smith v. State* (1997, 823).
30 *State v. Kelly* (1984).
31 *State v. Kelly* (1984, 377).
32 Ohio Rev. Code Ann. § 2945.392(B) (2016).
33 Kempe et al. (1962).
34 Amaral (2015).
35 *State v. Janes* (1993).
36 *State v. Janes* (1993).
37 Moreno (1989).
38 *State v. Janes* (1993).
39 Fletcher (1995).
40 Hubbard (2012).
41 Noble (1996).
42 The content of this section is drawn in part from Hafemeister and Stockey (2010).
43 Falk (1996).
44 Bonnie et al. (2004).
45 Weintraub (1997).

46 APA (2013, 271).

47 Clarke (2001).

48 Weintraub (1997).

49 Weintraub (1997).

50 USBJS (2008); USNIJ (2003).

51 Chananie (2007).

52 Kan. Stat. § 22-3219 (2017).

53 *Clark v. Arizona* (2006).

54 *Finger v. State* (2001).

55 *State v. Searcy* (1990).

56 *State v. Bethel* (2003).

57 *State v. Korell* (1984).

58 *State v. Herrera* (1995).

59 See, for example, Asokan (2016); Slobogin (2007, 5–6).

60 But see *Clark v. Arizona* (2006), discussed below.

61 The provisions enacted by the federal government apply only to criminal cases tried in a federal court and are not applicable to criminal cases adjudicated in a state court.

62 See, for example, 18 U.S.C. § 17 (2017); Tex. Code Crim. Pro. Art. 46C.153 (2017).

63 See, for example, Ky. Rev. Stat. 504.150(1) (2017).

64 *Brown v. Plata* (2011); *Estelle v. Gamble* (1976).

65 The "diminished capacity" defense generated considerable public outcry and ultimately led to its abolition in California following the acquittal of Dan White for what came to be known as his "Twinkie defense." See *People v. White* (1981); Cal. Penal Code § 28(b) (2017); Borum and Fulero (1999, 389).

66 Morse and Hoffman (2007). Ohio, for example, no longer recognizes the defense of diminished capacity, but does recognize a mens rea "defense" (*State v. Fulmer*, 2008; *State v. Poppelriter*, 2015).

67 Margolick (1994).

68 Borum and Appelbaum (1996); Pandya et al. (2013).

69 Smith (1957).

70 *Fulcher v. State* (1981); *Starr v. State* (2014); McCrory (2001). Alternatively, although less likely to qualify for an automatism/unconsciousness defense but perhaps eligible for a more traditional insanity defense, a person who experiences a traumatic brain injury may undergo a personality change whereby he or she now becomes routinely anxious, paranoid, or violent; quick-tempered and impulsive; liable to engage in aggressive attacks on others; and lacking the ability to control their thoughts, emotions, impulses, and conduct (Winslade, 2003; Wood and Agharkar, 2015). Recent attention has also focused on chronic traumatic encephalopathy (CTE), a brain injury that results from repeated blows to the head, such as football or hockey players experience, and that may result in violent behavior, as well as memory loss, confusion, and severe mood disorders (Lee, 2016).

71 APA (2013, 298).

72 Melton et al. (2007); Sharma et al. (2015).

73 *People v. Lisnow* (1978).

74 Lyon (2009); Schenck (2005).

75 Siclari et al. (2010).

76 Cartwright (2004).

77 Cox (2009).

78 Clark (1979).

79 MPC § 2.01(2)(c) (1985).

80 If a state authorizes the death penalty, there may be a crime referred to as "capital murder" or something similar, which establishes certain types of homicides as being particularly egregious and which may justify the imposition of the death penalty. See, for example, Va. Code § 18.2-31 (2017).

81 Washington, for example, permits expert testimony if a "diminished capacity" defense is explicitly raised by the defendant prior to the commencement of the trial (*State v. Clark*, 2017).

82 *State v. Mott* (1997).

83 Cal. Penal Code § 28(a) (2017).

84 *State v. Wilcox* (1982); *State v. Fulmer* (2008).

85 *Stamper v. Commonwealth* (1985).

86 FRE 704(b) (2017).

87 It should be noted that some jurisdictions do recognize an *involuntary intoxication* defense. If the defendant can prove that the intoxication was not voluntary (i.e., that it was coerced, mistaken, pathological, or an unexpected reaction to medication) and that (a) psychotic symptoms that met the requirements of that jurisdiction's insanity defense resulted, (b) as a result of the involuntary intoxication, it was impossible for the defendant to form the necessary mens rea for the crime, or (c) the involuntary intoxication rendered the defendant's actions "automatic," the defendant can either avoid conviction or at least receive a reduced punishment (Melton et al., 2007, 229–230).

    Similarly, some jurisdictions recognize a "settled insanity due to intoxication" defense. "The underlying rationale for the 'settled insanity' doctrine is generally explained as an acknowledgement of 'the futility of punishment, since the defective mental state is permanent,' or, more commonly, as a compassionate concession that at some point a person's earlier voluntary decisions become so temporally and 'morally remote' that the cause of the offense can reasonably be ascribed to the resulting insanity rather than the use of intoxicants" (*State v. Sexton*, 2006, 1102). See also *Bieber v. People* (1993); Melton et al. (2007, 230–231).

88 The prosecution in this case had contended that the defendant had been playing music loudly in his pickup truck in an effort to lure a police officer to him.

89 With the USSC in *Clark* having established that mental health evidence must be allowed to play some role in criminal responsibility determinations, all states do permit the possible impact of mental disorders on criminal behavior to be introduced and considered in some way or another.

CHAPTER 10. PROCEDURAL ASPECTS OF INSANITY
DEFENSE DETERMINATIONS

1 *Dejarnette v. Commonwealth* (1881); *Thompson v. Commonwealth* (1952); *Price v. Commonwealth* (1984).

2 It is also worth noting that, as in many states, the Virginia appellate courts have not established a definition of the requisite "mental disease or defect" needed for a successful insanity defense, the Virginia legislature has indicated that a "significant" mental disease or defect (similar to what is required by the federal test) must have been present at the time of the offense for the insanity defense to be available. In the directions it provides to forensic evaluators compiling court-ordered reports concerning a defendant's sanity at the time of the offense, the Virginia legislature has established that they should include in their reports "whether [the defendant] may have had a *significant* mental disease or defect which rendered him insane at the time of the offense" (Va. Code § 19.2-169.5(D) (2017); emphasis added.

3 See Chapter 11, Title 19.2, of the Code of Virginia.

4 The defendant may share this information with the prosecutor if exonerating or mitigating evidence is uncovered or the defendant hopes to persuade the prosecutor to not contest the defendant's insanity plea.

5 Although denied access to the evaluator and the evaluator's report, the prosecutor may discover via means independent of the evaluation and introduce into evidence related information unfavorable to the defendant.

6 Va. Code § 19.2-168 (2017).

7 Va. Code § 19.2-168.1(A) (2017).

8 Tex. Code Crim. Pro. Art. 46C.051 (2017).

9 Tex. Code Crim. Pro. Art. 46C.052 (2017).

10 Tex. Code Crim. Pro. Art. 46C.101 (2017).

11 Tex. Code Crim. Pro. Art. 46C.104 (2017).

12 N.Y. Crim. Pro. L. § 250.10 (2017).

13 Iowa Rule 2.11(11)(b)(2) (2017).

14 Va. Code § 19.2-169.5(A) (2017).

15 Va. Code § 19.2-175 (2017); Supreme Court of Virginia (2018).

16 Va. Code § 19.2-168.1(A) (2017).

17 The primary limitations that mental health professionals who are not physicians face in most states is that they are not allowed to write prescriptions for medications and they cannot independently admit patients into hospitals for treatment. See Slobogin et al. (2014, 120–146).

18 Va. Code § 19.2-169.5(A) (2017).

19 Tex. Code Crim. Pro. Art. 46C.102 (2017).

20 Tennessee State Courts Rule 12.2(c)(1) (2017).

21 Va. Code § 19.2-169.5(B) (2017).

22 For a lawsuit filed in federal court challenging these long delays while the defendant is incarcerated, asserting that this is a violation of defendants' due process rights, see *Ward v. Hellerstedt* (2016).

23 Va. Code § 19.2-169.5(B) (2017).

24 Va. Code § 19.2-169.5(D) (2017).

25 N.Y. Crim. Pro. L. § 250.10(4) (2017).

26 *Brady v. Maryland* (1963).

27 Va. Code § 19.2-169.5(C) (2017).

28 Va. Code § 19.2-168.1(A) (2017).

29 N.Y. Crim. Pro. L. § 250.10 (2017).

30 Va. Code § 19.2-169.5(E) (2017).

31 Va. Code § 19.2-168 (2017).

32 Va. Code § 19.2-169.5(E) (2017).

33 Tex. Code Crim. Pro. Art. 46C.101 (2017). The defendant is still permitted to secure his or her own expert to examine the defendant (Tex. Code Crim. Pro. Art. 46C.107 (2017)).

34 Tex. Code Crim. Pro. Art. 46C.105 (2017).

35 Va. Code § 19.2-169.5(A) (2017).

36 Va. Code § 19.2-175 (2017); Supreme Court of Virginia (2018).

37 Tex. Code Crim. Pro. Art. 46C.103 (2017).

38 Slobogin (1989).

39 FRE 704(b) (2017).

40 Va. Code § 19.2-169.5(D) (2017). As discussed in a previous note, the Virginia insanity test established by the judiciary does not attach the "significant" qualifier to the "mental disease or defect" requirement, but with this provision the Virginia legislature seems to indicate that a relatively severe mental disorder (similar to what is required by the federal test) must be present at the time of the offense for the insanity defense to be available.

CHAPTER 11. DISPOSITIONS FOLLOWING A SUCCESSFUL INSANITY DEFENSE AND RISK ASSESSMENTS

1 If a jury trial was held, typically the jury will not be informed of the possible dispositions of a defendant found NGRI, purportedly so the jury's decision will not be influenced by the availability and nature of these dispositions.

2 For the relatively similar approach to the disposition of insanity acquittees used in Texas, see Tex. Code Crim. Pro. Chap. 46C (2017).

3 Va. Code § 19.2-182.2 (2017). For a similar approach employed in Iowa, see Iowa Rule 2.22(8)(b) (2017).

4 Va. Code § 19.2-182.3 (2017).

5 Tex. Code Crim. Pro. Art. 46C.002 (2017).

6 The following is drawn in part from D. Herr, personal communication, September 30, 2008.

7 *Addington v. Texas* (1979).

8 It has been suggested that, in mathematical terms, a "clear and convincing evidence" standard requires that 75 percent of the evidence supports the verdict, while the "beyond a reasonable doubt" standard (the other widely used legal standard, which is employed in criminal trials to determine a defendant's guilt) requires that 95 percent of the evidence supports the verdict.

9 Keep in mind that in many jurisdictions judges are elected and such adverse publicity may impair their reelection chances.

10 As noted, in Texas an NGRI acquittee may not be committed to a psychiatric facility or be required to undergo outpatient or community-based treatment and supervision for a cumulative period that exceeds the maximum term provided for the charge of which the acquittee was tried (Tex. Code Crim. Pro. Art. 46C.002 (2017)).

11 *Mercer v. Commonwealth* (2000).

12 APA (2013, 659).

13 Va. Code §§ 19.2-182.2 through 19.2-182.16 (2017).

14 As noted above, in Iowa the duration of this initial custody period is set at fifteen days, with a possible extension of another fifteen days (Iowa Rule 2.22(8)(b) (2017)).

15 In contrast, in Iowa, "The defendant may have a separate examination conducted at the facility [where the defendant is being housed] by a licensed physician of the defendant's choice and the report of the independent examiner shall be submitted to the court" for consideration (Iowa Rule 2.22(8)(c) (2017)).

16 In Iowa, continued custody will be ordered if the insanity acquittee is deemed to be mentally ill and dangerous to him- or herself or to others (Iowa Rule 2.22(8)(e) (2017)).

17 Va. Code § 19.2-182.3 (2017).

18 In Iowa, in contrast, the insanity acquittee will remain hospitalized following the initial commitment hearing until the chief medical officer at the facility where he or she is committed reports to the court—with reports required at intervals that may not exceed sixty days—that the individual is no longer mentally ill and is no longer dangerous to him- or herself or others. Even then, the court can override this report if the court determines after a hearing that "continued custody and treatment are necessary to protect the safety of the defendant's self or others" (Iowa Rule 2.22(8)(e) (2017)).

19 Va. Code § 19.2-182.7 (2017).

20 Texas, for example, has such a provision, with a previously compiled victim impact statement used to identify who should be notified (Tex. Code Crim. Pro. Art. 46C.003 (2017)).

21 The following is drawn in part from M. Dennis, personal communication, November 11, 2010.

22 APA (2013).

23 Melton et al. (2007).

24 Spiegel (2011).

25 For a description of the various risk assessment instruments employed, see Melton et al. (2007, 309–314).

26 Melton et al. (2007, 299).

27 Glancy et al. (2015, S46). Another potential issue is whether it is ethical for a mental health provider/clinician to conduct an evaluation that may contribute to an adverse outcome for the person being evaluated (e.g., recommending that an insanity acquittee's request for conditional release or release be denied). Although the task force of the American Academy of Psychiatry and the Law concluded that ethics guidelines do not preclude such evaluations, it did caution that it would be prudent before providing such an evaluation to consult ethics guidelines that apply to risk assessments in legal settings (Glancy et al. 2015, S45–S46).

28 McDermott et al. (2008).

29 Monahan (1981).

30 McDermott et al. (2008, 329–330). Among the reasons given for the failure to use structured risk assessment instruments in this setting are the labor-intensive nature of these assessments, the fact that they are not routinely conducted in forensic facilities, and concerns that they are relevant only when looking at summary data, with their accuracy decreasing substantially when applied to specific individuals (McDermott et al., 2008).

31 See, for example, Green et al. (2016); Heilbrun, Yasuhara, and Shah (2010); Laniado (2017); Oliver (2017); Otto and Douglas (2010); Singh, Grann, and Fazel (2011); Yang, Wong, and Coid (2010).

CHAPTER 12. ALTERNATIVES AND CLOSING REMARKS

1 Adapted from Hafemeister, Garner, and Bath (2012).

2 Compton et al. (2008); Watson and Fulambarker (2012).

3 Variations on this approach include mandatory outpatient treatment and assigning convicted offenders with a mental disorder to specialized mental health probation officers. See Munetz et al. (2014); Skeem, Manchak, and Montoya (2017). The content of this section is drawn in part from Hafemeister, Garner, and Bath (2012).

4 Lowder, Rade, and Desmarais (2018).

5 Wexler (1993).

6 Lurigio and Snowden (2009).

7 Boothroyd et al. (2003); Goldkamp and Irons-Guynn (2000); Redlich et al. (2006).

8 For evaluations of the efficacy of mental health courts, see Almquist and Dodd (2009); Loong, Bonato, and Dewa (2016); McNiel and Binder (2007); Sarteschi, Vaughn, and Kim (2011); Steadman, Davidson, and Brown (2001); Steadman et al. (2011). A recent meta-analysis found that mental health court participation does have a small effect on subsequent charge and jail time, although it did not significantly affect the likelihood of future arrest or conviction (Lowder, Rade, and Desmarais, 2018).

REFERENCES

Addington v. Texas, 441 U.S. 418 (1979).

Advocacy Center for the Elderly & Disabled v. Louisiana Department of Health & Hospitals, 731 F. Supp. 2d 603 (E. D. La. 2010).

Almquist, L., and E. Dodd. 2009. *Mental health courts: A guide to research-informed policy and practice*. New York: Council of State Governments Justice Center.

Amaral, B. 2015. Courts grapple with abuse defense when kids kill their parents. NJ.com, February 13. www.nj.com.

American Psychiatric Association (APA). 2013. *Diagnostic and statistical manual of mental disorders: Fifth edition (DSM-5)*. Washington, DC: American Psychiatric Publishing.

American Psychiatric Association (APA). 2010. *Practice guidelines for the treatment of patients with schizophrenia*, 2nd ed. Washington, DC: American Psychiatric Association.

American Psychiatric Association (APA). 2000. *Psychiatric services in jails and prisons*, 2nd ed. Arlington, VA: American Psychiatric Association.

American Psychiatric Association (APA). 1994. *Diagnostic and statistical manual of mental disorders: Fourth edition (DSM-IV)*. Washington, DC: American Psychiatric Association Publishing.

American Psychological Association (AmPA). 2013. Specialty guidelines for forensic psychology. *American Psychologist* 68, no. 1: 7–19.

Angell, M. 2011. "The illusions of psychiatry": An exchange; Marcia Angell replies. *New York Review of Books*, August 18. www.nybooks.com.

Appelbaum, P. S. 1994. *Almost a revolution: Mental health law and the limits of change*. New York: Oxford University Press.

Argersinger v. Hamlin, 407 U.S. 25 (1972).

Aristotle. 1999 [350 BCE]. *Nicomachean ethics*, translated by W. D. Ross. Indianapolis: Hackett Publishing.

Arrillaga, P. 2006. Does Eric Clark deserve life in prison? *Arizona Daily Sun*, April 14. http://azdailysun.com.

Asokan, T. V. 2016. The insanity defense: Related issues. *Indian Journal of Psychiatry* 58, no. Suppl. 2: S191–S198.

Associated Press. 2011. Court won't bar forced medication of Tucson suspect. *New York Times*, July 23. www.nytimes.com.

Baldwin v. New York, 399 U.S. 66 (1970).

Ball, J. 2012. Loughner faces victims in being sentenced to life in prison without parole. *Washington Post*, November 8. www.washingtonpost.com.

Bardwell, M. C., and B. A. Arrigo. 2002. *Criminal competency on trial: The case of Colin Ferguson*. Durham, NC: Carolina Academic Press.

Belt, R. 2015. When God demands blood: Unusual minds and the troubled juridical ties of religion, madness, and culpability. *University of Miami Law Review* 69, no. 3: 755–794.

Bernstein, R., and T. Seltzer. 2003. Criminalization of people with mental illnesses: The role of mental health courts in system reform. *University of the District of Columbia Law Review* 7, no. 1: 143–162.

Bieber v. People, 856 P.2d 811 (Colo. 1993).

Black, R. C., and J. C. Spriggs II. 2008. An empirical analysis of the length of U.S. Supreme Court opinions, *Houston Law Review* 45, no. 3: 621–682.

Blasier, R. B. 2009. The problem of the aging surgeon: When surgeon age becomes a surgical risk factor. *Clinical Orthopaedics and Related Research* 467, no. 2: 402–411.

Bonnie, R. J. 1992. The competence of criminal defendants: A theoretical reformulation. *Behavioral Sciences and the Law* 10, no. 3: 291–316. doi:10.1002/bsl.2370100303.

Bonnie, R. J., A. M. Coughlin, J. C. Jeffries, and P. W. Low. 2004. *Criminal law*, 2nd ed. St. Paul, MN: Foundation Press.

Boothroyd, R. A., N. G. Poythress, A. McGaha, and J. Petrila. 2003. The Broward Mental Health Court: Process, outcomes and service utilization. *International Journal of Law and Psychiatry* 26, no. 1: 55–71.

Borum, R., and K. L. Appelbaum. 1996. Epilepsy, aggression, and criminal responsibility. *Psychiatric Services* 47, no. 7: 762–763.

Borum, R., and S. M. Fulero. 1999. Empirical research on the insanity defense and attempted reforms: Evidence toward informed policy. *Law and Human Behavior* 23, no. 3: 375–394.

Boykin v. Alabama, 395 U.S. 238 (1969).

Boyles, S. 2009. Schizophrenia linked to early death: Suicide, cancer, heart disease leading causes of death in schizophrenics. *WebMD Health News*, June 22. www.webmd.com.

Bradshaw v. Commonwealth, 228 Va. 484 (1984).

Brady v. Maryland, 373 U.S. 83 (1963).

Bram v. United States, 168 U.S. 532 (1897).

Brinegar v. United States, 338 U.S. 160 (1949).

Brooks, A. 1987. The right to refuse antipsychotic medication: Law and policy. *Rutgers Law Review* 39, nos. 2–3: 339–376.

Brown v. Plata, 563 U.S. 493 (2011).

Brown, J. 2016. State must hire independent consultant to track mental competency evaluations for inmates. *Denver Post*, August 2. www.denverpost.com.

Brubaker, H. 2017. A year after ACLU settlement, little change in delays for court-ordered mental health treatment. *Inquirer*, January 25. www.philly.com.

Buckley v. Valeo, 424 U.S. 1 (1976).

Cal. Penal Code §§ 28, 1367, 1368, 1369, 1369.1, 1370, 1375.5 (2017).

Carey, B. 2017. Are mass murderers insane? Usually not, researchers say. *New York Times*, November 8, A10.

Carter v. Superior Court, 46 Cal. Rptr. 3d 507 (Cal. Ct. App. 2006).

Cartwright, R. 2004. Sleepwalking violence: A sleep disorder, a legal dilemma, and a psychological challenge. *American Journal of Psychiatry* 161, no. 7: 1149–1158.

Centers for Disease Control and Prevention (CDC). 2016. *Injury prevention and control: Traumatic brain injury and concussion.* www.cdc.gov.

Centers for Disease Control and Prevention (CDC). 2011. Mental illness surveillance among adults in the United States. *Morbidity and Mortality Weekly Report* 60, no. 3: 1–32. www.cdc.gov.

Chananie, J. 2007. Violent videogames, crime, and the law: Looking for proof of a causal connection. *Developments in Mental Health Law* 26, no. 1: 27–38.

Chatterji, P., M. Alegria, and D. Takeuchi. 2008. *Psychiatric disorders and employment: New evidence from the Collaborative Psychiatric Epidemiology Surveys.* National Bureau of Economic Research, Working Paper No. 14404.

Clark v. Arizona, 548 U.S. 735 (2006).

Clark, L. 1979. Hypnosis as a defense. *University of Baltimore Law Forum* 10, no. 1: 14–16.

Clarke, G. W. 2001. Urban survival syndrome: A new defense. *Law Enforcement Quarterly* 30, no. 2: 16–17.

Cochrane, R. E., B. L. Herbel, M. L. Reardon, and K. P. Lloyd. 2013. The *Sell* effect: Involuntary medication treatment is a "clear and convincing" success. *Law and Human Behavior* 37, no. 2: 107–116.

Cohen, T. H., and B. A. Reaves. 2006. *Felony defendants in large urban counties, 2002.* Washington, DC: US Department of Justice, Office of Justice Programs, Bureau of Justice Statistics. doi:10.1037/e513962006-001.

Colorado v. Connelly, 479 U.S. 157 (1986).

Colton, C. W., and R. W. Manderscheid. 2006. Congruencies in increased mortality rates, years of potential life lost, and causes of death among public mental health clients in eight states. *Preventing Chronic Disease* 3, no. 2: A42.

Compton, M. T., M. Bahora, A. C. Watson, and J. R. Olivia. 2008. A comprehensive review of extant research on Crisis Intervention Team (CIT) programs. *Journal of the American Academy of Psychiatry and Law* 36, no. 1: 47–55.

Cooper v. Oklahoma, 517 U.S. 348 (1996).

Cooper v. State, 889 P.2d 293 (Okla. Ct. Crim. App. 1995).

Correll v. Commonwealth, 232 Va. 454 (1987).

Council of State Governments. 2002. *Criminal justice/mental health consensus project.* www.ncjrs.gov.

Cox, L. 2009. Sleepwalking domestic violence? *ABC News*, January 9. http://abcnews.go.com.

Cronin, C. 2009. *Forensic psychology: An applied approach*, 2nd ed. Dubuque, IA: Kendall Hunt Publishing.

Cruzan v. Director, Missouri Department of Health, 497 U.S. 261, 292 (1990).

Dallas, M. E. 2012. Disabled adults more apt to be victims of violence: Those with mental illness are the most vulnerable, researchers find. *HealthDay*, February 27. http://consumer.healthday.com.

Darani, S. 2006. Behavior of the defendant in a competency-to-stand-trial evaluation becomes an issue in sentencing. *Journal of the American Academy of Psychiatry and the Law* 34, no. 1: 126–128.

Dawes, S. E., B. W. Palmer, and D. V. Jeste. 2008. Adjudicative competence. *Current Opinion in Psychiatry* 21, no. 5: 490–494. doi:10.1097/YCO.0b013e328308b2ee.

Deane, M. W., H. J. Steadman, R. Borum, B. M. Veysey, and J. P. Morrissey. 1999. Emerging partnerships between mental health and law enforcement. *Psychiatric Services* 50, no. 1: 99–101.

Death Penalty Information Center (DPIC). 2017. Jared Loughner: Arizona shootings. https://deathpenaltyinfo.org.

Dejarnette v. Commonwealth, 75 Va. 867 (1881).

Domino, G., and D. D. Affonso. 1990. A personality measure of Erikson's Life Stages: The inventory of psychosocial balance. *Journal of Personality Assessment* 54, no. 3–4: 576–588. doi:10.1080/00223891.1990.9674021.

Drope v. Missouri, 420 U.S. 162 (1975).

Duncan v. Louisiana, 391 U.S. 145 (1968).

Durham v. United States, 214 F.2d 862 (D.C. Cir. 1954).

Dusky v. United States, 295 F.2d 743 (8th Cir. 1961).

Dusky v. United States, 362 U.S. 402 (1960).

Dusky v. United States, 271 F.2d 385 (8th Cir. 1959).

Elbogen, E. B., and S. C. Johnson. 2009. The intricate link between violence and mental disorder: Results from the National Epidemiologic Survey on Alcohol and Related Conditions. *Archives of General Psychiatry* 66, no. 2: 152–161.

Erikson, E. H. 1950. *Childhood and society*. New York: W. W. Norton.

Estelle v. Gamble, 429 U.S. 97 (1976).

Estelle v. Smith, 451 U.S. 454 (1981).

Faigman, D. L. 1986. Note: The Battered Woman Syndrome and self-defense: A legal and empirical dissent. *Virginia Law Review* 72, no. 3: 619–647.

Falk, P. J. 1996. Novel theories of criminal defense based upon the toxicity of the social environment: Urban psychosis, television intoxication, and black rage. *North Carolina Law Review* 74, no. 3: 731–811.

Faretta v. California, 422 U.S. 806 (1975).

Federal Rules of Evidence (FRE) 601, 704 (2017).

Felthous, A. R. 2012. The involuntary medication of Jared Loughner and pretrial jail detainees in nonmedical correctional facilities. *Journal of the American Academy of Psychiatry and the Law* 40, no. 1: 98–112.

Feuerstein, S., V. Coric, F. Fortunati, S. Southwick, H. Temporini, and C. A. Morgan. 2005. Malingering and forensic psychiatry. *Psychiatry* 2, no. 12: 25–28.

Finger v. State, 27 P.3d 66 (Nev. 2001).

Fitch, W. L. 2007. AAPL Practice Guideline for the Forensic Psychiatric Evaluation of Competence to Stand Trial: An American legal perspective. *Journal of the American Academy of Psychiatry and the Law* 35, no. 4: 509–513.

Fla. Stat. § 985.19 (2017).

Fletcher, G. P. 1995. *With justice for some: Victims' rights in criminal trials.* Boston: Addison-Wesley.

Fogel, M. H., W. Schiffman, D. Mumley, C. Tillbrook, and T. Grisso, T. 2013. Ten year research update (2001–2010): Evaluations for competence to stand trial (adjudicative competence). *Behavioral Sciences and the Law* 31, no. 2: 165–191.

Foucha v. Louisiana, 504 U.S. 71 (1992).

Fradella, H. F. 2007. From insanity to beyond diminished capacity: Mental illness and criminal excuse in the post-*Clark* era. *University of Florida Journal of Law and Public Policy* 18, no. 1: 7–91.

Frances, A. 2010. The forensic risks of DSM-V and how to avoid them. *Journal of the American Academy of Psychiatry and Law* 38, no. 1: 11–14.

Frank, R. G., and S. A. Glied. 2006. *Better but not well: Mental health policy in the United States since 1950.* Baltimore, MD: Johns Hopkins University Press.

From Daniel M'Naghten to John Hinckley: A brief history of the insanity defense. 2002. *Frontline*, October 17. www.pbs.org.

Fulcher v. State, 633 P.2d 142 (Wyo. 1981).

Garcia-Rill, E., and E. Beecher-Monas. 2001. Gatekeeping stress: The science and admissibility of post-traumatic stress disorder. *University of Arkansas Little Rock Law Review* 9, no. 1: 18–40.

Garrett, B. L. 2016. Why plea bargains are not confessions. *William and Mary Law Review* 57, no. 4: 1415–1444.

Gideon v. Wainwright, 372 U.S. 335 (1963).

Glancy, G. D., P. Ash, E. P. Bath, A. Buchanan, P. Fedoroff, R. L. Frierson, . . . and M. Norko. 2015. AAPL practice guidelines for the forensic assessment. *Journal of the American Academy of Psychiatry and the Law* 43, no. 2 Suppl.: S3–S40.

Godinez v. Moran, 509 U.S. 389 (1993).

Goldkamp, J. S., and C. Irons-Guynn. 2000. *Emerging judicial strategies for the mentally ill in the criminal caseload: Mental health courts in Fort Lauderdale, San Bernardino, and Anchorage.* Washington, DC: Bureau of Justice Assistance. http://ncjrs.gov.

Gøtzsche, P. C., A. H. Young, and J. Crace. 2015. Does long term use of psychiatric drugs cause more harm than good? *British Medical Journal* 350 (May 12): h2435. doi:10.1136/bmj.h2435.

Gover, E. M. 2008. Iraq as a psychological quagmire: The implications of using post-traumatic stress disorder as a defense for Iraq War veterans. *Pace Law Review* 28, no. 3: 561–587.

Grabowski, D. C., C. M. Campbell, and M. A. Morrisey. 2004. Elderly licensure laws and motor vehicle fatalities. *Journal of the American Medical Association* 291, no. 23: 2840–2846. doi:10.1001/jama.291.23.2840.

Green, D., M. Schneider, H. Griswold, B. Belfi, M. Herrera, and A. DeBlasi. 2016. A comparison of the HCR-20V3 among male and female insanity acquittees: A retrospective file study. *International Journal of Forensic Mental Health* 15, no. 1: 48–64.

Grisso, T. 2005. *Clinical evaluations for juveniles' competence to proceed: A guide for legal professionals.* Sarasota, FL: Professional Resource Press.

Grisso, T. 2003. *Evaluating competencies: Forensic assessments and instruments,* 2nd ed. New York: Kluwer Academic/Plenum Publishers.

Hadfield's case, 27 How. St. Tr. 1282 (1800).

Hafemeister, T. L. 2004. Parameters and implementation of a right to mental health treatment for juvenile offenders. *Virginia Journal of Social Policy and the Law* 12, no. 1: 61–139.

Hafemeister, T. L. 1996. Protecting child witnesses: Judicial efforts to minimize trauma and reduce evidentiary barriers. *Violence and Victims* 11, no. 1: 71–91.

Hafemeister, T. L., S. G. Garner, and V. E. Bath. 2012. Forging links and renewing ties: Applying the principles of restorative and procedural justice to better respond to criminal offenders with a mental disorder. *Buffalo Law Review* 60, no. 1: 147–223.

Hafemeister, T. L., and J. George. 2012. The Ninth Circle of Hell: An Eighth Amendment analysis of imposing prolonged Supermax solitary confinement on inmates with a mental illness. *Denver University Law Review* 90, no. 1: 1–54.

Hafemeister, T. L., and N. A. Stockey. 2010. Last stand? The criminal responsibility of war veterans returning from Iraq and Afghanistan with Posttraumatic Stress Disorder. *Indiana Law Journal* 85, no. 1: 87–141.

Hafemeister, T. L., and R. Vallas. 2016. Intimate partner violence and victims with a mental disorder: What do you do when it seems like all your choices are lousy and screaming for help just makes things worse. Unpublished manuscript.

Hagen, M. 1997. *Whores of the court: The fraud of psychiatric testimony and the rape of American justice.* New York: ReganBooks.

Harcourt, B. E. 2007. The mentally ill, behind bars. *New York Times,* January 15, A15.

Hartmann, M. 2011. Jared Loughner's condition worsens, judge allows forcible medication. *Jezebel,* August 28. http://jezebel.com.

Heilbrun, K., D. DeMatteo, G. Marczyk, and A. M. Goldstein. 2008. Standards of practice and care in forensic mental health assessment. *Psychology, Public Policy, and Law* 14, no. 1: 1–26.

Heilbrun, K., K. Yasuhara, and S. Shah. 2010. Violence risk assessment tools: Overview and critical analysis. In *Handbook of violence risk assessment,* edited by R. K. Otto and K. S. Douglas, 1–18. New York: Routledge.

Helderman, R. S. 2012. Senate rejects treaty to protect disabled around the world. *Washington Post,* December 4. www.washingtonpost.com.

Hiroeh, U., L. Appleby, P. B. Mortensen, and G. Dunn. 2001. Death by homicide, suicide, and other unnatural causes in people with mental illness: A population-based study. *Lancet* 358, no. 9,299: 2110–2112.

Hoge, C. W., C. A. Castro, S. C. Messer, D. McGurk, D. I. Cotting, and R. L. Koffman. 2004. Combat duty in Iraq and Afghanistan, mental health problems, and barriers to care. *New England Journal of Medicine* 351 (July 1): 13–22.

Hoge, S. K., R. J. Bonnie, N. Poythress, and J. Monahan. 1992. Attorney-client decision-making in criminal cases: Client competence and participation as perceived by their attorneys. *Behavioral Sciences and the Law* 10, No. 3: 385–394. doi:10.1002/bsl.2370100308.

Hubbard, A. 2012. Menendez brothers convicted in parents' murder 16 years ago. *Los Angeles Times*, March 20. http://latimesblogs.latimes.com.

Hughes, K., M. A. Bellis, L. Jones, S. Wood, G. Bates, L. Eckley, . . . and A. Officer. 2012. Prevalence and risk of violence against adults with disabilities: A systematic review and meta-analysis of observational studies. *Lancet* 379, no. 9,826: 1621–1629. doi:10.1016/S0140-6736(11)61851-5.

Human Rights Watch. 2003. *Ill-equipped: U.S. prisons and offenders with mental illness.* New York: Human Rights Watch.

Ibn-Tamas v. United States, 407 A.2d 626 (D.C. Ct. App. 1979).

Inbau, F. E., J. E. Reid, J. P. Buckley, and B. C. Jayne. 2013. *Criminal interrogation and confessions*, 5th ed. Burlington, MA: Jones & Bartlett Learning.

Indiana v. Edwards, 554 U.S. 164 (2008).

Insanity Defense Reform Act of 1984.

Institute of Medicine (IOM). 2006. *Improving the quality of health care for mental and substance-use conditions.* Washington, DC: Institute of Medicine.

Introduction: The insanity defense in the District of Columbia. 1973. *Washington University Law Quarterly 1973*, no. 1: 19–37.

Iowa Code § 701.4 (2017).

Iowa Rule 2.11(11), 2.22(8) (2017).

Jackson v. Indiana, 406 U.S. 715 (1972).

Jacobellis v. Ohio, 378 U.S. 184 (1964).

Jacobs, S., D. Filipov, and P. Wen. 2013. The fall of the House of Tsarnaev. *Boston Globe*, December 16. www.bostonglobe.com.

James, D. J., and L. E. Glaze. 2006. *Mental health problems of prison and jail inmates.* Washington, DC: US Department of Justice, Bureau of Justice Statistics.

J. D. B. v. North Carolina, 564 U.S. 261 (2011).

Johnson v. Zerbst, 304 U.S. 458 (1938).

Johnson, K. 2010. Verdict is guilty in abduction of Elizabeth Smart. *New York Times*, December 10. www.nytimes.com.

Jones v. United States, 463 U.S. 354 (1983).

Julien, R. M. 2013. *A primer of drug action: A concise nontechnical guide to the actions, uses, and side effects of psychoactive drugs, revised and updated.* New York: Owl Books.

Kan. Stat. § 22-3219 (2017).

Kansas v. Crane, 534 U.S. 407 (2002).

Kansas v. Hendricks, 521 U.S. 346 (1997).

Keedy, E. R. 1917. Insanity and criminal responsibility. *Harvard Law Review* 30, no. 6: 535–560.

Kempe, C. H., F. N. Silverman, B. F. Steele, W. Droegemueller, and H. K. Silver. 1962. The battered-child syndrome. *Journal of the American Medical Association* 181 (July 7): 17–24.

Ky. Rev. Stat. 504.150 (2017).

Kessler, R. C., P. Berglund, O. Demler, R. Jin, K. R. Merikangas, and E. E. Walters. 2005a. Lifetime prevalence and age-of-onset distributions of DSM-IV disorders in the National Comorbidity Survey Replication. *Archives of General Psychiatry* 62, no. 6: 593–602.

Kessler, R. C., W. T. Chiu, O. Demler, and E. E. Walters. 2005b. Prevalence, severity, and comorbidity of twelve-month DSM-IV disorders in the National Comorbidity Survey Replication. *Archives of General Psychiatry* 62, no. 6: 617–627.

Killer's manifesto: "You forced me into a corner." 2007. CNN.com, April 18. www.cnn.com.

Kinchin, D. 2007. *A guide to psychological debriefing: Managing emotional decompression and post-traumatic stress disorder.* London: Jessica Kingsley Publishers.

Kingdon, D., T. Sharma, and D. Hart. 2004. What attitudes do psychiatrists hold towards people with mental illness? *Psychiatrist* 28, no. 11: 401–406. doi:10.1192/pb.28.11.401.

Klein, D. W. 2009. Unreasonable: Involuntary medications, incompetent criminal defendants, and the Fourth Amendment. *San Diego Law Review* 46, no. 1: 161–204.

Knoll, J. L., and P. J. Resnick. 1999. *U.S. v. Greer*: Longer sentences for malingerers. *Journal of the American Academy of Psychiatry and the Law* 27, no. 4: 621–625.

Kohlberg, L. 1976. Moral stages and moralization: The cognitive-developmental approach. In *Moral development and behavior: Theory, research, and social issues,* edited by T. Lickona, 31–53. New York: Holt, Rinehart, & Winston.

Kuby, R. L., and W. M. Kunstler. 1995. So crazy he thinks he is sane: The Colin Ferguson trial and the competency standard. *Cornell Journal of Law and Public Policy* 5, no. 1: 19–26.

Kupers, T. 1999. *Prison madness: The mental health crisis behind bars and what we must do about it.* San Francisco: Jossey-Bass.

Laniado, S. 2017. *Toward better discharge decision-making for violent offenders in forensic mental health settings: A critical analysis of the literature.* https://search.proquest.com.

Larson, M. K., E. F. Walker, and M.T. Compton. 2011. Early signs, diagnosis and therapeutics of the prodromal phase of schizophrenia and related psychotic disorders. Expert Review of Neurotherapeutics 10, no. 8: 1347–1359.

Lave, T. R. 2011. Throwing away the key: Has the Adam Walsh Act lowered the threshold for sexually violent predator commitments too far? *University of Pennsylvania Journal of Constitutional Law* 14, no. 2: 391–429.

Lawrence, E. D. 2014. When should elderly people stop driving? *USA Today*, January 20. www.usatoday.com.

Lee, B. Y. 2016. Could concussions become a legal defense? *Forbes*, February 5. www.forbes.com.

Leo, R. A. 1996. The impact of Miranda revisited. *Journal of Criminal Law and Criminology* 86, no. 3: 621–692.

Leonard, K. 2014. Under Obamacare, mental health lacking. *U.S. News & World Report*, October 29. www.usnews.com.

Lithwick, D. 2002. Moussaoui hijacks the legal system: An accused terrorist puts the U.S. courts on trial. *Slate*, May 1. www.slate.com.

Loong, D., S. Bonato, and C. S. Dewa. 2016. The effectiveness of mental health courts in reducing recidivism and police contact: A systematic review protocol. *Systematic Reviews* 5, no. 123: 1–5. doi:10.1186/s13643-016-0291-8.

Lowder, E. M., C. B. Rade, and S. L. Desmarais. 2018. Effectiveness of mental health courts in reducing recidivism: A meta-analysis. *Psychiatric Services* 69, no. 1: 15–22. doi:10.1176/appi.ps.201700107.

Lurigio, A. J., and J. Snowden. 2009. Putting therapeutic jurisprudence into practice: The growth, operations, and effectiveness of mental health court. *Justice System Journal* 30, no. 2: 196–218.

Lyon, L. 2009. 7 criminal cases that invoked the "sleepwalking defense." *U.S. News & World Report*, May 8. http://health.usnews.com.

Mackler, D., and M. Morrissey. 2010. *A way out of madness: Dealing with your family after you've been diagnosed with a psychiatric disorder*. Bloomington, IN: AuthorHouse.

Maeder, T. 1985. *Crime and madness: The origins and evolution of the insanity defense*. Scranton, PA: Harper & Row.

Manderscheid, R. W. 2006. Saving lives and restoring hope. *Behavioral Healthcare* 26, no. 9: 58–59.

Margolick, D. 1994. Lorena Bobbitt acquitted in mutilation of husband. *New York Times*, January 22. www.nytimes.com.

Massey v. Moore, 348 U.S. 105 (1954).

Maxwell, V. 2009. This won't hurt a bit, really: Dating after mental illness. *Psychology Today*, April 18. www.psychologytoday.com.

McCrory, P. 2001. The medicolegal aspects of automatism in mild head injury. *British Journal of Sports Medicine* 35, no. 5: 288–290.

McDermott, B. E., I. V. Dualan, and C. L. Scott. 2013. Malingering in the correctional system: Does incentive affect prevalence? *International Journal of Law and Psychiatry* 36, nos. 3–4: 287–292. doi:10.1016/j.ijlp.2013.04.013.

McDermott, B. E., C. L. Scott, D. Busse, F. Andrade, M. Zozaya, and C. D. Quanbeck. 2008. The conditional release of insanity acquittees: Three decades of decision-making. *Journal of the American Academy of Psychiatry and the Law* 36, no. 3: 329–336.

McNiel, D. E., and R. L. Binder. 2007. Effectiveness of a mental health court in reducing criminal recidivism and violence. *American Journal of Psychiatry* 164, no. 9: 1395–1403.

Medina v. California, 505 U.S. 437 (1992).

Medina v. Chappell, 781 F.3d 1076 (9th Cir. 2015).

Melton, G. B., J. Petrila, N. G. Poythress, and C. Slobogin. 2007. *Psychological evaluations for the courts: A handbook for mental health professionals and lawyers*, 3rd ed. New York: Guilford Press.

Melton, G. B., J. Petrila, N. G. Poythress, and C. Slobogin. 2004. *Psychological evaluations for the courts: A handbook for mental health professionals and lawyers*, 2nd ed. New York: Guilford Press.

Meltzer, H., P. Bebbington, M. S. Dennis, R. Jenkins, S. McManus, and T. S. Brugha. 2013. Feelings of loneliness among adults with mental disorder. *Social Psychiatry and Psychiatric Epidemiology* 48, no. 1: 5–13. doi:10.1007/s00127-012-0515-8.

Menaster, M. 2011. Psychiatric illness associated with criminality. *Medscape*, June 27. http://emedicine.medscape.com.

Mental Health America. 2008. *Position statement 52: In support of maximum diversion of persons with serious mental illness from the criminal justice system*. www.mentalhealthamerica.net.

Mental Health Early Intervention, Treatment, and Prevention Act of 2000, S. 2639, 106th Cong. 2000.

Mercer v. Commonwealth, 523 S.E.2d 213 (Va. 2000).

Meyer, J. P. 2015. The James Holmes "Joker" rumor. *Denver Post*, September 18. www.denverpost.com.

Miller, R. D. 2003. Hospitalization of criminal defendants for evaluation of competence to stand trial or for restoration of competence: Clinical and legal issues. *Behavioral Sciences and the Law* 21, no. 3: 369–391. doi:10.1002/bsl.546.

Miranda v. Arizona, 384 U.S. 436 (1966).

Missouri v. Frye, 566 U.S. 133 (2012).

Missouri (Mo.) Rev. Stat. § 552.020(1) (2017).

Model Penal Code (MPC) § 2.01(2) (1985).

Monahan, J. 1981. *The clinical prediction of violent behavior*. Washington, DC: Government Printing Office.

Montana v. Egelhoff, 518 U.S. 37 (1996).

Moran v. Godinez, 972 F.2d 263 (9th Cir. 1992).

Moreno, J. A. 1989. Killing daddy: Developing a self-defense strategy for the abused child. *University of Pennsylvania Law Review* 137, no. 4: 1281–1307.

Moriarty, J. C. 2001. *The role of mental illness in criminal trials*. New York: Routledge.

Morse, S. J. 2017. Involuntary competence in United States criminal law. In *Fitness to plead: International and comparative perspectives*, edited by R. Mackay and W. Brookbanks, 207–230. New York: Oxford University Press, 2018. http://scholarship.law.upenn.edu.

Morse, S. J., and M. B. Hoffman. 2007. The uneasy entente between legal insanity and mens rea: Beyond *Clark v. Arizona. Journal of Criminal Law and Criminology* 97, no. 4: 1071–1149.

Moyer, K. S., and M. Nakic. 2016. Forced medication to restore competency. *Journal of the American Academy of Psychiatry and the Law* 44, no. 2: 280–283.

Munetz, M. R., C. Ritter, J. L. Teller, and N. Bonfine. 2014. Mental health court and assisted outpatient treatment: Perceived coercion, procedural justice, and program impact. *Psychiatric Services* 65, no. 3: 352–358. doi:10.1176/appi.ps.002642012.

National Alliance on Mental Illness (NAMI). 2007. *Mental illnesses: Treatment saves money and makes sense.* www2.nami.org.

National Institute of Justice (NIJ), Office of Justice Programs. 2014. *From juvenile delinquency to young adult offending.* http://nij.gov.

National Institute of Mental Health (NIMH). 2017a. *Any mental illness (AMI) among adults.* www.nimh.nih.gov.

National Institute of Mental Health (NIMH). 2017b. *Serious mental illness (SMI) among U.S. adults.* www.nimh.nih.gov.

National Institute of Mental Health (NIMH). 2015. *Schizophrenia.* www.nimh.nih.gov.

National Minimum Drinking Age Act of 1984, 23 U.S.C. § 158 (1984).

New York Criminal Procedure Law §§ 60.20, 220.15, 250.10, 730.10, 730.20, 730.50, 730.60, 730.70 (2017).

Noble, K. B. 1996. Menendez brothers guilty of killing their parents. *New York Times,* March 21. www.nytimes.com.

Nussbaum, D., M. Hancock, I. Turner, J. Arrowood, and S. Melodick. 2007. Fitness/competency to stand trial: A conceptual overview, review of existing instruments, and cross-validation of the Nussbaum Fitness Questionnaire. *Brief Treatment and Crisis Intervention* 8, no. 1: 43–72. doi:10.1093/brief-treatment/mhm026.

O'Dell v. Commonwealth, 234 Va. 672 (1988).

Ohio Rev. Code Ann. § 2945.392(B) (2016).

Olfson, M., C. Blanco, and S. C. Marcus. 2016. Treatment of adult depression in the United States. *Journal of the American Medical Association: Internal Medicine* 176, no. 10: 1482–1491. doi:10.1001/jamainternmed.2016.5057. http://archinte.jamanetwork.com.

Oliver, H. 2017. *Predicting modification and revocation of insanity acquittees on conditional release using the Short-Term Assessment of Risk and Treatability.* http://digitalcommons.georgefox.edu.

Oregon Advocacy Center v. Mink, 322 F.3d 1101 (9th Cir. 2003).

Otto, R. K., and K. S. Douglas, eds. 2010. *Handbook of violence risk assessment.* New York: Routledge.

Pandya, N. S., M. Vrbancic, L. D. Ladino, and J. F. Téllez-Zenteno. 2013. Epilepsy and homicide. *Neuropsychiatric Disease and Treatment* 9 (May 13): 667–673.

Pate v. Robinson, 383 U.S. 375 (1966).

People v. Burnett, 188 Cal. App. 3d 1314 (1987).

People v. Horton, 906 P.2d 478 (Cal. 1995).

People v. Jablonski, 126 P.3d 938 (Cal. 2006).

People v. Jones, 931 P.2d 960 (Cal. 1997).

People v. Kaplan, 57 Cal. Rptr. 3d 143 (Cal. Ct. App. 2007).

People v. Lawley, 38 P.3d 461 (Cal. 2002).

People v. Lisnow, 151 Cal. Rptr. 621 (Cal. Ct. App. 1978).

People v. O'Dell, 23 Cal. Rptr. 3d 902 (Cal. Ct. App. 2005).

People v. Pokovich, 141 P.3d 267 (Cal. 2006).

People v. Rells, 996 P.2d 1184 (Cal. 2000).

People v. Serravo, 823 P.2d 128 (Colo. 1992).

People v. White, 172 Cal. Rptr. 612 (Cal. Ct. App. 1981).

Perlin, M. L. 2017. The insanity defense: Nine myths that will not go away. In *The insanity defense: Multidisciplinary views on its history, trends, and controversies*, edited by M. D. White, 3–22. Santa Barbara, CA: Praeger.

Perlin, M. L. 1994. *The jurisprudence of the insanity defense.* Durham, NC: Carolina Academic Press.

Perr, I. N. 1991. Crime and multiple personality disorder: A case history and discussion. *Bulletin of the American Academy of Psychiatry and the Law* 19, no. 2: 203–214.

Pershing, B. 2008. Craig loses appeal in bathroom sting case. *Washington Post*, December 9. http://voices.washingtonpost.com.

Pescosolido, B. A., J. Monahan, B. G. Link, A. Stueve, and S. Kikuzawa. 1999. The public's view of the competence, dangerousness, and need for legal coercion of persons with mental health problems. *American Journal of Public Health* 89, no. 9: 1339–1345.

Pfeiffer, M. B. 2007. *Crazy in America: The hidden tragedy of our criminalized mentally ill.* New York: Carroll & Graf.

Phillips, J., A. Frances, M. A. Cerullo, J. Chardavoyne, H. S. Decker, M. B. First, N. Ghaemi, et al. 2012. The six most essential questions in psychiatric diagnosis: A pluralogue part I: Conceptual and definitional issues in psychiatric diagnosis. *Philosophy, Ethics, and Humanities in Medicine* 7, no. 3: 6–19. doi:10.1186/1747-5341-7-3.

Piaget, J. 2000. Piaget's theory of cognitive development. In *Childhood cognitive development: The essential readings*, edited by K. Lee, 33–47. Malden, MA: Blackwell.

Possley, M. 1998. Doctor says Kaczynski is competent for trial. *Chicago Tribune*, January 21. http://articles.chicagotribune.com.

Powell v. Alabama, 287 U.S. 45 (1932).

Poythress, N. G., R. J. Bonnie, S. K. Hoge, J. Monahan, and L. B. Oberlander. 1994. Client abilities to assist counsel and make decisions in criminal cases: Findings from three studies. *Law and Human Behavior* 18, no. 4: 437–452. doi:10.1007/BF01499049.

Poythress, N. G., R. J. Bonnie, J. Monahan, R. Otto, and S. K. Hoge. 2002a. *Adjudicative competence: The MacArthur Studies.* New York: Kluwer Academic/Plenum Publishers.

Poythress, N. G., J. Petrila, A. McGaha, and R. Boothroyd. 2002b. Perceived coercion and procedural justice in the Broward Mental Health Court. *International Journal of Law and Psychiatry* 25, no. 5: 517–533.

Preidt, R. 2017. Nearly 1 in 5 U.S. adults has mental illness or drug problem. *HealthDay*, July 21. https://medlineplus.gov.

President's New Freedom Commission on Mental Health. 2003. *Achieving the promise: Transforming mental health care in America.* http://store.samhsa.gov.

Price v. Commonwealth, 228 Va. 452 (1984).

Quinn, R. 2011. Court: Loughner can refuse meds: No forced medication for Tucson suspect while appeal is pending. *Newser,* July 13. http://www.newser.com.

Radnofsky, L. 2015. Where are the mental-health providers? As more patients seek help, advocates scramble to expand providers' ranks. *Wall Street Journal,* February 16. www.wsj.com.

Ray, I. 1838. *A treatise on the medical jurisprudence of insanity.* Boston: Little, Brown.

Redlich, A. D., H. J. Steadman, J. Monahan, P. C. Robbins, and J. Petrila. 2006. Patterns of practice in mental health courts: A national survey. *Law and Human Behavior* 30, no. 3: 347–362.

Regina v. Oxford, 9 Car. & P. 525, 173 Eng. Rep. 941 (1840).

Rex v. Arnold, 16 How. St. Tr. 695 (1724).

Riggins v. Nevada, 504 U.S. 127 (1992).

Roesch, R., and S. L. Golding. 1980. *Competency to stand trial.* Champaign: University of Illinois Press.

Roesch, R., and S. L. Golding. 1979. Treatment and disposition of defendants found incompetent to stand trial: A review and a proposal. *International Journal of Law and Psychiatry* 2, no. 3: 349–370. doi:10.1016/0160-2527(79)90012-8.

Roesch, R., P. Zapf, and D. Eaves. 2006. *Fitness Interview Test—revised.* Sarasota, FL: Professional Resource Press/Professional Resource Exchange.

Rogers, R., and R. P. Granacher. 2011. Conceptualization and assessment of malingering. In *Handbook of forensic assessment: Psychological and Psychiatric perspectives,* edited by E. Y. Drogin, F. M. Dattilio, R. L. Sadoff, and T. G. Gutheil, 659–678. Hoboken, NJ: John Wiley & Sons.

Rogers, R., N. Grandjean, C. E. Tillbrook, M. J. Vitacco, and K. W. Sewell. 2001. Recent interview-based measures of competency to stand trial: A critical review augmented with research data. *Behavioral Sciences and the Law* 19, no. 4: 503–18. doi:10.1002/bsl.458.

Roid, G. H. 2003. *Stanford-Binet intelligence scales.* Itasca, IL: Riverside Publishing.

Rosinia, N. 2012. How "reasonable" has become unreasonable: A proposal for rewriting the lasting legacy of *Jackson v. Indiana. Washington University Law Review* 89, no. 3: 673–703.

Sarteschi, C. M., M. G. Vaughn, and K. Kim. 2011. Assessing the effectiveness of mental health courts: A quantitative review. *Journal of Criminal Justice* 39, no. 1: 12–20. doi:10.1016/j.jcrimjus.2010.11.003.

Schenck, C. H. 2005. *Paradox lost: Midnight in the battleground of sleep and dreams.* Minneapolis, MN: Extreme-Nights.

Schwarzbold, M., A. Diaz, E. T. Martins, A. Rufino, L. N. Amante, M. E. Thais, J. Quevedo, A Hohl, M. N. Linhares, and R. Walz. 2008. Psychiatric disorders and traumatic brain injury. *Neuropsychiatric Disorders and Treatment* 4, no. 4: 797–816.

Sell v. United States, 539 U.S. 166 (2003).

Senator pleaded guilty, reportedly after bathroom stall incident. 2007. *CNN: Politics*, August 27. www.cnn.com.

Shannon, B. D. 2017. Competency, ethics, and morality. *Texas Tech Law Review* 49, no. 4: 861–880.

Sharma, P., M. Guirguis, J. Nelson, and T. McMahon. 2015. A case of dissociative amnesia with dissociative fugue and treatment with psychotherapy. *Primary Care Companion for CNS Disorders* 17, no. 3. www.ncbi.nlm.nih.gov.

Shields, C., K. Damphousse, T. Sours, P. Roberts, and B. Smith. 2007. The Unabomber: Theodore John Kaczynski. In *Crimes and trials of the century*, edited by F. Y. Bailey and S. Chermak, 43–60. Westport, CT: Greenwood Publishing.

Siclari, F., R. Khatami, F. Urbaniok, L. Nobili, M. W. Mahowald, C. H. Schenck, M. A. C. Bornemann, and C. L. Bassetti, 2010. Violence in sleep. *Brain: A Journal of Neurology* 133, no. 12: 3494–3509.

Silverthorne Lumber Co. v. United States, 251 U.S. 385 (1920).

Singh, J. P., M. Grann, and S. Fazel. 2011. A comparative study of violence risk assessment tools: A systematic review and metaregression analysis of 68 studies involving 25,980 participants. *Clinical Psychology Review* 31, no. 3: 499–513. doi:10.1016/j.cpr.2010.11.009.

Skeem, J. L., and S. L. Golding. 1998. Community examiners' evaluations of competence to stand trial: Common problems and suggestions for improvement. *Professional Psychology: Research and Practice* 29, no. 4: 357–367.

Skeem, J. L., S. Manchak, and L. Montoya. 2017. Comparing public safety outcomes for traditional probation vs specialty mental health probation. *Journal of the American Medical Association: Psychiatry* 74, no. 9: 942–948. doi:10.1001/jamapsychiatry.2017.1384.

Slobogin, C. 2007. *Proving the unprovable: The role of law, science, and speculation in adjudicating culpability and dangerousness*. New York: Oxford University Press.

Slobogin, C. 1989. The "ultimate issue" issue. *Behavioral Sciences and the Law* 7, no. 2: 259–266. doi:10.1002/bsl.2370070209.

Slobogin, C., T. L. Hafemeister, D. Mossman, and R. Reisner. 2014. *Law and the mental health system: Civil and criminal aspects*, 6th ed. St. Paul, MN: West Academic Publishing.

Slovenko, R. 2002. *Psychiatry in law*. New York: Brunner-Routledge.

Smith v. State, 486 S.E.2d 819 (Ga. 1997).

Smith v. State, 277 S.E.2d 678 (Ga. 1981).

Smith, R. P. 1957. Criminal law—Criminal responsibility of epileptic driver who causes death when stricken with sudden epileptic "blackout." *Notre Dame Law Review* 32, no. 4: 688–707.

Spiegel, A. 2011. Can a test really tell who's a psychopath? *NPR: All Things Considered*, May 26. www.npr.org.

The Spotlight Team. 2016. The desperate and the dead: Families in fear. *Boston Globe*, June 23. https://apps.bostonglobe.com.

Stamper v. Commonwealth, 324 S.E.2d 682 (Va. 1985).

Starr v. State, A-11250, 2014 WL 2834502 (Alaska Ct. App. June 18, 2014).

State v. Barzee, 177 P.3d 48 (Utah 2007).

State v. Bethel, 66 P.3d 840 (Kan. 2003).

State v. Clark, No. 92021-4 (Wash. 2017).

State v. Crenshaw, 659 P.2d 488 (Wash. 1983).

State v. Fulmer, 883 N.E.2d 1052 (Ohio 2008).

State v. Herrera, 895 P.2d 359 (Utah 1995).

State v. Janes, 850 P.2d 495 (Wash. 1993).

State v. Kelly, 478 A.2d 364 (N.J. 1984).

State v. Korell, 690 P.2d 992 (Mont. 1984).

State v. Mott, 931 P.2d 1046 (Ariz. 1997).

State v. Poppelriter, 50 N.E.3d 270 (Ohio 2015).

State v. Searcy, 798 P.2d 914 (Idaho 1990).

State v. Sexton, 904 A.2d 1092 (Vt. 2006).

State v. Wilcox, 436 N.E.2d 895 (Ohio 1982).

Steadman, H. J., S. Davidson, and C. Brown. 2001. Law and psychiatry: Mental health courts: Their promise and unanswered questions. *Psychiatric Services* 52, no. 4: 457–458.

Steadman, H. J., F. Osher, P. C. Robbins, B. Case, and S. Samuels. 2009. Prevalence of serious mental illness among jail inmates. *Psychiatric Services* 60, no. 6: 761–765.

Steadman, H. J., A. Redlich, L. Callahan, P. C. Robbins, and R. Vesselinov. 2011. Effect of mental health courts on arrests and jail days: A multisite study. *Archives of General Psychiatry* 68, no. 2: 167–172. doi:10.1001/archgenpsychiatry.2010.134.

Steenhuysen, J. 2010. Nearly 1 in 5 Americans had mental illness in 2009. Reuters, November 18. www.reuters.com.

Stroud, M. 2015. Will lie detectors ever get their day in court again? Bloomberg, February 2. www.bloomberg.com.

Substance Abuse and Mental Health Services Administration (SAMHSA), US Department of Health and Human Services. 2014. *Nearly 1 in 5 adult Americans experienced mental illness in 2013*, November 20. www.samhsa.gov.

Substance Abuse and Mental Health Services Administration (SAMHSA), Office of Applied Studies, US Department of Health and Human Services. 2008. *The National Survey on Drug Use and Health Report: Serious psychological distress and receipt of mental health services*. http://oas.samhsa.gov.

Substance Abuse and Mental Health Services Administration (SAMHSA), US Department of Health and Human Services. 2006. *National consensus statement on mental health recovery*. http://store.samhsa.gov.

Supreme Court of Virginia. 2018. Chart of Allowances. www.courts.state.va.us.

Supreme Court of Virginia. 2017. Rules, Part Three A, Criminal Practice and Procedure, Appendix, Form 6, Suggested questions to be put by the Court to an Accused who has pleaded guilty (Rule 3A:8). www.courts.state.va.us.

Tennessee State Courts Rule 12.2 (2017). www.tncourts.gov.

Teplin, L. A., G. M. McClelland, K. M. Abram, and D. A. Weiner. 2005. Crime victimization in adults with severe mental illness. *Archives of General Psychiatry* 62, no. 8: 911–921.

Terrell v. Commonwealth, 12 Va. App. 285 (1991).

Terry v. Hill, 232 F. Supp. 2d 934 (E.D. Ark. 2002).

Texas (Tex.) Code Crim. Pro. Chaps. 46B, 46C (2017).

Thompson v. Commonwealth, 193 Va. 204 (1952).

Torrey, E. F. 1997. *Out of the shadows: Confronting America's mental illness crisis.* New York: John Wiley and Sons.

Trangle, M., G. Mager, P. Goering, and R. Christensen. 2010. Minnesota 10 by 10: Reducing morbidity and mortality in people with serious mental illnesses. *Minnesota Medicine* 93, no. 6: 38–41.

Trueblood v. Washington State Department of Social & Health Services, 822 F.3d 1037 (9th Cir. 2016).

Turgal, J. 2012. Jared Lee Loughner sentenced in Arizona on federal charges in Tucson shooting. The FBI: Federal Bureau of Investigation, November 8. https://archives.fbi.gov.

Tyner, H. 2015. 5 mental illness myths debunked. *wecounsel*, January 2. www.wecounsel.com.

Tysse, J. E. 2005. The right to an "imperfect" trial: Amnesia, malingering, and competency to stand trial. *William Mitchell Law Review* 32, no. 1: 352–387.

Tysse, J. E., and T. L. Hafemeister. 2006. Amnesia and the determination of competency to stand trial. *Developments in Mental Health Law* 25, no. 2: 65–80.

United Nations. 2015. *Treaty collection: Convention on the rights of persons with disabilities.* https://treaties.un.org.

United Nations. 2006. *Convention on the rights of persons with disabilities.* www.un.org.

18 United States Code (U.S.C.) § 17 (2017).

United States Department of Health and Human Services (USDHHS). 1999. *Mental health: A report of the surgeon general.* Washington, DC: Department of Health and Human Services. http://profiles.nlm.nih.gov.

United States Department of Justice, Bureau of Justice Statistics (USBJS). 2008. *Crime and victims' statistics.* www.ojp.usdoj.gov.

United States Department of Justice, National Institute of Justice (USNIJ). 2003. *Fighting urban crime: The evolution of federal-local collaboration.* www.ncjrs.gov.

United States v. Binion, 132 Fed. Appx. 89 (8th Cir. 2005).

United States v. Brawner, 471 F.2d 969 (D.C. Cir. 1972).

United States v. Evans, 404 F.2d 227 (4th Cir. 2005).

United States v. Green, 532 F.2d 538 (6th Cir. 2008).

United States v. Greer, 158 F.3d 228 (5th Cir. 1998).

United States v. Harris, 542 F.2d 1283 (7th Cir. 1976).

United States v. Hernandez-Vasquez, 513 F.3d 908 (9th Cir. 2008).

United States v. Kaczynski, 239 F.3d 1108 (9th Cir. 2001).

United States v. Loughner, 672 F.3d 731 (9th Cir. 2012).

United States v. Meerbeke, 548 F.2d 415 (2d Cir. 1976).

United States v. Mitchell, 706 F. Supp. 2d 1148 (D. Utah 2010).

United States v. Preston, 751 F.3d 1008 (9th Cir. 2014).

United States v. Scheffer, 523 U.S. 303 (1998).

van Reekum, R., T. Cohen, and J. Wong. 2000. Can traumatic brain injury cause psychiatric disorders? *Journal of Neuropsychiatry and Clinical Neurosciences* 12, no. 3: 316–327.

Virginia (Va.) Code §§ 16.1-356, -357 (2017).

Virginia (Va.) Code § 18.2-31 (2017).

Virginia (Va.) Code §§ 19.2-168, -168.1, -169.1, -169.3, -169.5, -175, -182.2, -182.3, -182.4, -182.5, -182.6, -182.7, -182.8, -182.9, -182.10, -182.11, -182.12, -182.13, -182.14, -182.15, -182.16 (2017).

Virginia Tech Review Panel. 2007. Mass shootings at Virginia Tech, April 16. https://governor.virginia.gov.

Vrics, L. 2003. Sniper suspect: I do need lawyers. *CBS News*, October 23. www.cbsnews.com.

Walker, E. R., R. E. McGee, and B. G. Druss. 2015. Mortality in mental disorders and global disease burden implications: A systematic review and meta-analysis. *Journal of the American Medical Association: Psychiatry* 72, no. 4: 334–341. doi:10.1001/jamapsychiatry.2014.2502.

Ward v. Hellerstedt, No. 1:16-cv-00917 (W.D. Tex. July 29, 2016).

Washington v. Harper, 494 U.S. 210 (1990).

Washington v. United States, 390 F.2d 444 (D.C. Cir. 1967).

Wasser, T., and K. Trueblood. 2015. Forced medication to restore competency. *Journal of the American Academy of Psychiatry and the Law* 43, no. 1: 112–114.

Watson, A. C., and A. J. Fulambarker. 2012. The Crisis Intervention Team Model of police response to mental health crises: A primer for mental health practitioners. *Best Practices of Mental Health* 8, no. 2: 71. www.ncbi.nlm.nih.gov.

Weintraub, L. 1997. Inner-city post-traumatic stress disorder. *Journal of Psychiatry and Law* 25, no. 2: 249–286.

Weiss, R. 2005. Study: U.S. leads in mental illness, lags in treatment. *Washington Post*, June 7. www.washingtonpost.com.

West, D. J., and A. Walk, eds. 1977. *Daniel McNaughton: His trial and the aftermath.* London: Headley Brothers.

Wexler, D. B. 1993. Therapeutic jurisprudence and the criminal courts. *William and Mary Law Review* 35, no. 1: 279–299.

Williams, C. J. 2012. Forced medication of Jared Lee Loughner OK'd by court. *Los Angeles Times*, March 5. http://articles.latimes.com.

Williams Jr., D. O. 1955. Insanity, criminal responsibility and Durham. *William and Mary Review of Virginia Law* 2, no. 2: 103–113. http://scholarship.law.wm.edu.

Wilson v. United States, 391 F.2d 460 (D.C. Cir. 1968).

Winslade, W. J. 2003. Traumatic brain injury and criminal responsibility. *Medical Ethics* 10, no. 3: 4–12.

Wittchen, H. U., R. Lieb, H. Pfister, and P. Schuster. 2000. The waxing and waning of mental disorders: Evaluating the stability of syndromes of mental disorders in the population. *Comprehensive Psychiatry* 41, no. 2: 122–132.

Wood, S., and B. S. Agharkar. 2015. Traumatic brain injury in criminal litigation. *University of Missouri at Kansas City Law Review* 84, no. 2: 411–421.

Yang, M., S. C. P. Wong, and J. Coid. 2010. The efficacy of violence prediction: A meta-analytic comparison of nine risk assessment tools. *Psychological Bulletin* 136, no. 5: 740–767. doi:10.1037/a0020473.

Zapf, P. A., and R. Roesch. 2011. Future directions in the restoration of competency to stand trial. *Current Directions in Psychological Science* 20, no. 1: 43–47. doi:10.1177/0963721410396798.

Ziv, S. 2014. Report details Adam Lanza's life before Sandy Hook shootings. *Newsweek*, November 25. www.newsweek.com.

INDEX

abolition of mental health evidence, 252–53. *See also* insanity defense variations/alternatives

abolition of the insanity defense, 252. *See also* insanity defense variations/alternatives

actus reus "defense," 256–59. *See also* automatism defense; insanity defense variations/alternatives; mens rea "defense"; unconsciousness defense

ALI/MPC test. *See* Model Penal Code (MPC) test

alternatives to traditional criminal justice mental health, related proceedings, 312–17. *See also* crisis intervention teams; diversion; mandatory outpatient treatment; mental health courts; specialized mental health probation officers

amnesia impact on CST, 147–49. *See also* competence to stand trial

Angell, Marcia, 19, 321n70. *See also* psychiatric diagnoses

antisocial personality disorder, 37; prevalence, 322n111. *See also* personality disorders

anxiety disorders, 32–34, 42; agoraphobia, 34; generalized anxiety disorder, 34; panic disorder, 32–33; selective mutism, 34; separation anxiety disorder, 34; social anxiety disorder/social phobia, 33–34; specific phobia, 33. *See also* psychiatric diagnoses

automatism defense, 257–58, 341–42n15, 343n70; concussions, 257; dissociative fugue/fugue state/psychogenic fugue, 30, 257–58; epilepsy, 257; PTSD, 341–42n15; sleepwalking, 258; TBI, 343n70. *See also* actus reus defense; hypnotic state defense; insanity defense variations/alternatives; unconsciousness defense

avoidant personality disorder, 36, 39; prevalence, 323n119. *See also* personality disorders

battered child syndrome (BCS) defense, 247–50. *See also* insanity defense, variations/alternatives; Janes, Andrew; Menendez, Lyle and Erik

battered spouse syndrome (BSS) defense, 246–47, 249, 250, 342n26. *See also* insanity defense, variations/alternatives

battle of the experts, 143, 225, 281. *See also* CST assessment; insanity defense

behaviorism/social learning model, 16–17. *See also* mental disorders: explanatory models

Berkowitz, David ("Son of Sam"), 210, 340n16. *See also* insanity defense

bipolar disorders, 7, 18, 26–27, 65; bipolar I disorder (manic-depression), 26–27; bipolar II disorder, 27. *See also* mental disorders

Bobbitt, Lorena, 255–56; early release, 298. *See also* insanity defense, dispositions; psychological duress defense; temporary insanity defense

ABOUT THE AUTHOR

Thomas L. Hafemeister received a J.D. and a Ph.D. from the Law-Psychology Program at the University of Nebraska, served for almost five years as Assistant Counsel for the New York State Office of Mental Health, for over six years as Senior Staff Attorney/Research Associate at the National Center for State Courts, and for twelve years at the University of Virginia, where he was the Director of Legal Studies for the Institute of Law, Psychiatry, and Public Policy. He was also an Associate Professor at the University of Virginia School of Law. He is co-author of the leading textbook for law students on mental health issues, entitled *Law and the Mental Health System: Civil and Criminal Aspects,* as well as the author of a series of law review articles on various mental health and criminal justice issues.